The Web of Freedom

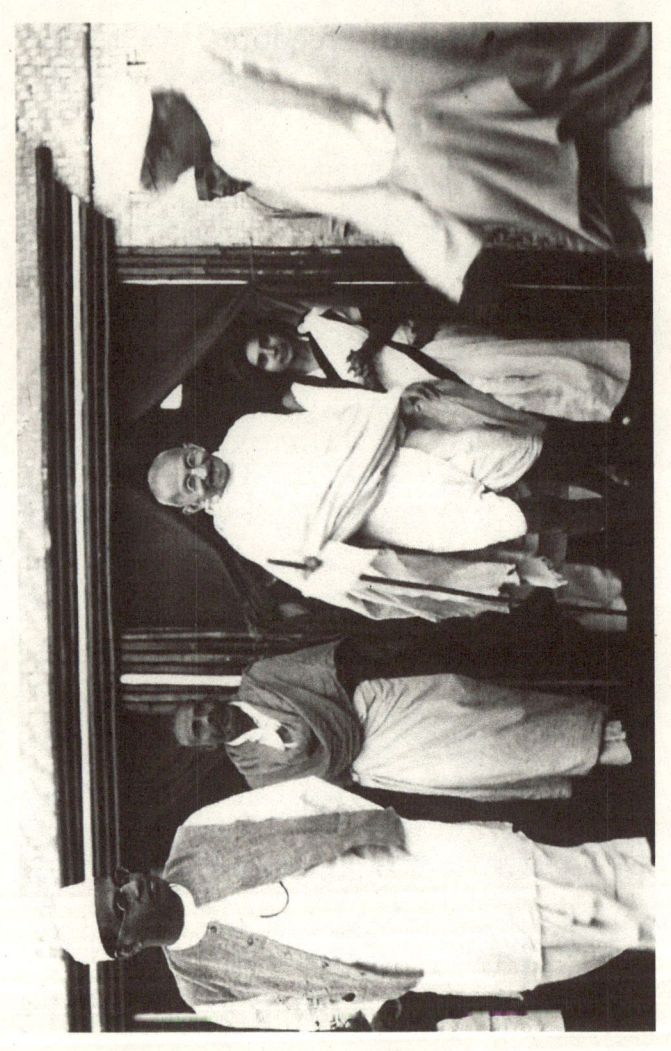

J. C. Kumarappa (extreme left) and Mahatma Gandhi at the Haripura Congress Session, 1938. Gandhi's compatriot and physician, Sushila Nayar, can be seen exiting the doorway to Gandhi's right. *Photograph courtesy of Baryalai Shalizi.*

The Web of Freedom

J. C. Kumarappa and Gandhi's Struggle for Economic Justice

Venu Madhav Govindu
and
Deepak Malghan

OXFORD
UNIVERSITY PRESS

Oxford University Press is a department of the University of Oxford.
It furthers the University's objective of excellence in research, scholarship,
and education by publishing worldwide. Oxford is a registered trademark of
Oxford University Press in the UK and in certain other countries.

Published in India by
Oxford University Press
YMCA Library Building, 1 Jai Singh Road, New Delhi 110 001, India

ISBN-13: 978-0-19-946081-6
ISBN-10: 0-19-946081-7

Typeset in Arno Pro 10.5/12.5
by Tranistics Data Technologies, Kolkata 700 091

To the many selfless workers of the
All-India Village Industries Association (1934–50)

Contents

Illustrations

Acknowledgements

The idea of writing this biography arose out of our belief that the life and work of J. C. Kumarappa (1892–1960) has important lessons for our own times. We have received much help and support from a number of individuals and institutions during the long period of working on this book.

The New India Foundation funded our work for a year (2006–7) through the grant of a fellowship. The Foundation is also a co-publisher of this volume and we are very grateful to its trustees for their generous support as well as their exemplary forbearance over the long period it took us to produce a manuscript.

The most important primary material used are the personal papers of Kumarappa that are archived at the Manuscripts Division of the Nehru Memorial Museum and Library (NMML), New Delhi. During our multiple visits to NMML we have benefited immensely from the help and cooperation of many, especially D. S. Routela, Deepa Bhatnagar, and N. Balakrishnan. Our work at the archives of the Sabarmati Ashram Preservation and Memorial Trust, Ahmedabad, was greatly aided by Durgesh Trivedi and Amritbhai Modi as well as Dina Patel and Kinnari

Bhatt. At Magan Sangrahalaya in Wardha—Kumarappa's home for some two decades—we were given free access to the available material by Vibha Gupta. The Sangrahalaya's copies of *Gram Udyog Patrika*, a journal edited by Kumarappa, were invaluable for our work. We are also very thankful to Vibha for her generous permission to use photographs from Kumarappa's personal collection. We are grateful to S. K. Bhatnagar and Y. P. Anand for their keen interest in our work and their help during numerous visits to the library of the National Gandhi Museum, Rajghat, New Delhi. We thank T. Kulashekar, Sita Sivaramakrishnan, and Lawrence Surendra for arranging unfettered access to books and papers at the Kumarappa Memorial Trust at Santhome, Chennai. Our lack of easy access to good libraries was significantly ameliorated by the treasure trove available online at the Digital Library of India.

Prior to being deposited at NMML, Kumarappa's personal papers were carefully preserved for many decades by his devoted disciple, the late M. Vinaik. We wish to record our gratitude to Vinaik for it would not have been possible to write this book without the availability of these personal papers or the immensely helpful outline provided by Vinaik's own biography of Kumarappa.

Over the years we have benefited from the support, advice, and research material provided by Gopalkrishna Gandhi, Ramachandra Guha, Srinath Raghavan, and E. S. Reddy. We are also thankful to the following individuals for providing us with useful research material: S. Theodore Baskaran, Satya Brink, Herman Daly, S. Chandrashekar, Raghabendra Chattopadhyay, Kanakmal Gandhi, Mark Lindley, Eric Lindquist, Arvind Krishna Mehrotra, Robert Nelson, Atmaram Saraogi, Solomon Victus, and Gomati Vinaik.

Many personal recollections were shared with us by Kumarappa's nephew, D. J. K. Cornelius, and nieces, the late Prita Kumarappa Shalizi and the late Sarah Chandy. Kumarappa's grand-nephew, Baryalai Shalizi, was most helpful with his prompt responses to a number of queries and his enthusiastic support. Baro also provided us with some wonderful photographs from the family collection.

We thank the team at Oxford University Press for shepherding the book through to publication.

Finally, we gratefully acknowledge the very useful and critical feedback provided on a first draft of the book by Rajmohan Gandhi, Ramachandra Guha, Srinath Raghavan, Amrita Shah, and Tridip Suhrud, as well as the two anonymous reviewers commissioned by the publishers. Needless to say, all errors and interpretations are those of the authors alone.

PERSONAL ACKNOWLEDGEMENTS

In addition to the individuals and institutions listed above, my work on this book was facilitated by the staff of many libraries, including the Gandhi Memorial Museum, Madurai; Mani Bhavan Gandhi Sangrahalaya, Mumbai; and the Goa State Central Library, Panaji. At the Gandhi Niketan Ashram, T. Kallupatti, Kumarappa's last place of residence, I was welcomed and helped by R. Venkataswami and his colleagues.

I acknowledge the help received from my students Avishek Chatterjee and Sk. Mohammadul Haque. Avishek designed the *charkha* icon used as a separator and processed many of the images used. Mohammad created a high-resolution version of the cover photograph using image super-resolution techniques developed as part of his research work.

In the early years of scouting for research material, I have freely availed of the hospitality of many friends: Khushman and Arati Gandhi in Ahmedabad, Supratik Chakraborty, Bibha Rani Chakraborty, and Lata P. M. in Mumbai, Sandhya and Shekhar Deshmukh in Wardha, and P. V. Madhusudhan Rao in New Delhi.

I owe a special debt of gratitude to my doctoral adviser, Rama Chellappa, who greatly aided the pursuit of my intellectual interests in computer vision. His free-spirited generosity and support has also been a vital enabling factor in the writing of this book. Ravindra R. P. played an instrumental role in seeding the idea of this biography and has been an unwavering source of support and friendship. A. G. Menon, Sugata Srinivasaraju, and Rosy D'Souza are the most generous of friends.

My parents, Saraswati and Krishna Murthi, and my brother, Suresh, provided their unconditional love as well as support for my atypical pursuits.

To Neeta I owe more than I can express here.

—*Venu Madhav Govindu*
Bengaluru
October 2015

U. N. 'Ravi' Ravikumar and Surendra 'Dada' Koulagi first introduced me to Kumarappa on a birdwatching trip in 1996. Ashok Rao, Santosh Koulagi, and Suresh Malghan facilitated access to the Gandhi Peace Foundation library at Dharwad, which was the site of my first textual engagement with Kumarappa.

I thank Ravindra R. P., Rajesh Kasturirangan, and Vinay Kumar for their support during the earliest stages of this project.

My doctors in Bengaluru and Chennai, combining skill, learning, and humility in equal measures, have been instrumental in seeing me through a significant health setback during the course of this project. I am grateful to the Indian Institute of Management Bangalore (my employer) for the generous health plan that has provided me access to doctors and hospitals. A long train journey shared with the redoubtable late Narayan Desai not only deepened my understanding of the history of constructive work but also gave me renewed strength to confront my medical problems. His creative and extempore reinterpretation of Gandhi's *Ekadash Vrat*, inscribed on the book that I was reading on the train, has continued to serve as a source of strength and inspiration. Ravi Rajan has been another source of immense wisdom on all things medical, and much else.

Venu and Neeta shared their warmth, friendship, home, and hearth. Their home in Goa and especially the long evening walks on the beach at Miramar was where this project took shape. Venu's uncommon comradeship, generosity, and forbearance have all been central to sustaining this project.

My family's support has been crucial during this project. My mother, Jyoti, has been a constant source of support despite upheavals in her own life. Arunima provides unalloyed joy, and is a life-affirming force. I am not even going to make an attempt to record Hema's love and sacrifice through the years. This is a debt that I cannot repay in any measure. She is—therefore, I am.

—*Deepak Malghan*
Bengaluru
October 2015

Abbreviations

AISA	All India Spinners Association
AIVIA	All-India Village Industries Association
ARC	Congress Agrarian Reforms Committee
CPB Survey	Industrial Survey Committee, Government of the Central Provinces and Berar
CWC	Congress Working Committee
CWMG	*The Collected Works of Mahatma Gandhi*
GUP	*Gram Udyog Patrika*
NPC	National Planning Committee
RBI	Reserve Bank of India

1 Introduction

The twentieth century was the age of ideologies applied on a mass scale. Millions of people were exploited in the service of one ideology or another. Life was no better under creeds meant to emancipate humankind. Amidst this welter of political chaos, there arose the still voice of Mahatma Gandhi, who eschewed talk of the masses but insisted on the indivisible and ineffable primacy of the ordinary individual, of Everyman. While consumed by the exigencies of the fight against British rule, Gandhi's vision went far beyond the task of winning India's political freedom. He ambitiously sought to address the social, economic, cultural, and spiritual freedom of the individual. Gandhi recognized that true emancipation of the individual is only possible when every person is afforded the conditions to live a healthy, well-rounded, and uncoerced life. And yet, the conditions for such equality had to be created in a context of existing grave inequalities and long histories of oppression and injustice. Therefore, notwithstanding the endowment and enforcement of rights by the state, building a wholesome life hinged on binding people into a moral compact based on mutuality and cooperation. This was the basis for his approach to 'constructive work' that included the promotion of *khadi*, development of village industries, a new pedagogical approach to education, and many other interventions. Gandhi could not convince most of his political compatriots of the value of constructive work, but a small band of like-minded colleagues applied themselves to this task. Looking beyond the immediate political affairs of the time, these constructive workers addressed themselves to the harder challenge of building a new order of human life in accordance with the principles enunciated by the Mahatma.

Of these individuals, easily the most interesting and original life is that of Joseph Cornelius Kumarappa (1892–1960). Born into a Tamil Christian family, Kumarappa trained as an accountant in London and studied public finance in the United States. His understanding of the colonial exploitation of India led him to abandon a successful career as a chartered accountant and join a small circle of constructive workers. In a short period of time, he was thrust into the Civil Disobedience campaigns of 1930–1 and became instrumental in running Gandhi's weekly journal *Young India* at a crucial point in modern India's political history. As a consequence, Kumarappa served time in jail. From then on, he dedicated his life to furthering the cause of rural India and its agrarian economy.

Owing to his direct and lifelong engagement with the countryside, Kumarappa had a deep understanding of its problems and concerns. He presented his views and arguments through numerous essays, pamphlets, and books that offer much insight and wisdom. These writings include his most well-known work, *Economy of Permanence*, written while he was imprisoned during the Quit India movement. Apart from deploying the written word, for more than two decades Kumarappa also worked on practical means to improve and rationalize a number of village industries that provided livelihood for many in rural India.

After India achieved independence, he became a consistent critic of its governments for their neglect of the many millions who depended on the agrarian economy. During the 1950s, he also argued against American involvement in India's economic development and courted controversy with his views on Russia and China. In an India that was seeking to rapidly achieve industrial modernity, Kumarappa's criticism and positions were unattractive to many. The result was a long period of neglect of his ideas and a corresponding lack of an appraisal of his true worth.

Fashioned as an intellectual biography, this book is an exercise in rehabilitation. Kumarappa's life is illuminating in three fundamental senses. First, as biography, it presents a fascinating story of self-transformation. Born at the high noon of Empire, he became a prosperous urban professional, only to exchange success and comfort for the uncertain life of a freedom fighter. In doing so, the Westernized Kumarappa traversed a great social and cultural distance to identify with the lives of ordinary Indians. By shedding the material and psychological shackles of colonialism, through a life that continually sought to bridge the gap between precept and practice, he provided a creative, if demanding, answer to the eternal human quest for identity and meaning in life.

Second, upon entering public life, the cosmopolitan Kumarappa quickly became the principal expositor of the values of *satya* and *ahimsa* applied to political economy and economic philosophy. Here it is particularly striking that his intellectual development is independent of but in agreement with the views of the Mahatma. In the course of his growth as a thinker, he addressed many fundamental questions and inflected them with moral understanding.[1] Indeed, the contribution to ecological thought, for which he is often recognized, is only one constituent of a deeply coherent and integral vision of life. The same characterization applies to his views on normative economics, social questions, and his insightful interpretation of Christian thought in light of Gandhian values. In the process of developing his philosophy and applying it to real-world problems, Kumarappa contributed significantly to the development of a Gandhian perspective on economic questions. From the early 1930s, he also directly influenced Gandhi's own understanding of economic issues.[2]

Kumarappa's comprehensive vision of life should not be confused with the advocacy of a foggy New Age spiritualism. At the same time, unlike analytic philosophers who are primarily driven by theoretical consistency and elegance, Kumarappa's vision was grounded in the material certitudes of life. Always concerned with the immediate betterment of the lives of the poor and the dispossessed, he was amongst the few individuals who established a dialectical relationship between theoretical insight and

[1] Throughout this biography, we have perforce ramified his integral vision into its multiple constituents for ease of comprehension. The reader is urged to bear in mind throughout that Kumarappa's moral vision encompassed all aspects of life as a whole.

[2] Thus, the title of a recent study of Kumarappa by Mark Lindley, *J. C. Kumarappa: Mahatma Gandhi's Economist* (henceforth *Gandhi's Economist*) (Mumbai: Popular Prakashan, 2007). Other recent works devoted to Kumarappa include those by the Madurai-based theologian Solomon Victus.

practical experience. Thus, during the period when he developed and refined his theoretical vision, Kumarappa was also spending much of his time as the prime mover behind the All-India Village Industries Association (AIVIA), an organization founded by Gandhi in Wardha to rationalize and improve India's village industries. Arguably, such a theory–praxis dialectic enriched both his philosophical vision as well as his understanding of the very material concerns of daily living. Much of Kumarappa's insight that has enduring value was wrested out of the struggle to address the practical problems he encountered.

A fundamental characteristic of the modern age is the economic ideology of large-scale industrialization and its socio-political siblings of growth and development. A corollary to the rise of this view is the precipitous decline of the village in the modern imagination. For technocratic modernists, the Indian village remains a stigmatized site that represents an irredeemable, collective burden. In challenging this view, Kumarappa emerged as a feisty, relentless, and original champion of rural India and its people. He painstakingly applied himself to revivifying the village through a robust, local economy. In the process, Kumarappa presented a searching examination of modern political economy and its implicit assumptions. His work also clarified, through a *theory of decentralization*, that the Gandhian advocacy of an agrarian economy was not a harkening to a hoary past. Rather, it arose from the need to preserve the essential freedoms of an individual in the face of massive political and economic inequalities in modern societies.

By forging a new idiom for contemporary times, Kumarappa shed light on some of the most fundamental questions that continue to haunt our contemporary social, political, and economic landscape. He made contributions to our understanding on a wide range of economic and political questions, such as the human ecology of industrialization and mass production, the role of machinery and industrial efficiency, the nature of an economic agent, the role of money in the modern economy, economic value, the meaning of work and the principles of democracy, as well as concepts such as well-being and standard of living. Similarly, he developed a comprehensive philosophical framework that addressed itself to questions pertaining to social evolution, human nature, value theory, and the place of humans in their larger ecological setting.

The third significant aspect of this biography is that it engages with the history of the three decades of his public life (1929–60). Roughly centred on the pivotal year 1947, this was the period when the future of India's polity and economy was debated and many fundamental choices were made. The implications of these choices continue to reverberate through our lives today. Indeed, while much of the scholarly literature is shaped by the colonial–postcolonial divide, Kumarappa's consistent engagement with public issues from the 1930s through to the 1950s helps us better understand the nature of the transition effected in 1947. As we shall see later, while the transition from a British colony to an independent nation was momentous, the neglect of the needs of rural India persisted to a significant degree.

As a pragmatic champion of the agrarian economy, Kumarappa spent an enormous amount of time keenly dissecting both positive economics as well as India's political economy. In the process of his engagement with issues of vital public significance, Kumarappa's life illuminates many aspects of modern India's economic history. Throughout his life, he mounted a challenge to the 'big idol' of materialism and positivist theories of growth and development that shaped the economic debate of his times. Thereby, he laid bare the common assumptions of industrialization and mass production that undergirded the dominant ideologies of capitalism and socialism. In particular, unlike many a leader of the freedom movement, Kumarappa demonstrated an acute historical understanding of the intimate and invidious relationship between European development through industrialization and the exploitation of the people and natural resources of the colonies. He remained deeply sceptical of the ability of large-scale industrialization to address India's problems as well as that of the modern bureaucratic state to provide equity and justice. Through his relentless critique of the colonial state and that of independent India, he explained the deep nexus between large-scale, capital-intensive industries and the instrumentality of modern state policy. The corollary was the inherent policy bias against village and small-scale industries that has grave consequences for individual, social, and ecological well-being.

Kumarappa's life also helps us to understand the precise manner in which the Congress eventually abandoned the moral legacy of Gandhi to pursue conventional politics by embracing the logic of liberal democracy as well as an industrial basis for the economy. His life also points to the reasons for the failure of the Gandhians to mount a meaningful political challenge to the Congress in the post-Independence era. Additionally, an examination of Kumarappa's public engagement provides us with crucial insights into the role and nature of Indian planning in the 1930s, the limited impact of agrarian reform in independent India, and the influence of Cold War politics on the development strategy of the Indian state in the 1950s. At the same time, Kumarappa sheds light on an important aspect of the turbulent Indian history of the 1940s that remains largely unexamined in popular literature. Through an incisive critique of colonial economic policy, he provides us with a vivid understanding of the systematic and devastating exploitation of Indian society by the British during the Second World War. The consequences of British policy were massive inflation, deprivation, and untold suffering throughout India, including the Bengal famine of 1943.

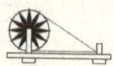

While we seek to present an intellectual biography of Kumarappa, we recognize that our exposition necessarily departs from the conventional attributes of this genre. It is crucially important to understand the dialectical relationship between Gandhian philosophy and constructive work in the real world. This objective is best achieved by an examination of Kumarappa's ideas in relation to the debates, politics, and political economy of the period of their development. Through such an examination of his life work, this biography also seeks to address a significant gap in our understanding of Gandhi's social vision and contribute towards a history of constructive work. Unlike the politics of India's freedom movement, which has been extensively studied, much of Gandhi's attempts at social reconstruction through constructive work as well as the development of Gandhian theory has not been examined with the seriousness it deserves. Indeed, while there are some sound expositions on Gandhian moral and political philosophy, the existing studies by both critics and admirers of 'Gandhian Economics' leave much to be desired. Moreover, while the role of khadi in India's struggle for freedom has received a measure of scholarly interest, very little attention has been paid to the equally important work on village industries and the rural economy in which Kumarappa played a central role. In a broader sense, one of the central arguments of this biography is that the development and evolution of the principles and practices of constructive work cannot be properly understood without attention to the specific historical context.

Yet the insights from Kumarappa's life's work transcend the historical specificity of his times as they are grounded in an understanding of universal truth. In this sense, they leapfrog the many decades and vastly changed circumstances that separate our times from his own. Apart from its intrinsic value, there is much in Kumarappa's life that speaks to ours. Finally, although this is a biography of Kumarappa, Gandhi is an inalienable and overarching presence in this book by the very nature of his decisive role in Kumarappa's life as well as in the India of his times. It will be evident to the reader that Kumarappa's lifespan naturally divides into three distinct phases: *before* Gandhi (1892–1929), *with* Gandhi (1929–48), and *after* Gandhi (1948–60).

2 The Great Transformation

In June 1929, India was in political ferment. With rising nationalist sentiment there was a run on khadi in Indian cities. A well-known Khadi Bhandar on Kalbadevi Road in Bombay (now Mumbai) saw brisk business as many proclaimed their political allegiance by wearing handspun. The shop was frequented by customers from all sections of society, but when a thirty-seven-year-old man walked in, he stuck out like a sore thumb. A chartered accountant with a flourishing practice, he was dressed every inch in the manner of a Westernized oriental gentleman. Exuding the confidence that comes with success and affluence, he accosted a salesman and demanded that he be 'measured up' for a *dhoti*! The bemused salesman had to educate his unusual customer that dhotis came in fixed lengths. Although he had never worn an Indian garment in his life till then, the customer purchased half a dozen dhotis, *kurtas*, caps, and long coats and marched out of the shop. Always a whole-hogger, he took to khadi and never dressed in Western clothes again.

Trading a three piece suit for a khadi dhoti and kurta was not the only unusual move he had made in this period. A few weeks earlier, in a bid to better identify with his countrymen, he had filed an affidavit in a Bombay court. In that affidavit, Joseph Chelladurai Cornelius renounced his said name and proclaimed that he was to be henceforth known as Joseph Cornelius Kumarappa. Shedding an alien name and habit for Indian ones were both of a piece. A successful and hitherto complacent middle-class, anglicized professional was rapidly moulting into a most dogged and creative fighter for justice.

To understand the significance of this transformation, we begin with the origins of Joseph's family that are intimately tied to the growth of Christianity in eighteenth-century Tamil country. The Protestant Church in present-day Tamil Nadu owes its origins to political changes in faraway Europe.[1] Following the 1648 Peace of Westphalia, a major political revolution reshaped Europe and established new sovereign states. It was in these changed political circumstances that in the German city of Halle 'Evangelical Pietism and Enlightenment thought were blended into an explosive new missionary movement' that eventually arrived in India at Tranquebar.[2] From its epicentre in Tranquebar—present-day Tarangambadi in Nagapattinam district of Tamil Nadu—a wave of Protestant Christianity spread to other centres like Thanjavur, Tiruchirapalli, and the original home of the Cornelius family, Palayamkottai in Tirunelveli. The initial wave of converts to Pietism were largely from the dominant landowning Vellalars—a peasant caste that was low in the ritual hierarchy but dominated the local agrarian economy. Amongst these sub-castes were the Tirunelveli Saiva Pillais—the caste of Joseph's ancestors from Palayamkottai—who were worshippers of Shiva, vegetarians, and considered themselves to be at the top of Vellalar hierarchy.

In 1750, the German Protestant missionary Christian Frederick Schwartz arrived at Tranquebar. Over the subsequent decades, Schwartz played a pivotal role in the spread of the Protestant faith in south India and amongst the Tamils in Jaffna in present-day Sri Lanka. The Jaffna connection pertains to the contest between European powers for political dominance in the region. The Tamil Vellalars of Jaffna were among the earliest converts to Catholicism in South Asia as the Portuguese controlled Sri Lanka from

---

[1] Robert Eric Frykenberg, *Christianity in India: From Beginnings to the Present* (New York: Oxford University Press, 2008), p. 142. Also see D. Dennis Hudson, *Protestant Origins in India: Tamil Evangelical Christians, 1706–1835* (Grand Rapids: William B. Eerdmans Publishing Company, 2000), pp. 5–9. [We are thankful to S. Theodore Baskaran for his help in understanding the history of Tamil Christianity.]

[2] Frykenberg, *Christianity in India*, p. 144.

the early part of the sixteenth century until the Dutch defeated them a century and a half later. With political power changing hands, religious activity followed suit. Eighteenth-century missionaries like Schwartz were able to draw a large number of these Catholic Vellalars into the Lutheran Pietist congregation. Pietism not only had the advantage of being ritually simpler than Catholicism, it also offered more material advantages. The evangelical need to spread Biblical knowledge through the written word had led to the introduction of modern education in south India. This newly available education was eagerly adopted by many Protestant families including those of Joseph's ancestors as it afforded access to jobs and economic mobility in the newly emergent administration of the East India Company. In this period of social and political turmoil, Schwartz's evangelical success lay in recruiting indigenous preachers—many of whom were sent to the seminaries in Jaffna for training.[3]

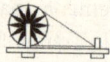

Joseph Chelladurai Cornelius was born in Thanjavur on 4 January 1892 as the ninth child of Esther Rajanayakam (1856–1924) and Solomon Doraiswamy Cornelius (1851–1917) who was the eldest son of Rev. John Cornelius of Palayamkottai.[4] While they had earlier belonged to

[3] Foremost among Schwartz's Tamil lieutenants who led the new converts was Nellaiyan Vedanayakam Pillai from Palayamkottai, one of Joseph's forbears on his distaff side. On Vedanayakam's significance in Tamil Christianity, see Indira Peterson, 'Bethlehem Kuruvanci of Vedanayaka Sastri of Tanjore: The Cultural Discourses of an Early-Nineteenth-Century Tamil Christian Poem', in *Christians, Cultural Interactions and India's Religious Traditions*, edited by Judith Brown and Robert Frykenberg (Grand Rapids: William B. Eerdmans Publishing Company, 2002).

[4] Of the twelve children born to his parents, two older boys died in childhood as did one sister in early adulthood. Information about Joseph's first eighteen years comes from a biographical essay by his sister, Elizabeth Appaswamy, 'Boyhood and Youth', in *The Economics of Peace: The Cause and the Man*, edited by S. K. George and G. Ramachandran (New Delhi: Peace Publishers, 1992). Additional details are from the first English biography of Kumarappa authored by his disciple, M Vinaik, *J. C. Kumarappa and His Quest for World Peace* (henceforth *Quest*) (Ahmedabad: Navajivan Publishing House, 1956). This volume can be taken to be authentic in its details as it was scrutinized by his brother Bharatan Kumarappa, and Kumarappa was himself induced to read the galley proofs. However, the updated 1987

the Catholic faith, the Cornelius family was amongst the earliest converts to the Protestant congregation. As was common practice, the Cornelius family name was derived from that of a missionary in the Tirunelveli area. Although from Palayamkottai, John and his brother James had trained in Jaffna to be clergymen, which was by then an established career path.[5] The different caste groups within the Pietist congregation had independent churches and following his training in Jaffna, John Cornelius preached to his fellow Vellalars at the East Gate Church in Madurai.

By the time of Joseph's birth, the Cornelius family belonged to the anglicized class with firm roots in the colonial administration. Solomon was employed in the Madras Public Works Department and was influential within his community.[6] The extended Cornelius family consisted of members who were judges, professors, physicians, and other professionals in the service of the British Raj. The family lived comfortably in houses that were large enough to accommodate more than a dozen people, including a small retinue of household help. In keeping with the original Pietist tenets, and unlike others of their social class and stature, Joseph's parents made no distinction between girls and boys when it came to education. The Cornelius family took the unusual step of sending the girls away to study at a school in faraway Poona (now Pune) and eventually out of the country to study medicine or science. The most significant departure from the norms of the time was that Solomon and Esther 'were not keen on early marriage of their children'.[7] Dowry was neither given nor received at any of the weddings in the Cornelius family.

The emphasis on good education meant that all of Joseph's siblings were academically well trained and would go on to lead accomplished and productive professional lives. The eldest of five sisters, Sornam Elizabeth Appaswamy (b. 1878) was a member of the Madras City Corporation besides serving on the senate of the Madras University and founding a well-known Chennai school. Kamala Gertrude (b. 1893) was trained at the present-day Chatham University in the United States and was a professor of

---

version of the biography, *The Gandhian Crusader: A Biography of J. C. Kumarappa* (Gandhigram: Gandhigram Trust, 1987), is hagiographic and unreliable in some sections. Elizabeth Appaswamy's essay also has several errors, including dates.

[5] M. Vinaik, 'The Great Sacrifice', unpublished manuscript, July 1991.

[6] At the time of Joseph's birth, Solomon served as the secretary of the Indian Christian Association as well as the Christian Provident Fund.

[7] George and Ramachandran, *Economics of Peace*, p. 4.

Chemistry at the Madras Christian College whereas Grace Pappammal (b. 1891) studied liberal arts in New York and later married into the Godfrey family of South Africa who were early collaborators of Gandhi. Jane Rajamani (b. 1882) was a physician who had a flourishing private practice in Coimbatore, and the youngest sister, Prema Margaret (b. 1895), was an obstetrician-gynaecologist trained in Dublin and served in several of the major hospitals in India. His older brother James Thambidurai Cornelius (b. 1889) was a physician and public health researcher who had studied in three prestigious institutions in the West. He served the United Provinces government's health department and later worked as a professor at the Christian Medical College in Vellore.

Joseph's nationalist sympathies were most closely shared by two of his brothers who also changed their names from Christian versions to Hindu ones. The eldest brother, Jagadisan Mohandas Kumarappa (1886–1957)—originally John Jesudasan Cornelius—was an accomplished social scientist with graduate degrees from Harvard and Columbia where he wrote a doctoral dissertation on Tagore's educational experiments. He went on to become the founding director of the Tata Institute of Social Sciences and also served a term as a nominated member of the Rajya Sabha. The most intellectually distinguished of the siblings was the youngest, Bharatan Kumarappa (1896–1957), whose Christian name was Benjamin Cornelius. Bharatan had originally trained in theology at the Hartford Theological Seminary in the United States, an experience that turned him into an agnostic! He later trained as a philosopher and a Sanskrit scholar. In the process, he obtained two doctoral degrees, from the University of Edinburgh and from London's School of Oriental Studies, studying the ethics of John Dewey and Ramanuja's Vishishtadvaita Vedanta theology, respectively.[8] Bharatan later joined Joseph in the nationalist cause and was involved in the running of the All-India Village Industries Association (AIVIA) and editing its journal, *Gram Udyog Patrika* (GUP). On account of his profound learning and deep understanding of Gandhi's thought, in the 1950s Bharatan became the founding editor of that monumental work of scholarship, *The Collected Works of Mahatma Gandhi* (CWMG).

---

[8] His London dissertation was the first work in English to systematically delineate the differences between Adi Sankara's metaphysical approach and Ramanuja's realism and was published as a well-received book, *The Hindu Conception of the Deity: As Culminating in Ramanuja* (London: Luzac and Co., 1934).

Along with the emphasis on education and professional success, the Cornelius household also instilled in the children a strong moral and ethical sense. Joseph would recollect years later the foundational role played by his modestly lettered mother in imparting a sense of empathy for the less privileged. In keeping with the Halle Pietist idea of using everyday chores for moral training, Joseph and his siblings would raise chicken and turkey for the market and all the profits would be used by Esther to support her pet charities. The poultry business was meant to be a lesson in basic arithmetic, economic literacy, and hygiene as well as to nurture the 'joy of giving out of [one's] own efforts'.[9] Later, working as an accountant in Bombay, Joseph would set aside a portion of his monthly income as a tithe for his mother to use for charity, but her definition of a tithe was more liberal than the biblical one-tenth!

When Joseph was twelve years old, the Cornelius family moved to Madras (now Chennai) following Solomon's retirement. Joseph now attended the Doveton European School for Boys that provided vastly greater opportunities than his earlier schooling. Doveton mainly served Europeans and Anglo-Indians but also had a sprinkling of upper-crust Christian boys whose parents served the Raj. His friends and classmates at Doveton were all anglicized boys whose pursuits included regular games of tennis that Joseph took to with great enthusiasm. As a young boy, he was fascinated by the workings of mechanical devices and retained a childlike curiosity for machines. However, at Doveton he did not do well enough in the matriculation exam to study mathematics in college as a prelude to the engineering degree that he desired. Instead, he took an honours degree in history from the Wesleyan Mission College.

Joseph was an active scout at high school and his scout master arranged for an accountancy apprenticeship with a prominent incorporated accounting firm in London. Thus, in 1913, Joseph departed for England to build a career as a chartered accountant. During the time Joseph was studying for his final accountancy examinations in 1917, his father passed away in India, but the ongoing war prevented him from travelling back home. After five years of apprenticeship, Joseph was made a partner at his

---

[9] George and Ramachandran, *Economics of Peace*, p. 2.

firm and took on the title 'Esquire', a common practice among people of his rank in the legal and accounting professions. While we know precious little about his England years, it is unlikely that nationalist politics was on the mind of J. C. Cornelius, Esq., who aspired to greater professional success. Although urged by his tutor to prepare for the Solicitors' Examination to improve his career prospects, under pressure from his mother, Joseph returned to India in 1919.[10]

During his time in England, India had undergone a tremendous political transformation with Gandhi's return home and elevation to national leadership. But Joseph seems to have remained untouched by nationalistic considerations during this period. However, a fundamental change occurred in his understanding of the relationship between the church and the state. In his early days in England, Joseph was a regular churchgoer.[11] The outbreak of the First World War, however, brought about a sudden and dramatic change in his attitude. He found the church's active support of war repulsive as it repudiated everything he had understood to be a true Christian's calling. Coming under the indirect influence of Christian Pacifists and other war resisters, he started questioning the role of the church. He was particularly impressed by the example of Bertrand Russell who resisted the draconian Defence of the Realm Act and criticized the church's support of the War, and chose to suffer 'exile and privation rather than conceal [his] light under a bushel'. Joseph was shocked to see 'Popes and Bishops blessing the banners, [and] Pulpits raising their vituperative voices against the Hun and inviting the youth to stand up for God, King and Country'. The hymn 'God Save the King' now took on new meaning when he considered the support religious leaders gave to what he thought was the 'organized butchery of men'. Decades later, Joseph would develop on this theme but the first psychological steps that led him away from his early moorings were taken in England.

The only surviving autobiographical account from this time is replete with anecdotes of life in London during the War years.[12] Joseph was particularly struck by the fact that 'the barriers of class distinction that were

[10] Letter from D. F. de'Hoste Ranking to J. C. Cornelius, 27 October 1919, Correspondence Files, J. C. Kumarappa Papers, Manuscripts Division, Nehru Memorial Museum and Library (NMML) (henceforth Kumarappa Papers); George and Ramachandran, *Economics of Peace*, p. 4.

[11] Letter from J. C. Kumarappa to Muriel Lester, 28 January 1936, Correspondence Files, Kumarappa Papers.

[12] Speeches and Writings, 7, pp. 33–8, Kumarappa Papers.

very noticeable before [were] set aside' in the face of adversity. While he was opposed to the War, he was moved by the patriotism and sacrifice that was on display in wartime London. But the War also sowed the first seeds of doubt in Joseph's mind about the economic structures underlying the British Empire. The 'luxurious carpets of civilization on which the nations [had] hitherto been reposing', he noted, had been torn apart by the War.[13] In a few years, however, he would himself arrive at an understanding of how Britain's luxurious carpet was woven out of the wealth of India and other colonies.

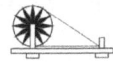

Back in India, Joseph moved to Bombay, the centre of Indian business and a most promising place for an aspiring incorporated auditor to begin his independent career. He very briefly worked for an English accounting firm in Bombay before setting up an incorporated partnership, Cornelius and Davar. His partner Sohrab Davar was the author of a popular accountancy textbook and proprietor of the pre-eminent college of accountancy in India where Joseph also served as a lecturer. With professional success at an early age, Joseph led an economically secure life in Bombay. For instance, while on vacation in Kodaikanal with the family in the early 1920s, his mother, Esther, collected donations towards famine relief in China. Joseph's contribution was a substantial sum of fifty rupees.[14] After three years of working with Davar, Joseph was now looking to follow his other siblings in higher academic pursuits. In 1923, he considered becoming a reader in commerce and accountancy at the University of Lucknow, an academic institution of some distinction at the time. The primary impetus for this idea was probably the presence of his brother, James Thambidurai who had just moved to Lucknow. We do not know if the 'master of his subject' and a 'successful teacher' got an offer but in any event Joseph did not move to Lucknow.[15] Instead, having built a substantial nest egg, Joseph would move to the United States to pursue graduate studies. During his time of professional success in Bombay, he was also searching anew for spiritual

[13] Speeches and Writings, 7, p. 38, Kumarappa Papers.
[14] Vinaik, *Quest*, p. 4. The 1920–1 famine killed an estimated half a million (1 million = 10 lakh) people in southeast China.
[15] Letter of recommendation from S. Davar, 25 April 1923, Correspondence Files, Kumarappa Papers.

bearings after his disillusionment in London. Unlike fellow Pietist Tamil Christians who were now well integrated into the Anglican Communion, Joseph had psychologically broken away from the Church of England. However, he was not yet ready to fully reject the organized church and did serve as the Secretary for the Bombay Baptist Church. In the summer of 1927, the thirty-five-year-old Joseph set sail for the United States armed with letters of recommendation from his church.[16] While he did carry the letters, it is unlikely he ever used them as arriving in America led to a radical transformation. The devout Christian and successful accountant would in a short while become a fierce nationalist who would reject the Raj and find himself at the epicentre of the Indian freedom struggle.

---

[16] The Baptist congregation in India was established by William Carey who also played an important role in the founding of the Baptist Church in the United States.

3   An American Interlude

I n 1927, after many years of a successful career in Bombay, Joseph set
sail for the United States. His eldest brother, then living in America,
had persuaded Joseph to visit on a long holiday. En route he vacationed
in Italy, Switzerland, France, and other European nations and eventually
arrived in America in the summer.[1] By this time, all three of Joseph's
brothers and a sister had already been educated in America, and it was
perhaps natural that he would seek to do the same. A month after arriving
in the United States, Joseph decided to enrol at Syracuse University in
upstate New York for an undergraduate degree in business administration.
He was awarded a degree in 1928 after a year of study as his 'five years of
training as an Incorporated Accountant was taken into consideration'.[2]
His undergraduate thesis on the fiscal consequences of income-tax
exemptions earned him an 'A'.[3] Giving early notice of his views on

---

[1] 'Educator from India, Student in Syracuse Summer School', *The Post-
Standard*, Syracuse, 6 July 1927, Press Clippings, Kumarappa Papers.

[2] Vinaik, *Gandhian Crusader*, p. 38.

[3] Joseph's thesis was a study of the economist Charles Hardy's recently
published *Tax-Exempt Securities and Progressive Surtax*. See Bound Volume, 1,
Kumarappa Papers. We thank Mark Lindley and Y. P. Anand for providing us a
copy of this thesis.

public finance, in this thesis Joseph argued that one had to go beyond merely counting revenue gains and losses and examine the distributive implications of tax policies. In addition to determining *what* the benefits were, Joseph held that any conception of public good also needed to ask *who* benefited.

The move to America offered him a new perspective on his own society. While Joseph had lived in England as a subject of an empire, he was now exposed to the American sensibility of freedom. Moreover, unlike his time in England during the First World War, Joseph's American sojourn coincided with a period of relative stability in American society. The First World War had ended almost a decade ago and the Great Depression lay ahead. Nevertheless, in this period of political calm, America did directly expose Joseph to a different problem of great consequence—race. A year prior to Joseph's arrival, India had entered the American public imagination in a rather negative way through the publication of Katherine Mayo's infamous, polemic *Mother India*, a book that Gandhi thought was 'the report of a drain inspector sent out with the one purpose of opening and examining the drains of the country'.[4] While Mayo had written her book with the express intent of turning American public opinion against India, thereby justifying British rule, it had a secondary effect of providing ammunition for racially motivated measures to deny American citizenship to people of Indian origin.[5] Joseph was exposed to the shrill debate on the race question as applied to Indians, and while he might have agreed with Mayo's critique of Indian social ills such as child marriage, he was deeply outraged by her attempt to buttress British imperialism.[6] It took a long period of dogged work by expatriate activists to undo the damage done to the Indian nationalist cause in America by Mayo's book. Many of them publicly questioned both her data and conclusions. Joseph's eldest brother, J. J. Cornelius, unsuccessfully challenged Mayo to a public debate in New York.

During this period, J. J. Cornelius was enrolled at Columbia University in New York City and was writing a doctoral dissertation on Tagore's

[4] Drain Inspector's Report, 15 September 1927, *CWMG*.

[5] See 'Introduction' in Katherine Mayo, *Selections from Mother India*, edited and with an introduction by Mrinalini Sinha (New Delhi: Kali for Women, 1998). Mayo vigorously opposed granting of citizenship rights to expatriate Indians living in the United States.

[6] Subject File, 4, Kumarappa Papers.

educational work.[7] He was seriously involved in Indian questions and by this time had developed strong nationalist leanings. He wrote frequently and eloquently in American news media presenting the Indian case. He also wrote in Indian newspapers explaining American social and political phenomena. Although Joseph does not record it anywhere, without a shred of doubt, it was the social and political leanings of J. J. Cornelius that played the most important role in his 'Indian' education in America. As illustrations of the source of such influence, one may cite two representative essays of J. J. Cornelius that were published in the influential *Harper's Monthly Magazine*, 'An Oriental Looks at Christian Missions' in 1927 and 'Gandhi and His Spinning Wheel' in 1928. Although Joseph would later emerge as a prime expositor of Gandhi's economic thought, in 1928 it was the older brother who was unknowingly shaping Joseph's eventual destiny as a constructive worker and colleague of the Mahatma.

In early 1928, on the advice of a Syracuse faculty member, Joseph moved to Columbia University to pursue a masters degree in public finance.[8] Given his interests, it was perhaps inevitable that Joseph would come to work under E. R. A. Seligman, a pre-eminent American economist of his generation. Seligman was acknowledged as an early pioneer of the modern theory of taxation and as a distinguished historian of economic thought.[9] He also had important India connections. He had befriended and helped Lala Lajpat Rai in explaining the Indian cause to America and was also the adviser of the most famous of Columbia's Indian graduates, B. R. Ambedkar. The training in public finance and the history of economic thought under Seligman helped Joseph develop the hallmark of his approach, that is, the use of historical, institutional, and normative ideas to illuminate economic questions. It is also likely that Joseph's exposure to sociology sparked a lifelong penchant for developing taxonomies to describe the economic and sociological evolution of human societies.

Apart from the influence of Seligman, Joseph's intellectual commitments were given concrete shape by an encounter of a different kind. At Columbia,

---

[7] This dissertation was published as *Rabindranath Tagore: India's Schoolmaster: A Study of Tagore's Experiment in the Indianization of Education in the Light of India's History* (New York: Columbia University Press, 1928).

[8] Vinaik, *Gandhian Crusader*, p. 38.

[9] Seligman was highly accomplished, being the editor-in-chief of the landmark *Encyclopedia of the Social Sciences*, the editor of the influential *Political Science Quarterly* as well as a founder of the New School of Social Research that promoted a pluralistic approach in economics.

he took a seminar conducted by Herbert Davenport, an economist of the Austrian School. Davenport was a radical proponent of individualism in economic theory and viewed economic thought that brought in social considerations as 'a system of apologetics'. He propounded this view in a series of books that culminated in *The Economics of Enterprise*, which was the basis for the Columbia seminar class. Davenport took the idea of individual pursuit of profit to its logical extreme and with 'ruthless consistency ... he reduce[d] ... economic phenomena to terms of individual activities in pursuit of gain'.[10] Thus, he regarded robbery as productive economic activity and the tools used for theft as 'instruments of production'. Evidently, Davenport was 'by nature a controversialist, and it was perhaps his greatest pleasure, in speech and writing, to cross swords with a worthy foe'.[11] Joseph's sense of decency was outraged by Davenport's thesis and in the seminar he fought back tooth and nail. Joseph's fellow-students advised him to tone down his criticisms, lest they offended the professor. The counter-arguments did offend Davenport, but also earned Joseph the highest grade in the class. More significantly, Davenport's shocking arguments also drove Joseph out of 'complacently being a party to capitalistic and imperialistic organization, and to rethink his own economics'.[12] An obituary of Davenport argued that a true measure of his work would only be available after the posthumous publication of his book on Alfred Marshall.[13] One may add that by provoking Joseph, Davenport had enabled contributions to economic thought that he would wholly have disapproved of.

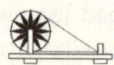

Living in New York brought Joseph into contact with John Haynes Holmes, a minister at the Community Church in New York who was well known for bringing Gandhi into American consciousness by equating the greatness of the Mahatma with that of Jesus. Some decades later, Joseph would himself boldly and creatively interpret the message of Jesus in light of the contemporary ideal of *Sarvodaya*. As educated Indians in

---

[10] Wesley C. Mitchell, 'Review of *The Economics of Enterprise*', *American Economic Review*, vol. 4, no. 3 (September 1914): 602–5.

[11] Paul T. Homan, 'Herbert Joseph Davenport: 1861–1931', *American Economic Review*, vol. 21, no. 4 (December 1931): 696–700.

[12] Vinaik, *Quest*, p. 12.

[13] Homan, 'Herbert Joseph Davenport'.

America were wont to do in that era, Joseph soon began giving expository lectures and magic lantern talks on a variety of Indian issues in churches and other fora in New York.[14] Compared to his insight in later years, Joseph's knowledge of many of the issues he spoke on was understandably superficial. Indeed, later in life he never commented on these novice efforts, but his New York audiences enjoyed them and Holmes complimented Joseph for his 'precision and charm of presentation that were most delightful'.[15] In the process of preparing the lectures, in a short period of time, Joseph was led to a self-study of Indian culture and civilization. Moreover, the controversy over American racism and the anti-imperialist and nationalist sensibilities of his brother forced Joseph to examine his own views. Soon, from a believer in the essential benevolence of British rule in India, Joseph turned into one of its dogged foes. Similarly, in alliance with his brothers, Joseph had also begun an examination of his Christian roots that eventually led him away from the organized church to strike out on an individual spiritual quest. All in all, Joseph was undergoing a Pauline conversion where he was re-examining many of his personal views and values as well as his understanding of both economic theory and the historical role of British rule in India.

The growing importance of moral imperatives in Joseph's thinking are visible in a term paper he wrote in his first semester at Columbia. In this essay, he examined the economic implications of the Versailles Treaty that was forced upon Germany at the end of the First World War.[16] The orthodoxy on the subject was derived from John Maynard Keynes' best-seller *The Economic Consequences of the Peace*. Published in 1919, this book was hailed by the opponents of war who were also against the Carthaginian peace achieved by imposing economically ruinous reparations on Germany. Undeterred by the book's cult status, Joseph presented a scathing critique of Keynes. He argued that while Keynes appeared to be ameliorating the conditions imposed on Germany, 'in the remedies for the

[14] The topics were diverse and included 'The Place of Women in the Indian Social Order', 'Hindu Marriage', 'Art and Architecture in India', 'Civilisations: Oriental and Occidental', 'India's Reaction to Western Influence', 'Problems of Foreign Missionaries in India', and so on. See Subject File, 4, Kumarappa Papers.

[15] Letter from John Haynes Holmes to J. C. Cornelius, 21 November 1928, Subject File, 1, Kumarappa Papers.

[16] J. C. Cornelius, 'An Examination of Some of the Policies Involved in the Solution of the Reparations and Inter-Allied Debt Problems', Speeches and Writings, 11, Kumarappa Papers.

Reparations tangle suggested by Mr Keynes he stands out pre-eminently as a Britisher rather than as a Scientist'. Joseph argued that Keynes' proposals were largely protectionist measures in favour of Britain's mercantile interests against the Germany of the future. In the aftermath of the Second World War, Joseph would have occasion once again to harshly criticize the imperial motives of Keynes, this time in the context of India. Joseph's analysis mirrored the sentiments presented in a famous review of Keynes' book by the American sociologist Thorstein Veblen.[17] At Columbia, Joseph also read Veblen's pioneering critique of middle-class consumerism, *The Theory of the Leisure Class*, and was certainly influenced by both Veblen's argument as well as his wry humour.

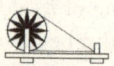

Joseph's self-study of Indian history, culture, society, and polity helped clarify many issues, including the nature of the colonial subjugation of India. One of the talks that he gave, 'Why, Then, Is India Poor?' impressed Seligman who encouraged his student to abandon plans to study the finances of the Bombay Municipality and focus on the larger question posed in the lecture. The result was Joseph's master's thesis *Public Finance and India's Poverty* that Seligman deemed 'an unusually able essay'.[18]

A striking and unique aspect of early Indian nationalism was its economic critique of British rule.[19] Indeed, one may argue that Indian nationalism originated in an economic critique of colonial exploitation. In his thesis, Joseph also added his own contribution to this lineage with many an illustrious predecessor like Dadabhai Naoroji and R. C. Dutt.[20] While we closely follow Kumarappa's position in this

[17] Thorstein Veblen, 'Review of John Maynard Keynes, *The Economic Consequences of the Peace*', *Political Science Quarterly*, vol. 35, no. 3 (1920): 467–72.

[18] Letter of recommendation from E. R. A. Seligman, 29 January 1929, Subject File, 1, Kumarappa Papers.

[19] This is well documented in Bipan Chandra, *Rise and Growth of Economic Nationalism in India: Economic Policies of Indian National Leadership, 1880–1905* (New Delhi: People's Publishing House, 1960).

[20] Dadabhai Naoroji, *Poverty and Un-British Rule in India*, London: S. Sonnenschein, 1901; Romesh Chandra Dutt, *The Economic History of India under Early British Rule* (London: Kegan Paul, Trench, Trubner and Co. Ltd., 1906).

biography, we recognize that the historiographic debates on the colonial period of Indian economic history have been complex and vigorous, and continue to this day. Indeed, the imperialist position that sees British rule as a largely positive experience has also had many advocates. Such authors, along with their 'revisionist' descendants, have contested virtually every aspect of the anti-imperialist critique of British rule including the 'drain theory' and the 'deindustrialisation of India'.[21] This historiographic turn towards revisionism has also been effectively critiqued.[22]

Given his background in accountancy and keen interest in public finance, Joseph chose to focus on British colonial financial policy. He began the thesis by presenting a rapid survey of the state of the Indian economy at the beginning of the nineteenth century. Strikingly, although he was developing strongly nationalist views, Joseph did not take easy recourse to

[21] A modern exemplar is the controversial position of Morris D. Morris, which is available—along with critical responses—in Morris D. Morris, Toru Matsui, Bipan Chandra, and Tapan Raychaudhuri (eds), *Indian Economy in the Nineteenth Century: A Symposium* (Delhi: The Indian Economic and Social History Association, 1969). The revisionist position is also reprised in more recent writings such as Dharma Kumar (ed.), *The Cambridge Economic History of India, Volume II, c. 1757–2003* (New Delhi: Orient Longman, 2005); and Tirthankar Roy, *The Economic History of India: 1857–1947*, third edition (New Delhi: Oxford University Press, 2011). Snapshots of the multiple dimensions of the debate are presented in G. Balachandran (ed.), *India and the World Economy: 1850–1950* (New Delhi: Oxford University Press, 2003), whereas a recent overview is David Washbrook's 'The Indian Economy and the British Empire', in *India and the British Empire*, edited by Douglas M. Peers and Nandini Gooptu (Oxford: Oxford University Press, 2012), pp. 44–74.

[22] Some notable responses are Irfan Habib, 'Studying a Colonial Economy—without Perceiving Colonialism', *Modern Asian Studies*, vol. 19, no. 3 (1985): 355–81; and Aditya Mukherjee, 'The Return of the Colonial in Indian Economic History: The Last Phase of Colonialism in India', *Social Scientist*, vol. 36, nos 3–4 (2008): 3–44. Much of the recent revisionist argument views the colonial Indian economy in terms of the 'flows' and 'exchange' located within the larger context of global trade. Such a position fails to account for the economic impact on people, as well as the social and moral implications of one society colonizing another.

the imagery of a golden age in India's past. Instead, he argued that 'although for centuries past Indian history alternated with prosperity and adversity, peace and war ... benevolence and tyranny', on the whole, 'we find India enjoyed a remarkable share of peace and prosperity' in comparison with other nations.[23] To describe the utter poverty and destitution of later times, Joseph took recourse to British witnesses like William Digby and Prime Minister Ramsay MacDonald. The thesis provided a clear delineation of the sources of Public Revenue and their utilization as Public Expenditure and presented three central observations.

First, Joseph showed how public finance was used as an instrument of fiscal policy to further Britain's imperial interests rather than that of India. Second, he made a direct connection between economic subjugation, and political, social, and cultural stagnation in British India. Third, *Public Finance* showed that if the fiscal policy framework was calculated to promote British commercial interests, the utilization of revenue under public expenditure was also exceedingly lopsided. Instead of ploughing back the revenue receipts into long-term capital formation that would benefit Indian society, colonial expenditure was designed as a novel way to drain money from India. If the maintenance of a huge army was an egregious example of India paying for its own subjugation, the so-called Home Charges—that used Indian money to pay for interest on debt, pensions for retired British administrators of India, and other similar expenditures—were no less controversial. A third expenditure incurred on 'behalf' of the Indian people was public debt in the form of railway bonds and other capital investments that were no less exploitative. Joseph revealed the cumulative injustice of these factors in a stark comparison. If one considered the spending on debts, the military, and administration in the United States, in 1925–6 they constituted 49 per cent of net revenue. In contrast, in British India, these expenditures used up a whopping 94 per cent of the revenue receipts, leaving nothing for public works.[24] Even out of the little monies spent on public requirements such as education, much was geared towards the welfare of the European population in India. On a per head basis, the British spent Rs 25 on educating a European child in India 'while it dole[d] out a beggarly four annas per head on the children of the land'. In fiscal terms, British rule in India was nothing but parasitic.

[23] J. C. Kumarappa, *Public Finance and Our Poverty: The Contribution of Public Finance to the Present Economic State of India* (Ahmedabad: Navajivan Press, 1930), p. 6.

[24] J. C. Kumarappa, *Public Finance*, p. 18.

Being a master's thesis, the scope of Joseph's work was limited and only provided a broad examination of Indian public finance. One limitation was that the analysis was based on publicly available government data that left a great deal to be desired and made it very difficult to make accurate comparisons over the years.[25] However, in personal terms, working on the thesis was immensely useful to Joseph as it finally shattered his belief in the moral legitimacy of British rule in India. The methodology he adopted in the writing of *Public Finance* is also of great significance. Unlike other Indian academic exercises on colonial public finance at that time, Joseph does not shirk from harshly criticizing the colonizers for the exploitation of their hapless subjects.[26] The primary value of *Public Finance* lies in its consistent focus on the distributional impacts of public finance. Joseph argued that any claim on public revenues and assets in terms of 'national interest' had to demonstrate its social value. At the same time, all of the hallmarks of his lifelong concerns with freedom, justice, and autonomy are already evident in this work. Remarkably, over his long and often controversial public life of three decades, one finds great consistency and continuity of these ideas and values that were first expressed, admittedly in an inchoate form, in *Public Finance*. Although Joseph made only a limited contribution to the understanding of colonial public finance, his frank exposition as well as prescriptive remedies were refreshingly free from the obtuseness of typical academic theses. It is these characteristics of *Public Finance* that would make a positive impression on the person who mattered most in India at that time—Mahatma Gandhi.

Up to a point, Joseph was following in the footsteps of the great Indian economic nationalists of the past and indeed he drew on their ideas, including the drain theory, to understand the nature of colonial taxation. He had certainly read the works of Naoroji, Dutt, Gokhale, and Ranade, but in his own work, Joseph makes a radical departure. Although he agreed with the criticism of British economic policy, Joseph rejected the arguments of Ranade and others who held that the remedy for India's problems lay in its rapid industrialization. Joseph's departure from the early economic nationalists is clearly visible in his analysis of India's railways. While he recognized that policies discriminating

---

[25] J. C. Kumarappa, *Public Finance*, p. 31.

[26] In part, this was made easier by the thesis being written at an American university where the academics had no need or desire to defend British colonialism from criticism. A similar exercise would have been harder to carry out at a Cambridge or an Oxford in 1928.

in favour of foreign goods over Indian products had a serious impact on indigenous industries, his critique directly questioned the basic premise for the existence of India's vast railway network. Contrary to the present-day popular understanding that sees the Indian railways as an unalloyed blessing bestowed upon the nation by the British, Joseph clearly recognized that by 1925, the railways had been developed far in excess of real demand with 'the result that large amounts of Government revenue ha[d] to be diverted to maintain these unnatural and parasitic growths'.[27] Indeed, railway bonds in India were a sure-shot financial bargain for investors in London as the Government of India[28] had guaranteed high rates of return to be serviced out of India's public revenues. Thus, while the railways were built to earn interest for British capital, the development of the network was also skewed in favour of the metropolitan economy. Apart from discriminatory railway tariff structures that favoured British imports, the railway network was laid out on trunk lines that linked India's hinterland to the major ports. The expected result was the easy drain of India's 'reserves of food grains for [sale in] distant markets'.[29] Indeed, the railways were a contributing factor to that recurring crisis of life in colonial India, the scourge of famine.

Joseph argued that the land revenue policy under the British *ryotwari* system that was tied to the extent of landholding rather than the actual produce was an important factor in causing famines.[30] He pointed out that before the advent of the British, 'famines devastated the country in parts, but never the whole land at any one time. The chief cause was mainly the shortage of grain following a drought, not the lack of purchasing power. It was a natural calamity rather than the result of the economic situation'. While he wrote this from the academic refuge of Columbia, in a few years Joseph would be directly involved in a critique of the impacts of ryotwari taxation policy in Gujarat. More significantly, this understanding would play an important role in his response to British policy on the eve of the Bengal Famine of 1943.

[27] J. C. Kumarappa, *Public Finance*, p. 24.

[28] Please note that depending on the context, in this book, the term 'Government of India' refers to either the colonial regime or the government of independent India.

[29] J. C. Kumarappa, *Public Finance*, p. 25.

[30] J. C. Kumarappa, *Public Finance*, p. 8; here Joseph was following the views of A. Loveday, *The History and Economics of Indian Famines* (London: G. Bell and Sons Ltd., 1914).

Along with the distorted nature of railway investments and taxation policy, and the general neglect of public welfare, Joseph dwelt upon a key attribute of British fiscal policy in India that was to play an even greater role in India's exploitation in later years—the stability of the Indian rupee. In *Public Finance*, he noted that 'the Government is … not concerned with the stability of the purchasing power of the rupee which affects the welfare of the people'.[31] Rather it was solicitous of the 'maintenance of the stability of the rupee in terms of the sovereign to meet the interests of those engaged in foreign trade'. Till the end of British rule in India, colonial monetary policy was dictated by the financial interests of Britain at an enormous price that was paid for by the ordinary Indian.

While British colonialism had been subjected to an economic critique by many writers, perhaps the most valuable contribution of Joseph's thesis is its argument that there is nothing more 'closely related to the well-being of the nation' than its public finance.[32] He identified the stewardship of a society's ecological resources as the responsibility of a wise Government 'as short-sighted private ownership might waste and exhaust them in a brief period of time', since individuals 'in their anxiety [tend] to crowd into their span of three score years and ten as much of economic production as possible'. The tempering role of the state, Joseph argued, was not merely to curb the profligacy of the individual. Rather, it was necessary to limit the danger that wasteful use of resources 'may entail on the coming generations'. In explicitly foregrounding the rights of future generations in his fiscal analysis, he anticipated the modern debate in economics by several decades. If the rights of the unborn generations were to be protected, it was equally imperative that public policy be tested against the touchstone of individual well-being as opposed to the conventional 'monetary standard of wealth'.[33] Joseph agreed with John Ruskin when he asserted that 'there is no wealth but life'.[34]

Apart from laying out the purposes of public finance and good governance, Joseph's thesis is also marked by its clear-eyed statement of how a government ought to gather revenues as well as utilize them. Joseph commended indirect taxes but recognized that such taxation demands great care and responsibility in its deployment. Thus, if 'Hindu literature likens

---

[31] J. C. Kumarappa, *Public Finance*, p. 27.
[32] J. C. Kumarappa, *Public Finance*, p. 1.
[33] J. A. Hobson quoted by J. C. Kumarappa in *Public Finance*, p. 3.
[34] J. C. Kumarappa, *Public Finance*, p. 2.

[indirect taxation] to the process by which the bees suck the honey without the flowers knowing it', Joseph warned that 'this quality in its nature calls for the exercise of great caution on the part of those who are entrusted with this high duty'.[35] In figures of speech that take on ecological meaning in modern times, he alludes to the Kautilyan dictum that 'taxes should be obtained as the fruit that is plucked when ripe without injury to the plant' and not like the act of a 'charcoal dealer who cuts down the trees, burns them' and makes a profit. Joseph argues that the value of public administration cannot be measured in terms of mere profitability or efficiency. Rather it has to be judged 'on the touchstone of prosperity of the general mass of people'.[36] His line of ecological arguments for principles of public finance culminates in his commendation that

> [t]he laying out of the revenue so obtained should be such as to increase the productivity of the people. To use a classical figure, the taxes should rise as the vapour from the sea, from the section of the populace who could best pay, and should be precipitated like rain on the needy, as when the rich are taxed to pay for the education of the poor.[37]

During his years as an accountant in England, Joseph had implicitly believed in 'the trusteeship of the British Government, their well-meaning bureaucracy and their God-sent mission' in India.[38] But his short American interlude irrevocably changed his understanding of the world and his place in it. He came to recognize the source of his privileged position in society as well as the grave injustice being meted out to his less fortunate countrymen. Indeed, he might very well have asked himself, 'After such knowledge, what forgiveness?'[39]

By February of 1929, Joseph was preparing to depart for India and bade goodbye to his new-found friends in Syracuse and New York. That his time in the United States was one of a great churning of the mind is evident in a reminder sent by his Syracuse landlady.[40] She wrote and

---

[35] J. C. Kumarappa, *Public Finance*, p. 3.

[36] J. C. Kumarappa, *Public Finance*, p. 4.

[37] Here, Joseph is obviously borrowing the metaphor of taxes as rain from R. C. Dutt's *The Economic History of India under Early British Rule*, pp. xi–xii.

[38] Vinaik, *Gandhian Crusader*, p. 39.

[39] The quote is from the poem 'Gerontion' by T. S. Eliot.

[40] Letter from Isabelle Darby to J. C. Cornelius, 30 January 1929, Correspondence Files, Kumarappa Papers.

asked him not to forget his friends in his mad rush to acquire his liberty. In a prescient warning that Joseph would soon ignore, she also asked him not to 'allow the big cause to swallow [him] ... body and soul to the exclusion' of their friendship. Soon Joseph set sail from New York, but neither he nor his correspondents would have guessed what life had in store for him in India.

Figure 1 The Cornelius family, circa 1901. The nine-year-old Joseph is standing in the back row (second from right, with a bow-tie) and his parents, Solomon Doraisamy Cornelius (1851–1917) and Esther Rajanayakam (1856–1924), are seated in the middle. *Photograph courtesy of Magan Sangrahalaya Samiti, Wardha (Maharashtra).*

Figure 2 Holidaying on the beach at Mandwa, 1925. *Photograph courtesy of Magan Sangrahalaya Samiti, Wardha (Maharashtra).*

Figure 3   On a picnic with friends in England, sometime between 1913 and 1919. *Photograph courtesy of Magan Sangrahalaya Samiti, Wardha (Maharashtra).*

Figure 4   Joseph taught accountancy at Davar's College in present-day Mumbai. The college was founded by Sohrab Davar, Joseph's partner in the firm Cornelius and Davar. *Photograph courtesy of Magan Sangrahalaya Samiti, Wardha (Maharashtra).*

Figure 5 Just in case you thought selfies were a new phenomenon.
Joseph took these in early 1927 and captioned them (*a*) 'Reflections',
(*b*) 'The Denationalised One',

(c) 'The Pathan', and (d) 'The Shah'. *Photographs courtesy of Magan Sangrahalaya Samiti, Wardha (Maharashtra).*

Figure 6   As a student in Syracuse in the winter of 1927–8. *Photograph courtesy of Magan Sangrahalaya Samiti, Wardha (Maharashtra).*

4 Waiting for the Mahatma

I n 1929, after a three-month sojourn in Europe, Joseph returned to Bombay and resumed his flourishing practice with Sohrab Davar.[1] Although he was still committed to a professional career, he was now driven by an inner urge and was seeking new avenues to be of 'service to the country'.[2] An important clue to Joseph's state of mind during this period is given by a significant decision he made along with two of his three brothers. While a Westernized upbringing and education offered many material advantages under the Raj, Joseph and some of his siblings felt that their anglicization had alienated them from the rest of Indian society. While this continues to be a source of anxiety in some elements of India's English-speaking elite, in 1929, Joseph and

[1] Letter from J. C. Cornelius to Mrs Stewart, 3 May 1929, Correspondence Files, Kumarappa Papers.

[2] Letters from J. C. Coomarappa to Mahatma Gandhi, 22 and 31 May 1929, S. N. 32027 and 32028 respectively. The initials S. N. stand for 'Sabarmati Nidhi' and refer to items from the Archives of the Sabarmati Ashram Preservation and Memorial Trust, Ahmedabad (henceforth S. N.). During this period he was elected a Life Fellow of the Royal Economic Society. See Letter from J. C. Cornelius to Mrs Stewart, 3 May 1929, Correspondence Files, Kumarappa Papers.

his brothers made the unusual decision to discard their Christian names in favour of the original family name. On 10 May 1929, Joseph Chelladurai Cornelius filed an affidavit in Bombay stating that he was henceforth to be known as Joseph Cornelius Coomarappa.[3] His brothers even changed their given names to Hindu ones. Thus, John Jesudasan Cornelius and Benjamin Cornelius became Jagadisan Mohandas Kumarappa and Bharatan Kumarappa respectively. After some time, Joseph too adopted the orthography of their family name and became Joseph Cornelius Kumarappa. In the remainder of this biography we will refer to him as Kumarappa.

While the question of identity was sorted out, Kumarappa's ambiguity of purpose also did not last long as he sought a meeting with that great 'fisher of men', Mahatma Gandhi. In 1947, Kumarappa wrote an account of this encounter for a collection of anecdotes on Gandhi.[4] Perhaps due to the passage of almost two decades between the event and its recollection, the essay is incorrect on certain counts. The other recountings of Kumarappa's first visit to Sabarmati Ashram that exist have replicated these factual errors. Furthermore, internal histories of the Gandhian movement have sought to portray Kumarappa's first meeting with the Mahatma as one of instantaneous 'conversion' and utter devotion to Gandhi.[5] While the notion of an immediate conversion can be easily discounted, the process of transmission and retelling of this story is a fascinating example of mythification, a process that transmutes a real historical event into a *katha* with a didactic purpose. Similarly, as we shall see, an important eyewitness account of Kumarappa's visit also does not square with the

[3] Affidavit reproduced in J. D. Chakkanatt, *Of God and Mammon: J. C. Kumarappa's Religious Theory of Economics as a Counterpoint to the Religion of Economics* (New Delhi: Intercultural Publications, 2001). Evidently, Joseph wished to retain the family name of Cornelius in some form and transposed it to become his middle name. In *Gandhi's Economist* (p. 4), Mark Lindley states that the new name was Joseph Chelladurai Kumarappa. This is incorrect and contradicts evidence, including that of the affidavit.

[4] J. C. Kumarappa, 'Lessons from His Life', in *Incidents of Gandhiji's Life*, edited by Chandrashanker Shukla (Bombay: Vora and Co. Publishers Ltd., 1949), pp. 131–43.

[5] While Vinaik makes no such claims in the first biography of Kumarappa he wrote in 1956, in the 1987 version he claims, 'At the end of the interview, a complete transformation overtook Kumarappa' (*Gandhian Crusader*, p. 5).

historical record. Thus, with time, there are different ways this meeting is remembered by the various actors themselves that gives the story a Rashomon-like effect.

Although the archival record is sparse, in conjunction with the biographical material available we can reconstruct the broad contours of Kumarappa's life during this critical period. Impressed by the quality of his work, Seligman had advised Kumarappa to publish his master's thesis.[6] Now back in Bombay, Kumarappa was scouting for a publisher. Given the nature of the thesis, a friend felt that Gandhi would probably be interested and suggested that Kumarappa seek his advice on the matter. In his essay, Kumarappa places the date of his meeting with Gandhi at Sabarmati Ashram as 9 May 1929. While we do not know if it was an error on Kumarappa's part or that of the printer, we do know that on that day Gandhi was nowhere near Ahmedabad. In fact, he was on tour in the Andhra region, then part of Madras Presidency, and was speaking at Polavaram.[7] Gandhi arrived in Bombay on the night of 22 May 1929 and was staying at Mani Bhavan on Laburnum Road in Gamdevi. Kumarappa's first letter addressed to Gandhi is also dated 22 May 1929 and he probably went to Mani Bhavan on 24 May. In any event, as Kumarappa recalled, on arriving at Mani Bhavan dressed in European clothes, he went 'up the staircase, and the door was answered by someone who [he] ... took to be a servant clad in dhoti and [shirt]'. On being told that Gandhi was busy in a Congress Working Committee (CWC) meeting, and since the person spoke good English, Kumarappa surmised that he was 'worthy of taking a message' and handed over his manuscript and the letter. In the letter, Kumarappa sought Gandhi's advice on publishing it and also asked for an appointment. The presumed 'servant' was Pyarelal, one of Gandhi's secretaries, who called back later and advised Kumarappa to arrive in Ahmedabad in a week's time for his appointment with Gandhi.[8]

[6] Letter from J. C. Coomarappa to Mahatma Gandhi, 22 May 1929, S. N. 32027.

[7] C. B. Dalal (comp.), *Gandhi: 1915–1948 A Detailed Chronology* (New Delhi: Gandhi Peace Foundation, 1971), p. 77.

[8] J. C. Kumarappa, 'Lessons from His Life' in *Incidents*, pp. 131–2.

On the morning of the appointment, 30 May 1929, Kumarappa arrived at Sabarmati Ashram and was shown into his guest room.[9] Much used to the elaborate clutter of anglicized living, Kumarappa was horrified at the bareness of his room that 'was devoid of all furniture excepting a *charpai*'. To make matters worse, his accommodation had, what Kumarappa quaintly called, 'squatting toilet arrangements'. The portents were not good. With plenty of time to kill before his 2:30 p.m. appointment, Kumarappa spent some time enjoying the beauty of the Sabarmati and walked back towards the settlement. What followed is best described in his own words:

On the way up, I saw an old man seated under a tree on a neatly cleaned cow-dunged floor, spinning. Having never seen a spinning wheel before, I leaned on my walking stick and standing akimbo was watching, as there were still ten minutes for the appointment. This old man after about five minutes opened his toothless lips, and with a smile on his face enquired if I was Kumarappa. It suddenly dawned on me that my questioner might be no other than Mahatma Gandhi. So I, in my turn, asked him if he was Gandhiji; and when he nodded I promptly sat down on the cow-dunged floor regardless of the well-kept crease of my silk trousers! Seeing me sitting with stretched legs, more or less in a reclining position, someone from the house came rushing down with a chair for me, and Gandhiji asked me to get up and sit in the chair more comfortably. I replied that since he was seated on the floor I did not propose to take the chair.[10]

What transpired between Kumarappa and Gandhi is not clear but it is unlikely that Gandhi would have had the time in the intervening week to actually read Kumarappa's thesis. Again in his anecdotal recollections Kumarappa suggests that Gandhi proposed to publish his essay in a serialized form in the journal *Young India*. However, it was actually many months later that Gandhi wrote to Kumarappa mentioning that he had nearly finished reading the essay and desired to publish it in *Young India*, and later as a pamphlet.[11] Nevertheless, during the first meeting Gandhi

[9] This date is inferred on the basis of his letter to Gandhi on 31 May 1929 wherein he states 'after seeing you yesterday'. But if the date was actually 29 May then we can explain the use of '9 May' in the essay in *Incidents* as a printer's error.

[10] J. C. Kumarappa, 'Lessons from His Life' in *Incidents*, pp. 132–3. It is puzzling that in 1929, Kumarappa seemed unaware of what Gandhi looked like.

[11] Letter to J. C. Kumarappa, 14 November 1929, *CWMG*. The serialization ran between 28 November 1929 and 23 January 1930 and was subsequently published by Navajivan Press as *Public Finance and Our Poverty: The Contribution of Public Finance to the Present Economic State of India* in 1930. Kumarappa added a

had shrewdly grasped the worth of his somewhat unusual visitor and sent him to meet both Kaka Kalelkar and Shankerlal Banker who headed the Gujarat Vidyapith and the All India Spinners Association (AISA), respectively. While Kalelkar was the considerate person who had offered a chair to Kumarappa, their subsequent meeting did not go well. Kalelkar felt that Kumarappa's ignorance of both Hindi and Gujarati rendered him unfit for the Vidyapith where learning was imparted in the vernacular. Similarly Banker did not feel that the AISA could avail itself of Kumarappa's services. The temperamental Kumarappa got into a huff and returned to Bombay from where he dashed off a letter to Gandhi explaining that his meetings were disappointing but he reiterated his desire to work for the country.[12]

Gandhi, however, understood the potential of Kumarappa as a worker and prevailed upon Kalelkar to change his mind.[13] A chastened Kalelkar now wrote to Kumarappa inviting him to join the Vidyapith! Given the shortage of dedicated workers, Kumarappa could be accommodated despite his language handicaps. However the Vidyapith, like other nationalist institutions, was run on meagre resources and Kumarappa was offered a monthly salary of Rs 75 and a housing allowance of Rs 15, a far cry from Kumarappa's earnings in Bombay at the time.[14] In later years, Kalelkar and Kumarappa became close comrades, and the former was perhaps embarrassed at his initial rebuff of his younger visitor. In a Festschrift for Kumarappa published in 1952, Kalelkar elided the actual chain of events and instead claimed that sometime after his meeting with Gandhi, Kumarappa wrote to him 'expressing a wish to join the Gujerath Vidyapith' and consequently Kalelkar 'sent him a reply warmly welcoming him to the Vidyapith'.[15]

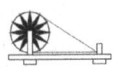

In contrast to writings about the political leadership of India's freedom

chapter on public debts to the second edition in 1931 and another on the sterling credits to the third edition in 1945.

[12] Letter from J. C. Coomarappa to Mahatma Gandhi, 31 May 1929, S. N. 32028.

[13] Years later, Gandhi told Kumarappa that while Kalelkar was unable to size him up, Gandhi himself knew that this was a young man he had to 'grab'. J. C. Kumarappa, 'Lessons from His Life', in Incidents, p. 134.

[14] Letter from D. B. Kalelkar to J. C. Coomarappa, 2 June 1929, S. N. 32030.

[15] D. B. Kalelkar, 'My Reminiscences of Kumarappa', in Economics of Peace, p. 346.

movement, the literature on the inner lives of constructive workers is sparse. The decision to relinquish the comfort of a secure life in favour of an uncertain future is always a hard one. In Kumarappa's case, he was making the transition from a Westernized accountant aspiring to a four-digit monthly income to a public servant who lived out his ideals in a life of greatly reduced means. While his initiation into the nationalist movement was comparatively quick, it was by no means instantaneous or unambiguous. In reply to Kalelkar's invitation to join the Vidyapith, Kumarappa sought some time as he had to extricate himself from his practice of a decade. Moreover, his partner, Sohrab Davar, was anxious not to dissolve the partnership right away. Kumarappa himself felt that it would be wiser to go to the Vidyapith on probation without remuneration for a few months. While keen on joining the Vidyapith, he was as yet not ready to 'burn the bridge'.[16] Curiously, for a man who was fiercely independent-minded, Kumarappa wrote to his two elder brothers, J. M. Kumarappa and J. T. Cornelius, seeking their counsel. The responses were as contrasting as they could possibly be. An anxious Thambidurai wrote back from Lucknow advising Kumarappa to 'stick at Bombay and build up' his practice. Further, he wanted Kumarappa to refrain from social work for ten years which would make him 'financially quite independent and allow ... greater freedom of action'. Alarmed at the prospect of his brother taking such a drastic decision, Thambidurai also suggested that for some time he should avoid politics 'like the devil' and 'remain tactful and silent and not give free expression' to his feelings on political issues. Thambidurai took a dim view of the Gujarat Vidyapith and was apprehensive about Kumarappa 'working under a wholly Indian managed organization under present conditions'.[17] In contrast, J. M.'s wife, Ratnam Kumarappa, enthusiastically endorsed Kumarappa's plans. Writing on behalf of her absent husband, she felt that J. M. would not object to the probation at the Vidyapith, rather 'he may be only too pleased, as it falls quite in line with his present views and outlook'.[18]

Despite writing to his brothers for advice, Kumarappa's mind was already made up and he told Kalelkar that he would arrive at the Vidyapith

---

[16] Letter from J. C. Coomarappa to D. B. Kalelkar, 4 June 1929, S. N. 32031.

[17] Letter from J. T. Cornelius to J. C. Coomarappa, 8 June 1929, S. N. 32033.

[18] Letter from C. K. Ratnam to J. C. Coomarappa, 10 June 1929, filed under Press Clippings, Kumarappa Papers.

by the end of June 1929.[19] While we are not privy to his state of mind at this time, it was by all means a momentous choice. In Kumarappa's case, he was also consciously traversing the considerable cultural distance between his upbringing in a Tamil Christian family and the largely unfamiliar north Indian milieu of Gandhi's establishment in Ahmedabad. The most striking example of this cultural gap is evident in the first letter he wrote to the Mahatma. In the careless orthography that persists even today in Western writings, Kumarappa addressed his note to 'Mahathma Ghandi'.[20]

Since everyone at the Vidyapith wore only khadi as a 'practical symbol of ... identification with the masses', Kalelkar advised Kumarappa to procure his clothing in Bombay.[21] It was this suggestion that had prompted Kumarappa's khadi bhandar visit that we described earlier. When Kumarappa arrived at the Vidyapith on 1 July 1929, 'with a Gandhi cap on his head and dressed in a khadi kurta' a bemused Kalelkar was pleasantly surprised but also noted that 'neither fitted him well and his appearance was somewhat ludicrous'.[22] The novelty of Kumarappa's determined attempt to Indianize himself is further underscored by Kalelkar's remembrance of what followed that day. The presence of a Christian in the Vidyapith was a rarity and Kalelkar saw it as a chance to break the taboo of interdining. With this in mind, he decided to join the students in the dining room and took the new arrival along. To make Kumarappa comfortable, Kalelkar had arranged for a table and a chair. To this courtesy 'Kumarappa retorted that he was not yet so old as to be unable to change from the chair to the floor' and dine with everyone else. Thus Kumarappa did sit on the floor but could not cross his legs like everyone else. Instead 'he sat twisting the whole body in the shape of an irregular N' and proceeded to eat. As Kalelkar recalled, the students 'had the good manners not to burst into laughter'.

[19] This is inferred from a letter from D. B. Kalelkar to J. C. Coomarappa, 12 June 1929, S. N. 32034. Kalelkar was presumably responding to Kumarappa's letter. Since the letter from his brother Thambidurai warning him against joining the Vidyapith is dated 8 June 1929 from Lucknow, it is reasonable to infer that by the time it arrived in Bombay, Kumarappa's mind was already made up.

[20] Letter from J. C. Coomarappa to Mahatma Gandhi, 22 May 1929, S. N. 32027.

[21] Letters from D. B. Kalelkar to J. C. Coomarappa, 7 and 12 June 1929, S. N. 32032 and S. N. 32034 respectively.

[22] D. B. Kalelkar, 'My Reminiscences of Kumarappa', in *Economics of Peace*, p. 346. The date of Kumarappa's arrival is inferred from the letter from D. B. Kalelkar to J. C. Coomarappa, 22 June 1929, S. N. 32035.

While such cultural differences were amusing, the apprehensions of Davar and Thambidurai about Kumarappa's trial period of nationalist work were not entirely misplaced. As a chartered accountant in Bombay, Kumarappa's clients were predominantly European and Parsi firms whose interests were tied to the fortunes of the British Raj. Since these businessmen would not 'tolerate a man with Gandhian sympathies', Kumarappa was seriously jeopardizing his professional prospects in Bombay. However, once he landed in jail, his bridges to life in Bombay were well and truly burnt. As Kumarappa tellingly points out, 'It was *after* this that I threw in my lot with Gandhiji.'[23]

While Kumarappa's unusual background held novelty value at the Gujarat Vidyapith, it also presented Kalelkar with the problem of finding suitable work for a man who knew no Hindi or Gujarati. Soon, this problem resolved itself as the Gandhians embarked upon a study of the agrarian crisis of Gujarat.

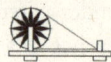

By the end of the nineteenth century, the institutionalization of new forms of land tenure meant that taxation was a major burden for the peasants. At the same time, the development of a railway network and growth of exports left the rural Indian economy vulnerable to the fortunes of international trade. In the ryotwari areas of Gujarat, the assessed land revenue which was collected in an uncompromising manner led to serious consequences when compounded with natural disasters. In particular, the famine of 1899–1900 had a devastating impact and wiped out a fifth of Gujarat's population.[24] In 1918, although the peasantry had partly recovered from the effects of this famine, a combination of poor rainfall and high inflation on account of the First World War took a severe toll.[25] While the 'revenue code' allowed for a full remission of land revenue due to poor yields, the administration was unyielding. The resultant discontent led to the first agrarian *satyagraha* in Kheda district in 1918 headed by Gandhi and

[23] J. C. Kumarappa, 'Lessons from His Life', in *Incidents*, p. 134; emphasis added.

[24] A. Yagnik and S. Sheth, *The Shaping of Modern Gujarat: Plurality, Hindutva and Beyond* (New Delhi: Penguin Books India, 2005), pp. 133–5.

[25] D. Hardiman, *Peasant Nationalists of Gujarat: Kheda District, 1917–1934* (New Delhi: Oxford University Press, 1981), pp. 86–7.

Vallabhbhai Patel. Despite the relative success of the Kheda satyagraha, the level of peasant discontent remained high and land revenue continued to be a major bone of contention. Inevitably, it led to another major confrontation with the government in 1928, in Bardoli *taluka* of Surat district. The Bardoli satyagraha was keenly watched and its success in bending the will of the mighty Raj was met with a chorus of applause. It also evoked interest in the agrarian questions that plagued the Indian peasantry. While this wider interest was fleeting, the constructive workers had a deeper commitment to Gandhi's agenda of rural renewal.

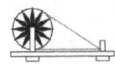

From the late nineteenth century, sociological and economic studies of Indian villages had become popular. Mostly supervised by Englishmen, they did not address the concerns of Indian nationalists.[26] During this period, wary of a contentious debate, many studies of Indian villages completely avoided references to land revenue.[27] This was also true of the Royal Commission on Agriculture of 1928 that scrupulously avoided any discussion of either land revenue or taxation.[28] If this situation was to be redeemed, the Gandhians decided that they would have to apply themselves to the problem. Given his academic training and inability to teach at the Vidyapith, Kumarappa was the natural choice to carry out a survey to understand the condition of the villages. Till then, the little that he knew of rural India was gleaned from the writings of others. Now, the survey offered direct contact with villages which was to profoundly shape Kumarappa's understanding of the problems of India's agrarian economy.

Although the survey by Kumarappa was a new endeavour for the Gandhians, its rationale was presented in the recognizable terms of immiseration due to the pernicious land revenue policies. In November 1929, a committee to survey fifty-four villages of Matar taluka was

---

[26] Notably Gilbert Slater's *Some South Indian Villages* (1918) and Harold Mann and N. V. Kanitkar's *Land and Labour in a Deccan Village* (1921).

[27] For example, John Matthai's *Village Government in British India* (1915) and J. B. Shukla's *Life and Labour in a Gujarat Taluka* (1937).

[28] This point was made in chapter eight of G. T. Wrench, *The Restoration of the Peasantries: With Especial Reference to that of India* (London: C. W. Daniel Company, 1939).

appointed with Sardar Patel as the chairman and Kumarappa as director. It was explained that Matar taluka was chosen as the survey area due to its 'history of revenue settlements' and consequent impoverishment. It was stated that in line with Gandhi's commitment to a truthful inquiry, the survey committee would try to obtain a true picture of the conditions and 'gauge the true measure of the people's impoverishment'.[29] It is possible that the choice of Matar for the survey was also motivated by the expectation of public support. During the Kheda satyagraha of 1918, due to the tireless work of the political activist Indulal Yagnik, the agitation was most vigorous in Matar taluka.[30] This support for the nationalist movement was further consolidated after the much-appreciated relief work undertaken by Gandhians during the floods of 1927.[31]

The survey villages were carefully chosen to be representative of different agrarian conditions caused by differential access to irrigation. While the Navagam villages had good irrigation facilities due to an 1843 treaty with the British, the southern villages around Limbasi were poorly irrigated and drought-prone. The level of access to water in the villages around the town of Matar lay somewhere in between. Fieldwork for the survey by Kumarappa and nine students of the Vidyapith began in December 1929 and concluded on 11 March 1930, a day before Gandhi set out for the shores of Dandi. However, with the country engulfed in the Civil Disobedience movement the report was eventually published during the last days of 1931.[32]

[29] M. Desai, 'An Economic Survey', *Young India*, 28 November 1929.

[30] Hardiman, *Peasant Nationalists of Gujarat*, pp. 102–3.

[31] J. C. Kumarappa (Director), *A Survey of Matar Taluka: Kaira District* (Ahmedabad: Gujarat Vidyapith, 1931), p. 2. Also see Appendix VII-A of B. Pattabhi Sitaramayya, *History of the Indian National Congress (1885–1935)* (Madras: Working Committee of the Congress, 1935).

[32] The multiple surveys in Gujarat in this period have led the historian David Hardiman to club Kumarappa's Matar Survey preceding the Civil Disobedience campaign of 1930–1 with the assessments made prior to the launch of the satyagrahas of Kheda and Bardoli. This led him to conclude 'that such work tended to have very radical consequences'; see D. Hardiman, *Gandhi in His Time and Ours* (New Delhi: Permanent Black, 2003), p. 81. First, the Matar Survey and the rapid assessments in Kheda and Bardoli were very different in their nature and objectives. The latter only verified local claims before launching a no-revenue campaign. Second, Kalelkar's 'Prefatory Note' is dated 21 December 1931, hence, the published report could not have influenced the no-tax campaign of 1930–1 or the Civil Disobedience movement itself.

Agrarian discontent in Gujarat was primarily due to the relentless increase in land revenue that the British considered as rent and not as taxation in the ryotwari areas. The administration and nationalist agitators were divided on the question of the government's right to arbitrarily assess the quantum of land revenue in a manner that was independent of actual crop yields. This has given rise to a perception of the Matar Survey as a nationalist polemic against land revenue policies. However, in Kumarappa's hands, the published survey took on a distinct character that went beyond an anti-tax diatribe. The survey did address itself to land revenue policy and a general lack of governmental solicitude towards the peasantry, but in its main thrust it sought a basis for village revitalization. Although not noticed in the din of political rhetoric, this new direction was due to the distinct remit given to the survey team by Gandhi. While the Congress had a limited interest in such issues, for Gandhi, crafting an economic vision for rural India was a fundamental task. Aware of the unpopularity of his agenda amongst the educated sections, Gandhi wished that a new Indian economics be built on a sound foundation of empirical data. Therefore, he wanted the survey to arrive at a posteriori inferences based on rigorous reasoning that 'no amount of jugglery could controvert'.[33]

The findings of the survey confirmed the claims the nationalists had been making for a long time. The extortionate land revenue policy was indeed the main reason for driving a relatively prosperous region into penury. The true effect of government policy was evident when revenue was assessed in terms of productivity. Estimated in terms of actual yield, land revenue varied from 71 per cent in Limbasi to as much as 215 per cent in Traj.[34] Kumarappa pointed out that the revenue was paid by the farmer as the only other alternative was starvation.[35] He found that 60 per cent of the families examined were unable to pay their dues on time forcing them to frequently borrow money. The farmers' problems were compounded by the transfer of large amounts of Indian capital to England during this period. The resultant contraction of money supply and a complex chain of linkages to the metropolitan economy meant that the Indian villager ended up servicing his debt at a very high interest rate. The impact of all of these factors was severe as it drove farmers further into debt. While

---

[33] Kalelkar, 'Prefatory Note', in *Survey of Matar Taluka*.

[34] *Survey of Matar Taluka*, p. 86.

[35] *Survey of Matar Taluka*, p. 92. The same argument is also presented in Dietmar Rothermund, *Government, Landlord and Peasant in India: Agrarian Relations under British Rule, 1865–1935* (Wiesbaden: Franz Steiner Verlag GmbH, 1978), p. 39.

government officials castigated farmers for profligate spending on marriages and other social occasions, Kumarappa turned the argument around and pointed out that if even for small pleasures and social necessities the farmer had to resort to borrowing, it surely meant that their occupation was hardly remunerative. In contrast to the oft-repeated charge of Gandhian romanticization of villages, Kumarappa remarked: 'Life in a village is drab enough and an occasional entertainment or festivity is indulged in to relieve this monotony.'[36]

The empirical evidence assembled in the report was extensive and has served as an invaluable basis for a long-term study of economic change in the region.[37] This richness in data is complemented by Kumarappa's observations which, for a novice in the field, are sharp and insightful. Expectedly, the treatment of land rent and its impact was extensive in the Matar Survey. But the bulk of the report studies the agricultural practices of the Matar peasantry with extensive chapters on crop cultivation and the use of manure. In both cases, Kumarappa felt compelled to defend the peasant against various charges which according to him were unfair and not borne out in the field. A lack of interest in using a heavier plough than the traditional one was often cited as an example of the backwardness of the Indian peasant. Using his own evidence and drawing from other studies Kumarappa demonstrated that the farmers' choice was a well-considered one since their farm animals were not strong enough for the heavier versions that had the disadvantage of also being substantially more expensive. Kumarappa also disputed the claim of the Royal Commission on Agriculture that the use of cow dung cakes for domestic fuel was a wasteful practice. He extended the debate on this seemingly mundane issue by connecting it with the vagaries of irrigation and unavailability of enough farmyard nutrients. Kumarappa's nuanced insights are best illustrated by his comments on the role of bullocks in the agrarian economy. While it was usual to condemn the backwardness of Indian villages, he argued against the use of oil pumps for irrigation and motorized transport. Drawing on his data, Kumarappa demonstrated that the maintenance of bullocks was the largest item of expenditure for farmers. This expenditure on bullocks was inevitable. Since bullocks were needed to plough the fields, they had

[36] *Survey of Matar Taluka*, p. 114.

[37] The existence of this survey has inspired many resurveys in more recent times. The differential access to water that existed in 1931 changed with the introduction of canal irrigation. This has also made it possible to study the impact of irrigation on the region.

to be maintained. In such a scenario, oil pumps and motorized transport would only add to the cost. He argued, '[A]s long as the organization of our present rural economy remains what it is, mechanization of particular parts' was not desirable, since the additional expenditure incurred would not offset the benefits.[38]

While Kumarappa was quick to champion the peasant's cause and attack the deplorable conditions in the villages due to government policy, he was not a partisan who took absolute positions. He also criticized Matar's peasants when warranted. He discounted the repeated complaint of failure of rains since 1900 and showed that the five-year averages of rainfall statistics told a different story.[39] The farmers and artisans were also criticized for their failure to effect any improvement in the quality of their seeds and for not bettering their implements. The general lack of hygiene also came in for criticism, and Kumarappa pointed out that changing this situation would need a well-directed effort. In this context he found the condition of the untouchables deplorable. While the caste people were generally well provided with drinking water, this was rarely the case with the untouchables. In one egregious instance, Kumarappa noted that while the cattle were provided with a nicely cemented trough, the untouchables had to use a stagnant pool.[40]

Although empirically sound and insightful, on sociological issues Kumarappa was on weaker ground. At this point in time, with no real experience, his understanding of the organizational principles of Indian society was largely a reflection of Gandhi's own views on caste and hereditary occupation. Thus, the central problem was that the 'caste system had petrified into a system of hereditary professions carrying special rights and privileges or disabilities'.[41] The challenge was to restore the dignity of labour and delink caste from various occupations in the agrarian economy. Keeping in mind the economic and psychological impact of idleness, Kumarappa recommended that peasants should cease to be 'gentleman farmers' and work on the land themselves.[42] Even for a region that had participated in satyagraha, this was wishful thinking.

By the time he finished the fieldwork for the Matar Survey, Kumarappa's intellectual preparation for his role in the Gandhian fold was complete. This

[38] *Survey of Matar Taluka*, p. 49.
[39] *Survey of Matar Taluka*, p. 41.
[40] *Survey of Matar Taluka*, pp. 117–18.
[41] *Survey of Matar Taluka*, pp. 63–4.
[42] *Survey of Matar Taluka*, p. 20.

was possible since he, unlike many of his compatriots, had arrived at his convictions prior to meeting Gandhi. As Gandhi himself put it, Kumarappa had arrived 'ready-made'.[43] The Civil Disobedience campaign that followed the march to Dandi was to make heavy demands on Kumarappa. In the process of addressing the challenges that rapidly presented themselves, he was to finally make his transition from being a successful urban professional to a lifelong champion of the Indian village and the villager.

[43] Gandhi made this remark in a conversation with Madan Mohan Malaviya; see Vinaik, *Quest*, p. 12.

5 Baptism by Fire

During Kumarappa's years in America, the political temperature
in India had been steadily on the rise. By the time he arrived at
Sabarmati Ashram to meet Gandhi in May 1929, the countdown
to a mass struggle had already begun. On the morning of 12 March 1930,
with a pledge to return to the ashram only after India was liberated,
Gandhi set out with a select band of compatriots on a path that criss-
crossed the Gujarat countryside. Arriving at the village of Dandi, by the
simple act of picking up a pinch of salt, Gandhi inaugurated an extensive
campaign of civil disobedience that was to forever alter the balance of
power between the rulers and the ruled.

In the meanwhile, since the December of 1929, Kumarappa and his
team quietly laboured away in Matar. But when Kalelkar wrote asking for
a few pen sketches of village life, Kumarappa claimed to have no gift for
writing and was 'not prepared to air [his] ignorance for the amusement of
the public'.[1] While he needed time to think through the rural issues that he
was confronting for the first time, Kumarappa was also anxious that the
survey be seen as 'a scientific one worthy of the impartial judgement of a

---

[1] Letter from J. C. Kumarappa to D. B. Kalelkar, 20 December 1929,
Subject File, 6, Kumarappa Papers.

National University'. As the survey area lay right on the path chosen from Sabarmati to Dandi, Kumarappa did not want his work to appear to be mere political propaganda. But soon he was propelled by circumstances into the eye of the nationalist storm.

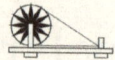

On 20 April 1930, Kumarappa visited Gandhi in Karadi to discuss the latter's foreword to *Public Finance and Our Poverty*. Perhaps in consideration of Gandhi's time, Kumarappa had typed up the foreword himself and presented it to Gandhi for his signature! An amused Gandhi laid the typescript aside and told Kumarappa that the foreword would be his own.[2] As chairman of the survey committee for Matar, Sardar Patel was much impressed by Kumarappa's diligence and had conveyed this to Gandhi who now invited Kumarappa to contribute regularly to the columns of his weekly journal, *Young India*.[3] Kumarappa demurred on the grounds of inexperience and instead offered his skills at 'auditing dusty ledgers'. In response, Gandhi answered that as the editor it was he who was to judge the fitness of a writer. Since Gandhi had expected to be arrested at any point during the Salt March, he had nominated Mahadev Desai to become the editor in the event of his arrest. Next in the line of succession was a young English Quaker, Reginald Reynolds, who had become well known when he was hand-picked to personally deliver Gandhi's letter to the Viceroy before Dandi. As it transpired, Mahadev Desai was arrested in the early days of the campaign and by the time of Gandhi's arrest, *Young India* ended up with two acting editors. However, Reynolds quit soon owing to

the impossibility of co-operating with a new Acting Editor of *Young India*, whose authority had eventually been established after much argument. He was a man whom I have since learnt to respect; but as he is still considered a difficult person to work with, I may have had good reason for my criticisms of him.[4]

[2] J. C. Kumarappa, 'Lessons from His Life' in *Incidents*, pp. 131–43.

[3] J. C. Kumarappa, 'Vallabhbhai', *Gram Udyog Patrika*, January 1951.

[4] Reginald Reynolds, *A Quest for Gandhi* (New York: Doubleday and Company, 1952), p. 68.

That querulous and difficult acting editor was Kumarappa! The confusion arose when in early May, with both Gandhi and Mahadev Desai under arrest, the trustees of Navajivan invited Kumarappa to help run *Young India*.[5] The 15 May 1930 issue appeared with Kumarappa named as the *pro tempore* editor. Writing from Yeravda Jail, Gandhi expressed his happiness at this arrangement.[6] Gandhi felt Kumarappa was worthy of the job, but perhaps he had spoken prematurely. By the next week, the question of editorship was sorted out in favour of Jairamdas Daulatram who remained the named editor till his incarceration in August. Daulatram, a Sindhi nationalist from Karachi of the same age as Kumarappa, was probably preferred as the editor given his longer involvement with the nationalist struggle.[7] Although Kumarappa had earlier baulked at wielding the journalist's pen, it is not difficult to understand the reasons for a change of heart. For one, most of the leaders were either busy organizing protests or had earned their rest in prison. As a result, there were not many capable hands left in Ahmedabad. Besides, there would have been fewer still who could handle English with ease. More significantly, the march of events in 1930 was to have a profound impact on Kumarappa's mind and deeply influence his resolve to commit his life to the nationalist cause.

The Civil Disobedience campaign of this period was characterized by a remarkable combination of fearlessness and self-discipline on the part of the *satyagrahis*. While this was by no means universal or even durable, beyond a doubt a new idiom of politics had been invented. As the struggles and protests played out all over the country, *Young India* sought to both inform and steer the progress of the campaign along the lines of satya and ahimsa. Apart from the editorial work of organizing the material sent in by Congress workers from all over the country, Kumarappa's own writings centred on countering British propaganda, and addressing the nationalists on ideological issues as well as examining the attitude of Christians to the nationalist upsurge in India. However, Kumarappa's most significant contribution during this period was ensuring the uninterrupted publication of the weekly despite the Navajivan Press being seized. From May 1930 till his imprisonment in early 1931, he edited, organized, and wrote many of the columns of *Young India*, which was a major vehicle for communication at a time of great turmoil all over India.

[5] J. C. Kumarappa, 'Lessons from His Life' in *Incidents*, pp. 131–43.

[6] Letter to Narandas Gandhi, 18/21 May 1930, *CWMG*.

[7] Years later, after the death of Bharatan in 1957, Daulatram was for a brief period the editor-in-chief of *The Collected Works of Mahatma Gandhi*.

While providing a political and economic critique of British rule was easy for Kumarappa, he was remarkably forthright in his assessment of the satyagraha campaigns, as exemplified by his essay on the Dharasana salt raids.[8] By the time of his arrest, Gandhi was planning to break the stalemate following the end of the Salt March by a more proactive raid on the salt depots at Dharasana. In his absence, a mass action plan was executed on 21 May 1930. What transpired on that day has since passed into history. Column after column of unflinching volunteers walked towards the salt deposits till they were brutally clubbed down by the *lathis* of policemen. Although the waiting crowd seethed with anger, a remarkable degree of discipline was achieved and no one broke ranks to set upon the policemen in revenge. The injuries inflicted were severe and the calculated brutality of the police stood in stark contrast to the steely courage of the satyagrahis. Kumarappa observed that the events at Dharasana had exposed 'the Government in all its ugliness and ferocity' which had decided on the brutal assault not 'at a moment of heat but under cool deliberation'. Raiding the salt reserves was only a means to expose the government, and here the satyagrahis had 'succeeded beyond measure'. However, in its overall objectives Kumarappa felt that the raids were only a partial success since the satyagrahis were raw and untrained. Their campaign, he explained, was unique in the history of the world and any failures and limitations served as lessons for the future course of action.

Although *Young India* was not immediately suppressed, this was certainly not due to a lack of intent. Gandhi had urged all pressmen to refuse to furnish securities and forfeit their presses if necessary.[9] Now, in early July of 1930, a security deposit of Rs 2,000 was demanded of *Young India* which it refused to pay and the press was confiscated. But for the workers and many volunteers at Navajivan Press, keeping the journal afloat under all circumstances became a point of honour. From 10 July 1930, *Young India* appeared in cyclostyled form and an astonishing seven thousand copies were made and distributed.[10] Remarkably, not a single issue was missed. Till his own incarceration, Kumarappa shouldered the burden of editing and writing most of the material in each issue. In its new

[8] J. C. Kumarappa, 'The Message of Dharasana', *Young India*, 29 May 1930.
[9] M. K. Gandhi, 'Veiled Martial Law', *Young India*, 8 May 1930.
[10] See M. K. Gandhi, 'Young India', *Young India*, 12 March 1931. Gandhi, however, evinced some displeasure with the modus operandi of the clandestine publication of the weekly which though effective was, in his opinion, 'less in keeping with the spirit of Ahimsa and Truth which know no secrecy'.

avatar as a cyclostyled sheet, *Young India* was pruned to two pages. But at a time when press censorship had imposed a severe drought of information, *Young India* managed to speak truth to power.[11]

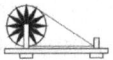

By the end of 1930, the British position in India was greatly undermined by the Civil Disobedience campaign. Salt, it must be remembered, was only one part of a three-pronged attack. If the defiance of the Empire with a pinch of salt was dramatic, the picketing of liquor shops and the boycott of foreign cloth was to have a more direct economic effect. According to the budget presented by the Finance Member, the Government of India in 1930–1 had a deficit of Rs 13.56 crores to deal with, as against an expected surplus of Rs 86 lakhs.[12] The boycott campaign more than halved India's import of British cloth. The impact of Civil Disobedience could not have been more telling. Besides, the 'constitutional' measures were looking increasingly unworkable. The widening of the struggle to no-revenue and no-rent campaigns in more areas was wearing down the administration and affecting its public image. In January 1931, in a dramatic departure from its earlier position, the Raj released Gandhi and all other leaders on the CWC. While the powers in Delhi had sued for peace, the provincial ones had a mind of their own. Incensed by Kumarappa's strident and relentless criticism, in early February of 1931, the district officials issued him a show-cause notice as to why he should not be made to execute a bond for good behaviour for a year.[13] The official charge was similar to the one made against Gandhi in 1922—of writing seditious articles in *Young India* 'so as to cause feelings of contempt and disaffection amongst the public against the Government by law established'.[14] Kumarappa had his day in court where he refused to participate in the proceedings except for reading a prepared statement.

---

[11] Kumarappa noted, presumably with some satisfaction, that the Nizam of Hyderabad had banned *Young India* in his dominions (*Young India*, 2 October 1930).

[12] N. N. Mitra (ed.), *The Indian Annual Register: An Annual Digest of Public Affairs in India* (Calcutta: The Annual Register Office, January–June, 1931), p. 28.

[13] Vinaik, *Gandhian Crusader*, p. 19.

[14] Supplement to *Young India*, 26 February 1931.

In his statement, he shredded to pieces the premise of the show-cause notice. While all loyal citizens were bound to obey the law as it embodied the 'will of the people', Kumarappa took umbrage to the idea that the Government of India was 'by Law established'. This could not be true as the Government was established by an Act of the Parliament of Great Britain which represented the people of Britain. Consequently, the Government of India was at best 'an illegal association' and Indians owed it as much allegiance as to the 'man in the moon'. Turning the tables, he stated, that since there was no cause for a genuine bond or affection between Indians and their government, he could not be guilty of spreading disaffection. As regards the question of causing contempt, he pointed out that it was the Government's own officials who were creating the contempt by their actions. In a manner reminiscent of Gandhi's appeal in court in 1922, Kumarappa pleaded that the Indian Magistrate resign his humiliating position and sever his

disreputable connection with a soulless machine that drinks deep of the blood of your people and descending from the throne of the usurper which you now occupy, come and stand by your own in the hour of their need.

The proceedings had no bearing on the ultimate sentence to be passed, since the choice of sentence was usually predetermined by the Executive which was in British hands. On 25 February 1931, Kumarappa was sentenced to one year of simple imprisonment. Despite his bitter denunciation, there was no ill will between him and the Magistrate. After the pronouncement of the sentence, the Magistrate invited Kumarappa and his admirers in court to his own chamber and offered them some refreshments while awaiting the arrival of the jail van.[15] Kumarappa was now one of some ninety thousand men and women who had gone to jail for their country during this period. Gandhi told the readers of *Young India* that one could be proud of Kumarappa's statement in court. While in 1929 he had sensed the potential in Kumarappa, now he came to recognize that 'his was a pure and full sacrifice in more ways than one'.[16]

[15] Vinaik, *Quest*, p. 41. The accord was reciprocal. When the Magistrate was ill and admitted to the Vadilal Sarabhai Hospital at Ahmedabad in 1932, Kumarappa sent his greetings and good wishes from Nasik Prison through his correspondent who was a matron at the same establishment. See letter from J. C. Kumarappa to W. B. Lazarus, 26 April 1932, Subject File, Loose, Kumarappa Papers.

[16] M. K. Gandhi, 'Kumarappa', *Young India*, 5 March 1931.

Locked up in jail, Kumarappa was in good company. He occupied the cell recently vacated by Sardar Patel and had the Mahatma's youngest son, Devadas Gandhi, for a neighbour. Meanwhile, the stage was set for major political changes when the Viceroy entered into negotiations with Gandhi that led to the Gandhi–Irwin Pact. One of the consequences of the Pact was the release of satyagrahi prisoners and, by the end of March, Kumarappa was freed.[17] When he left America, a friend had expressed the hope that 'the richest blessings life has to offer await you in your homeland'.[18] That benediction had come true, albeit in an unusual manner. It had been a remarkable year for the accountant from Bombay who had embarked on 'a year of probation'. Although his time in prison was short, Kumarappa had crossed the psychological barrier that held back many from the struggle. What he had exclaimed to the heroic men at Dharasana, one could now say of Kumarappa himself—'*Purna Swaraj* is within you'.[19]

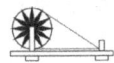

Prior to his imprisonment, besides editing and writing for *Young India*, Kumarappa was also analysing the Matar Survey data. This work progressed at a slow pace, and in any event had to await a less chaotic period for its eventual publication in December 1931. As if this was not enough, he was often invited to address many public events, probably because most of the recognizable leaders were by now the guests of His Majesty. By this time, the Navajivan Press had been seized and since *Young India* had very little space, many of Kumarappa's speeches were reported in the eponymous weekly, the *Indian Social Reformer*. The speeches that he delivered testify to the profound evolution he had undergone in the few months he had been part of the Civil Disobedience campaign. In September 1930, Kumarappa inaugurated a *swadeshi* exhibition in Surat, where he delivered two addresses titled 'Khaddar: Our Refuge' and 'Gandhiji's Place in History'. Taken together, these talks present a keen understanding of the economic and political situation that lay at the root of the national upheaval then under way. Khadi, Kumarappa argued, played a vital role in providing much-needed work to the millions who, due to the decimation of

[17] Vinaik, *Gandhian Crusader*, pp. 22–3.

[18] Letter from Harriet Stanten Place to J. C. Cornelius, 1 February 1929, Correspondence Files, Kumarappa Papers.

[19] J. C. Kumarappa, 'The Message of Dharasana', *Young India*, 29 May 1930.

the village economy, were largely idle. He argued that the overwhelming dependence on agriculture highlighted the gravity of the problem in the countryside. If we aim at providing for the needs of the masses, Kumarappa argued, the 'subsidiary industry is the foundation on which we have to reconstruct economic India'.[20] In 1930, at a point when few saw beyond khadi, Kumarappa was already envisioning a future where khadi would only be the *primus inter pares* among the many village industries needed to build a cohesive economic whole. It is this insight that made the development and propagation of village industries his life-mission.

Talking of Gandhi's place in history, Kumarappa likened him to Moses who was to 'deliver his people from bondage'.[21] In a broad sweep, he went on to assess Gandhi's radical role in the spiritual, moral, political, and economic spheres of national life. The address made an impression on Kalelkar who thought that it was 'nice and penetrating'.[22] The commendation would have pleased Kumarappa as it came from a man who had known the Mahatma intimately since 1915. Kalelkar went on to state that this perception was shared by the editor of the *Indian Social Reformer*, K. Natarajan, who now put Kumarappa in the ranks of C. F. Andrews and Richard Gregg. The English priest Andrews was a friend of both Tagore and Gandhi and his staunch advocacy on behalf of the Indian poor earned him the epithet *Deenabandhu*. Gregg was a Boston lawyer who spent a lifetime developing a theory of non-violent resistance. Having arrived at Sabarmati Ashram in its early days, Gregg wrote manuals on spinning and also what would qualify as the first book on Gandhian economics, *Economics of Khaddar*.[23] Natarajan's implication was obvious, given Kumarappa's spiritual and economic insights and the Christian connection. However, Kalelkar himself was not impressed with the analogy. Andrews and Gregg, he wrote, were sympathetic outsiders, whereas Kumarappa was 'a live Indian with the Hindu outlook'. Perhaps this was a greater compliment. The man

---

[20] J. C. Kumarappa, 'Khaddar: Our Refuge', an address delivered at the opening of an exhibition at Surat on 19 September 1930, Speeches and Writings, 3, Kumarappa Papers.

[21] J. C. Kumarappa, 'Gandhiji's Place in History', an address at a public meeting in Surat on 19 September 1930, published in *Indian Social Reformer*, 27 September and 4 October 1930, Speeches and Writings, 4, Kumarappa Papers.

[22] Letter from D. B. Kalelkar to J. C. Kumarappa, date not known, S. N. 32051.

[23] Gregg's *The Power of Nonviolence* interpreted Gandhi's philosophy to an American audience and had a deep influence on Martin Luther King Jr.

who had rebuffed his Westernized visitor who spoke no Hindi, was now eagerly claiming Kumarappa as one of his own!

On 5 November 1930, Kumarappa delivered a talk in Lahore titled 'Rebuilding India' where he presented his own fundamental views in a rather incongruous setting.[24] The occasion was the third All-Punjab Students' Conference. In previous years the presidential addresses were delivered by Lajpat Rai and Subhas Bose. The conference was meeting just a month after the sensational event of the death-sentence being handed to Bhagat Singh for the assassination of a British policeman. In a meeting charged with the revolutionary message, it is doubtful if any of the listeners was interested in the philosophical import of Kumarappa's exposition. His talk laid out the desiderata for the rebuilding of the Indian social order which lay in a shambles. Unenamoured of a socialist revolution, Kumarappa was quietly but firmly positing a different view when he pointed out that the task was one of rebuilding and not merely building. Such reconstruction necessitated a careful study of the nature of the underlying ground on which the edifice of a new India was to be erected. Kumarappa argued that a land and its people were not a *tabula rasa* and that it was imperative that the new social order erected be in alignment with the core values of Indian society. The fundamental characteristics of India were that it was rural and its genius lay in decentralization. The idea of decentralization pervaded the social, economic, and political organizations in India, and perhaps was taken to its extreme limit in every Hindu having a favourite god unto himself. If the nature of the change was to be informed by an understanding of the past, so must the pace of this transformation. National life, a result 'of thousands of years of adaptation', could not be 'summarily dismissed and new ways formed in the course of a few years'. Forcing an unnatural pace would be akin to building on sand.

Turning to the central role of education in this process, Kumarappa averred that an essential aim of education was to equip people for this task of 'delving into the past' with an eye to the future. In this regard, Macaulay and others had succeeded extremely well in turning out clerks instead of 'Indians glowing with a sense of duty towards their country'. Unlike Englishmen who emptied their universities when called up to defend their country, the full benches of Indian colleges attested to the success of the British scheme. Perhaps drawing from his own education, Kumarappa complained of the deep alienation induced by a learning process 'from an

[24] J. C. Kumarappa, 'Rebuilding India', Speeches and Writings, 10, Kumarappa Papers.

alien point of view with the help of an alien language'. He also mounted a vigorous plea for making the village the centre of the nation's economic life. He pointed to the problem that 'hardly anything [was]... done in the villages to promote education', and all large institutions were located in towns. Going further, he rebuked national institutions, including his own Gujarat Vidyapith, which despite being 'started under Gandhiji's inspiration ... [had] ... blindly followed government practice' in locating itself in a city.

By the time the Gandhi–Irwin accord was concluded, much had changed in India. Ironically a succinct presentation of the Indian position came from a most unlikely quarter—Viceroy Irwin. His willingness to negotiate with Gandhi earned him the displeasure of London and Irwin was replaced by an unyielding defender of the colonial ideal, Willingdon. Perhaps unhappy with the manner of his ejection from India, Irwin gave vent to his feelings in a farewell speech. Warning that the 'good old days of paternal administration' were over, he went on to remark that

> Indian self-consciousness is finding expression in two fields, firstly in the natural demand for political control by Indians of their own affairs, and the economic development of India's resources for India's good.... No Englishman can, without being false to his own political history and in recent years to his own pledges can [*sic*] take objection to pursuit by others of their own political liberty, nor have I ever been able to appreciate the attitude of those who might be the first in Great Britain, particularly to the Conservative Party, to exhort their countrymen only to buy British goods, and yet would regard a movement for encouragement of *swadeshi* industry in India as something reprehensible, and almost, if not quite, disloyal.[25]

While Gandhi's formulation of purna swaraj encompassed both the political and economic dimensions of freedom, it was at the Karachi Congress session of 1931 that the Congress averred that if exploitation of the masses was to end, 'political freedom must include real economic freedom

[25] Mitra, *Indian Annual Register*, Jan–June 1931, pp. 85–6. Interestingly, the official published version of the speech is a sanitized one where the reference to the Conservatives has been removed; see *Speeches by Lord Irwin*, vol. 2, Simla: Government of India Press, 1931, pp. 357–8.

of the starving millions'.[26] The resolutions on Fundamental Rights and Economic Programme laid down in great detail the basic civil rights that an independent India would guarantee. But if the economic changes were to be pursued in right earnest, a prerequisite was to figure out the nation's monetary balance sheet. The question of the public debt was considered in 1922 at the Gaya session of the Congress where a resolution was passed to the effect that any future liabilities incurred by the Government would stand repudiated. This foray into public finance arose out of an increasingly 'crystallised public opinion against Government monetary policy'.[27] At the Lahore session in 1929, public debt emerged as a key issue and Jawaharlal Nehru argued that 'every obligation and concession to be inherited by independent India will be strictly subject to investigation by an independent tribunal'.[28]

As our discussion of Kumarappa's *Public Finance* volume detailed, much Indian wealth was transferred to Britain under various devices and passed off as India's public debt. For a long time, investing in India was an extremely safe and lucrative proposition. While European governments were accountable to their people and faced the peril of being thrown out of office, the British in India did not feel compelled to show much solicitude towards public welfare. Despite a heavy burden of taxation on the people, a very small fraction of the revenues was spent on public works. Instead, colonial policy was geared to service British financial interests in India, such as the debts incurred by offering large payouts on railways, and as in recent times, made a fetish out of balancing the budget. Thus, while the peasants starved, India's high credit rating in the global money market was assiduously maintained. The Lahore pronouncement sent shivers down the spines of British investors, and the value of Government securities floated in London took a hit.[29] Irwin condemned the idea of debt repudiation which, he felt, 'would strike a fatal blow at India's economic life' as it was India's credit that was pledged.[30] Irwin's denunciation was

---

[26] B. Pattabhi Sitaramayya, *History of the Indian National Congress*, p. 779.

[27] G. Balachandran, 'Towards a "Hindoo Marriage": Anglo–Indian Monetary Relations in Interwar India, 1917–35', *Modern Asian Studies*, vol. 28, no. 3 (1994): 615–47.

[28] N. N. Mitra (ed.), *The Indian Quarterly Register: Being a Quarterly Journal of Indian Public Affairs* (Calcutta: The Annual Register Office, July–Dec 1929), p. 310.

[29] J. C. Kumarappa, 'Buccaneering Commission', *Young India*, 20 February 1930.

[30] Irwin's speech in the Legislative Assembly on 25 January 1930, reported in *Indian Annual Register*, Jan–June 1930, p. 209.

only part of a greater outcry against the new rebellious mood. Given the general confusion and propaganda, Kumarappa tried to clarify the Congress' position. He pointed out that the debt ought not to be considered as National Debt as India did not have a National Government that had incurred it on behalf of the public. Thus, the Government of India had no business pledging India's credit. The professed fears, Kumarappa contended, were unfounded as any liability that a future national government of India refused to recognize should be carried over to those who had incurred it in the first place—the Government of Britain.

While the British sought to portray the Congress position as a repudiation of India's liabilities, the Congress was only asking for a fair squaring of the books. However, aware of the controversial nature of the issue, it decided to get 'powder and shot ready for the battle that would necessarily rage over the subject'.[31] Thus, at the Karachi session, the CWC appointed a committee 'to carry out a scrutiny into the financial transactions of the East India Company and the British Government in India and the so-called Public Debt of India and to report on the obligations which should in future be borne by India or England'.[32] While the committee was made up of old hands like the lawyers D. N. Bahadurji and Bhulabhai Desai, and the economist K. T. Shah, the appointment of Kumarappa as its convenor was in recognition of his recent work on public finance. Tasked with working on the committee report, Kumarappa located back to Bombay for a few months. Drawing largely on the earlier work of Kumarappa and Shah, the report was ready in early July of 1931 and created a public stir upon its release.

The *Report on the Financial Obligations between Great Britain and India* was a comprehensive statement by the Congress on the debts incurred by the Government of India. In the report, Kumarappa introduced the crucial distinction between the 'public debt' and 'national debt', and argued that the 'debts had been incurred really by Great Britain and imposed upon India'.[33] Since they had been 'involuntarily imposed upon the revenues of India', he maintained that all aspects of the debt had to be ratified before a future independent Indian state could take on the burden of the so-called

[31] B. Pattabhi Sitaramayya, *History of the Indian National Congress*, p. 783.

[32] J. C. Kumarappa (Convenor), *Report on the Financial Obligations between Great Britain and India*, vol. 1 (Bombay: All-India Congress Committee, 1931), p. 1.

[33] J. C. Kumarappa (Convenor), *Report on the Financial Obligations between Great Britain and India*, vol. 1, p. 3.

'public debt' of India.[34] In turn, the report examined the debts incurred by the British East India Company and those by the British Crown, and finally placed its own recommendations. The report was also at pains to stake out a responsible position by demonstrating a willingness to accept those debts that had been taken up 'for the benefit of the people of India'. Thus, all items of debt were examined in terms of whether they were productive or unproductive from an Indian point of view.

The depths of the sense of injustice could be seen when the debts were examined item-wise. Many of the wars of conquest fought to establish British rule were charged to the Indian exchequer to the tune of Rs 35 crores. Far more egregious was the Rs 40 crores paid out of Indian revenues to suppress the 1857 'mutiny'. If Kumarappa and his colleagues did not see why Indians should willingly pay for their own bondage, neither did they recognize the validity of the Rs 37 crores spent in liquidating the East India Company when the British Government took over in 1858. The rather unrepresentative nature of British rule in India was most clearly demonstrated in the further expenditure of funding external wars. By the dawn of the twentieth century, British loot of India had taken on a veneer of sophistication which was demonstrated by the sleight-of-hand method of accounting used in 1918. In fighting the First World War, the British had incurred heavy expenditures and their counterpart, the Government of India, was most sympathetic to the Crown's economic predicament. In a fit of generosity, the colonial Indian government presented a 'gift' of Rs 190 crores to the British exchequer. In the report, Kumarappa also argued that a significant part of the expenditure incurred by the Indian Army—Rs 171 crores—that fought in Europe during the Great War, should truly be charged to Britain as India was not a party to the War.

As regards public investments, the *Financial Obligations Report* was willing to accept a significant part of the debts incurred towards expenditure on railways, irrigation, and post and telegraphs as they had resulted in infrastructure assets. However, an important argument introduced in the report was on the expenditure on the building of the railway networks in India far in excess of requirements at the time. Not only did this result in easy extraction of food exports from the hinterland, but the Government of India had, by assuring a very high rate of yield, made British investment in the railways extremely lucrative. Thus, by the expedient of paying out very

[34] J. C. Kumarappa (Convenor), *Report on the Financial Obligations between Great Britain and India*, vol. 1, p. 4.

high returns, large amounts of Indian revenue were transferred to Britain. Through a careful analysis, the report argued that Britain owed India to the tune of Rs 83 crores towards the 'unproductive' component of the colonial crony capitalist investments in the railways.

In 1931, the 'public debt' of India as estimated by the British was to the tune of Rs 1,100 crores. Although it decried the injustice of British occupation of India, the report was rather business-like in its accounting exercise. The attempt was to make reasonable arguments based on the principles of natural justice to stake out a position on the question of the public debt. It argued that the undue benefits that Britain obtained by the suppression of Indian industry and forcible extraction of tribute in various forms should be sufficient reason to transfer all external liabilities of India to the shoulders of Great Britain 'from every moral and equitable point of view'.[35] Nevertheless, the *Financial Obligations Report* recommended that India claim only Rs 729 crores out of India's public debt. Additionally, Kumarappa argued that Britain should be charged for the annual expenditure of the maintenance of the Indian Army—as it was primarily an army of occupation—as well as interest charges for the specific items of expenditure claimed. All of this amounted to more than Rs 1,000 crores, which by itself would suffice to wipe out the public debt of India completely.

In 1931, the world was still reeling from the effects of the Great Depression, and India's woes were compounded when Britain went off the gold standard. This move set off a complex chain of causal relationships, and in conjunction with the sterling–rupee ratio controversy it resulted in a disgorging of gold from India, creating further hardships for the Indian peasantry.[36] Written in this context, the *Financial Obligations Report* was important for its normative statement on future financial settlements. In particular, published on the eve of the Second Round Table Conference, it signalled the Congress' commitment to seek justice on the question of India's public debt. In discussing the salient features of the *Financial Obligations Report*, Gandhi himself argued that the Congress would 'seriously follow the matter to the end' as India could not 'afford to be generous at the expense of the dumb millions who after all have to make the largest contribution

[35] J. C. Kumarappa (Convenor), *Report on the Financial Obligations between Great Britain and India*, vol. 1, p. 61.

[36] During this period, the rate of conversion between the British pound and Indian rupee was artificially fixed by the British Government and was chosen in favour of British economic interests.

towards the payment of any liabilities that may be undertaken'.[37] The *Financial Obligations Report* was intended to publicly state the policy of the Congress and clear the ground for staking these claims on India's public debt whenever independence arrived. However, by the time Britain transferred power into Indian hands, both the material circumstances as well as the mindset of the Congress leadership had undergone an enormous shift on this matter of vital public importance. As we shall see later, in 1947, it was left to Kumarappa to recall the lessons of the 1931 *Financial Obligations Report*.

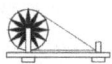

By the time he came to work on the *Financial Obligations Report*, Kumarappa had validated Gandhi's assessment that he was a self-made man worth grabbing for the cause. But the value that Kumarappa brought to the Gandhian fold also exacted a price. Kumarappa proved to be a difficult person to deal with and apart from the difficulties of Reginald Reynolds, Gandhi's long-time English disciple Mirabehn was known to be hurt by Kumarappa's rejection of many of her articles submitted to *Young India*.[38] Moreover, once the Navajivan Press was seized, Mira was upset with Kumarappa continuing to clandestinely publish the weekly in cyclostyled format, an act she believed went against Gandhi's tenet of satya. Gandhi's correspondence from Yeravda are full of references to these problems and he repeatedly urged Mira to be charitable towards Kumarappa.[39] Upon hearing of more such complaints, Gandhi pleaded helplessness as Kumarappa was from Madras and had too much chilli in his blood![40]

[37] M. K. Gandhi, 'Bahadurji Committee's Report', *Young India*, 23 July 1931.

[38] Online transcript of the oral interview of Kamala V. Nimbkar, Centre of South Asian Studies, University of Cambridge, available at http://www.s-asian. cam.ac.uk/archive/audio/item/interview-mrs-kamala-v-nimbkar/, accessed on 8 August 2012.

[39] See, for instance, Letter to Mirabehn, 7/12 January 1931, *CWMG*. While Mira had numerous problems with Kumarappa in 1930, years later she came to appreciate his intense commitment to the cause. With the death of Gandhi in 1948, she was drawn to Kumarappa as a kindred spirit. Thus, her references to Kumarappa in her memoir, *The Spirit's Pilgrimage*, were warm and showed nothing of the bitterness of the past.

[40] Vinaik, *Gandhian Crusader*, p. 8.

Despite his angularity, Kumarappa had demonstrated a strong sense of commitment during a difficult period and had established himself as a valuable worker. In 1929, while introducing *Public Finance* in *Young India*, Gandhi felt it necessary to mention that Kumarappa had not yet committed himself to a permanent position at the Vidyapith. But, by the time he came to commend the *Financial Obligations Report*, the earlier ambiguity had vanished. While thanking the other members of the team for their time working on the report, Gandhi pointed out that for Kumarappa it was no additional burden as he was now 'a registered national servant ... [whose] time and labour were already at the disposal of the Congress'.[41] Towards the end of August, Gandhi agreed to attend the Round Table Conference in London and left Simla (now Shimla) in a hurry. En route to Bombay, Gandhi wrote to Kumarappa asking him to look after the editorial work of *Young India*. Thus, Kumarappa found himself editing *Young India* once again but not without a gentle admonishment to 'make as little criticism as possible but give as many facts and figures as possible'.[42]

By the time Gandhi returned from the failed Round Table Conference and landed at Bombay on 28 December 1931, British officialdom in India had made up its mind to crush the mood of rebellion abroad. Willingdon refused to entertain any form of negotiation. On the day Kumarappa turned forty in Ahmedabad, Gandhi was thrown back into jail. Attempting to undo Irwin's policy of accommodation, a wave of violence and repression was unleashed on the Congress which was declared illegal and whose funds were confiscated, and many nationalist institutions were occupied by the police.[43] The arrests, arbitrary trials, and summary sentences, and the chronology of events of the early months of 1932 as laid out in the *Indian Annual Register* make for compelling reading. In a fell swoop, most prominent Congressmen in Ahmedabad, including Kumarappa, were arrested on 7 January 1932 and lodged at Sabarmati Jail.[44] On 2 February 1932 he was released on parole on the condition of a restraining order.[45] However, Kumarappa was not one to toe the line and was rearrested *that very afternoon* and hauled up

[41] M. K. Gandhi, 'Bahadurji Committee's Report', *Young India*, 23 July 1931.

[42] Letter to J. C. Kumarappa, 28 August 1931, *CWMG*.

[43] Bipan Chandra, Mridula Mukherjee, Aditya Mukherjee, K. N. Panikkar, and Sucheta Mahajan, *India's Struggle for Independence* (New Delhi: Penguin Books India, 2000), p. 288.

[44] *Indian Annual Register*, Jan–June 1932, p. 3.

[45] That he was given a restraining order is based on material in Vinaik's *Quest* volume.

before the District Magistrate of Ahmedabad.[46] An infuriated Kumarappa argued that it was 'the height of absurdity' for the Government to demand that he desist from participating in Civil Disobedience.[47] Having stated his views on the jurisdiction of the court about a year earlier, Kumarappa reiterated that 'it is impossible for any self-respecting citizen whose soul is not quite so dead, to sit still and watch the stalking of lawless law through the land without doing his duty to his motherland'. For his pains, he was fined Rs 2,000.[48] He refused to pay and was sent to jail again for thirty months of rigorous imprisonment.

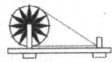

Soon Kumarappa was transferred to Nasik Road Central Prison, which during this period held many a nationalist, including his brother Bharatan. Kumarappa would have found life in prison dull and boring in comparison with the roller-coaster ride he had been on in recent years. The brothers spent some time every day spinning on a *charkha* and took to wearing khadi woven out of their own yarn. Much of Kumarappa's time in prison was spent in reading books supplied by friends, which included many volumes on economics, in particular the writings of his adviser at Columbia, Seligman. Along with Bharatan, he also read a Hindi edition of the Mahabharata. Making up for the cultural enrichment that their education had failed to provide, the brothers diligently applied themselves to the task with the aid of a Hindi–English dictionary that they managed to obtain. In the letters Kumarappa wrote from prison, we occasionally get glimpses of the world he had left behind. Kumarappa had been jailed just a day after he approved the final proofs of two volumes he had worked on, that is, the *Survey of Matar Taluka* and a volume he edited with C. Rajagopalachari on Gandhi's visit to England for the Round Table Conference, *The Nation's Voice*. Now he anxiously enquired about their public reception. From prison, he also diligently kept track of the lives of a large family and many friends. The steady news of their lives in the outside world kept him in good cheer and in rare instances one sees a wry sense of humour. In recalling the Macleans, old friends from his England years, Kumarappa affectionately hoped that they

[46] Letter from J. C. Kumarappa to W. B. Lazarus, 2 February 1933, Subject File, Loose, Kumarappa Papers.

[47] Vinaik, *Quest*, p. 46.

[48] *Indian Annual Register*, Jan–June 1932, p. 9.

had bought his 'valuable publications in the normal course of commerce without waiting like true Scots for presentation copies'.[49]

By May of 1933, Bharatan was freed and Kumarappa himself began counting down towards his own release. His life lately had been tumultuous and he would have to reconcile with the many losses that a nationalist had to suffer. If the loss of a steady and significant income was not to be underplayed, neither was the disappearance of the manuscript of a textbook on public finance he was working on before landing in jail.[50] The life that lay ahead of him was uncertain, but now there was no turning back. Thus, while Bharatan desired that they both move back to south India, Kumarappa felt that

> it is not possible to go down south. My life is cast and bound up amongst and with those with whose ideals I have my sympathy. Once we are grown up, our brothers and sisters are those who share a common purpose. I should not look back once I had put my hand to the plough.[51]

By the end of September 1933, Kumarappa was released from prison. He had suffered from poor health during his imprisonment and needed to recuperate. However, in a few months, he would be drawn back into public life.

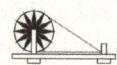

On 15 January 1934, northern Bihar was hit by a catastrophic earthquake affecting an area of 30,000 square miles with a population of a crore and a half. Unofficial estimates put the death toll at a massive twenty thousand people.[52] As both material and donations poured into Bihar, the Congress formed the Bihar Central Relief Committee to manage the relief work.

[49] Letter from J. C. Kumarappa to W. B. Lazarus, 11 October 1932, Correspondence Files, Kumarappa Papers.

[50] Letter from J. C. Kumarappa to W. B. Lazarus, 12 July 1932, Correspondence Files, Kumarappa Papers. Kumarappa had sketched out a plan of eighteen chapters and written five of them. The manuscript was never recovered and the textbook he had in mind never saw the light of day.

[51] Letter from J. C. Kumarappa to W. B. Lazarus, 9 September 1933, Correspondence Files, Kumarappa Papers.

[52] D. G. Tendulkar, *Mahatma: Volume Three (1930–1934)* (New Delhi: Publications Division, 1961), p. 246 and p. 258.

The seriousness of the devastation wrought by the earthquake brought momentary peace between the government and the Congress in Bihar and many political prisoners, including an ailing Rajendra Prasad, were released to help with relief work. The scale of the relief efforts sorely tested the organizational skills of the Congress leaders who had rushed to the area.

Aware of the magnitude of the operations and the contributions that poured in, Gandhi deputed Jamnalal Bajaj to act as the treasurer of the Bihar Central Relief Committee.[53] In turn, Bajaj asked Kumarappa to arrive in Patna and take charge of the accounts. Thus, a few years after his offer to Gandhi to help with auditing dusty ledgers, Kumarappa's accounting skills were put to the test. By the time of his arrival, funds of around Rs 19 lakhs had accumulated, which would eventually grow to over Rs 26 lakhs. With two thousand workers spread over twelve districts, and receiving '300 money orders a day', the task of accounting for the funds 'was assuming formidable proportions'.[54] But for Kumarappa, Prasad remarked, the Congress relief efforts 'would have been in a terrible mess'. Helped by a team of volunteers, Kumarappa tackled the task of accounting for the money and material with ferocious energy. As Kalelkar realized on arriving at the relief camp, Kumarappa had arrived in Patna with 'only one shirt which he managed to wash and put on as best as he could ... [and never] said a word about his difficulties to anybody'.[55] If the large donations given to the Congress were testimony to the implicit trust the public had in its leadership, the organization also managed to fulfil its goal. Writing many decades after the events in Bihar, Acharya Kripalani, who was 'in charge of the general organization and supervision of the relief work', recalled those days with a touch of pride. 'I do not think,' he claimed, 'that any public funds were ever so honestly, scrupulously, and usefully spent as the Bihar Relief Fund.'[56]

The scrupulous adherence to the tenets of public accountability paid off in earning the Congress greater credibility and, more specifically, countering the extensive malicious propaganda unleashed by the Government. Thanks to Kumarappa's meticulous accounting and stringent control of expenditure,

[53] Vinaik, *Quest*, p. 51.

[54] Rajendra Prasad, *Autobiography* (Bombay: Asia Publishing House, 1957), p. 367.

[55] Kaka Kalelkar, 'Kumarappa—The Christian Saint', *Asian Reader*, vol. 1, no. 4 (1968): 4.

[56] J. B. Kripalani, *My Times: An Autobiography* (New Delhi: Rupa and Co., 2004), p. 232.

it was possible for the Congressman Bhulabhai Desai to effectively counter the Government's allegations in the Legislative Assembly.[57] Rajendra Prasad had every reason to be grateful as Kumarappa had 'saved the honour of Bihar'.[58]

When Kumarappa arrived in Patna he sought to curb excessive expenditure in a characteristically heavy-handed manner. He decreed that 'the daily allowance for food of volunteers should not exceed three annas' and introduced tight controls that 'caused a certain amount of dissatisfaction'.[59] When Gandhi arrived with his entourage in Patna, Kumarappa disallowed their 'bills in regard to food and motor car travel'.[60] Gandhi summoned Kumarappa and protested that if the sole reason for his trip to Patna was to help with relief work he failed to understand why Kumarappa would refuse to debit his expenses. Kumarappa explained that the rules he had set down helped curb extravagance and his 'delicate position' would be jeopardized if he paid for Gandhi's expenses beyond the limits. Gandhi accepted Kumarappa's argument and earned the latter's admiration for his willingness to 'subject himself to the discipline that the administration called for'. Kumarappa's strictness with Gandhi had a salutary effect.[61] It also earned him the epithet of 'Colonel Sahib' within Gandhi's inner circle.[62]

[57] See *Indian Annual Register*, Jan–June 1936, p. 131; Bhulabhai Desai, *Speeches of Bhulabhai J. Desai: 1934–38* (Madras: G. A. Natesan and Co., 1938), p. 327.

[58] Vinaik, *Quest*, p. 53.

[59] J. C. Kumarappa, 'Lessons from His Life' in *Incidents*, p. 136.

[60] J. C. Kumarappa, 'Lessons from His Life' in *Incidents*, p. 137.

[61] See Letter to J. C. Kumarappa, 8 June 1934, *CWMG*. In fact, this is a letter *from* Kumarappa *to* Gandhi and not the other way round as its presence in the *CWMG* would imply.

[62] This was stated to the first author of the present work, Venu Madhav Govindu, by the veteran Gandhian Narayan Desai. Desai also recalled being sent to the railway station to receive Kumarappa on the first visit of the latter to Wardha. Interview of Narayan Desai at Vedchhi on 23 July 2003.

6   Breaking Ground

The mass political upsurge of 1930 was a rare moment when many disparate forces were welded together into a common cause. However as this unity of purpose rapidly faded, Gandhi could comprehend the underlying social and political problems with greater clarity. Apart from a lack of Muslim participation in the Civil Disobedience campaigns, on the political front the divide between the Swarajists and the socialists within the Congress had grown into a first-rate crisis. Akin to the differences of an earlier era, a sizable group in the Congress was desirous of entering the legislatures, whereas an ascendant left wing was pushing for a more radical position. For Gandhi, *swaraj* included the material and moral rejuvenation of some seven lakh Indian villages, whereas for many others it largely meant Indian control over political affairs. Neither the Swarajists nor the socialists had any interest in social renewal through constructive work.[1]

A decade earlier, Gandhi had identified khadi or handspun, handwoven cloth as a pivot of his agenda of social reconstruction. With the decimation of India's traditional industries during the growth and expansion of colonial rule, the employment crisis in rural India was grave. Gandhi recognized

---

[1] Much of this chapter is devoted to understanding Gandhi's position in this period as it was a fundamental determinant in shaping Kumarappa's life work.

that the large numbers of unemployed and underemployed needed to be provided with an alternative source of livelihood, as agriculture itself could not absorb the vast numbers seeking work. However, given the limited education, skills, and resources available in the countryside, the approach to take the pressure off the land needed to work within several constraints. The answer lay in khadi, which simultaneously answered many disparate needs. It was a low-cost approach that did not demand much skill, broke the traditional idea of spinning being a woman's activity as well as the barriers of class. In due course, khadi emerged as an emblem of India's self-emancipation and rejection of colonial rule. However, for Gandhi it represented the first element of a larger programme of social revitalization through constructive work. For him, khadi was the foundation on which a new agrarian economy was to be erected.

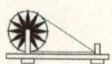

In November 1933, following his fast against a separate electorate on caste lines and the subsequent political settlement known as the Poona Pact, Gandhi embarked on a year-long nationwide campaign against untouchability. Thanks to his extensive travels across the country on the Harijan Tour, he got a first-hand sense of the state of affairs across India.[2] The countryside had not yet recovered from the severe economic dislocation caused by the combined effects of the Great Depression and Britain's 1931 decision to get off the gold standard.[3] While the agrarian economy was crying for immediate redress, Gandhi was also confronted

[2] The term 'Harijan' has been superseded by 'Dalit', the self-description of the oppressed castes. Our usage of the term 'Harijan Tour' here is in keeping with historical fact. Gandhi received no support for this campaign to end untouchability from his colleagues in the Congress who saw it as a distraction from the political task in hand.

[3] A significant indicator of the attendant hardship for rural India was the extraordinary volumes of gold sold in distress. The dropping of the gold standard resulted in the economic bloc known as the Sterling Area, which would have enormous consequences for India's economy during the Second World War. For details on the effects of the Great Depression, see the chapter 'The Consequences of the Great Depression' in Dietmar Rothermund, *An Economic History of India: From Pre-Colonial Times to 1991* (New York: Routledge, 1993), as well as his full-length study, *India in the Great Depression: 1929–1939* (New Delhi: Manohar Publications, 1992).

with evidence that khadi had its limitations as a means of economic sustenance. Thus, at a time when the urban leadership was keen on rapid industrialization, Gandhi concluded that the needs of rural India could wait no more. He decided to widen the message of self-sufficiency and self-reliance by reviving other village industries.[4]

The challenge was to enable ordinary people with limited assets, skills, and education to become meaningful economic actors. This, Gandhi argued, was only feasible with a revival and scientific rationalization of India's many village industries. Such a move would enable the village to make the best use of its resources and thereby stem the flight of economic surplus from the village to the city. The development of the village economy was meant to be an appropriate answer to the debate between the prevalent economic ideologies of capitalism and communism. However, Gandhi could neither carry Congress opinion with his political convictions nor generate enthusiasm for constructive work. Therefore, desiring 'complete detachment and absolute freedom of action', in October 1934, at the Bombay session, he resigned from primary membership of the Congress.[5] At the Bombay session, the Congress politely rejected many of Gandhi's proposals but agreed to put into effect the agenda of the revival and improvement of village industries with Kumarappa being chosen to lead the effort. On 28 October 1934, the Andhra leader Pattabhi Sitaramayya moved a resolution proposing the formation of the All-India Village Industries Association (AIVIA), also known in Hindustani as the Akhil Bharat Gram Udyog Sangh.[6]

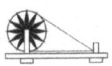

Given its importance in Kumarappa's life, it is useful to consider the resolution which, in its entirety, read as follows:

Whereas organizations claiming to be swadeshi have sprung up all over the country with and without the assistance of Congressmen, whereas much confusion has arisen in the public mind as to the true nature of

[4] Chandrashanker Shukla, who acted as the Mahatma's secretary during this period, dates this idea to a specific interview with a khadi worker in Guruvayur on 11 January 1934. See *Incidents*, pp. 320–1.

[5] Statement to the Press, 17 September 1934, *CWMG*.

[6] *Indian Annual Register*, July–December 1934, p. 256. The resolution was seconded by Khan Abdul Ghaffar Khan.

swadeshi, whereas the aim of the Congress has been from its inception progressive identification with the masses, whereas village reorganization and village reconstruction is one of the items in the Congress constructive programme, whereas such reconstruction necessarily implies revival and encouragement of dead or dying village industries, besides the central industry, hand-spinning, and whereas this work is possible only through concentrated special effort unaffected by and independent of the political activities of the Congress, Mr. J. C. Kumarappa is hereby authorized to form under the aegis of the Congress and as part of its activities, an autonomous organization under the advice and guidance of Gandhiji called the All-India Village Industries Association with power to frame its own constitution, to raise funds and to perform such acts as may be considered necessary for the advancement of its objects.[7]

The framing of the AIVIA resolution can only be understood in the context of Gandhi's extended public debates in the preceding year on the very definition of swadeshi. In order to benefit from public sentiment, a variety of products were being sold under the swadeshi label solely because the manufacturing companies were owned by Indians. This was especially true of mill-made textiles that cashed in on the upsurge of patriotic feelings and competed against khadi for mass patronage. The result was enormous confusion amongst both khadi workers as well as the public at large. Angered by such opportunism, Gandhi issued a harsh condemnation that 'the existing practice was an unconscious fraud upon the public'.[8] To counter such mala fide practices, Gandhi provided a new definition of swadeshi as covering 'useful articles manufactured in India through small industries' and excluded 'articles manufactured through the large and organized industries' that were perfectly capable of taking care of themselves.[9] Gandhi's formulation of 'cent-per-cent' swadeshi as he called it, along with the formation of the AIVIA, was specifically meant to address a vital issue.[10] It was increasingly clear that India would achieve independence in due course, but Gandhi raised questions about the quality of freedom that the ordinary Indian would obtain. Indeed, his lifelong battle for economic

[7] Appendix to Statement to the Press, 15 October 1934, *CWMG*.

[8] M. K. Gandhi, 'Swadeshi', *Harijan*, 10 August 1934.

[9] Interview with All-India Swadeshi League delegation, 17 June 1934, *CWMG*.

[10] Gandhi also had the CWC reiterate its position on swadeshi and he spent much time in 1935 giving a new orientation to khadi and the work of the AISA.

justice for India's millions took on a new urgency and the AIVIA was his attempt to channel the spirit of swadeshi to this end.

If experience was any guide, Gandhi was well justified in delinking the AIVIA from the Congress. Given the widespread indifference and irritation amongst the urban intelligentsia towards constructive work, Gandhi needed some independence to effect his village reconstruction agenda. In fact, the new definition of swadeshi that he offered to the All-India Swadeshi League had stirred up a controversy. The league, headed by Madan Mohan Malaviya, was unhappy with the Mahatma's definition and argued that all Indian manufactures were worthy of the swadeshi label. Curiously enough, both Malaviya and Gandhi accepted Kumarappa as the arbitrator of this dispute. Upon examination of the arguments on both sides, Kumarappa ruled in favour of Gandhi and opined that mere exploitation of raw materials while neglecting the potentialities of the individual producer 'could never tend to establish human equality'.[11]

In the face of colonial exploitation or rank indifference, many village industries had either withered away or were in poor shape. When the AIVIA began work, there was very little systematic knowledge available on the processes and products of Indian villages. If the agrarian economy was to be built anew and if it was to withstand the assault of the modern industries, it needed to be put on a sound footing. While the AISA had handled all aspects of khadi production, including organizing the weavers and marketing their products, the mandate for the AIVIA had to necessarily be restricted due to the great variety of village industries and the limited funds and technical manpower available at its disposal. However, although the AIVIA was to be highly decentralized in its work, it still needed some basic infrastructure for its offices and experimental work.

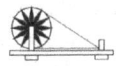

The man who met these vital needs was a wealthy Marwari businessman in Wardha and long-time follower and confidant of Gandhi, Jamnalal

---

[11] Vinaik, *Gandhian Crusader*, p. 62. It seems likely that Kumarappa was brought in as the arbitrator at the suggestion of Lilavati Munshi who was then the secretary of the All-India Swadeshi League that was headed by Malaviya. See Letter to Lilavati Munshi, 21 August 1934, *CWMG*.

Bajaj.[12] In this period, Gandhi had himself moved to Wardha and he accepted Bajaj's offer of his garden house and an attached orange orchard for the headquarters of the AIVIA that was officially founded on 14 December 1934 at a meeting in Wardha.[13] During this meeting the objectives and rules of the organization were framed and the first Board of Management was constituted. Shrikrishnadas Jaju, a lawyer and long-time khadi worker, was elected president and treasurer and Kumarappa was designated as organizer and secretary of the association. Gandhi's insistence that the members of the AIVIA could not participate in any campaign of Civil Disobedience indicated the degree of separation he wanted between the Congress and his new association.[14] Although Bajaj's generous donation of a building and land was to be availed of by the AIVIA, it was originally earmarked as a memorial to Maganlal Gandhi. A nephew of the Mahatma, Maganlal was the chief architect of the development and spread of khadi as the centrepiece of Gandhi's constructive programme in the 1920s. The khadi movement was dealt a severe blow in 1928 with Maganlal's untimely death.[15] Although there were plans to build a memorial to Maganlal, they had to be shelved for years due to political uncertainties. Finally, in the

---

[12] For an account of the life of Bajaj, see B. R. Nanda, *In Gandhi's Footsteps: The Life and Times of Jamnalal Bajaj* (New Delhi: Oxford University Press, 1990).

[13] M. K. Gandhi, 'The New Baby', *Harijan*, 21 December 1934.

[14] The other members of the board were Prafulla Chandra Ghosh, a future chief minister of Bengal, Gosibehn Captain, a granddaughter of Dadabhai Naoroji and a keen advocate of khadi in Bombay, Shoorji Vallabhdas, a businessman in Bombay and an organizer of khadi centres and a swadeshi bazar, Laxmidas P. Ashar and Shankerlal Banker, who were Gandhi's intimates in Ahmedabad and were closely involved in the running of the AISA, and Dr Khan Saheb Behram Khan, who served in lieu of his brother, Khan Abdul Ghaffar Khan, who was incarcerated during this period. Gandhi also enlisted prominent personalities to serve as advisers to the AIVIA. Amongst the many who agreed to do so were the luminaries Rabindranath Tagore, J. C. Bose, P. C. Ray, and C. V. Raman, businessmen G. D. Birla and Purshottamdas Thakurdas, the English clergyman and agriculturalist Sam Higginbottom and nutritionist Robert McCarrison, as well as stalwart Congressmen and physicians Jivraj Mehta, M. A. Ansari, and B. C. Roy. The advisers, however, seem to have signed up out of deference to the Mahatma's wishes and never played any role in the work of the AIVIA.

[15] For more on Maganlal Gandhi, see C. Shambu Prasad, 'Gandhi and Maganlal: Khadi Science and the Gandhian Scientist', in *Mahatma Gandhi and His Contemporaries*, edited by B. Puri (Shimla: Indian Institute of Advanced Study, 2001).

relative quiet of late 1934, Gandhi and Bajaj agreed that the land donated would house both a memorial museum as well as the offices of the AIVIA.[16] Thus, Bajaj's lands, now named Maganvadi, came to be the location for the headquarters of the AIVIA and also Kumarappa's home for more than two decades.

By early February of 1935, both Gandhi and Kumarappa had taken up residence in Maganvadi and worked towards establishing the AIVIA. In the early days, Kumarappa occupied one corner of the spacious accommodation and tried to avoid the nuisance created by some of the other inmates of Maganvadi.[17] However, it was scarcely possible for Kumarappa and others to avoid being experimented upon by the food faddist in Gandhi who dictated the meals in the common kitchen. Gandhi's Maganvadi experiments with nutritious but unappetizing soya beans have been remarked upon by many writers. If the unappetizing lumps of boiled beans could somehow be tolerated, both Kumarappa and his brother Bharatan seem to have been particularly affected by Gandhi's experiments with a chutney of neem leaves! Writing many years later, both brothers recalled Gandhi's paternal indulgence towards them which took the form of additional doses of this culinary delicacy. Bharatan was a new arrival into the Gandhian fold having chosen to follow his brother into public service. As a result, he was regularly seated next to Gandhi who plied his ward with extra helpings of goodies like boiled soya beans, orange-skin marmalade, raw garlic, and 'bitter as quinine' neem chutney.[18] On one occasion, Kumarappa himself was a recipient of similar munificence when Gandhi placed a spoonful of the chutney on his *thali* (plate). This act of love was witnessed by Vallabhbhai Patel who wryly remarked, 'You see, Kumarappa, Bapu started with drinking goat's milk, and now he has come to goat's food!'[19]

Gandhi's experiments might have led to some humour, but the intent behind them was serious. When he wrote to many scientists asking for

---

[16] Letters to Jamnalal Bajaj and Shankerlal Banker, 18 November and 6 December 1934 respectively, *CWMG*.

[17] Mirabehn, *The Spirit's Pilgrimage* (London: Longmans, 1960), p. 191.

[18] Bharatan Kumarappa, 'The Great Experimenter' in *Incidents*, pp. 123–31. While Bharatan had endured the neem chutney, his cultural sensibility was scandalized when the Maganvadi kitchen served tamarind water that had 'the colour of mud and tasted much like it' and called it *rasam*. As he recalled, 'we who were from the South justly felt insulted that so famed a preparation of ours ... was caricatured thus'.

[19] J. C. Kumarappa, 'Lessons from His Life' in *Incidents*, p. 143.

scientific information on common Indian foods, Gandhi drew a blank. No such information was available, which led him to wonder: 'Is it not a tragedy that no scientist should be able to give me the chemical analysis of such a simple article as *gur*?'[20] It was precisely this lack of attention towards the needs of the agrarian economy that AIVIA was meant to address. But, as is the case today, during his lifetime Gandhi's agenda of constructive work was deeply misunderstood. Thus, the widening of the constructive agenda to encompass village industries invited great ridicule. Echoing the socialist critique of Gandhi's economic programme, his old acquaintance V. S. Srinivasa Sastri characterized the newly formed association as part of Gandhi's 'endless and quixotic war against modern civilization'.[21] Gandhi, in turn, pointed out to his critics that the cry of 'back to the village' was not meant to be a setback to progress but was merely a demand 'to render unto the villagers what is due to them'. If all the needs for raw materials were to be met by the village, Gandhi wondered why the villagers should not be taught to work on it themselves instead of being exploited by the more resourceful city-dwellers.[22]

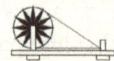

While the AIVIA was conceived by Gandhi, Kumarappa's role in the organization could not be that of a mere implementer of Gandhi's ideas. In fact, right from the time of the Matar Survey, Kumarappa had been developing his own understanding of the Indian rural problem. His numerous speeches from the period give notice of a line of understanding that was congruent with Gandhi's values but quite independent in its conception and articulation. Earlier, Kumarappa had himself come to recognize the limits of khadi as an ameliorative measure to address the dire needs of India's multitudes who were groaning under the burden of poverty.[23] Although spinning was of universal application, Kumarappa

[20] Speech at Gandhi Seva Sangh, on or before 30 November 1934, *CWMG*.

[21] Letter from V. S. Srinivasa Sastri to Mahatma Gandhi, 23 November 1934, extract given as footnote to Letter to V. S. Srinivasa Sastri, 17 November 1934, *CWMG*.

[22] Speech at Gandhi Seva Sangh, on or before 30 November 1934, *CWMG*.

[23] J. C. Kumarappa, 'The Task before Us', address delivered to the Conference of Village Workers of Gujarat, Ahmedabad on 12 April 1931, Bound Volume, 10, Kumarappa Papers.

averred that 'further industries of local interest' ought to be encouraged to increase the productivity and, consequently, the purchasing power of the rural populace. The problem of India's chronic underemployment and poverty needed the development of village industries as a subsidiary activity to cultivation. However, in the absence of active government support, it was up to the nationalists to propagate such industries as the foundation on which the economic reconstruction of India was to be erected in the future. The task was to demonstrate the 'way we can help home industries' and in 'showing to the people what things are available in our own country and in educating them to the idea of Swadeshi'.[24] While 'the spirit of swadeshi is a natural expression of an awakened nationalism', Kumarappa did not want it to be merely a 'boycott of foreign goods' born out of a sense of hatred of the British.[25] Rather, he argued that although we must 'broaden our outlook to one of universal brotherhood, before we can reach the uttermost parts of the earth, we have to make a start with our next-door neighbour', the poverty-stricken Indian villager.[26] Thus, Kumarappa was distinguishing swadeshi from a virulent form of nationalism and developing its meaning as self-reliance in moral terms. He also argued that if swadeshi allowed itself to generate profits for wealthy Indian businessmen, it would only be servicing the 'wolf of avarice ... hidden by an apparently noble purpose in the lambskin of patriotism'. In line with Gandhi's new definition, he contended that interpreting swadeshi as the slogan of 'Buy Indian' undermined its objective by 'giving help to those who are well able to look after themselves'.

While Kumarappa argued against an insular idea of swadeshi and capitalist profiteering, he did not indulge in mere rhetoric. He was keenly aware that the village industries could not be revived out of mere empathy with the village. On observing the state of village crafts at an exhibition in Lucknow in 1936, he warned that 'unless we bestir ourselves and adapt our production to everyday needs, our skill, art and craftsmanship will be found soon only in museums'.[27] While he went on to list out his remedies,

[24] J. C. Kumarappa, 'Khaddar: Our Refuge', an address delivered at the opening of an exhibition at Surat on 19 September 1930, Speeches and Writings, 3, Kumarappa Papers.

[25] Address delivered by Mr Kumarappa at the Opening Ceremony of Azad Bazaar, 21 July 1930, Speeches and Writings, 10, Kumarappa Papers.

[26] J. C. Kumarappa, 'Our Exhibitions', Harijan, 21 December 1935.

[27] J. C. Kumarappa, 'Some Thoughts on the Lucknow Exhibition', Harijan, 25 April 1936.

Kumarappa also emphasized, albeit implicitly, the principle of *local production for local consumption*. He argued for 'the production of utility articles' that could find a local market as opposed to the case of craftsmen turning to the curio trade, which resulted in 'the market becoming distant, the trade [shrinking] into the hands of a few, throwing several out of employment', while the price included 'a large share for the middleman, and it [went] to feed luxury trades'. In contrast, despite the low remuneration available, trade in utilities was preferable as here the wealth generated 'was more or less evenly distributed'.

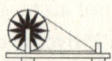

Along with organizing exhibitions to educate the public about the value of the village economy, constructive workers felt a strong need for a permanent exhibition that would feature the various aspects of production of khadi and other village industries. Therefore, it was decided that the memorial to Maganlal Gandhi would be a museum that would archive material and designs of khadi and village industries from all over the country. As with the AIVIA, Gandhi had intended the museum to act as a nodal agency that would collect, assimilate, improve, and eventually transmit the knowledge of craft and economic production. The museum was intended to be different from conventional institutions that largely collected 'curios and rarities'.[28] Rather it was conceived as 'a central organization which would furnish specimens both from past and present art, craft, designs and workmanship'. In May 1935, Kumarappa travelled to Santiniketan for an interview with Tagore on the plans for the museum.[29] While Tagore's appeal for attention to the languishing crafts of India did make its impression on the agenda for the museum, its core concern remained one of providing an educative experience in ways to 'enrich the life of the villagers' and all exhibits were 'subordinated to this aim'.[30]

---

[28] J. C. Kumarappa, 'Exhibits for the All India Village Industries Museum', *Harijan*, 7 May 1938.

[29] For Tagore's comments, see K. Kripalani, *Faith and Frivolity* (New Delhi: Malancha, 1962), pp. 25–6, We are thankful to Shri Y. P. Anand for providing us this reference. Also see, Interview to *Bombay Chronicle*, 22 May 1935, *CWMG*.

[30] R. V. Rao, *Sevagram: Gandhiji's Ashram and Other Institutions in Wardha*, third edition (Sevagram: Ashram Pratisthan, 1969), pp. 48–9.

Although it was decided in early 1935 to build the museum, work progressed at a slow pace for care had to be taken in designing and building a permanent edifice; also, the project was handicapped by a lack of funds. During construction, Kumarappa took personal responsibility for errors that had to be rectified and defrayed the costs by skipping a meal every day for a period of time. A decade after Maganlal Gandhi's tragic death, a memorial—the Magan Sangrahalaya—was inaugurated by Gandhi on 30 December 1938.[31] It was Maganlal who 'combined painstaking application to detail with skill, artistic sense and organizing ability' thereby making Gandhi's work on khadi possible.[32] And it was this pioneering work on khadi that provided the AIVIA with 'the nucleus around which the village industries movement' was being built.[33] The entrance to the grounds of Maganvadi was through a thoughtfully constructed gateway that one could describe as an amalgam of the aesthetic sensibilities of Gandhi and the influence of artists like Nandalal Bose. The gateway had pillars adorned by the figures of a man and woman on either side who were didactically depicted as 'healthy and vigorous, showing the way to physical welfare through the development of industries'.[34] Over the arch were two plaques depicting the classical Indian motifs of the eighteen-petalled lotus and ornamental peacocks. Above these motifs were 'two bulls in repose— the silent and ubiquitous motive power available to the villagers'.[35] An additional, thoughtful feature of the compound was the availability of a hieroglyphic plan to enable illiterate persons to find their way around.[36]

On the same day as the opening of the Magan Sangrahalaya, Gandhi also inaugurated the Gram Udyog Bhavan that housed the workshops of the various industrial departments of the AIVIA. Although brick and mortar was used when needed, most of the structures were of 'bamboo, wood and mud' and were designed 'to be within the means of villagers'.[37] In his

[31] The building was designed by Surendranath Kar, a cousin of the Santiniketan artist Nandalal Bose. For more on Kar and his work, see 'Surendranath Kar, the Architect', *Modern Review*, vol. 58, no. 6 (July 1935): 118.

[32] J. C. Kumarappa, 'Magan Sangrahalaya', *GUP*, January 1939.

[33] Speech at Opening of Magan Sangrahalaya and Udyog Bhavan, 30 December 1938, *CWMG*.

[34] *Guide to Maganvadi* (Wardha: published by J. C. Kumarappa), n.d., p. 2.

[35] J. C. Kumarappa, 'Magan Sangrahalaya', *GUP*, January 1939. The Sangrahalaya also exhibited some of the watercolours done by Nandalal Bose and his associates for the 1938 Haripura session of the Congress.

[36] *Guide to Maganvadi*, p. 3.

[37] *Guide to Maganvadi*, p. 3.

address at the inauguration, Kumarappa referred to the building as rural in style. However, Gandhi was quick to point out that the buildings were 'still far above the rural standards of living as they obtain in our country today'.[38] Rather, they stood as 'a futurist symbol of what artisans' dwellings should be and would be in the rural India of the AIVIA's dreams'.[39]

[38] Speech at Opening of Magan Sangrahalaya and Udyog Bhavan, 30 December 1938, *CWMG*.

[39] Speech at Opening of Magan Sangrahalaya and Udyog Bhavan, 30 December 1938, *CWMG*.

7　The Natural Order

I n his work as an advocate of the village economy and as a strident
critic of the policies of independent India, Kumarappa was concerned
with ameliorating the life of the weakest members of society. However,
his commitment to pragmatic remedies was always informed by a
deeper philosophical vision. Indeed, the entire body of his writings and
organizational work is shot through with an original and profound world
view. This chapter departs from our historical narrative and is entirely
devoted to an examination of Kumarappa's moral and philosophical vision.
In the next chapter we shall examine his social and political philosophy
and detail his views on the political economy of industrial societies.
His ecological understanding and prescriptions will be considered in a
separate chapter.

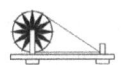

By the time he came to work with Gandhi in 1929, Kumarappa had
assimilated a range of intellectual ideas. But much of his later insight arose
out of everyday observation and problem-solving over a lengthy period of
engagement with rural India. For Kumarappa, theoretical insight fulfilled
its purpose only when deployed to address the fundamental concerns

of the ordinary individual. This dialogue between theory and practice is reflected in his two major expository texts, *Why the Village Movement?* published in 1936, and *Economy of Permanence* that appeared in 1945. The first editions of both books consisted primarily of theoretical material while successive editions added sections on the practical implementation of his ideas. However, Kumarappa's discussion of practice necessarily had to fall short of the ideal as it grappled with real-world constraints. As a result, the significance of his philosophical argument was masked by a patchwork of prescriptions and practice.[1]

Owing to his use of metaphorical allusions to nature and his ecological prescriptions, Kumarappa has been recognized as an ecological thinker. Important as these ideas are, we wish to also recognize his significant contributions to moral philosophy with political and economic implications. In contrast with philosophical expositions of contemporary times, Kumarappa was at pains to simplify his presentation to make it accessible to the layperson. Often he chose examples and idioms from the daily experiences of ordinary Indians. Kumarappa also dispensed with the scholarly apparatus of annotation and attribution and was quite eclectic in borrowing and adapting ideas and theories that he encountered. Often he would take an idea and imbue it with a meaning that was different from—and sometimes richer than—the original one. While it makes his argument clear, this style of writing raises difficulties in clearly tracing the genealogy of his intellectual ideas.[2] With this caveat, we proceed to examine Kumarappa's philosophical understanding as well as the light it sheds on various aspects of the human predicament.

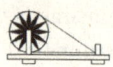

Kumarappa begins his most well-known work, *Economy of Permanence*, by asking a fundamental question: 'What is permanent? What is transient?'[3]

---

[1] For instance, such interplay between theory and practice makes it hard to strictly categorize Kumarappa's ethical theory as either deontological or teleological.

[2] For instance, as discussed earlier, the writings of his eldest brother played a pivotal role in the making of Kumarappa the nationalist, but one would not know this from Kumarappa's own writings.

[3] J. C. Kumarappa, *Economy of Permanence: A Quest for a Social Order Based on Non-Violence* (henceforth *EOP*), reprint of second edition (Varanasi: Sarva Seva Sangh Prakashan, 1997), p. xi.

His answer is that nothing can be said to be permanent other than transcendental God, that is, the conception beyond human comprehension of 'Time and Space'.[4] Except for this eternal God, everything else that human beings can comprehend has finitude in Time and Space, including the *ur*-source, Nature. While the material Nature *exists*, Kumarappa yokes it to a moral framework of ontological relationships, that is, the 'Natural Order'. Indeed, all of his wisdom and insight flows from the constant relationship and interaction he establishes between the moral and material worlds. This moral–material relationship leads to Kumarappa's specific notion of Permanence. He argues that human life is 'transient' when *compared* to the lifespan of the universe that defines the 'permanence' of nature. It is worth emphasizing that Kumarappa's permanence is not a material concept but a moral one with material implications.

To understand and interpret the universe in moral terms, Kumarappa borrowed and significantly modified a key concept of Western philosophy, that is, the Great Chain of Being.[5] Defined as a hierarchical ordering of all living and non-living things in the universe, for centuries the conception of the chain was determined by Christian theology that placed the perfection of God at the top of the chain. All living species and other entities had a fixed location in the hierarchical chain depending on their degree of 'perfection'. The epoch-making work of Darwin put an end to the idea of individual species having a fixed location on the chain. The phenomena of the world were no longer seen as divinely ordained but had a material explanation. One consequence of the rejection of theological dogma is that modern forms of knowledge explain phenomena or processes but refuse to judge or evaluate them. A noteworthy exception is the work of the American sociologist Thorstein Veblen that exercised great influence on Kumarappa's own thinking. Veblen utilized Darwinism but also vigorously argued that all human economic activity is undertaken with a purpose in mind, in other words, it is teleological.[6]

---

[4] This conception of God should not be thought of as the commonplace form in most religions, but as a spiritual abstraction.

[5] A modern exposition is A. O. Lovejoy, *The Great Chain of Being: A Study of the History of an Idea* (Cambridge, MA: Harvard University Press, 1936).

[6] Thorstein B. Veblen, 'Why Is Economics Not an Evolutionary Science?', *The Quarterly Journal of Economics*, vol. 12, no. 4 (1898): 373–97. However, Veblen merely acknowledged the existence of a teleological purpose in economic activity; he did not specify it. Veblen's use of Darwinian ideas should not be confused with Social Darwinism.

Although such Western ideas had their influence, Kumarappa's most significant intellectual debt was to the man who decisively shaped his life, Mahatma Gandhi. Writing in 1949, Kumarappa asserted:

> If there is anything that characterises Gandhiji's life, it is his devotion to Truth and Non-violence. Any economy that is associated with his name should, therefore, answer to these fundamental principles.[7]

While this formulation was framed for economics, its principles pervade all of Kumarappa's philosophy as well as his understanding of society or civilization. Indeed, in many instances, Kumarappa used the terms 'economy' and 'society' interchangeably. It is also here that we see the deft manner in which he infuses new meaning into extant ideas. In Kumarappa's 'Natural Order' the epitome of perfection at the top of the chain is not the Christian God, but is implicitly replaced by Gandhi's conception 'Truth is God'. Thus, the ultimate reality of existence is satya, and ahimsa is the means to realize it. Put differently, satya is the teleological objective in the Natural Order and one conforms to this cardinal principle to the extent that one practises ahimsa in all aspects of life. Kumarappa interprets the Natural Order not as a hierarchy, but as a web of interdependence and ethical obligations. While no being is perfect, the degree of perfection is judged by the extent to which mutual rights and obligations are respected. The novelty of Kumarappa's ideas lies in the relationship he establishes between the moral and material worlds.[8] Although one lives and acts in the material world, the meaning and value of one's actions is to be judged by their moral implications. By fusing his ideas with those of Gandhi, Kumarappa taps into a long tradition of Indian thought on the fundamental interconnectedness of the universe. However, unlike the quest for spiritual salvation in much of Hindu thought, Kumarappa was more interested in the welfare of fellow human beings. Like Gandhi, his concern was 'dharma, rather than moksha, the Moral Law rather than personal salvation through political disengagement'.[9] Indeed, in his preface to Economy of Permanence, Kumarappa argued that

---

[7] J. C. Kumarappa, *The Gandhian Economy and Other Essays*, second edition (Wardha: The All-India Village Industries Association, 1949), p. 1.

[8] By specifying a teleological objective in moral terms, Kumarappa also moves far beyond Veblen's ideas.

[9] Raghavan Iyer, *The Moral and Political Thought of Mahatma Gandhi* (New Delhi: Oxford University Press, 1973), p. 20.

his was an attempt to apply the concepts of 'eternal life' or 'Union with Godhead' to 'the everyday life of man'.[10]

Drawing from Gandhi's philosophy, he assumes that individuals are endowed with the agency or ability to act. The common view of swaraj as political freedom from British rule is a negative conception of liberty, that is, an absence of constraining forces.[11] Gandhi's swaraj encompasses a positive conception of freedom that hives closer to the idea of autonomy, which means that the individual is endowed with the ability to act on his or her own free volition.[12] His emphasis on autonomy is an innovation in Indian thought as it foregrounds the individual. Unlike the traditional caste-based notions of kinship, Gandhi and Kumarappa were fundamentally interested in the preservation of the autonomy of the individual in the modern context of a political state and industrial economy. We may add that their conception of swaraj also departs from liberal theories in its scepticism of the ability of the modern state to uphold truth and justice without intruding on the autonomy of the individual citizen.

Kumarappa argued that the degree of individual autonomy available in a society is a measure of its freedom, and the extent to which individuals honour their obligations reflects the social and moral evolution of that society.[13] He also examined the implications of privileging duties over rights, as well as critiqued the utilitarian theory of value. Kumarappa begins by recognizing that economic activity starts with satisfying

[10] J. C. Kumarappa, *EOP*, p. v.

[11] For a modern Indian enunciation of the distinction between positive and negative conceptions of liberty by Bipin Chandra Pal, see Dennis Dalton, *Indian Idea of Freedom: Political Thought of Swami Vivekananda, Aurobindo Ghose, Mahatma Gandhi and Rabindranath Tagore* (Gurgaon: The Academic Press, 1982), pp. 99–101. In modern Western philosophy, this distinction is primarily attributed to the work of Isaiah Berlin.

[12] For an authoritative interpretation of Gandhi's conception of autonomy, see Ronald Terchek, *Gandhi: Struggling for Autonomy* (New Delhi: Vistaar Publications, 2000).

[13] J. C. Kumarappa, *Why the Village Movement? A Plea for a Village-Centred Economic Order in India* (henceforth *WVM*), reprint of the fifth edition (Kashi: Akhil Bharat Sarva Seva Sangh, 1960), p. 28.

basic needs, of which hunger is the most primeval. In examining the 'economies' that are obtained in nature, he classifies them according to the degree to which they conform to the moral imperatives of the Natural Order. We may also bear in mind that here Kumarappa's use of the term 'economy' can be interchanged with 'society'. Borrowing from the natural need to satisfy want, he classifies the 'types of economy in nature' into five ordered categories: Parasitic Economy, Predatory Economy, Economy of Enterprise, Economy of Gregation, and Economy of Service.[14] In the parasitic and predatory economies, there is no recognition of rights, obligations, or even the Natural Order. In an Economy of Enterprise, individuals improve on earlier categories as they 'take something that is of their own effort and making'.[15] While not overtly violent, individual self-interest continues to be the central characteristic. There is some recognition of rights and obligations that govern the Natural Order but the absence of altruism makes an Economy of Enterprise susceptible to violence and represents the most elementary stage of social evolution.[16] In the next stage of social evolution, 'man becomes more and more conscious that no one lives unto himself but that there are certain ties that bind and man develops a gregarious attitude'.[17] The individuals in an Economy of Gregation, like the honeybees, 'do not work for their own respective individual gains but for the common benefit of the whole colony' which represents 'an extension from self-interest to group-interest and from acting on immediate urge of present needs to planning for future requirements'.[18] The evolution from individual self-interest to group interest demonstrates a limited degree of enlightenment, as the recognition of duties towards others is limited to within the group. It does not preclude the possibility of violence as obligations are not yet accorded precedence over rights.

A society that is organized on the basis of 'higher cultural values' is built on a 'consideration of duties' rather than an emphasis on rights. Such an economy that leads 'to an evaluation of each life in terms of the others' will make way for an economy of permanence or an Economy of Service.[19] An example of this 'highest form of economy' is to be seen in the care of the young by a parent. In its endless scouring of the jungle

---

[14] J. C. Kumarappa, *EOP*, pp. 5–8.

[15] J. C. Kumarappa, *EOP*, p. 6.

[16] J. C. Kumarappa, *WVM*, p. 26.

[17] J. C. Kumarappa, *WVM*, p. 27.

[18] J. C. Kumarappa, *EOP*, pp. 6–7.

[19] J. C. Kumarappa, *WVM*, p. 28; J. C. Kumarappa, *EOP*, p. 7.

for food for its young chicks, a mother bird 'functions neither for its present need nor for its personal future requirement'.[20] This disinterested service 'comes nearest to what may be called a non-violent economy of permanence'. Although no human society had achieved this high-water mark of a moral economy, Kumarappa viewed Gandhi's life work as an attempt towards such an Economy of Service. One may remark here that although he uses metaphors from the natural world, Kumarappa's yardstick for judging the evolution of a society is neither biological nor sociological, but decidedly moral.[21] For him, participants in the Natural Order have a duty to fulfil their moral obligations and are to be judged accordingly. In the Natural Order, moral obligations are the source of all rights and individual autonomy is essential for both rights and obligations to flow without obstruction. This emphasis on autonomy is not a means of spiritual indulgence but, as we develop later, it is essential for economic and political freedom.

Although all of the above discussion on the Natural Order is presented in abstraction, Kumarappa was no ingénue in his understanding of both human behaviour or the difficulty in applying eternal principles to real life. Indeed, the second part of *Economy of Permanence* deals with practical issues in terms of an Economy of Gregation rather than an Economy of Service or the Economy of Permanence. In other words, while the Economy of Service is an ideal, real societies are far from it in their moral stature. Indeed, human beings often fail to recognize the true nature of their place in the Natural Order. Nevertheless, compared to other beings, humans have a special moral obligation as their failure in discharging their obligations results in the severest moral and material violence.[22]

Kumarappa is best remembered today for his prescient observations about the environmental crisis inherent in large-scale industrialization. Writing at least four decades before global recognition of the ecological consequences of industrial civilization, Kumarappa's critique was centred on the use of false scales of values that dominate modern society, especially

[20] J. C. Kumarappa, *EOP*, p. 7.

[21] Such biological metaphors had been commonly used by moral philosophers, the most famous example being that of Bernard de Mandeville's use of the beehive metaphor in *The Fable of the Bees* (published in 1714) to argue that individual pursuit of self-interest results in the better welfare of all. Kumarappa's choice of bees in his metaphor can be seen as a symbolic refutation of Mandeville's theory.

[22] J. C. Kumarappa, *EOP*, pp. 11–12.

the emphasis on money and material possessions.[23] Although human beings need to use material resources, Kumarappa enjoins them to correctly discharge their moral responsibility in the process. He distinguishes between two fundamentally different kinds of resources available in nature, that is, the finite supplies of materials such as minerals, petroleum, and so on, and those that are relatively inexhaustible in that they could be renewed by natural processes and human effort, such as timber, cotton, water, and so on. Terming these two types of resources as the Reservoir Economy and Current Economy respectively, Kumarappa advocates great prudence in using materials from the former category.[24] He advocates that societies be built primarily on renewable flows of natural resources rather than by a profligate mining of their bequest of non-renewable resources, making him one of the earliest of ecological seers of the modern world. We shall examine his ecological prescriptions in detail in an independent chapter but remark here that the emphasis on the Current Economy stems from Kumarappa's understanding that to achieve a measure of permanence and reduce moral and material violence, human consumption ought to align itself with the cycle of life, thereby harmonizing itself with the Natural Order which includes other living beings as well as the inanimate world. However, recognizing that humans often fail to behave according to the moral imperative, Kumarappa also presents his argument in pragmatic terms: 'Nature is unforgiving and ruthless. Therefore, self-interest and self-preservation demand complete non-violence, co-operation, and submission to the ways of nature if we are to maintain permanency by non-interference and by not short-circuiting the cycle of life'.[25]

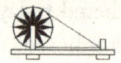

In Kumarappa's view individuals or societies are not frozen in place but can progress towards the top of the Natural Order. The ability to progress in this manner is predicated on two closely related concepts that pervade philosophical debate through the millennia—the existence of human freewill as well as the perfectibility of human nature. He argued that while animals live by instinct, it is only human beings who have the capacity for freewill or the ability 'either to make or mar the orderly

[23] J. C. Kumarappa, *EOP*, p. 50.
[24] J. C. Kumarappa, *WVM*, p. 25.
[25] J. C. Kumarappa, *EOP*, p. 2.

functioning of Nature'.[26] In the short run, man might manage to interfere with the workings of Nature, but in the long run he would do so at his own peril. Thus, for moral as well as instrumental reasons, Kumarappa argues that man ought to exercise his freewill in a *conscious* manner to bring about 'greater co-operation and co-ordination with nature's units than any other living being'.[27]

This capacity for choice is related to a fundamental question addressed in all religious and philosophical traditions, that is, whether and how it is possible for human beings to achieve perfection or a full comprehension of one's place in the universe. Indeed, Gandhi's entire social and political project assumes that *all* human beings are endowed with the capacity for good. It is in this sense that satyagraha can be seen as an aid that enables the oppressor to discover his truer self. At the height of the Civil Disobedience campaign and in the face of extreme provocation by the Raj, Kumarappa vehemently argued that 'the ultimate goodness of human nature persuades us to believe in the ultimate triumph of Satyagraha'.[28] Indeed, for him, human nature is perfectible and human fulfilment lies in 'consciously working towards, if not attaining, an Economy of Permanence'.[29]

Kumarappa's notion of human perfectibility differs from most religious doctrines in fundamental ways. While Christian theology assumes that such perfectibility is only possibly by the grace of God, in Indic traditions the quest for perfectibility is extended across lives and is tied to the *karmic* belief in rebirth.[30] Despite the different approaches, both these positions focus largely on the spiritual quest of the individual believer. Kumarappa implicitly rejects such positions and insists that the quest for perfectibility cannot be carried out in the luxury of isolation but has to be exercised in the here and now. If humans are endowed with the 'gift of freewill', it comes with attendant responsibilities.[31] He argues that 'the noblest faculty man possesses

---

[26] J. C. Kumarappa, *EOP*, p. 9. Kumarappa renders the term as 'freewill' instead of the more commonly used form of 'free will'.

[27] J. C. Kumarappa, *EOP*, p. 11.

[28] J. C. Kumarappa, 'Implications of Satyagraha: Our Attitude in the Present Struggle', Speech at the Bombay International Fellowship, 1 February 1931, Speeches and Writings, 10, Kumarappa Papers.

[29] J. C. Kumarappa, *EOP*, p. 10.

[30] For a comparative exposition, see Harold Coward, *The Perfectibility of Human Nature in Eastern and Western Thought* (Albany: State University of New York Press, 2008).

[31] J. C. Kumarappa, *EOP*, p. 18.

in excelsis is his capacity for love and to express it in the form of 'selfless service' to fellow beings.[32] For Kumarappa, it is through the service of fellow beings that man carries out his quest for perfection. For him, working for the 'happiness of those in need' is the 'permanent blessed way of love'. In other words, just as man does not live by bread alone, he cannot find spiritual salvation if others are denied their bread.[33]

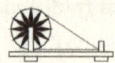

To exercise their freewill in an enlightened manner, humans need a means of judging their actions, that is, a 'scale of values'. In his early years as a nationalist, Kumarappa was smitten by a Baul song that he commended for its rapier wit:

> A goldsmith, methinks, has come into the flower garden.
> He would appraise the lotus, forsooth,
> By rubbing it on his touchstone![34]

Working in an India that was undergoing enormous transformations, Kumarappa was worried about the increasing use of purely material considerations in daily transactions, resulting in 'self-centered' societies instead of 'altruistic' ones.[35] As a result, he consistently and vehemently rejected modern economic theory which assumes people to be selfish and atomized individuals who are solely concerned with increasing their personal benefit. While he recognized the success of neoclassical economics and the Marginal Revolution in explaining economic activity, Kumarappa held that purely utilitarian arguments were false from a normative perspective. For him, 'altruistic and objective standards' were a 'prerequisite to the achievement of permanence'.[36] Although irritated by 'ignorant tradespeople' who used self-centred valuations, Kumarappa reserved his anger for the 'renowned universities of the world' that 'are used

---

[32] J. C. Kumarappa, *EOP*, p. 17.

[33] Gandhi repeatedly expressed this view in his pronouncements on bread labour.

[34] Rabindranath Tagore, *The Religion of Man* (Boston: Beacon Press, [1931] 1961), p. 213.

[35] J. C. Kumarappa, *EOP*, p. 31.

[36] J. C. Kumarappa, *EOP*, pp. 35–6.

as hotbeds for raising theorists who will rationalize and support' selfishness as an economic virtue.[37]

Kumarappa was not naive about human capacity for selfishness, but nevertheless argued that our ideals should inform our actions and not the other way around. Thus, while humans may act in a self-interested manner in the course of daily activity,

> [t]o lead to any degree of permanence, the standard of value itself must be based on something apart from the person valuing, who is after all perishable. Such a basis, detached and independent of personal feelings, controlled by ideals which have their roots in the permanent order of things, are *objective* and so are true and reliable guides.[38]

It was incorrect to view human economic activity as a mere means of earning material profit while stripping it of a multitude of moral values and imperatives that were encoded in it. Instead of building an economy on the principle of self-interest, Kumarappa argued that humans should strive to overcome self-centred considerations. For him, defining a value theory was not an academic exercise, but a matter of utmost urgency. He wished that India would avoid the dangers of rapid and unthinking industrialization that neglected fundamental social, economic, and ecological considerations. Hence, it was essential that Indian society redefined its values and learnt to look deeper into the various dimensions of economic activity and their role in developing a non-violent social order. Kumarappa illustrates the problem through a personal story. Once, while touring the Travancore region he learnt that the craft of making pine mats had been decimated within a lifetime. Whereas the previous generations were 'wealthy enough to build two-storied houses', their descendants 'cannot even afford' to keep their homes in good repair.[39] The mat-weavers wanted the visitors to explain where the problem lay, and Kumarappa found the answer when he accepted an invitation to lunch at the house of the headman. While everyone was seated on pine mats, as a special guest Kumarappa was seated on an imported Japanese mat. Not known to pull his punches, Kumarappa pounced upon this and castigated his host. If the mat-weaver himself valued the Japanese mat over his own products, Kumarappa demanded to know how he could 'blame others doing likewise'.[40] The fault lay in

---

[37] J. C. Kumarappa, *EOP*, p. 43.
[38] J. C. Kumarappa, *EOP*, p. 36; emphasis added.
[39] J. C. Kumarappa, *EOP*, p. 48.
[40] J. C. Kumarappa, *EOP*, p. 49.

the weaver's own scale of values and this episode presented 'a picture in miniature of what [was] happening all over the country'. The increasing commodification of society as well as an unthinking thrust towards mass production disturbed Kumarappa as it led to a loss of economic autonomy of the ordinary individual.

The proponents of rapid industrialization charged that Kumarappa's economic vision would result in a low standard of living. He responded by questioning the underlying premises of concepts such as 'progress' and 'standard of living'. One may recognize the contemporaneity of these debates if we consider familiar terms such as 'growth' and 'development'. Kumarappa argued that such terms were 'delightfully vague' and demanded clarity on whether our definitions were to be based on 'an economic basis or follow cultural considerations or social needs'.[41] Arguing against a purely materialist basis, he questioned the assumption that any form of industrialization would automatically qualify as progress. He observed:

> Progress signifies both the search after knowledge and truth as found in nature and its application to satisfy human needs. In the measure in which we are able to pull alongside nature's dictates, we shall be progressing in the right direction. But in so far as we are pulling against the course of nature, we shall be creating violence and destruction which may take the form of social conflicts, personal ill-health and the spread of anti-social feelings, such as, hatred, suspicion and fear. From these symptoms we shall know whether we are progressing scientifically or not. If our course of action leads to goodwill, peace and contentment, we shall be on the side of progress, however little the material attainments may be; and if it ends in dissatisfaction and conflict, we shall be retrogressing, however much in abundance we may possess material things.[42]

Kumarappa argued that standards of living were to be judged by the extent of creative autonomy they afforded the individual, that is, 'everything that affords him opportunities for the free expression of the whole man—his body, mind and spirit—for all that will make him approach perfection'.[43] We wish to emphasize here that such a definition did not advocate 'poverty' as many interpretations of Gandhian thought wrongly claim. Rather, Kumarappa suggested that one's material possessions are not mere inanimate artefacts but are stamped by the standards of value prevalent

[41] J. C. Kumarappa, *EOP*, pp. 75–6.
[42] J. C. Kumarappa, 'What Is Progress?', *Harijan*, 13 April 1947.
[43] J. C. Kumarappa, *EOP*, p. 77.

in society. Although a certain level of material welfare is a moral imperative, Kumarappa was not enamoured of the modernist claim that material wealth leads to a fundamental emancipation of the individual. The real problem confronting an individual is one of choosing between 'complex' and 'simple' material standards of living rather than between 'high' and 'low' material standards.[44] Indeed, he asserted that this error is a wilful deception 'devised to convey a psychological preference for the complex standard which is the foundation' of the modern consumer economy. Kumarappa argued that what is commonly referred to as a 'high' material standard is in reality a 'multiplicity of material wants [that are] artificially created'.[45] The need to earn the high income to maintain a complex lifestyle meant that individuals ended up with less freedom, or as he put it, a 'complex standard converts a devotee into a drudge'.[46]

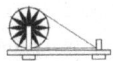

In the early 1940s, India had already embarked on the trajectory of commodification and mass production. Apart from an economic perspective, Kumarappa also critiqued mass production on cultural and aesthetic grounds. He was acutely aware of the culturally corrosive effects of colonialism which were perhaps more harmful than economic exploitation. Likening life to a great canvas and one's values to paints, Kumarappa argued that it is with 'the firm strokes of his brush of freewill' that man 'brings into existence his indelible work of art, which he will leave behind him to help or retard human progress'.[47] Every individual has both an 'opportunity *and* responsibility' to lead an autonomous life and should not 'leave his life meekly in the hands of others'.[48] With the zeal of a taxonomist, he categorized human societies into houses. The lowest is the House of Imitation characterized by 'self-love and pleasure-seeking by the easiest route' with no opportunity for any creativity.[49] Most prominent in this category was the leisure class who only consume without creating anything worthwhile on their own. The House of Adoption is a marginal

[44] J. C. Kumarappa, *EOP*, p. 78.
[45] J. C. Kumarappa, *EOP*, p. 77.
[46] J. C. Kumarappa, *EOP*, p. 78.
[47] J. C. Kumarappa, *EOP*, pp. 52–3.
[48] J. C. Kumarappa, *EOP*, p. 53; emphasis added.
[49] J. C. Kumarappa, *EOP*, p. 55.

improvement as its denizens adopt the 'creations of others' but lack any distinctive 'claim to originality'.[50] Thus, the Indian babu will wear his shirt outside the trousers, use chappals instead of shoes and dispense with the tie.[51] While this presented an 'eyesore to the whole-hogger', given the Indian climate such sartorial adoption is an improvement on the *pucca* version. Nevertheless, it lacks real autonomy for having adopted Western clothes in the first place.

Those living in the House of Material Creations are more evolved than the earlier ones, but while they lead profligate lives based on consumerism, these individuals are unable to dictate the direction of their consumption and are swayed by marketing, advertising, and propaganda. A classic example of such behaviour is to be seen in the herd mentality of the elite who meekly accept being told what is most fashionable in a given year. Echoing Ruskin, Kumarappa's critique here dwells on the utter loss of originality and creative autonomy in mass production and consumption which 'leads to the benumbing of the higher faculties which spells death to progress and development'.[52] The abandonment of any sense of taste by the Indian elite angered him. It was even possible to find wonderful specimens of art in an old cemetery, Kumarappa argued, 'but not in a modern Bombay flat'! Stuffed with modern comforts, these houses were aesthetic wastelands where, for instance, the furniture exhibited 'no variety, no imagination, no original ideas'. Moving along the scale, analogous to the Economy of Gregation was the House of Social Innovations exemplified by nations that carried out large-scale social engineering directed by the state. Writing during the Second World War, for Kumarappa, the communist Soviet Union and the fascist nations of Italy and Germany were examples where an 'individual citizen may be crushed and turned into an unquestioning automaton'.[53] Thus, if the homo economicus presented a sterile version of human life in capitalistic societies, so did the *homo gregarious* of regimented societies. The loss of human autonomy was common to both of these modern mass ideologies.

At the apex of Kumarappa's ordering is the House of Sublimation that mirrors an Economy of Service. In this House, committed individuals use their own lives to work out solutions for the problems of society 'from a

---

[50] J. C. Kumarappa, *EOP*, p. 57.

[51] J. C. Kumarappa, *EOP*, p. 58.

[52] J. C. Kumarappa, *EOP*, p. 61.

[53] J. C. Kumarappa, *EOP*, p. 75.

selfless, detached and long-range point of view'.[54] 'In a country bristling with socio-economic problems' Kumarappa presented this ideal of moral living as a challenge to individuals who would share their lives with the masses, 'and having experienced in their own being the sufferings of those around them, [would] ... proceed to find a suitable remedy'. In our tour of Kumarappa's philosophy we have now come full circle. If he borrowed from Western philosophy to define an idealized Natural Order representing a moral economy, unlike intellectuals satisfied with propounding theoretically consistent world-views, for Kumarappa precept and practice went together. Not only did he propound ideal standards of ethical life, as a lifelong constructive worker, he lived in the House of Sublimation and participated in an Economy of Service.

[54] J. C. Kumarappa, *EOP*, p. 72.

8   A New Deal

Much of Kumarappa's time as the prime mover of the All-India Village Industries Association (AIVIA) was spent in applying his philosophical ideas to everyday practical problems. Keenly aware that philosophers in dealing with the higher aspects of life tend to forget 'mundane applications', he argued that a clear conception of the eternal principles of satya and ahimsa can only be had by 'watching them in everyday action'.[1] As a result, he forged a distinct and perceptive understanding of the 'economic question' and its relationship to individual and social well-being. Kumarappa argued that economic questions were not merely technical exercises but were tied to fundamental considerations. Therefore, if an economy is 'well-conceived it will afford *free play* to all creative faculties of *every* member of society'.[2] He looked beyond economic growth and was focused on the goal of human development, that is, 'the needs of the human being—body, mind and spirit—apart from the material needs of the animal man'.[3] While mindful that the material deprivation of

---

[1] J. C. Kumarappa, 'Swaraj through the Village', *The Statesman*, 13 April 1939, Speeches and Writings, 2, Kumarappa Papers.

[2] J. C. Kumarappa, *EOP*, p. 66; emphasis added.

[3] J. C. Kumarappa, 'Large-Scale Industries and Human Development', *Harijan*, 5 October 1947.

India's emasculated masses must be addressed, Kumarappa insisted that an exclusively material focus on economic organization could not address the challenge of human development. This view on human welfare led him to consistently examine and challenge the received economic wisdom. For going against the grain, he had to contend with critics who argued for the merits of large-scale industrialization and the virtues of mass production. Consequently, a central and recurring theme in Kumarappa's work is a wide-ranging and coherent analysis of the modern economy.

Gandhi and Kumarappa shared an objective of building a non-violent social and economic order that promoted equity and justice for all individuals. Their social and economic understanding led them to conclude that 'the only path to true democracy in political life, and to peace among nations' was a decentralized economic and political system where, necessarily, the 'rewards were moderate'.[4] In a world where economic growth has assumed the proportions of theological doctrine, this view continues to be misunderstood. The confusion between 'simplicity' and 'poverty' existed even during Gandhi's lifetime. The Mahatma's arguments were 'often attributed to the strain of the ascetic in him', and thereby discredited.[5] But Kumarappa explained that Gandhi's views stemmed from the fact that 'simplicity is the basis of any economy aiming at permanence'. However, there was some recognition of the moral imperative writ large over the Gandhian espousal of the village economy. Indeed, as a well-known economist remarked, this 'system of economic thought cannot be adequately appraised merely in terms of [the assumptions of] current economic theory' since 'it is a challenge to those assumptions themselves'.[6]

Gandhi and Kumarappa did not wholly depend on the intrinsic goodness of human beings to achieve the objectives of a non-violent economic order. Rather, they attempted to organize society around essential principles that would create conditions conducive to desirable outcomes. Gandhi and Kumarappa believed that economic progress was not to be measured in monetary terms alone. Apart from ensuring the essential necessities of life, the ideal social order should afford every individual the fullest measure of political, economic, social, and spiritual autonomy to fulfil their creative potential. However, such an individual pursuit could not be

---

[4] J. C. Kumarappa, *WVM*, p. 31.

[5] J. C. Kumarappa, 'Is It Ascetism?', *Harijan*, 5 October 1947.

[6] J. J. Anjaria, 'The Gandhian Approach to Indian Economics', *Indian Journal of Economics*, vol. 22, no. 3 (1941–2): 357–66.

acceptable at a cost to the welfare of others, especially when every society had great inequalities in both wealth and opportunity. Therefore, it was imperative that every individual pursues his or her own calling aimed at the welfare of society as a whole. It is these considerations that led Kumarappa to develop what may be termed a *moral political economy*.

The experience as an exploited colony had turned Indian opinion against capitalism and, as a consequence, the socialist model as exemplified by Russia appealed to many in the freedom movement. For Kumarappa, this dichotomy was deeply unsatisfactory. Although politically opposed to each other, both the creeds of capitalism and socialism share a deep commitment to the centralized, urban industrial model as the 'only panacea for all the economic ills'.[7] However, large centralized industries by their very nature are inimical to the autonomy of the individual and are ultimately an impediment to social progress. Thus, 'if the individual is to be liberated from economic slavery either to the machine or to the capitalist, there appears no other course open to us than to adopt decentralization of production'. While 'there is no doubt that material goods can be increased by standardization and centralisation', unfettered industrialization has profoundly negative consequences on the material, moral, and cultural well-being of individuals in a society.[8] Such social implications led Kumarappa to reject large-scale industrialization as a remedy worse than the disease. For him, decentralization was a natural answer to the search for an economic approach that afforded and preserved individual autonomy while promoting social and economic justice. While Gandhi laid out the broad contours of an argument for swadeshi, it was Kumarappa who out of a prolonged engagement shaped it into a *theory of decentralization*.

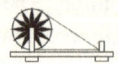

Kumarappa argued that large-scale industries, which were totemic of centralized economies, had an internal logic that played out as a set of

[7] J. C. Kumarappa, 'Is It Economic Anarchism?', *Harijan*, 4 May 1935.
[8] J. C. Kumarappa, 'Ahimsa and Industrialisation', *Harijan*, 12 February 1938.

specific outcomes. The high levels of investment of capital required for heavy machinery meant that they had to be run at high levels of production on a continual basis in order to reduce the marginal costs of the investment. Often, in a capitalist economy, situations arise when 'accumulated capital seeks investment' and then desires 'close control' over the production process itself to ensure high returns.[9] This thirst for profits means that economic activity has no 'reference to the needs of the market ... and every producer produces in competition with his neighbour to secure for himself the greatest advantage'.[10] In other words, 'the incentive for large production without regard to the existing market is in the very nature of a system of production' that is based on capital investment.[11] For such large investments of capital, greater profitability could be achieved by producing goods that command a high price in the marketplace and not necessarily goods that serve a social purpose. The resultant herding of production towards satisfying the needs of the rich effectively shuts most people out of the economic cycle of production and consumption. Moreover, with their vast resources, industrialists can influence the state to increase their own profits rather than aim to achieve the welfare of society at large. But, Kumarappa argued that this was not the full story. To survive, 'capitalism has to create a clientele for itself by setting up social customs and fashions which people will follow without questioning their rationale'.[12] The result is a consumerist culture driven by 'advertisements which by mere repetition makes the public believe it wants what it does not really want and induces it to part with its purchasing power'.[13]

Under capitalist investment, production has no reference to real demand and leads to two consequences. First, one needs a steady and assured source of large volumes of raw materials. Second, having overproduced goods, the capitalist seeks an assured market. Since the raw materials and resources used in the modern industrial economy have to be drawn from the four corners of the world, it is necessary to obtain and then maintain control over the lands where such resources exist. In addition,

[9] J. C. Kumarappa, 'Ahimsa and Industrialisation'.

[10] J. C. Kumarappa, Summary of Speech at Mysore Swadeshi Exhibition, 30 May 1936, Bound Volume, 10, Kumarappa Papers.

[11] J. C. Kumarappa, WVM, p. 86.

[12] J. C. Kumarappa, 'The Groundwork for Independence', Harijan, 12 July 1942.

[13] J. C. Kumarappa, 'The AIVIA as the Happy Mean', Speeches and Writings, 2, Kumarappa Papers.

since distribution follows production, 'keen competition to dispose of surplus production leads to a struggle for markets'. All these factors dovetail into an enterprise that leads to imperialism and its associated violence on the subject peoples. In fact, Kumarappa argued, 'wherever we see the seeds of centralised industries germinating we find also a soil ready for imperialism'.[14] Such imperialism is not a deliberate design on other nations but a 'gradual and natural growth out of circumstances demanded by centralized industries for their own development and maintenance'. While the imperialism of the old is long gone, the perceptive link that Kumarappa drew between the industrial mode of social organization and the associated need for control of raw materials and markets has an ominous resonance in contemporary times. In discussing this linkage between the capitalist mode of production and organized violence, Kumarappa argued that the 'extension of markets in their turn call for the Army, Navy and the Air Force to control them in the interests of particular nations'.[15] In support of his argument, Kumarappa cited the case of Britain's need for cotton when supplies were cut off during the American Civil War, resulting in Britain turning to India as a source.[16] Thus, the appetite of Britain's textiles mills for cotton intensified the British grip over India and 'to ensure against any political disturbances upsetting her economic order, [Britain] felt it necessary to control our country's economic life'.

Here, reference may be made to Say's Law which in modern times has been formulated as 'supply creates its own demand' and critiqued by the economist John Maynard Keynes. Kumarappa's own view on this matter was shaped by the experience of colonial control in the era of

[14] J. C. Kumarappa, 'The Parent of Imperialism', *GUP*, January 1947.

[15] *WVM*, p. 121. Recognition that 'free markets' are actually based on the use of such brute force also comes from a cheerleader of American expansionism who pointed out: 'The hidden hand of the market will never work without a hidden fist .... McDonald's cannot flourish without McDonnell Douglas, the designer of the U.S. Air Force F-15. And the hidden fist that keeps the world safe for Silicon Valley's technologies to flourish is called the U.S. Army, Air Force, Navy, and Marine Corps' (Thomas Friedman, *The Lexus and the Olive Tree: Understanding Globalization* [New York: Picador, 2012], p. 464).

[16] J. C. Kumarappa, 'The Parent of Imperialism', *GUP*, January 1947. For a useful summary see F. A. Logan, 'India—Britain's Substitute for American Cotton, 1861–1865', *The Journal of Southern History*, vol. 24, no. 4 (November 1958): 472–80. Logan, however, draws entirely different conclusions on the value of this cotton trade for the Indian peasantry.

mass production. After two centuries of capitalist production, the world was 'groaning under the load of over-production due to the efficiency of the machine, dire need due to maldistribution of goods, scarcity of necessities due to misdirection of production and abject poverty due to accumulation of profits in a few hands'.[17] The colonizing West was ever in need of markets for their goods leading to the attempts to 'civilize backward peoples and the resultant Imperialism'. Under these circumstances, India's markets operated according to Say's Law since the 'consumer [had] ... no voice in calling for his goods', and it was a misnomer to call such economic transactions 'demand'.[18] This colonial economy was the antithesis of Kumarappa's normative ideal of the Natural Order where it is demand that leads to supply as exemplified by the saying 'necessity is the mother of invention'.[19] For Kumarappa, any economy that operated under Say's Law would necessarily lead to violence. Indeed, as we shall see presently, Kumarappa's attempt to link producers and consumers of economic goods into a tight web of relationships was designed to avoid the violence inherent in an economy that operated according to Say's Law.

While this critique of the capitalist enterprise was accepted by many, the socialists surmised 'that the only development for the present economic stage is towards large-scale production under social ownership ... [and] that such production would not only end exploitation and violence but would also raise human life and civilization to an unprecedented level'.[20] Kumarappa was unconvinced by the socialist assumption that state control of the means of production would expunge industrialization of the excesses due to private ownership. While one could perhaps cleanse industrialization of the taint of greed and the private monopoly over markets, the socialist model retained centralization of industries which

[17] J. C. Kumarappa, Foreword to Kropotkin's *Conquest of Bread*, 1935, Speeches and Writings, 1, Kumarappa Papers. To the best of our knowledge this foreword was never published.

[18] J. C. Kumarappa, *WVM*, p. 47.

[19] J. C. Kumarappa, *WVM*, p. 46.

[20] J. P. Narayan, *Socialism versus the All-India Village Industries Association: A Pamphlet*, 1935, in *Jayaprakash Narayan: Essential Writings (1929–79)*, edited by B. Prasad (New Delhi: Konark, 2002), p. 140.

'entails concentration of power'.[21] Both capitalism and socialism failed to address Kumarappa's fundamental critique 'that centralisation of industries is inimical to the development of democracy in politics'. Arguably, here Kumarappa was a lone voice in the 1930s to draw a perceptive link between the economic system of production and its implications for our democratic objectives. He agreed that in overthrowing the feudal order in Russia, the Bolshevik Revolution had 'succeeded in guiding production by social ideals and not by profit'.[22] However, the problem was not solved but rather exacerbated since the resultant 'dictatorship of the proletariat' had 'aimed at the masses having power in their hands but in effect the few at the top [held] ... the reins'.[23] Therefore, while capitalism and communism were locked in a deep and often violent ideological combat, it was a spurious struggle since both ideologies were 'based on a consideration of material values forgetting that such a myth as the "Economic Man" does not exist'.[24]

Kumarappa's decentralization was not a rigid principle that brooked no exception. Since the methods of production 'are but instruments for social and economic ends' the nature and degree of decentralization in different areas of economic activity was to be determined by a careful consideration of social objectives.[25] Thus, while the quest for 'true democracy' meant that 'centralized production in consumption goods' needed to be abandoned in favour of decentralized village industries, this approach did 'not preclude all centralized industries'.[26] Partly in concession to his critics, Kumarappa argued that the scrutiny of 'the method of mass production by centralisation' was 'mainly in terms of producing consumer goods as distinct from public utilities or key industries'.[27] Indeed, he agreed that 'there are various functions, which can be performed most economically and efficiently only by centralized

[21] J. C. Kumarappa, 'Preface to the Fourth Edition', WVM.

[22] J. C. Kumarappa, 'Mahatma's Challenge to Capitalism', 16 April 1935, source unknown, Press Clippings, Kumarappa Papers.

[23] J. C. Kumarappa, 'Communism and the Common People', Special Number of The Students Outlook, Allahabad University, 17 November 1935, Speeches and Writings, 1, Kumarappa Papers.

[24] J. C. Kumarappa, 'Preface to the Fourth Edition', WVM.

[25] J. C. Kumarappa, WVM, p. 167.

[26] J. C. Kumarappa, WVM, p. 151.

[27] J. C. Kumarappa, War: A Factor of Production (Rajahmundry: Hindustan Publishing Co. Ltd., 1938), pp. 1–2.

methods'.[28] Kumarappa advocated such a qualified approach to the question of decentralization since certain public utilities like 'finance, transport and supply of power are naturally centralized functions' and needed large investments from the state. Thus, 'in the village movement there is a definite place for centralized industries, not for their own sakes, but as adjuncts and subsidiaries to decentralized units'.[29] In Kumarappa's conception, the argument for decentralized industries was not dictated by a fetish against industries *per se*. The existence of these large-scale industries in the decentralized economy was not an anomaly. Rather, his was an attempt to allocate a decisive role for decentralized means of production in the economy and thereby contain the monopolistic tendencies inherent to large-scale production by centralized industries. This, Kumarappa argued, was not a contradiction since even in 'the political sphere a democracy does not eschew Government control and regulation when it is directed towards the better realization of individual development and expression'.

Kumarappa's position on a decentralized economy significantly influenced Gandhi's own economic thought. This is exemplified by Gandhi's famed October 1945 letter to Nehru laying out fundamental differences on the shape of the future economy of an independent India. Gandhi argued that 'the individual person should have control over the things that are necessary for the sustenance of life. If he cannot have such control the individual cannot survive'. But Gandhi could 'still envisage a number of things that [would] ... have to be organized on a large scale' and, borrowing from Kumarappa, he mused that 'perhaps there will even be railways and also post and telegraph offices'.[30]

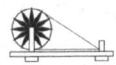

Kumarappa recognized that much of modern machinery and technological advancement was designed to enable large-scale standardized production which was a result of the demands of capitalism. This approach had resulted in the loss of autonomy and cultural self-expression of the ordinary

[28] Interview with J. C. Kumarappa, *Searchlight*, Patna, 3 April 1935, in *Jayaprakash Narayan: Essential Writings (1929–79)*, edited by B. Prasad (New Delhi: Konark, 2002), p. 290.

[29] J. C. Kumarappa, *WVM*, p. 107.

[30] Letter to Jawaharlal Nehru, 5 October 1945, *CWMG*.

individual who was either left out of the production process or made into an appendage to large-scale production. Although machines were not in themselves evil, their use in certain circumstances enabled a single man 'to obtain the labours of thousands'. While 'this does not argue that we should abandon machinery forever ... it cautions us to restrict the use of machinery within limits so that it does not become a means of exploitation'.[31] Thus, the argument was not against machinery *per se* but opposed the 'type of machinery that has been evolved by Western civilization' which was chiefly devised either as aid in circumstances of 'scarcity of labour'—as in the case of the settling of America—or as a means of exploitation that concentrated profits in a few hands.[32] Therefore, such labour-saving machinery was to be avoided in a society like India where labour was abundant and was 'the best means of distribution of wealth'. In the prevailing intellectual climate of the time, Kumarappa's arguments were often misrepresented and attacked though he repeatedly clarified that when a machine 'is used to increase the personal efficiency of the individual it is welcome' but was objectionable when it was 'used as a lever to exploit our neighbour'.[33] This was the difference between the bicycle as a means of transport that increased an individual's efficiency and a rickshaw that became a means of exploitation. A real-life illustration of this attitude towards machinery was provided in the case of the manufacture of hand-made paper. The Board of the AIVIA voted to allow the use of machinery for pulp manufacture since the 'labour involved is too heavy or dangerous for men' and the mechanization did not 'put any workers out of employment'.[34] Indeed, Kumarappa's personal position was neither a romantic view of rural life nor a Luddite reaction to automation. On occasion, he warned against the reductionist 'idea that doing things by hand is good and by machine is bad'.[35] Instead, one needs to 'see if these things promote ahimsa'.

The Gandhian attitude towards machinery stemmed from the understanding that mere mechanical efficiency was not the sole desiderata of economic organization. Rather it was tied up with the *who*, *what*, and *how* of production of goods. The desirability and role of machines

---

[31] J. C. Kumarappa, 'The AIVIA as the Happy Mean'.

[32] J. C. Kumarappa, *WVM*, p 105.

[33] J. C. Kumarappa, Review of *Technique of Rural Reconstruction* by R. K. Parmar, Speeches and Writings, 1, Kumarappa Papers.

[34] *WVM*, p. 107. For specific details of this story, see J. C. Kumarappa, 'When Machine Power', *Harijan*, 15 March 1942.

[35] J. C. Kumarappa, 'Speech delivered at convocation of Samagra Vidyalaya of Sevagram', 22 March 1954, Speeches and Writings, Loose, Kumarappa Papers.

and the large-scale industrial mode of production in the social order was to be determined by their implications for the welfare of the labouring classes and of society at large. But it must be emphasized that this attitude towards machinery did not lead to an immutable principle. The impulse against mechanization of economic production beyond a limited point was a provisional ethic dictated by the need to provide wholesome employment to millions of poor people who had rather limited skills, almost no capital to invest, and were desperate for a worthwhile livelihood.

Kumarappa was often accused of promoting inefficient village industries when industrial mass production made the best use of resources. An Indian academic asked Kumarappa whether one hoped 'to utilize our resources to the best advantage by means of cottage units', and he cited 'the meat packing industry of Chicago as an instance of a complete utilisation of by-products in large scale industries' which thereby resulted in the 'cheapening of the goods to the consumer'.[36] In a perceptive response, Kumarappa unpacked the assumptions of the question, 'viz. (1) that complete utilization of bye-products is *only* possible in large-scale industries, (2) that large-scale industries are *always* economical in the utilization of resources, (3) that low price is an *invariable* desideratum'.[37] Kumarappa's response to the question is strikingly insightful and sets the Gandhian approach apart from a naive attack on modernity. By considering this reply at length, we see how the Gandhians sought an original pathway to convert the moribund village economy into a vibrant decentralized solution to the needs of employment and efficient production.

While admitting that large-scale industries did utilize their resources well, Kumarappa argued that it was wrong to ascribe this to such industries alone. He pointed out that while the contemporary cottage tanners were indeed wasteful in their processing of the available resources, it had more to do with ignorance and was not because 'such utilisation [was] ... foreign to cottage units'. As a specific example Kumarappa pointed to a tannery run by the constructive worker Satish Dasgupta which made use of all parts of animal carcasses. In an indictment of the practice of science that is as valid today as in 1942 when he wrote it, Kumarappa argued that if the small-scale industries were unable to make proper use of their resources 'the remedy is not to abandon cottage units but to bring the *light of science* to cottage workers. This is where we have failed, and selfless scientists with the necessary initiative to adapt their knowledge to the simplicity

---

[36] J. C. Kumarappa, 'Some False Assumptions', *Harijan*, 22 March 1942.

[37] J. C. Kumarappa, 'Some False Assumptions'; emphasis in the original.

of cottage resources are the desideratum, and not the large-scale units'.[38] If the urban intelligentsia viewed the village economy as irredeemable, Kumarappa sought to turn the tables by challenging them to address and solve the technical, economic, and organizational challenges that arose in the rural context. Unfortunately, the urban professional classes did not find these rural challenges interesting enough to warrant their attention. The founding of the AIVIA was in part an attempt to address this apathy towards the village.

However, the issue was not one of efficiencies of scale alone. Indeed, Kumarappa argued that if large-scale units were economical in reducing overheads, they did not make economical use of resources. In fact, such units were 'the most extravagant when we look at it from the national viewpoint'. Taking the example of paper-making, Kumarappa pointed out that every large factory virtually needed 'a forest of bamboos at its disposal', while the village unit made use of discarded material. So fresh-cut bamboo was first used as baskets, mats, and so on, and then when they were no longer usable, they could be converted to paper. This was a much more economical utilization of resources as the bamboo was put to a much more extended period of use than directly feeding it into a paper factory. Indeed, large-scale industries that seemed highly efficient were often 'subsidised by public expenditure'. In contrast, while the 'expensive researches of scientific institutions' were lavishly underwritten by the public exchequer, 'the village artisan hardly ever [derived] ... any benefit' from it. Thus, the many 'handicaps placed on village industries [were] ... counted towards their inability to compete' with factory produce that enjoyed unfair advantages in the form of subsidies.[39] The example of the paper industry that Kumarappa described is particularly telling when read in conjunction with other narratives of recent vintage. In *Ecology and Equity*, the authors point out that while bamboo was 'made available to paper mills at a throwaway price, as low as Rs 1.5 per tonne', the market price of bamboo in cities 'was of the order of Rs 3,000 per tonne'. Thus, 'while poor basket weavers paid a hefty price for this vital raw material, industry was given virtually free access to stocks on reserved forest lands'.[40] Similarly, Kumarappa argued that while mill-made cloth would always be cheaper than khadi, this was not due to the inherent superiority of large-scale production in this context. Rather,

---

[38] J. C. Kumarappa, 'Some False Assumptions'; emphasis added.

[39] J. C. Kumarappa, '"The Inefficiency" of Village Industries', *GUP*, April 1947.

[40] M. Gadgil and R. Guha, *Ecology and Equity: The Use and Abuse of Nature in Contemporary India* (New Delhi: Penguin Books India, 1995), p. 46.

it was because of the many subsidies afforded to factories, including large amounts of power produced using public money and 'supplied to the mills at arbitrary rates', which is 'a great injustice to the nation'.[41]

Arguably, Kumarappa's correspondent had chosen one of the worst possible examples of mass production, that is, the Chicago meat industry. Notorious for its unhygienic conditions and exploitation of labour, the Chicago meat-packing industry was actually totemic of what was *wrong* with the industrial mode of production. The pathetic conditions and the 'wage slavery' of the Chicago meat-workers were the subject of a much-acclaimed 1906 novel, *The Jungle*, by Upton Sinclair.[42] Given the irony of the example proffered, one can only surmise that neither his correspondent nor Kumarappa was aware of Sinclair's damning exposé. Otherwise, most certainly, this particular example extolling the virtues of mass production would not have escaped from being subjected to Kumarappa's acerbic wit.

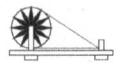

Like large-scale industries, money also played a fundamental role in the modern economy. As a result, Kumarappa also spent a significant amount of time analysing the role of money in human life. Since his years as a student in America, Kumarappa was acutely aware of the role of public finance and monetary policy in the transfer of wealth from India to Britain. He recognized that the European empires that encompassed the world '[could] ... only exist because of the facilities afforded by money'.[43] The artificial manipulation of the conversion ratio between the Indian rupee and the British sterling was a key issue that had exercised Indian nationalists. While it placed Indian business at a distinct disadvantage, Kumarappa was more concerned with the impact that London's policies had on the Indian villager who, as an economic historian of India has argued, 'was subjected

[41] 'Questions levelled at Kumarappa by students at public meetings', no location or date given, Speeches and Writings, Loose, Kumarappa Papers.

[42] For a study of the environmental implications of the growth of Chicago's industries, see William Cronon, *Nature's Metropolis: Chicago and the Great West* (New York: W. W. Norton and Co., 1991).

[43] J. C. Kumarappa, *Gandhian Economy*, p. 23. We may recognize the validity of this statement today in the massive scale of global financial transactions that are facilitated by the availability of vast communication networks without which the modern globalized economy would not exist.

to the forces of the world market without really participating in it'.[44] A true sense of Kumarappa's perception of the financial dimension of the colonial enterprise will be clear when we discuss the effects of inflation and famine during the Second World War.

Over a period of time, Kumarappa developed a critique of the role of money in the modern economy. The growth of money had obvious advantages since it smoothed economic transactions by serving as a medium of exchange and as storage of purchasing power. However, Kumarappa argued that the dominant role of money in the economy was a problem, since a token of exchange had itself 'become a source of profit'.[45] The result was that 'means has been turned into an end'. The use of money in transactions distorts the exchange value involved as the same denomination is used to measure the utility of luxury goods consumed by the rich and bare necessities like food consumed by the poor. This impedes a proper valuation of goods in terms of their utility resulting in the 'obliterating of human values'.[46] The mobility of money allows the transfer of purchasing power from one location to another with ease. Under the colonial dispensation it meant the transfer of vast amounts of wealth from the Indian countryside to London and urban areas of India. The problem is further compounded when the state draws money from the villages and spends it on the cities without taking any measures to check prices. Indeed, 'for transfer of purchasing power, money and credit are unsurpassed'.[47] The relevance of Kumarappa's critique to our contemporary times is evident when we consider the overwhelming—some would say nightmarish—dominance of financial capital over our economies.

Kumarappa was also concerned about the exploitation that obtains with modern money. As early as his time in Columbia, he had remarked on the disadvantage it placed on the producer of economic goods.[48] Given the perishable nature of most consumer goods, the producer seeks to sell them as soon as possible. In comparison with such goods, the purchasing power of money is stable, allowing the buyer to wait till the opportune time. Thus, 'the bargaining power of a seller of perishable bananas or fish is not on a par with that of the buyer' resulting in the smothering of 'equity

---

[44] Rothermund, *An Economic History of India*, p. 85.

[45] J. C. Kumarappa, 'Advantages of Barter', *Harijan*, 24 July 1937.

[46] J. C. Kumarappa, 'Exchange and Human Values', *Harijan*, 3 May 1942.

[47] J. C. Kumarappa, *WVM*, p. 41.

[48] J. C. Kumarappa, Notebooks, 10, vol. 2, Kumarappa Papers.

and justice'.[49] As regards its role as a storage of purchasing power, any depreciation in prices is 'an increasing burden to the debtor and growing wealth to the creditor' thereby accentuating existing inequalities.[50] The millions living in a subsistence economy needed 'an unalterable storage of purchasing power'.[51] Based on the experience of the Second World War, Kumarappa argued that any intermediary like money should be designed so as to 'faithfully report the value received from one party to another' and that 'it should not change its value in the interval' between production and consumption.[52]

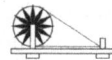

Kumarappa's critique of the role of money can also be understood in terms of value theory which is an idea central to economic philosophy. Although Kumarappa never explicitly used this technical term, by parsing his writings and pronouncements, we can establish his position on value in two recognizable senses. First, much of our earlier discussion of his philosophy—including his 'scale of values'—centred on the Natural Order would fall under the rubric of ethical theory. The second use is with regard to the source of economic value. Since the development of the modern industrial economy, a central debate in the history of economic thought has been on the source of economic value inherent in goods that are traded in the marketplace. Of relevance to us are the positions of the early French Physiocrats who held that all value arose out of agriculture, and that of Marx who critiqued the classical economists through his 'labour theory of value'. In terms of the Natural Order, Kumarappa's position was a moral one that went beyond the anthropocentrism of the debate between economists on the source of economic value. For him, in nature, work 'consists in the efforts put forth by various factors—insentient and sentient—which cooperate to complete [the] cycle of life'.[53] In other words, nature was the ultimate source of value. In moral terms, while the value of an economic good arose out of human activity that co-operated with the dictates of

[49] J. C. Kumarappa, *WVM*, p. 41.
[50] J. C. Kumarappa, 'Advantages of Barter', *Harijan*, 24 July 1937.
[51] J. C. Kumarappa, *EOP*, p. 138.
[52] J. C. Kumarappa, *Gandhian Economy*, p. 21.
[53] J. C. Kumarappa, *EOP*, p. 2.

nature, any undue extraction of economic value inevitably resulted in moral and temporal violence.

Economists distinguish between two types of value, that is, use and exchange value. While use value of a commodity represents its ability to satisfy human needs, roughly speaking, exchange value represents the 'price' the commodity commands in the marketplace. Kumarappa argued that the modern economy driven by money as the means of exchange introduces severe distortions in our understanding of value. In the era of mass production, this crisis is exemplified by the commodification of material goods, of which Kumarappa provided an illustration. In course of the AIVIA's work in promoting bee-keeping as a viable venture, Kumarappa was impressed by the success of a cooperative society that made good profits by selling honey. Upon meeting the daughter of the secretary of the society, he found that she knew a lot about bees and their hives. However, when asked if she liked the taste of honey, the little girl had a blank look and responded that she had never tasted honey! Given the high prices the honey commanded in urban markets, the father felt he could not afford to give his daughter the honey he produced. Angered by this situation where exchange value had trumped use value, Kumarappa damned such economics for 'enticing away honey from the mouth of the child to the overladen tables of the rich'.[54]

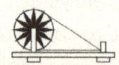

The dominance of exchange value as price resulted in a distortion of both wages and prices. Kumarappa argued that with their monopoly over money, the capitalists had 'cornered all the work available', which was doled out in the form of wage slavery to the labouring masses.[55] This was accompanied by constant attempts to keep wages down so that the prices of commodities were lowered and made competitive. For Kumarappa, low prices of commodities were not an unalloyed good as they did not take into account the proportion of the price that constituted the wages of the producer. Since in a capitalistic economy low prices are often obtained by exploitation of labour rather than efficiency in production, Kumarappa

[54] J. C. Kumarappa, *EOP*, p. 51.
[55] J. C. Kumarappa, 'Advantages of Barter', *Harijan*, 24 July 1937.

argued that 'if we aim at an equalitarian society based on social justice, we must be prepared for higher prices' which would lead to a better distribution of wealth.[56] To overcome the impacts of wage slavery and avoid exploitation and concentration of wealth, Kumarappa argued that labour had to be made the 'mainstream of wealth distribution' in society.[57] This view was succinctly enunciated by Gandhi in his reply to Charlie Chaplin in 1931 that he did not want mass production but 'production by the masses'.[58] The alternative of idleness imposed by unemployment was no leisure at all but only led to starvation.

Along with a consideration of just wages, Kumarappa also addressed an important, if neglected, aspect of economic activity, the very idea of work itself. With his deeply felt desire to place the individual at the centre of the economy, it was natural that he would pay particular attention to the impact of work on the individual worker. Indeed, it is in his philosophy of work that we find Kumarappa at his insightful and creative best. Beyond the economic dimension of labour, he argued that the very 'history of the human race has been moulded by the attitude man takes towards work'.[59] He pointed out that 'human nature being what it is', there is always an attempt to shift physical toil 'on to someone else'.[60] In the Indian context, Kumarappa implicitly saw it in its social organization. Acutely aware that 'it is no use preaching to the unfortunate [about] the dignity of labour', he wryly observed that if one were to pay a good salary to a tanner 'you will find the highest caste people elbowing each other to fill the place'.[61] In Western societies, Kumarappa located this attitude in the Judeo-Christian view of work as 'a curse from God' that man had to somehow circumvent.[62] The result was the continual exploitation of the weak by the powerful. In ancient times, this was justified by the Aristotelian view that slavery was ordained by nature. Later, it took on the form of serfdom under feudal

[56] J. C. Kumarappa, 'Equalitarian Society', *GUP*, November 1952.

[57] J. C. Kumarappa, 'Ahimsa and Industrialisation', *Harijan*, 12 February 1938.

[58] M. K. Gandhi, 'Mass Production v. Production by the Masses', in *Cent Per Cent Swadeshi or The Economics of Village Industries* (Ahmedabad: Navajivan Publishing House, 1948), pp. 118–23.

[59] J. C. Kumarappa, *The Philosophy of Work and Other Essays* (Wardha: The All-India Village Industries Association, 1949), p. 1.

[60] J. C. Kumarappa, *Philosophy of Work*, p. 3.

[61] J. C. Kumarappa, 'Unemployment and Swadeshi', Speeches and Writings, 8, Kumarappa Papers.

[62] J. C. Kumarappa, *Philosophy of Work*, p. 1.

appropriation of land, and in modern times the result is capitalist control over labour. In all instances, whole societies came to grief due to such unnatural approaches that 'in the moral sphere we call sin', and 'in the physical sphere' we know as violence.

The wage system that reduced labour to a commodity results in drudgery, whereby the labourer is soon made into a wreck only to be replaced by others in an endless cycle of exploitation. Kumarappa was once taken on a tour of a gold mine in Kolar district of present-day Karnataka and was asked for suggestions for the welfare of the miners. The forthright Kumarappa suggested that this would be best served by shutting down the mine! If this proposition was not acceptable to the management, he suggested that they could do the next best thing and 'provide more liquor shops to enable the men to drown their miseries'.[63] As in this instance, the employer looks only to his profit and 'takes the subjective, short-term view of life'.[64] The corrective, Kumarappa argued, had nevertheless to contend with providing work, since 'a nation cannot exist on doles and public works'.[65] There could be no other way for the worker but to earn his living. The solution to exploitation of the worker under capitalism could only be provided by various social means, 'the state, religion, or social organization', in the form of wholesome work that addressed itself to the needs of the worker.[66] Such wholesome work contained a small creative element along with much that was drudgery. If every individual was to be afforded creative satisfaction in their calling, work had to provide both physical and creative benefits.

Although he argued for holistic work, Kumarappa did recognize that division of labour was inevitable with the growth of civilization and that specialization of work undoubtedly brought great benefits. In Indian life 'such specialization has held sway since time immemorial and it has even gone to seed having become hereditary and caste-bound'.[67] In the modern context, division of labour as exemplified by the Fordian assembly line had 'broken up work into minute processes', making it synonymous with drudgery, 'with all the undesirable qualities of a curse'. Thus, division of labour should not be carried out beyond a limit whereby it 'concentrates

[63] J. C. Kumarappa, *EOP*, p. 107.

[64] J. C. Kumarappa, 'At What Cost Industrialisation?', Speeches and Writings, 1, Kumarappa Papers.

[65] J. C. Kumarappa, 'Unemployment', *Harijan*, 19 February 1938.

[66] J. C. Kumarappa, 'At What Cost Industrialisation?'.

[67] J. C. Kumarappa, *Philosophy of Work*, p. 12.

the pleasures in a few hands' and by shifting the toil to labourers, deprives their work of the 'germ of growth'.[68]

In line with the Gandhian view of individual autonomy, Kumarappa argued that the best form of work was not wage labour but 'exertion with a self-chosen purpose'.[69] Under such conditions, the unpleasant part of work is not always drudgery. Rather, 'the toil part of work is essential to enable one to grow through work' and achieve something of creative value.[70] 'No musician can aspire to be able to produce music merely by listening' but needs to go through 'the ordeal of practising' for years on end. Thus, more than the material productivity, 'perhaps the more important contribution of work' is its impact on the individual. The notion of leisure is also tied to the circumstances and nature of work. In an industrial setting, where the worker labours under a regimented schedule, leisure is provided in short intervals to counter the boredom of repetitive work and exhaustion from hard labour. The corollary is that when 'left no scope for the exercise of self-development and self-expression, sports [assumes] ... a special importance'.[71] With Veblenian overtones, Kumarappa argued that while one group has no energy left for leisure, the other needs to fill its time with recreation. In an argument that is guaranteed to alienate many Indians, Kumarappa pointed out that the 'most suitable game for the conditions described above is cricket'! Arguing against the industrial definition of leisure, Kumarappa agreed with Kropotkin that 'the satisfaction of physical, artistic, and moral needs, has always been the most powerful stimulant to work'.[72] Under such circumstances, work has an element of leisure built into itself, that is, 'leisure is not a complete cessation of all activities'.[73] Rather 'leisure is an integral part of work just as rest is an essential component of a musical note'. While engaging in wholesome work, beneficial leisure provides rest to certain faculties while exercising others.

Kumarappa's philosophy of work went far beyond mere economism and embodied an entire vision of life. He argued that 'if a man is truly religious', his actions should be imbued by this view.[74] Since ceremonial religion

[68] J. C. Kumarappa, 'At What Cost Industrialisation?'.

[69] J. C. Kumarappa, *Philosophy of Work*, p. 5.

[70] J. C. Kumarappa, *Philosophy of Work*, p. 2.

[71] J. C. Kumarappa, *Gandhian Economy*, p. 65.

[72] J. C. Kumarappa, Foreword to P. Kropotkin's 'Conquest of Bread', 1935, Speeches and Writings, 1, Kumarappa Papers.

[73] J. C. Kumarappa, *Philosophy of Work*, p. 14.

[74] J. C. Kumarappa, *WVM*, p. 58.

occupied a small part of one's life compared to daily work, Kumarappa argued that one should view work as 'the practical side of religion' and to 'deny man his opportunity to work is to deny' his very humanity. Kumarappa was to further develop this argument in his discussions on the purpose of religion in human life. Unlike thinkers who elevated creative freedom of the mind to the highest form of artistic self-expression, Kumarappa sought to ground it in the existential contingencies of ordinary life, that is, wholesome and uncoerced work. Thus, 'the economic activity of man shorn of greed and the cause of friction, affords an opportunity for the realisation of one's inner urge for self-expression'.[75] The ultimate goal of Gandhi's life, Kumarappa argued, was 'precipitating ahimsa in life by raising work to the dignity of a life purpose'.

Much of Kumarappa's critique of modern work mirrors Marx's theory of alienation obtained in capitalist society. Thus, he held that as long as capital wielded a disproportionate amount of power, labour unions were necessary to 'take concerted action to bring about equilibrium'.[76] Nevertheless, as is evident, the Gandhian conception of the role of work in human life was also a dramatic departure from a Marxist interpretation of the meaning of work and labour. In particular, Kumarappa's spiritualized interpretation of 'work as religion' sets it apart from the critique by the Young Hegelians of whom Marx was a prime example.

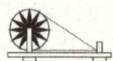

Kumarappa argued that the correct approach to judge any economic paradigm would be 'one which sorts out the methods of production according to the manner by which a system seeks to control the environment and circumstances of human beings'.[77] This led to his rejection of the dominant ideologies of the day since 'both under capitalism and communism human values are not fully taken into account'.[78] If capitalism saw human beings as mere 'gun-fodder', the socialist order did no better in viewing him

[75] J. C. Kumarappa, 'Note on Gandhi Jayanti', Speeches and Writings, 3, Kumarappa Papers.

[76] J. C. Kumarappa, The Philosophy of the Village Movement, Kovvur Sanivarapu Subba Rao, 1935, p. 41.

[77] J. C. Kumarappa, 'The Groundwork for Independence', Harijan, 12 July 1942.

[78] J. C. Kumarappa, WVM, p. 13.

as 'a cogwheel in a machine'. In contrast to the very material considerations of both these dominant ideologies, at its core, Kumarappa's theory of economic decentralization was a moral project.[79] In his view, economic activity was not merely for production of goods or monetary profit but must satisfy 'the needs of people, distribute wealth in the process, and contribute towards the happiness and well-being of mankind'.[80] For him the central challenge was to organize fruitful employment for millions of Indians who had no skills or assets to offer but their bodily labour. While recognizing the essential roles of the state and the market, he was fundamentally sceptical of their ability to deliver economic justice without intruding on individual autonomy. Under these circumstances, the only way people could earn their bread was through their own sweat.

Apart from not grudging higher prices if they meant better wages to the worker, Kumarappa argued for the recognition that one's own welfare was intimately bound up with that of those around us. He recognized that while it is easy to love an abstract God, 'it is difficult to show one's love of God in one's everyday dealings with one's neighbour'.[81] Yet this is precisely what Kumarappa demanded of every individual and, believing in the perfectibility of human nature, he reckoned that our 'economic life is capable of being projected into the eternal or the spiritual level'.[82] Thus, if distributive justice was to be achieved through economic activity without an excessive dependence on the munificence of the state or the market, there was no alternative but to marry the moral imperative to our daily economic activity.

Such a moral view of our relationship with others meant that 'wealth' did not imply the 'possession of materials in plenty'.[83] Rather, as its root word signified, wealth denoted welfare, that is, 'the wholesome reaction of material things to human well-being'. Following Ruskin, Kumarappa

---

[79] Indeed, it is from this moral perspective that Kumarappa argued after the Second World War that India should not accept reparations extracted from the defeated countries of Japan and Germany due to the moral taint attached to them. See 'A Share in the Booty', *GUP*, February 1947 and 'Are We Imperialists?', *GUP*, June 1947.

[80] J. C. Kumarappa, 'National Wealth', *Harijan*, 12 April 1942.

[81] J. C. Kumarappa, 'Abstract of Speech at Third Annual Meeting of the Guntur Hand-Pounded Rice Association', 1 November 1936, Bound Volume, 10, Kumarappa Papers.

[82] J. C. Kumarappa, *WVM*, p. 70.

[83] J. C. Kumarappa, 'National Wealth', *Harijan*, 12 April 1942.

asserted that life is wealth, and argued that an economy run on the principles of Gandhian sarvodaya 'would emphasize the human values in prices and cost rather than use them as guides in material production'.[84] In light of this perception, he rejected the attempt by the marginalist theoreticians to give economics a scientific footing like that of natural laws. He bemoaned the fact that by considering the atomized, selfish, and profit-maximizing individual as the fundamental unit, 'economic theory has gone to seed in mathematical formulae rather than being presented as a fascinating psychological study of human nature'. At the same time, Kumarappa recognized the limits to human altruism and held that the profit motive was not to be entirely rejected, and that 'it is necessary to allow a certain amount of self-interest'.[85] However, one would certainly 'curb the capacity of the individual to accumulate profits and wealth'. This balance of the personal interests and larger social considerations could only be achieved by binding individuals into a moral web of mutual obligations. He argued that an economy built on purely material considerations 'may appear efficient but lead to competition and violence' and could not provide equity and justice.[86] The only remedy was to build a society around the principles of co-operation—that may be arduous, but would, 'in the long run, support everybody, and lead to self-sufficiency and thereby bring about peace'.

Kumarappa illustrated his economic vision with Gandhi's advocacy of khadi. While most thought of khadi as 'merely the wearing of handspun and handwoven cloth', in reality it stood for 'an economic organization based on self-sufficiency and co-operation'.[87] In contrast to the 'present economic order which is based on competitive production', the rules governing a co-operative economy would be of a different order. Given the persistent myths on Gandhi's ideas, it is important to emphasize that the village economy being advocated here was far from an isolated, autarkic island. Nor was the thrust towards a localized economy based on self-sufficiency harkening back to a hoary past. Rather, it stemmed from a recognition of the severe distortions that existed in modern markets where the participants had vastly different levels of economic power and influence. Rejecting the idea of comparative advantage, Kumarappa argued that trade should occur only in surpluses. As seen in our earlier example of trade in

[84] J. C. Kumarappa, 'Economics of Sharing', *GUP*, May 1955.

[85] J. C. Kumarappa, *WVM*, p. 13.

[86] J. C. Kumarappa, 'The Ultimate Goal of All Gandhian Programmes', *GUP*, May 1954.

[87] J. C. Kumarappa, 'Khadi in Our Life', *GUP*, June 1947.

honey, the distortion introduced by exchange value robbed the villager of the far greater use value of the commodities they produced. In particular, Kumarappa wished to set aright the lopsided and exploitative economic equation between the town and the village. As Gandhi had envisioned in his 'oceanic circles' formulation of society, in an economy based on localized trade 'the outermost circumference will not wield power to crush the inner circle but will give strength to all within and derive its own strength from it'.[88] Far from sealing off the village to outside influences, Kumarappa was arguing for an alternative vision of modernity where the welfare of the individual was paramount.

He argued that the key modern economic crisis was the delinking of production and distribution and could only be remedied by placing 'the buyer and seller on an equal footing'.[89] It was only if the goods produced by the masses were consumed that one could expect a better distribution of wealth in society. The money economy had resulted in a long chain of links between the producer and the consumer with most of the profits being siphoned off by intermediaries. By encouraging consumption within a local region, this problem could be addressed and this would also halt the flight of wealth out of a region. Ideally, the dominance of money could be removed if one could trade in goods, but in a complex economy such barter was impracticable. Nevertheless, the spirit of equity inherent in a barter economy could be retained if one could 'reduce the chain of exchange and bring the producer and consumer together'. It is also important to recognize that in arguing for village-based production, both Gandhi and Kumarappa were consistently advocating *local production for local consumption*, thereby binding people in a moral web of producer–consumer relations. It may be pointed out that since India's independence, the Gandhian advocacy of village industries has increasingly—and often perversely—been interpreted as the encouragement of cottage industries to produce goods for urban markets. The production of curios and trinkets for the fickle tastes of the urban market is not the fate that Gandhi or Kumarappa had in mind for the economic actors in India's numerous villages.

Kumarappa laid much store on the duties of the consumer to ensure the operation of moral laws in the economic domain. He argued that an economy based purely on the rights of the consumer was nothing but

[88] M. K. Gandhi, 'Independence', *Harijan*, 28 July 1946. As we shall see later, Kumarappa developed a coherent model based on Balanced Cultivation that took a region as the basis for economic planning.

[89] J. C. Kumarappa, 'Advantages of Barter', *Harijan*, 24 July 1937.

barbarism.[90] Only in a localized economy could the violence inherent in the operation of Say's Law be neutralized. In a localized economy it was possible for production to closely follow demand as both producers and consumers were engaged in a direct relationship with few or no intermediaries. If the purchase of goods produced outside one's region was nothing but the importation of unemployment into one's neighbourhood, the act of importing goods also carried the potential of moral taint.[91] Applying a human standard of values behoves us to look into the antecedents of a product that we wish to purchase. If a commodity is made through exploitation, say cocoa 'obtained from plantations on the west coast of Africa', using 'forced native labour', the purchaser of the manufactured tin of chocolate unwittingly becomes a participant in the exploitation.[92] However, inquiring into the antecedents of every commodity produced in a far-off location is humanly impossible. Therefore, economic transactions should be, as far as possible, restricted to one's locality. Not only does mass production 'impoverish life' by 'laying waste personality and individuality', it is also antithetical to justice in the political economy.[93] This is the moral basis of swadeshi.

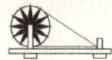

Kumarappa's economic decentralization was ambitious in its objectives of providing creative autonomy for the individual, which would form the basis for a durable and non-violent social order. The primacy accorded to the individual in the economic realm is naturally reflected in his views on democratic governance of the polity. He argued that democratic ideals 'do not begin and end with politics', as that definition would imply the acceptance of voting power as a means of public force, that is, a form of dictatorship of the majority or voting bloc.[94] The true democratic ideal is one where 'the scope of the individual for full development of his personality is not restricted, and where in developing himself he develops others'.[95] Much like an amateur cyclist who controls his motions

---

[90] J. C. Kumarappa, *Gandhian Economy*, p. 57.

[91] Gandhi's boycott and burning of British cloth was due to the moral burden such a fabric represented.

[92] J. C. Kumarappa, *WVM*, p. 78.

[93] J. C. Kumarappa, *EOP*, pp. 61–2.

[94] J. C. Kumarappa, *WVM*, p. 193.

[95] J. C. Kumarappa, *WVM*, p. 201.

in a deliberate and conscious manner, a 'functional democracy' is one in which people are guided by a handful of leaders. In contrast, when the democratic ideals are fully assimilated into the body politic, much like a seasoned cyclist, the individual carries out his or her responsibilities automatically and without conscious effort, leading to 'cultural democracy'. Kumarappa argued that while one may build 'functional democracies overnight, cultural democracies are products of millennia'.[96] But it is only the latter form that stands the test of time when the control or governance of the individual is from within and not imposed from without. The difference lies in the fact that while functional democracy is 'based on a widely diffused franchise', cultural democracy is based on 'the will of the people themselves which finds expression, not in mere votes, but in actual administrative power'.

Although he recognized the value of formal democracy, Kumarappa did not accord its mechanism a fundamental importance. Both during the colonial period and after India's independence, he remained sceptical of the ability and willingness of the state to deliver justice to the people at large. This scepticism stemmed from the fact that modern democracies represented an enormous concentration of political and economic power which was always inimical to individual autonomy and development. The complexity of modern bureaucracies meant that citizens could do little to prevent abuse of power vested in the instruments of the state. Without enough political and economic decentralization, it was not possible for individuals to exercise any significant control over their destinies. While modern states hid their undemocratic practices behind the formalities of franchise such as voting, their true nature was unmasked in times of social and political strife. Thus, in view of the behaviour of the European governments during the Second World War, Kumarappa argued that 'democracy, as we know it in the West, is a delegated autocracy, and differs little from the organization of totalitarian states'.[97] This view was reinforced by his deep disillusionment with the Congress-led Indian state after Independence. With power in hand, independent India's leaders comprehensively rejected Gandhi's vision and adopted the trappings of a liberal democracy where the urban industrial economy was accorded primacy and the village continued to languish in neglect.

Kumarappa recognized that Gandhi's historic role was in the deepening of democracy through the introduction of 'Dharma in all

[96] J. C. Kumarappa, *WVM*, p. 195.
[97] J. C. Kumarappa, 'The Choice', *GUP*, January 1942.

walks of life—including politics and the art of Government'.[98] Viewed from this vantage point, modern democracies that are organized on the basis of individual rights are inadequate and often fall short in their practice of public virtues. Kumarappa emphasized that a more mature form would be based on 'a consciousness of duties'. One may bear in mind that Kumarappa's argument here is for a normative ideal and his position should not be construed as a conservative argument for the preservation of the *status quo*. In fact, Kumarappa was taking a radical position here by arguing that 'the essence of democracy is that the executive and legislative power must be vested in each individual'. Under such ideal conditions, 'every citizen must be capable of being a law unto himself in an enlightened sense'. The argument, which echoes Tolstoy's views, is similar to the reasoning behind economic decentralization. While the autonomy of the individual has primacy as the normative ideal, given the acute inequalities and injustices that exist in society, it is to be tempered by a moral imperative that individuals exercise their freedom of agency in discharging their responsibilities towards others.

Kumarappa was not naive about the difficulty of the task of building a non-violent social order, but he insisted that a rights-based discourse inevitably leads to social or group conflict. The formal mechanisms of centralized, liberal democracies provide the trappings of democratic exercise, but are open to the abuse of power by the few leaders vested with political control. In contrast, 'when each citizen is so disciplined as to act on what is right from a detached view of affairs he can be entrusted with the executive and legislative powers without any fear of his misusing them'. This was the democratic ideal and 'in the measure in which we approximate to this ideal stage we are developing democracy'. In the context of the emphasis on duties, it is worth repeating that Kumarappa was not against the enforcement of rights. Properly conceived, he argued, such enforcement falls within the domain of the state, whereas the Gandhian constructive workers should work on 'the development of duty-mindedness' amongst the people towards others in society.[99]

Kumarappa's arguments for political and economic decentralization were centred on the primacy of the individual. Indeed, he argued that of the many contributions of Gandhi, 'not the least is the conferring of a unique dignity on man'.[100] But if the goal was to restore the dignity of man, not only did

---

[98] J. C. Kumarappa, 'The Dharma of Kings', *GUP*, February 1956.
[99] J. C. Kumarappa, 'Our Plans and Programmes', *GUP*, April 1956.
[100] J. C. Kumarappa, 'Dignity of Man', *GUP*, November 1949.

one have to contend with the might of the centralized state, one also had to reckon with that fundamental sociological fact of Indian society—caste.

Kumarappa's understanding of caste underwent an evolution as his personal circumstances changed. In his years in America, he held the then common perception that the original caste order was a guild that prevented severe competition and regulated society but had become corrupted at a later stage.[101] Apart from his limited understanding of caste in its operational form, in these early years he was also acutely aware of his position as a Christian nationalist. Caste had been identified as the Achilles' heel of Hinduism by Christian missionaries who relentlessly attacked the caste order as a symptom of Hindu depravity. Needless to say, Kumarappa was at pains to distance himself from this missionary position.

Starting with the Matar Survey, as he began to gain direct experience of rural India, Kumarappa came to understand caste as the key factor that cut across 'physical, economic, spiritual and social' institutions of agrarian India.[102] Whatever may have been its historical antecedents, the Indian countryside had fallen into a 'blind well of castes and subcastes tapering into untouchability and unapproachability' which affected social relations and shaped the physical environment. The 'unhygienic and insanitary conditions' that characterized Indian villages were a direct result of how the caste system operated. Thus, his position quickly evolved to one where he held that the rigidity of the *varnashrama dharma* rendered its values 'a total misfit in the modern world' where the primacy of the individual had to be restored.[103] This perception was shared by many nationalists including Gandhi.[104] But, unlike the proponents of

---

[101] Notes for lecture delivered in America on 'Women in India' in 1928, Subject File, 4, Kumarappa Papers.

[102] J. C. Kumarappa, 'The Land of Villages', 16 October 1935, Speeches and Writings, 2, Kumarappa Papers.

[103] J. C. Kumarappa, *EOP*, p. 25.

[104] The evolution of Gandhi's position was, in part, due to his political debate with Ambedkar. For an interpretation of the Gandhi–Ambedkar debate on caste as a dialectical process and its implications, see D. R. Nagaraj, *The Flaming Feet and Other Essays: The Dalit Movement in India*, edited by Prithvi Datta Chandra Shobhi (Ranikhet: Permanent Black, 2010).

urban industrialization, for constructive workers the 'liberation of the untouchable' was organically linked to the economic 'emancipation of the village'.[105]

Kumarappa believed that the 'freedom of the individual in a classless and casteless society' was a fundamental objective.[106] However, he did not believe that the task could be accomplished merely by calling for an end to caste. If the new India to be built was to avoid 'exploitation, unlimited accumulation of wealth and unrestrained competition', it was necessary to protect the poor from the vagaries of life in an urbanized society that offered no sense of kinship.[107] Aware that a rapid and complete dissolution of the indigenous social structures would create newer and greater problems than they attempted to solve, constructive workers had the unenviable task of clearing the space for a new social order in the village itself. Thus, Kumarappa argued that the freedom of the individual could only be ensured by binding people into a compact of reciprocal and equitable economic ties, and for this purpose, the social order in village India had to be reworked in situ.

While he rejected the ritual hierarchy and social injustice implicit in caste, Kumarappa nevertheless called for recognition that the 'caste system and the Joint Family system have a great deal to teach us in Economics and Sociology'. Therefore, he asserted that 'while we may be prepared to throw away the deposit we should strive to understand the chemical action that brought about the precipitation'. As today, in 1930 Kumarappa knew that he was apt to be misunderstood and felt it necessary to clarify that he had 'not been pleading for a reversion to old methods'. Rather, he wanted his audience to 'think on these lines, prove all things, [and] hold fast to that which is good'.

Kumarappa's position on caste came to be informed by his objectives as well as the nature of his audience. He wanted to end caste, but he also wished to widen the endemic value of caste kinship to encompass everyone in a village. Consider the case of a 1931 speech in which he argued that the caste system had played a role in the historic past in 'assuring to every

[105] Nagaraj, 'Self-Purification vs. Self-Respect: On the Roots of the Dalit Movement', in *The Flaming Feet and Other Essays*, p. 57.

[106] Letter from J. C. Kumarappa to Shankarrao Deo, 27 November 1947, Correspondence Files, Kumarappa Papers.

[107] J. C. Kumarappa, 'Rebuilding India', Speeches and Writings, 10, Kumarappa Papers.

individual the minimum of subsistence'.[108] Now, a contemporary reading of this position would characterize this as exceedingly conservative, even casteist in character. But, as a Christian, Kumarappa had no personal commitment to the institution of caste. What he was aiming to achieve here, albeit clumsily, was to make a case for mutually binding moral obligations in modern times. Indeed, an even greater source of misunderstanding is Kumarappa's occasional use of *varna* nomenclature to describe society.[109] In Kumarappa's typology, the classification of people into the four varnas was not according to the caste they were born into, but was based on their true worth in terms of contribution to society.

Even as he took on such positions, as his direct experience of rural India deepened, he began to criticize casteist practices. In the same speech mentioned above, he castigated the upper castes for their 'treatment of the untouchables [which] is worse than even the treatment given to animals' and wondered what the state would be of 'the country given over into the hands of people who could so tyrannise their own brethren'. Going further, Kumarappa argued:

> We are supposed to be a religious-minded nation. If we do not see God in the needs of our brethren, our religiosity is pure humbug. A Brahmin who hesitates to touch an untouchable should be an outcaste of society and it is a blasphemy to call him a priest. A true Brahmin is he who lays down his life in service of God as revealed in the needs of the helpless and the down-trodden.

Similarly, in discussing the true meaning of education, Kumarappa gave vent to his indignation at the practice of Brahminical learning. In describing his visit to a centre for Sanskrit learning, he was appalled that certain *mantras* were taught only to Brahmins and 'needless to say no Harijans were allowed into the college'.[110] The learning of ancient lore by rote in such a casteist manner, Kumarappa argued, was 'no more culture than vomiting is digesting'. True culture is obtained only when 'we learn ancient lore and by contact with present-day problems are able to convert

---

[108] J. C. Kumarappa, 'Speech delivered at the Ramadas Co-operative Training Institute Ltd.', Rajahmundry, 1931, Speeches and Writings, 5, Kumarappa Papers.

[109] See J. C. Kumarappa, 'Handicrafts and Cottage Industries', *The Annals of the American Academy of Political and Social Science*, vol. 233, no. 1 (1944): 106–12. Also see J. C. Kumarappa, *WVM*, pp. 22–4.

[110] J. C. Kumarappa, *WVM*, p. 180.

that knowledge to practice and transform the evils of present society into good'.[111] Going further he argued:

> Such institutions are parasitic and should be wiped out of existence. These are disease-germ breeding centres of our educational system. True education is above all castes and creeds. It transcends man-made bounds. Until we recognize the dignity of all human beings we shall be bound by so called 'sacred threads' to death's head and degradation. Let us shake ourselves loose from such bondage. If there be any who feels proud that he is a Brahmin may he know that India has to bow down her head in shame before the world because of such unnatural distinctions.

As the years progressed, Kumarappa's battles and arguments were with India's urban citizenry, and he spent much time in defending the village as a viable site of modern society. His focus was largely on criticizing the excesses of industrialization and protesting against the widespread injustice meted out to rural India. The caste question appeared less frequently in his writings although it reappeared in his public pronouncements during his 1948–9 tours of India as the chairman of the Agrarian Reforms Committee (ARC).[112]

Gandhi and Kumarappa worried that the dissolution of the caste order should not translate into the press-ganging of the lower castes into a faceless labour force that could be exploited for India's industrialization. Instead of destroying the village and its economy, Gandhi had argued that the solution to India's problem of social hierarchy lay in setting aright 'the divorce between intelligence and labour [that] has resulted in a criminal negligence of villages'.[113] However, the village economy held no value for independent India's planners who took the industrial road to modernity. The ironic result has been that India has managed to all but destroy the village but not the caste order.

[111] J. C. Kumarappa, *WVM*, p. 181.

[112] Once when the higher castes prevented a post office being set up in a predominantly Dalit village, Kumarappa wrote directly to Nehru to have the problem solved. Letter from J. C. Kumarappa to Jawaharlal Nehru, 16 December 1953, Correspondence Files, Kumarappa Papers.

[113] M. K. Gandhi, *Constructive Programme: Its Meaning and Place*, reprint of revised and enlarged edition (Ahmedabad: Navajivan Trust, [1945] 2005), p. 12.

9   The Lonely Furrow

While the work of the All-India Village Industries Association (AIVIA) was begun in real earnest, being 'in the nature of pioneer work, with no experience of the past to fall back upon', progress was inevitably slow.[1] As the AIVIA was dealing with a very broad set of industries, it was necessary for it to define its role as a facilitator rather than undertake the task of building the entire chain of operations from sourcing raw materials to the sale of finished products.[2] An early remit the AIVIA set for itself was to act as a clearing house of information that would help improve and rationalize village industries. The association sought to address this task by building a decentralized network of members, workers, and agents. As Gandhi put it, while the administration of the AIVIA was to be decentralized, he wanted 'centralization of thought, ideas and scientific knowledge'.[3] However, accurate and scientifically validated knowledge of the various technical

---

[1] *All-India Village Industries Association: Annual Report* (henceforth *AIVIA Annual Report*) (Wardha: The All-India Village Industries Association, 1939), p. 1.

[2] This approach of the AIVIA also distinguished it from other rural reconstruction efforts that typically focused on a small geographical region or a few villages.

[3] Speech at Gandhi Seva Sangh, on or before 30 November 1934, *CWMG*.

aspects of many village industries was either non-existent or hard to come by. By the 1930s, educated public opinion lay between apathy and hostility towards the AIVIA and 'even the most enlightened' were of the view that 'in this age of mechanization it is futile to revive village industries'.[4] Consequently, apart from the fact that 'no organised effort or scientific knowledge had been directed' towards addressing the needs of the village, the AIVIA could not attract competent workers towards its cause.[5] Kumarappa was under no illusion about the difficulty of the task and had warned that constructive work in the village entailed 'patience and plodding but India's future will depend on the foundations' laid in this manner.[6] Exhorting the workers not to be disappointed if their efforts did not yield quick results, he pointed out that although mushrooms grew overnight, they were aiming at raising the 'banyan tree [that] takes years of slow growth' which in its full maturity 'would yield shelter to all around it'. The problems of a lack of trained workers and an antagonistic public perception were acute and related. If, for Gandhi, the AIVIA was an attempt to 'revive and encourage the remunerative village industries', his critics continued to read it as part of his attack on modernity.[7] This misreading of the intent of the AIVIA persisted and throughout its existence it remained largely starved of the sort of talent and leadership that the political struggle would continue to garner.

However, one new worker was now available. During the founding of the AIVIA, Bharatan Kumarappa had been employed at the Indian Institute of Philosophy at Amalner.[8] In 1933 Bharatan had tried to persuade Kumarappa to move back to the south. But by the middle of 1935, Bharatan quit his job to throw in his lot with that of his brother and arrived in Wardha to work for the AIVIA.[9] In contrast to his acerbic brother, Bharatan was

---

[4] *AIVIA Annual Report*, 1939, p. 1.

[5] An earlier effort was made by Kaka Kalelkar who introduced a short-lived course on village work at the Gujarat Vidyapith. An early graduate of this course was Jhaverbhai Patel, who was a key AIVIA worker at Maganvadi. See Madho Prasad, *A Gandhian Patriarch: A Political and Spiritual Biography of Kaka Kalelkar* (Bombay: Popular Prakashan, 1965), pp. 196–8.

[6] J. C. Kumarappa, 'The Task before Us'.

[7] M. K. Gandhi, 'Its Meaning', 4 January 1935, *CWMG*.

[8] Unpublished note on Bharatan Kumarappa written by M. Vinaik.

[9] Letter to Vallabhbhai Patel, 17 June 1935, *CWMG*. It appears to be the case that the eldest brother, J. M. Kumarappa, might have followed them into public service but for the fact that he had a family to support.

mild-mannered. He endeared himself to Gandhi and was quickly assimilated into the community at Maganvadi.[10] With the few workers and limited means at its disposal, the new association set about the task of mapping the terrain of village industries.

The AIVIA's difficulties were compounded by the lack of village workers who could serve as exemplars and propagate village industries. The association began addressing this gap by organizing a school for village workers at Maganvadi, the Gram Sevak Vidyalaya. From 1936 to 1950, except for a period of three years during the Quit India movement when it was shut down, the Vidyalaya ran fifteen sessions in which about 600 students were trained to be technically competent, full-time village workers who could spread the message of the village movement all over the country.[11] The daily work-and-study regimen laid out for the students was highly demanding and was designed to teach them lessons in self-reliance and the value and dignity of manual labour.[12] This long period of sustained work at the Vidyalaya did not come easily but had to be wrested from the near-defeat of the enterprise in its early days. The teething problems arose as the AIVIA was itself struggling to assemble knowledge on village industries and doubts arose as to the viability of the venture.[13] Given the scant attention paid to the problems of village India in the educational system, the Gram Sevak Vidyalaya was a pioneering exercise that originated in the same period as Gandhi's radical and ambitious educational idea of *Nai Talim* or New Education.

[10] Given their learning, in that very year of 1935, the brothers wrote essays on topical subjects that were published on the occasion of the Golden Jubilee of the Congress. While Kumarappa wrote a volume titled *Public Debt of India*, Bharatan wrote *Village Industries and Reconstruction*. Over the years, the scholarly Bharatan emerged as an authentic interpreter of Gandhi's thought and was the first editor of *The Collected Works of Mahatma Gandhi*.

[11] Vinaik, *Gandhian Crusader*, pp. 89–90. The workers were taught a variety of technical skills as well as basic book-keeping, village economics, and the history of the Congress and of the AISA and AIVIA. See 'The School for Village Workers', *Harijan*, 7 December 1935.

[12] Rising at 4 a.m., the students and staff followed a packed schedule that allowed for periods of rest. In an era before electric lighting became available, the communal dinner was served before sunset and was followed by a postprandial walk and a community prayer at 7:30 p.m.

[13] Minutes of the Meeting of the Board of the AIVIA, 24 December 1936, NMML microfilm.

The AIVIA's remit was not confined to experimentation and training alone. Gandhi also demanded that it play a role in addressing important normative questions that concerned the welfare of the individual worker. Although the AISA had helped propagate the creed of khadi, Gandhi was unhappy that it had ended up placing a premium on low prices, which translated to low wages for the artisan. This was one of the proximate causes for the founding of the AIVIA. In 1935, Gandhi was determined to correct this anomaly, and rejected the view of his colleagues that it was infeasible to increase wages without destroying the khadi movement. He tasked the AIVIA with defining a minimum wage. In Gandhi's reckoning, without a minimum wage rate, 'there is every danger of the village artisan suffering, though it is for his sake that the AIVIA has been brought into being'.[14] If the AIVIA was to avoid ending up as an exploiter, it should not attempt to 'produce village articles as cheap as possible' but should 'provide the workless villagers with work at a living wage'. In effect, Gandhi was demanding that the consumer 'do justice to the toiling millions' instead of taking advantage of their helplessness by paying a wage that barely keeps the worker alive. After a careful consideration of nationwide conditions, brought to light through a questionnaire, the AIVIA determined that if the promotion of the welfare of the worker was to be made the central concern, 'it stands to reason that any industry that does not maintain the worker in fit physical condition is not worth the effort'.[15] At the very minimum, any industry that the AIVIA encouraged should enable the worker to earn enough for 'a well-balanced diet' based on 'eight hours of efficient work for a standard quality and quantity of produce', and prices of products were to be fixed accordingly.[16] This wage policy had two significant attributes. Its benchmark was based on a clear understanding of rights and duties of all parties involved. Thus, while the employers had to provide adequate compensation for labour, the workers were also enjoined to provide an adequate amount of productive work in return. It is also of interest to note that the AIVIA's definition of a standardized wage was 'the same for either sex for equal quantity of work' which, for its times, was a major normative advance towards gender equality.[17] Kumarappa was to reprise this position in 1950 when he countered the view that 'agriculture does

---

[14] M. K. Gandhi, 'Need for a Standard Wage', *Harijan*, 13 July 1935.

[15] *AIVIA Annual Report*, 1936, p. 1. We are grateful to Shri Kanakmal Gandhi for providing us some of these reports.

[16] *AIVIA Annual Report*, 1936, p. 2.

[17] M. K. Gandhi, 'Need for a Standard Wage', *Harijan*, 13 July 1935.

not pay'. He argued for the minimum wages to be fixed on the basis of the needs of the agricultural labourer rather than using norms defined for the industrial worker.[18]

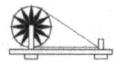

Given its mandate and the philosophical underpinnings defined by Gandhi, the AIVIA's pedagogy was immensely practical and took account of the real needs of village India. The Vidyalaya's courses were taught in Hindi and intended to both train workers in village industries as well as enable them to make a living through one of them. If the workers were to be able to convince their neighbours of the value and viability of village industries, it was essential that they demonstrate it through the medium of their own lives. Thus, it was found that it was 'important to let each worker specialize in one industry and base his further study and experience on that industry'.[19] Underpinning the entire exercise was the self-identification of the constructive workers with the fate of rural India. While this can be inferred through the institutional literature of the AIVIA such as its annual reports and other publications, a more intimate understanding can be had by considering the way of living adopted at Maganvadi. When Gandhi and Kumarappa moved into the bungalow of Jamnalal Bajaj, the entire property was well appointed with amenities that included such luxuries of the time as electric power, running water, and even a 'beautifully decorated wall panel by Jamini Roy'.[20] Gandhi and Kumarappa concurred that 'a mansion for the comfort of rich men' could hardly house the 'headquarters for serving the *Daridranarayana* in this land' and 'they voluntarily shed some of the facilities that were not generally available in the villages'. An electric pumpset was removed and running water was dispensed with.[21] Instead, the irrigation of the Maganvadi orchards and fields was carried out by means of a Persian wheel.[22] As the AIVIA added more industrial units it also needed to provide housing for the staff who arrived at Maganvadi. In the course of the construction of accommodation for the new arrivals,

---

[18] J. C. Kumarappa, 'Minimum Wages and Democracy', *GUP*, August 1950.

[19] *AIVIA Annual Report*, 1936, p. 1.

[20] Vinaik, *Gandhian Crusader*, p. 67.

[21] Vinaik, *Gandhian Crusader*, pp. 67–8.

[22] Minutes of the Meeting of the Board of the AIVIA, 7 November 1935, NMML microfilm.

a fire destroyed an old hut on the premises. Ever alert to proving a point, Kumarappa had the poles and tiles of the hut salvaged and they went into erecting a small hut for him. Despite Jamnalal Bajaj's pleading for a more spacious construction, Kumarappa's hut, his home for almost two decades, only measured 12 feet by 14 feet in size and cost a sum of Rs 150.[23] The size of Kumarappa's hut and his willingness to yoke personal practice to precept made an impression on many a visitor to Maganvadi.

Despite its tenuous hold on success, the value of the AIVIA's work lies in the ethos of constructive work that demanded perseverance in the face of inordinate odds. This commitment is exemplified in the case of a Pieta gifted to the AIVIA.[24] In the middle of nationwide turmoil in late 1946, the Pieta was erected at Maganvadi with an accompanying inscription that read:

> Grama Sevaks who obtain their training in the various departments housed in this Udyog Bhavan are expected to be imbued with the spirit of a true Satyagrahi. They should go out to serve the villagers dedicating all they have to such service. In the pursuit of their ideal they should be prepared to lay down even their lives if need be.
>
> To symbolize this spirit of vicarious suffering and sacrifice that should be the goal of all Satyagrahis, this sculpture is erected depicting Jesus being taken down from the Cross on which he was crucified by the leaders of his day, because with his life of purity and unrelenting championship of truth, he proved an unbearable critic of the evil customs and traditions prevalent at that time. He laid down his life to fulfil his ideals.[25]

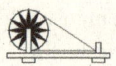

In addition to the early difficulties, a first-rate crisis was created by Kumarappa himself. In September 1936, a dispute arose between Kumarappa, who was the secretary of the AIVIA, and Srikrishnadas Jaju, on the interpretation of the latter's powers as the president. While Kumarappa felt that Jaju was interfering with his role as the secretary, Jaju felt that

[23] Vinaik, *Gandhian Crusader*, p. 68 and p. 105. The hut is till date in good repair and stands on the grounds of Maganvadi in Wardha.

[24] The Pieta was made by the sculptor Clara Quien Hopman, who had also made a bust of Gandhi; see Minutes of the Meeting of the Board of the AIVIA, 14 and 15 December 1946, NMML microfilm.

[25] Vinaik, *Quest*, p. 93.

as president of the association, his opinion prevailed in the event of a difference of opinion.[26] Kumarappa's angular nature is quite evident in this matter. With a penchant for pressing a point home, he refused to accede to Gandhi's request to reconsider his position.[27] Eventually, Jaju submitted his resignation, but the board sided with Jaju's interpretation and chose not to elect a new president.[28] Gandhi was hurt with the turn of events as Jaju was a veteran khadi worker. However, Kumarappa was aggrieved at the board's refusal to accept his interpretation of the dispute, and obtained an opinion from the AIVIA's legal adviser, Mangaldas Pakvasa. Pakvasa agreed with Kumarappa's interpretation of the AIVIA 'constitution in respect of the powers and authority of the President which was contrary to the opinion expressed by the majority of the Board'.[29] Although Gandhi did not accept the legal opinion offered by Pakvasa, he told Kumarappa that the 'opinion is a feather in your cap' and wanted it circulated amongst the board members.[30] That Kumarappa scored a technical point but lost the larger battle was soon made clear. On being presented the legal opinion, the board felt that since it still favoured Jaju's view, it was 'necessary to amend the Constitution so as to make it accord with the said opinion of the Board'.[31]

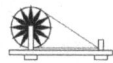

Kumarappa's obduracy and inability to accommodate the views of others would have a telling effect on his relationships with those who were not as charitable as Gandhi. While his stubbornness vexed Gandhi on occasion, a greater cause for concern was Kumarappa's health. The Bihar earthquake had interrupted Kumarappa's period of recuperation from illness due to the stint at Nasik Jail, and by August of 1935 he was unwell again with a low

[26] Minutes of the Meeting of the Board of the AIVIA, 24 March 1937, NMML microfilm.

[27] Letter to J. C. Kumarappa, 26 September 1936, *CWMG*.

[28] Minutes of the Meeting of the Board of the AIVIA, 24 March 1937, NMML microfilm.

[29] Minutes of the Meeting of the Board of the AIVIA, 16 September 1937, NMML microfilm.

[30] Letter to J. C. Kumarappa, 13 August 1937, *CWMG*.

[31] Minutes of the Meeting of the Board of the AIVIA, 16 September 1937, NMML microfilm.

but stubborn fever. The persistent illness was worrisome and Gandhi had Kumarappa examined by the local Civil Surgeon who recommended that the patient repair to a hill station.[32] While Gandhi could not provide for a holiday in the hills, he knew Amrit Kaur who could do so.[33] On a visit to Wardha in March 1935, Amrit Kaur met Kumarappa and they soon became close friends. This relationship was most certainly cemented by a shared background of a Westernized upbringing in a Christian household, eventual rejection of ties with the Raj, and commitment to the nationalist cause. Amrit Kaur had inherited a mansion in Simla and invited Kumarappa to spend time in the hills. Between September 1935 and February 1936, Kumarappa stayed at Amrit Kaur's Simla mansion, Manorville. While we do not have his own written account of his time in Simla, a large number of photographs taken by Kumarappa suggest that he quite enjoyed his stay. If the bracing climate and warm hospitality were a welcome break from life in Wardha, Kumarappa also had some friends for company.[34]

Gandhi had many considered views on health and believed that 'disease was caused by man's deviation from Nature's ways', and that the solution lay in bringing 'back our life in alignment with the requirements of Nature'.[35] Thus, when Kumarappa fell ill prior to a meeting, Gandhi joked that all 'illness should be regarded as misconduct punishable under the I.P.C.'[36] In faux despair, alluding to Kumarappa's rotundity, Gandhi claimed that he would reconcile himself to the absence of Kumarappa's 'bulky contribution to the debate'. However, a few years later, in 1940, the problem was grimmer and Kumarappa suffered a stroke that 'turned paralytic for a few hours'.[37] Alarmed at the situation, Gandhi scolded Kumarappa for such 'gross misbehaviour' and asked him to come to Sevagram for personal observation.[38] Further, out of his own long experience, Gandhi opined that

[32] Letter to Amrit Kaur, 23 August 1935, *CWMG*.

[33] Born into the royal family of Kapurthala to a father who had converted to Christianity, Amrit Kaur (1889–1964) had been educated in England. Drawn into the freedom struggle in the 1930s, she worked as Gandhi's personal secretary on occasion. Later, Amrit Kaur became independent India's first health minister.

[34] These included Gandhi's youngest son, Devadas, who was also recuperating from illness; Kasturba Gandhi; and one of Gandhi's secretaries, Pyarelal.

[35] J. C. Kumarappa, 'Lessons from His Life', in *Incidents*, p. 141.

[36] Letter to J. C. Kumarappa, 8 August 1937, *CWMG*.

[37] J. C. Kumarappa, 'My "Retirement"', *GUP*, July 1953.

[38] Letter to J. C. Kumarappa, 8 April 1940, *CWMG*.

the 'brain needs more rest than the body', which he felt was at the root of Kumarappa's problems. Soon, Gandhi the indefatigable experimenter was presented with an opportunity to test his hypothesis.

Following the detection of his blood pressure problem, Kumarappa was dispatched to Bombay and 'was at the mercy of specialists for three or four days', who, after a lengthy investigation, found 'nothing wrong organically'.[39] In July 1940, when the Englishwoman Emily Kinnaird visited Sevagram to persuade Gandhi to convert to Christianity, Gandhi hit upon a controlled test. He instructed his physician, Sushila Nayar, to take down Kumarappa's blood pressure before and after a fifteen-minute discussion with Kinnaird. This procedure was adopted for two other tasks for the patient, sawing a plank along a straight line and running a furlong. Running had the least effect on Kumarappa whereas his blood pressure shot up after his discussions with the visitor! From this Gandhi concluded that Kumarappa's problem was not due to physical fatigue but an overworked mind. Notwithstanding Gandhi's assessment, soon Kumarappa fell seriously ill with hepatitis and laboured under the burden of poor health for the rest of his life.

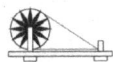

By 1937, the third year of the AIVIA's existence, the 'pioneering phase of fixing its policy and programme' was over.[40] However, given the mandate of propagating village industries and co-ordinating its efforts, the AIVIA sorely lacked a journal of its own and consequently space in the weekly *Harijan* was being used instead. Some readers had taken 'exception to the way in which the columns of Harijan [were] being occupied with the development of the village industries scheme' and Gandhi had to counter their criticism by insisting on an inalienable link between the welfare of the lowest castes and the fate of village industries.[41] However, it was decided to issue a monthly bulletin called the *Gram Udyog Patrika (GUP)* to be supplied to members and subscribers.[42] From July of 1937, the AIVIA began issuing the *Patrika* in English and Hindi on hand-made paper manufactured

---

[39] J. C. Kumarappa, 'Lessons from His Life'.

[40] *AIVIA Annual Report*, 1937, p. 1.

[41] 'Expansion of "Harijan"', *Harijan*, 21 December 1934.

[42] Resolution No. 8 of the Minutes of the Meeting of the Board of the AIVIA, 20 April 1937, NMML microfilm.

at Maganvadi.[43] Except for a period of political turmoil around the time of the Quit India movement when many AIVIA workers were imprisoned, the *Patrika* appeared with unfailing regularity till the end of 1956 when it ceased publication due to Kumarappa's ill health. Over two decades, the *Patrika* served as the journal of record for the village movement and is a gold mine of sociological, political, and technical knowledge on India's villages and their industries. A substantial part of the journal was devoted to a precise description of the experimental research on village industries that was carried out at Maganvadi and elsewhere. Its pages also faithfully chronicled the varying fortunes of the village industries in the crucial decades centred around Independence, and presented Kumarappa's understanding of the economic and political situation of the day. In understanding the fate of India's rural economy, the *Patrika* is an indispensable resource.

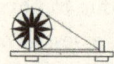

If the constructive programme was viewed with disfavour by the majority of nationalists, Gandhi set the cat amongst the pigeons with the radical proposal for the reform of education, Nai Talim. By designing a pedagogy that taught children through craft, Gandhi was demanding that Indian education make a clean break from the colonial models that enslaved minds by alienating them from their own culture while providing no practical skills. More importantly, by insisting on education through working on a craft, he wished to break down caste-based social barriers by neutralizing the upper-caste disdain for physical labour. In 1937, a committee headed by the eminent educationist Zakir Hussain—with Kumarappa as a member—undertook the task of designing an appropriate syllabus that was christened the Wardha Scheme of Education. While Kumarappa was most likely on the committee as a representative of the AIVIA, his presence was not merely by dint of his affiliation. A significant body of the literature on Gandhi's educational philosophy points to its similarities with that of the American philosopher John Dewey.[44] However, if knowledge

---

[43] We are grateful to Atmaram Saraogi and Krishen Laetsch for their invaluable help in procuring copies of some of the early issues. Unfortunately, the first two issues of July and August 1937 and the issues of October–December 1938 are untraceable till date.

[44] See, for instance, the entry on Gandhi written by the eminent educationist Krishna Kumar in *Thinkers on Education* (UNESCO Publishing, 1997). Available at

of educational philosophy was the sole consideration, Bharatan would have been a more suitable representative of the AIVIA, given that he had written a dissertation on Dewey's philosophy while at Edinburgh. But, for Gandhi, Kumarappa was eminently suited for the task, given his sound grasp of the philosophy of constructive work. Kumarappa's early recognition of the need for trained workers with an understanding of the philosophy of the AIVIA and an ability to make a living out of their skills is well reflected in the Wardha Scheme. While the education of the child was the central agenda, an equally strong emphasis was laid on the 'proper training of teachers [which] is perhaps the most important condition for the success of this scheme'.[45] In the following months, Kumarappa spent time explaining and defending the scheme in his public lectures. The extended public debate on the proposals of the scheme was an enriching experience for Kumarappa, and led to him to formulate his 'philosophy of work' that we have seen earlier.

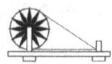

Despite his poor health Kumarappa spent a lot of time travelling around the country, canvassing on behalf of the village economy. Such propaganda inevitably ran foul of those with very different ideas on economics and development. By the early 1930s, Indian nationalism had reached a state of maturity. The struggle within the Congress was as much for political primacy as for the right to give shape to the future of India's polity and economy. While the two prominent modes of economic organization—capitalism and communism—were opposed to each other, both could hardly countenance the propounding of an alternative economic theory that centred itself on the needs of rural India. Although the criticism of Kumarappa arose from varied quarters, there were a few underlying themes that help us understand how the village movement ideas were perceived, and often misrepresented. Understanding the nature of such criticism also identifies the obstacles that the likes of Kumarappa encountered on a daily basis while advocating their cause.

---

http://www.ibe.unesco.org/en/services/publications/thinkers-on-education.html, accessed on 2 June 2009.

[45] *Basic National Education: Report of the Zakir Hussain Committee* (Wardha: Hindustani Talimi Sangh, 1938), p. 30.

The criticism of the AIVIA emerged as soon as it was founded. An editorial in the *Indian Express* dubbed Kumarappa's approach as 'economic anarchism' and accused him of presenting a seductive theory that provided a 'clever escape' to Indian feelings of inferiority.[46] The editorial argued against economic decentralization which, in its view, meant a turn towards the primitive. In response to such critics, Kumarappa accepted that there were certain economic functions that were naturally centralized, but he was worried that the unthinking introduction of powered machinery and centralized industries would result in the 'enforced idleness and starvation of millions'.[47] Decentralization was essential if one were to protect 'human beings from the indignity of being mere machine tools'. Interestingly enough, while rejecting Kumarappa's arguments, the counter-response of the *Express* argued that it would have been understandable if Kumarappa had excluded machinery altogether. His mixed line of reasoning about decentralization coupled with some naturally centralized industries was far more troublesome. In other words, the only acceptable position in the debate was that of the whole-hoggers, not of those like Kumarappa who advocated a mixed approach. This interpretation of Kumarappa's line of argument would remain a constant refrain. Instead of engaging with his plea to consider the larger social implications of technological choices, the choice of using machinery and industrial methods was reduced to a binary exercise. The Gandhian position on economic decentralization was consistently bedevilled by such a Manichaean interpretation by its critics.

Indeed, Gandhi himself was assailed by much criticism on account of his purported views on machinery and their role in social and economic regeneration. Thus, writing in 1938, the scientist Meghnad Saha revisited the question posed by Charlie Chaplin to the Mahatma in 1931. Chaplin, according to Saha, had asked if Gandhi would oppose industrialization even if one 'had a Government which organized industrial workers on modern lines' and provided people with 'all the amenities of modern life'.[48] Saha felt that Gandhi had failed to 'give any satisfactory answer' to this question and went on to propose his own 'philosophy of industrialization'. He argued that with better technology, 30 per cent of the people could produce adequate food for all, which left one with the question of what to

[46] 'Economic Anarchism', *Indian Express*, 17 April 1935, Press Clippings, Kumarappa Papers.

[47] J. C. Kumarappa, 'Is It Economic Anarchism?', *Harijan*, 4 May 1935.

[48] Meghnad Saha, 'The Philosophy of Industrialization', *Modern Review*, vol. 64, no. 2 (1938): 145–9.

do with the surplus labour dependent on the land. In chilling phraseology that is strikingly contemporaneous, Saha argued that the other 36 per cent rendered unemployed by modern agriculture were a problem and the 'only way to improve the villages is by drafting more villagers into cities, and by creating a larger number of cities based on industrial work'. Saha's impatience with the Gandhian approach was reproduced in newspapers and Kumarappa felt compelled to clarify that 'nobody objects to machinery as such, but the objection is to machinery which helps in the exploitation of other people's labour'.[49] Kumarappa averred that economic decentralization was not 'a return to primitive methods but an advance towards humanitarian systems of production and distribution'. With a Hegelian sense of history, Saha had argued that we could get a clear idea of the benefits that would accrue to India by comparing 'the kind of life pursued' in Western countries 'and the present system of industrial production' there and compare them with 'human life and industry in the same countries two centuries ago'.[50] But, for Kumarappa, comparative political economy held other lessons. 'Every country,' he retorted, 'that has taken to centralization of production has ultimately drifted towards Imperialism and armaments'.[51]

The village movement was perceived as a huge detriment to industrial growth and progress by some of the intelligentsia. So strong was the distaste for Kumarappa and the AIVIA in certain quarters that it elicited a fifty-page-long diatribe spread over three issues of a now-defunct monthly journal from Allahabad, *Twentieth Century*.[52] This lengthy invective was penned by P. S. Narayana Prasad, an economist who later worked at the Reserve Bank of India (RBI) and also served as the Indian executive director at the International Monetary Fund (IMF).[53]

In contemptuous terms, characteristic of the attitude of many towards village industries, Prasad argued that 'to many it is a cloak of tattered patches' whereas for others it was 'a museum exhibit of a cross-breed of economic fallacies and philosophical humanitarianism'.[54] To his mind,

---

[49] J. C. Kumarappa, 'Negation of Values: A Reply to Dr. Meghnath Saha', Press Clippings, Kumarappa Papers.

[50] Saha, 'The Philosophy of Industrialization'.

[51] J. C. Kumarappa, 'Negation of Values: A Reply to Dr. Meghnath Saha'.

[52] We are thankful to Arvind Krishna Mehrotra for obtaining this essay for us.

[53] These biographical details were provided by J. Krishnamurty in an email dated 25 March 2010.

[54] P. S. Narayana Prasad, 'The Philosophy of Village Industries: A Criticism', *Twentieth Century* (March 1938): 529.

the philosophy of village industries was based on Gandhi's ideas on economics 'inherited from the intellectual confusion of Ruskin and Carlyle' and its ingredients included the 'revolt of Ruskin against the worship of Mammon, the retreat of William Morris from the soullessness of machinery, the individual anarchism of Proudhon and Bakunin, and the religious humanitarianism of Tolstoy'.[55] It was into this pastiche, Prasad argued, that Kumarappa had poured in an 'economic potion' at the behest of the Congress, all in an attempt to conjure up 'a Swadeshi alternative to the imported ideas of Socialism'. As a mainstream economist, Prasad had no sympathies for socialism, but to him Kumarappa's philosophy was a form of anarchist thought that was worse than the ideas of the rising left. The 'insipid morality of non-violence' irritated him very much as did Kumarappa's views that suffered from 'utter neglect of allegiance to logic, not to speak of its wanton shyness of economic truth'.[56] Having concluded that Kumarappa did not understand elementary economics, Prasad explained that economics was about reconciling scarce means with alternative ends and the problem could be 'solved only through production based on division of labour'.[57] Kumarappa had argued that the central question of distribution was inseparable from that of production; Prasad clearly delinked the two and argued that since the problem 'lies in the domain of distribution', it was unwise to put constraints on productive capacities.[58]

In his essay, Prasad ignored the basic question of economic justice but alluded to his justification for doing so. In an approach that to this day remains at the heart of modern economic theory, Prasad maintained that there was a fundamental distinction between 'the *art* of political economy and the *science* of economics'.[59] Thus, while 'the maxims of normative economics may be *laid down*', they were subject to a variety of contingencies. In contrast, Prasad opined, 'the laws of economics are *not* laid down, but explored, and their immutability or universality is scarcely open to question'.[60] Thus, ethical questions were relevant to the 'art of economy ...

---

[55] Prasad, 'The Philosophy of Village Industries'; first phrase from part III, July 1938, p. 839 and the second is from part I, March 1938, pp. 529–30.

[56] Prasad, 'The Philosophy of Village Industries', part I, pp. 535–6.

[57] Prasad, 'The Philosophy of Village Industries', part II, June 1938, p. 710.

[58] Prasad, 'The Philosophy of Village Industries', part II, p. 715.

[59] Prasad, 'The Philosophy of Village Industries', part III, p. 839; emphasis in the original.

[60] Prasad, 'The Philosophy of Village Industries', part III, pp. 840–1; emphasis in the original.

but the body of economic science stands on a plane of neutrality to ethics'. Therefore, any attempt to 'superimpose ethical judgments on the findings of positive economics is an essay in irrelevance'.

Thus, on the one hand, Kumarappa was criticized for failing to recognize the lessons of economics which was akin to a natural science. On the other hand, faced with the challenge of the moral and ethical problems of their time, economists like Prasad took refuge behind the immutable laws of economic theory. According to such an argument, economics admitted of no ethical questions and was best left in the hands of economists. Given the vehemence of Prasad's attack, Kumarappa responded in the *Harijan* in a two-part essay.[61] Kumarappa felt that Prasad's essay was 'nothing new but ... a rehashing of the usual arguments of scholars soaked in traditional Western economic theories'.[62] The village movement was inspired by 'a desire for non-violence and truth in the economic sphere' and one would 'search in vain' to look for its affirmation in 'Western textbooks'. While Kumarappa's reply reiterates his arguments that we have seen earlier, it is the nature of his response that provides a key insight into his character and temperament. For a man known to be acerbic in his criticism, Kumarappa's response to a personal attack in this instance was utterly devoid of rancour or sarcasm.

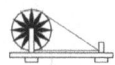

Apart from technocratic modernists like Saha and Prasad, Kumarappa was also targeted by the political left.[63] The man who led this attack was one of Gandhi's most trenchant socialist critics of the time, Jayaprakash Narayan, popularly referred to as JP. Both JP and Kumarappa had spent time in Nasik Jail and subsequently had worked on the relief efforts after the Bihar earthquake. By the 1950s, JP went on to be identified with the Gandhian movement. In 1935, however, as an avowed Marxist he had no patience with Kumarappa's ideas on decentralization. Kumarappa was interviewed by the Patna bi-weekly *Searchlight* which provoked a sharp critique by JP and a

[61] J. C. Kumarappa, 'Violence in Economic Activity', parts I and II in *Harijan* 23 July 1938 and 6 August 1938 respectively.

[62] J. C. Kumarappa, 'Violence in Economic Activity', part I.

[63] The contemporary eclipse of leftist thought in India should not obscure the fact that in the 1930s and 1940s, socialist thought had a significant number of votaries within the nationalist movement.

counter-response by Kumarappa.[64] Although it was brief, the Kumarappa–JP debate is valuable, for it is a searching examination of a central theme in modern Indian history—the relative merits of the Gandhian and socialist modes of political and economic thought. In fact, while the Gandhi–Nehru debate on economic development has served as a trope, the key issues at stake are far better clarified in the argument between Kumarappa and JP.

The *Searchlight* interviewer touched upon the same issues that were raised by the *Indian Express* editorial mentioned earlier. In a wide-ranging response, Kumarappa clarified that he did not 'hold out the ascetic ideals' or a primitive way of living as an objective.[65] As before, Kumarappa reasoned that there were many economic functions that were to be carried out 'efficiently only by centralized methods' but the bulk of economic activity could be carried out in a decentralized manner. Once more it was the familiar and vexed debate on the nature of decentralization and the relationship between production and distribution.

More than Kumarappa's argument, it was his criticism of Soviet Russia that upset JP.[66] JP's socialist response echoed that of Saha and Prasad. JP argued that while Gandhi's aims were modest, Kumarappa was 'more royalist than the king' and, by implication, not to be taken as faithful to the Mahatma's views. The bulk of JP's criticism centred on what he saw as fatal flaws in Kumarappa's theory of decentralization as well as the latter's understanding of the state of affairs in Russia. While Kumarappa had argued that decentralization was the only way to ensure that each man got just rewards for his labour, JP countered this view with the socialist vision of 'a thousand persons [who] *worked together*, not for a third party but *for themselves*, and *consumed together* all that they produced'.[67] This was far superior to Kumarappa's modest proposition since it retained the economies and efficiencies of scale. The key question here was that of exploitation of labour and the simplistic socialist answer assumed that the workers could easily be organized into one harmonious whole without a whiff of injustice or coercion.

<hr/>

[64] *Searchlight* was a bi-weekly founded in 1918 by Rajendra Prasad and other Patna-based leaders. The journal was eventually shut down by the British in 1942. See Rajendra Prasad, *Autobiography* (Bombay: Asia Publishing House, 1957), p. 131. *Searchlight* was later revived as a daily.

[65] Interview with J. C. Kumarappa, *Searchlight*, Patna, 3 April 1935, in *Jayaprakash Narayan: Essential Writings*, p. 291.

[66] J. P. Narayan, *Socialism versus the AIVIA*, p. 140.

[67] J. P. Narayan, *Socialism versus the AIVIA*; emphasis in the original.

In his critique of Kumarappa, JP effected a shift in the discourse, perhaps without realizing it. Having dismissed the merits of a decentralized economy, JP posed the question of how Kumarappa proposed to end the exploitation of industrial workers and the peasantry. This made sense as such workers and peasants formed the most important classes in Marxist theory and, in 1935, JP was as doctrinaire a leftist as any. Undoubtedly, Kumarappa did not have an answer as to how the exploitation of industrial workers or organized labour could be ended. But he had not set out to address such a question. Kumarappa's concern was the vast multitude of unorganized rural labour who were starved of meaningful employment of any sort.[68] While economists like Prasad felt it was heresy to mix up the question of equitable distribution with that of economic production, for socialists there was a simple answer. They argued that exploitation could be ended 'by abolishing private ownership and establishing ... the ownership of the community' which would be exercised by the state.

In his interview, Kumarappa also presented a prescient analysis of the state of affairs in Soviet Russia. In an era when Bolshevism was seen as holding great promise to colonial subjects, Kumarappa presented a contrarian view. The socialist answer to the problem of capitalist monopoly was state ownership of the means of production. Kumarappa argued that this was a case of 'being content with a remedy without curing the ailment' as the socialist state was similar to a capitalistic system in its reliance on a centralized industrial economy.[69] He went on to presciently predict—in 1935—that once the 'dam of idealism' broke, it would not take long to 'convert Soviet Russia of today into a Rockefeller organisation tomorrow'. Kumarappa felt that exploitation of the worker was inevitable under large-scale industrialization, whether under the capitalist or the socialist state.[70] The analogy he had used was that of the worker as a galley slave on a rowing ship. To the slave at the receiving end of the whip, it mattered little as to who owned the galley. To JP's mind, these were 'breath-taking statements' that betrayed 'a complete misunderstanding of the basis of socialism'.[71] JP claimed that the 'worker in Russia is anything but a galley

[68] This important distinction between the Gandhian agenda and socialist objectives got attenuated in the shrillness of the debate of the 1930s and remains so till date.

[69] Interview with J. C. Kumarappa, *Searchlight*, Patna, 3 April 1935.

[70] Or as a witticism attributed to the American economist J. K. Galbraith has it: 'Under capitalism, man exploits man. Under communism, it's just the opposite.'

[71] J. P. Narayan, *Socialism versus the AIVIA*.

slave' but a 'member of the ruling order'. In JP's view, the problem was not one of decentralization but of *private* versus *social ownership of the means of production*. Unaware of the terrible violence inflicted on the Russian people under Stalin, JP argued that it was only socialism that could solve the problem of distribution and usher in 'the Age of Plenty, the eternal dream of mankind'. While the socialists differed from the liberal view on the ownership question, they were both equally sanguine regarding the emancipatory power of science and technology. Thus, JP denounced Kumarappa's views on decentralization 'as a reactionary step' that 'turns back the productive forces of society'.

As in the case of Prasad, Kumarappa provided a measured response devoid of personal animosity. Describing JP's criticism as a 'well-reasoned and thought out statement', Kumarappa provided a comprehensive rebuttal.[72] Given the economic malady of the world, any move to bring alignment between economic production and 'the genius of man' was neither 'retrogression nor stagnation'. It was to guard against the use of centralization as 'an enormous instrument of exploitation' that Kumarappa desired to decentralize 'commodity production which satisfied primary needs'. Kumarappa's response also demonstrated a clear understanding of human nature itself. While he advocated decentralized production to help preserve the economic freedom of the masses, he also recognized the limitations of the 'individual view-point [which] is invariably self-centered and short-sighted'. Therefore, when the overall well-being of society required it, Kumarappa was not averse to 'a long-time view of affairs' where the need was to 'substitute individualism by collectivism'. This balancing act could be mediated through the state or co-operative organizations and local bodies of governance like the *panchayats*. Strikingly, it is this early view that Kumarappa develops further more than a decade later during his work as chairman of the Congress Agrarian Reforms Committee.

If Kumarappa acknowledged that centralized industries and organizations had a role to play in society, he was ever keen on limiting their scope. He refused to accept JP's simplistic claim of thousands of people voluntarily coming to work together. This, Kumarappa argued, was impossible without 'social coercion on a large scale' whereby violence is inevitable. Whatever be the original intent, 'the tendency of centralised

[72] 'Mr Kumarappa on Village Movement: To Make Exploitation Impossible', *Searchlight*, 26 June 1935, Press Clippings, Kumarappa Papers.

and controlled production is to vest the power in a few hands' which leads to 'concentration of power and withdrawal of liberty'. This was already the case as, by 1935, the Russian Revolution had 'resolved itself in practice into a dictatorship of a handful of men'. Much concerned with individual autonomy, Kumarappa argued that it was essential to 'stimulate the individual growth and personality of the citizen' and allow every worker 'the full benefit of his labour and develop on his own lines' of creativity. While the modern approach to economic production through centralization and division of labour led to increased productivity and perhaps 'more of material comfort', one lost out on 'individual initiative', and mechanical work was 'little different from slavery'. In the ultimate analysis, despite the allures of increased economic productivity and growth, the situation where a worker lost his own creativity and freedom was 'a greater loss to humanity'.

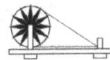

If Gandhi had resigned from the Congress in 1934 and formed the AIVIA to advocate his economic ideas, soon enough the modernists would find an opportunity to advocate their own vision for the economy of India. In 1937 the Congress had contested the elections to the provincial legislative assemblies and eventually accepted office in seven provinces, thereby inaugurating a new era in its own political evolution. The grudging espousal of khadi and village industries by the Congress was the price it was willing to pay for the Mahatma's indispensable leadership, as also for his popular appeal among the masses. With the first taste of power in the provincial governments, the underlying contradiction would be defined in full relief.

In October 1938, a conference of the industries ministers of various Congress-ruled provinces appointed a National Planning Committee (NPC). The prime advocate of planning in India, Jawaharlal Nehru, was made its chairman. Although it has now fallen into disrepute, the idea of planning to co-ordinate the myriad components of economic life had many adherents, since its impressive, albeit notorious, career in the Soviet Union of the 1920s. For its advocates, planning could only mean *large-scale industrial* planning, and the resolution behind the formation of the NPC argued that 'the problems of poverty and unemployment ... and of the economic regeneration in general cannot be solved without industrialisation', and called for a comprehensive scheme to develop key heavy industries.[73] The Congress was looking forward to taking charge of the country and a worried big business joined the NPC, as it would be easier to 'look after its interests better from inside the committee than from outside'.[74]

The formation of the NPC and the presence of Indian capitalists within it gave rise to public apprehension that the Congress would jettison its oft-stated commitment to khadi and village industries. The criticism was serious enough for Congress President Subhas Bose to argue 'that there was no inherent conflict between cottage industries and large-scale industries', a view shared by Nehru.[75] In an attempt to defuse criticism, Bose suggested that a representative of the AIVIA be co-opted into the NPC. Despite his dislike for the AIVIA's worldview, Nehru also recognized the need to carry public opinion and as chairman extended an invitation to Kumarappa to become a member of the NPC. An NPC that included 'practical industrialists, academic economists, laboratory scientists, men of the world, and business magnates' made Kumarappa sceptical of its value, and he declined the invitation.[76] Nehru now urgently wired Gandhi to use his influence and send Kumarappa to Bombay for the inaugural meetings that had commenced.

Gandhi himself had little faith in the NPC. However, when Kumarappa argued that his 'time would be ill-spent in merely trying to fence with the other interests' on the committee, Gandhi admonished him. Gandhi felt that this was not the approach of a true satyagrahi and declared that it was Kumarappa's duty to join the NPC and work with an open mind. Kumarappa remained unconvinced of Gandhi's argument since he felt that 'though we may be innocent as doves, we have also got to be wise as serpents, and we should not attempt the impossible'. Nevertheless, he acceded to Gandhi's demand and departed for Bombay to join the deliberations. By getting the Mahatma to intervene, Nehru did manage to defuse the crisis of perception that the NPC faced. However, Kumarappa was hardly the person to provide mere window dressing. At his first meeting he raised a fundamental point of order, that is, whether the NPC

[73] *Report of the National Planning Committee* (Bombay: Vora and Co., 1949), p. 5.
[74] Jawaharlal Nehru, *Discovery of India* (Calcutta: The Signet Press, 1946), p. 474.
[75] Meeting Minutes of the National Planning Committee, 17 December 1938, part 2, file no. 135, part-1, Jawaharlal Nehru Papers, NMML.
[76] J. C. Kumarappa, 'Lessons from His Life' in *Incidents*, pp. 138–9.

was going to comply with the resolutions of the Congress. Prior to his retirement in 1934, in the process of providing a new definition of swadeshi, Gandhi had the CWC pass a resolution to clear the air and define the scope of activities of the Congress. That resolution had asserted that 'large and organised industries which can or do command State aid are in no need of the services of Congress organization or any Congress effort in their behalf'.[77]

Compliance with the Congress resolutions was farthest from the minds of the NPC members, most of whom were intellectually committed to large-scale industries as the main vehicle of economic growth. Kumarappa's poser forced Nehru to prepare a lengthy note on the matter wherein he asserted that while 'the Congress would disapprove of any policy which came in the way of its development of cottage industries ... [there was] nothing in the Congress resolutions against the starting or encouragement of large scale industries, *provided* this does not conflict with the natural development of village industries'.[78] By now this was a familiar refrain and such bald assertions merely sidestepped the question of whether conflict could ever be avoided. Although he never quite explained himself, it is safe to conjecture that by *natural development*, Nehru probably meant benign neglect of village industries that in his view had no place in a modern social order. The key issue, however, was the interpretation of the 1934 CWC resolution. While Kumarappa felt that it prohibited the NPC from promoting large-scale industrialization, Nehru held the opposite view. Though agreeing that in 1934 the Congress felt that it need not promote large-scale industries, Nehru argued that it did not oppose large-scale industries either. And then he tellingly asserted that since the Congress was 'to some extent identifying itself with the State it cannot ignore the question of establishing and encouraging large-scale industries'. Therefore,

---

[77] *Indian Annual Register*, July–December 1934, p. 201.

[78] Meeting Minutes of the National Planning Committee, 21 December 1938, part 2, file 135, part 1, Jawaharlal Nehru Papers, NMML; emphasis added. It is interesting to contrast this with what Nehru had to say in entirely different circumstances. On 6 January 1948, Nehru, now India's prime minister, wrote to the Mahatma arguing that 'so far as the economic and communal matters are concerned, we are bound down by the Congress policy and decisions, and both of us [that is, Nehru and Patel], as well as other Congressmen, must necessarily work in accordance with them'. See Uma Iyengar and Lalitha Zackariah (eds), *Together They Fought: Gandhi–Nehru Correspondence, 1921–1948* (New Delhi: Oxford University Press, 2011), p. 520.

he concluded, not only was it within the scope of the NPC to consider the entire question of large-scale industries 'in all its aspects, but the Committee will be failing in its duty if it did not do so. There can be no planning if such planning does not include big industries. But in making our plans we have to remember the basic Congress policy of encouraging cottage industries'. Here, the amphibious character of the Congress was evident. If to Kumarappa's mind, the NPC was to follow the path of promoting a decentralized economy laid out by Gandhi for the Congress, Nehru was already anticipating the role the Congress would play in running the apparatus of an independent Indian state. If there was ever a 'moment of manoeuvre', it was this. Indeed, during the period 1937–9, we see a subterranean shift within the nationalist movement, away from Gandhi's ideas, and towards an industrial model that would later be identified with Nehruvian socialism. However, between 1940 and 1946, India lurched from one political crisis to another. By 1946, what emerged was a Congress that had in all but name rejected Gandhi.

The conflict between the Gandhian trajectory for the economy and that adopted by the NPC was quite evident, but in public it was continually asserted that the interests of the village industries would not be sacrificed. Exactly as intended, Kumarappa's presence on the committee was presented as evidence of the seriousness of the NPC in ensuring that the village economy would not suffer.[79] During the second session of the NPC in July 1939, the difference of opinion was starkly laid out in discussions on the role of cottage industries in the overall plan. Determined to fight for his cause, Kumarappa argued that all key industries, public utilities and methods of resource exploitation demanded the use of large-scale industries. To protect the larger social interest these industries could not be left to private parties but had to be under the control of the state. Since India was under a colonial dispensation, it served no useful purpose to concentrate on large-scale industries. Rather, Kumarappa argued, the Congress should focus on 'functional planning of cottage and village industries for the time being'.[80] In any event, Kumarappa's argument that economic and social violence was inherent to large-scale industrialization and that the main problem of distribution of wealth was automatically addressed through village industries was not accepted by the NPC. Instead, speaking in airy

[79] 'National Planning: Mr Giri on Bombay Discussions', *The Hindu*, 23 December 1938, Subject File, 11, Kumarappa Papers.

[80] Meeting Minutes of the National Planning Committee, 9 June 1939, Subject File, 11, Kumarappa Papers.

generalities that undercut Gandhi's logic in favour of village industries, Nehru said:

> The Congress had very rightly always laid stress on village industries because it wanted us to think in terms of the villager. We had got into the habit of ignoring him and his needs. He was the forgotten man in India although it was he who constituted India. That emphasis was essential and in all our work we must remember him. But the emphasis did not mean a turning away from big industry. The Congress thought that big industry was powerful enough to look after itself and to go ahead. It was the villager that wanted help and protection and the Congress gave him these.

Frustrated by the Congress' habit of speaking in multiple voices, Kumarappa pressed his case for clarity in a letter to Rajendra Prasad, who had by then become the president of the Congress. In his letter, Kumarappa pointed out that on the one hand there were the Congress resolutions, and on the other hand one saw Congress office-bearers happily inaugurating large-scale factories suggesting to the public that 'the Congress also supports large-scale industries under private enterprise'.[81] Prasad's reply was an ambiguous one that once again danced around the central question of a clear position of the Congress that Kumarappa was repeatedly demanding. Unwilling to provide cover for the NPC while it made a mockery of the AIVIA's agenda, after obtaining Gandhi's consent, Kumarappa resigned from his membership of the NPC. He had to resign, Kumarappa explained, as he 'felt like a fish out of water' on the NPC and 'had to get out for the sake of my very existence'.[82] Gandhi concurred that Kumarappa was better off spending his time doing useful work 'instead of listening to grand discourses' in the NPC meetings.[83]

Notwithstanding the disclaimers in favour of village industries, the proceedings of the NPC left no one in doubt as to the nature of things to come in an independent India. Gandhi himself took a dim view of the proceedings of the NPC but held his counsel. Nehru, in the meanwhile, had developed a personal distaste for Kumarappa. When Kumarappa refused to extend his co-operation to the NPC after his resignation, Nehru was angered enough to call him a 'worthless man' in a complaint to Gandhi.[84] This

---

[81] Letter from J. C. Kumarappa to Rajendra Prasad, 19 June 1939, *Congress Bulletin*, no. 3 (1939): 43–4.

[82] J. C. Kumarappa, 'Out of One's Element', *GUP*, September 1939.

[83] Letter to J. C. Kumarappa, 10 June 1939, *CWMG*.

[84] Letter to Jawaharlal Nehru, 5 January 1940, *CWMG*.

upset Gandhi who challenged Nehru to substantiate this characterization of a valuable worker like Kumarappa. Unable to do so, Nehru withdrew his comments but the animosity remained.[85] Kumarappa's refusal to toe the modernist line on the NPC led to a renewed public debate on Gandhi's attitude towards machinery and large industries. While Nehru gracefully retracted his allegations against Kumarappa, Meghnad Saha wrote a lengthy, rambling critique of Kumarappa and Gandhi. So sanguine was Saha of his superior understanding that not only did he declare Kumarappa to be wholly devoid of 'knowledge of elementary principles of economics', Nehru and the entire Congress were deemed to be equally guilty of ignorance.[86] Saha attributed many colourful statements made against Kumarappa in the NPC discussions to Nehru.

This forced Nehru to record a strongly worded repudiation of the statements attributed by Saha to him.[87] Nehru had good reason to be incensed since, when squared with the record of the meetings, Saha's characterization of the proceedings can only be termed as fictional. For instance, consider Saha's claim that Kumarappa had repeatedly argued 'that the use of machineries presents some kind of violence' although, Saha helpfully added, 'of what brand he was not quite sure!'[88] Characterizing Kumarappa as a latter-day Don Quixote made for colourful reading but, as an examination of the archival record demonstrates, he made no such foolish argument in the NPC meetings. However, in much of the literature on the NPC, this tendentious characterization of Kumarappa has reappeared despite the fact that the evidence indicates otherwise.[89] Thus a dissertation on Indian planning does recognize that the NPC 'only made it clear to all that the Gandhian notion of village economy was finally disregarded by the Congress leadership'.[90] However, Kumarappa's arguments are vaguely said to rely on 'the Congress view on Swadeshi and large industries', with no reference to the specific CWC resolutions

[85] Letter to Jawaharlal Nehru, After 5 January 1940, *CWMG*.

[86] Letter from M. N. Saha to Krishna Kripalani, 31 August 1939, M. K. Gandhi Papers, NMML.

[87] Letter from Jawaharlal Nehru to Krishna Kripalani, 29 September 1939 in Jawaharlal Nehru and others, *A Bunch of Old Letters*, Bombay: Asia Publishing House, 1958, p. 381.

[88] Letter from M. N. Saha to Krishna Kripalani.

[89] For instance, see *Together They Fought*, p. 387.

[90] Raghabendra Chattopadhyay, 'The Idea of Planning in India, 1930–1951', (PhD dissertation, Australian National University, 1985), p. 101.

that Kumarappa had upheld.[91] Further, this opposition is attributed to the Gandhian view that 'violence was inherent in machines and large-scale industries'.[92] Such a description fails to account for the fact that notwithstanding his personal views, Kumarappa was rightly pointing out that the NPC was indulging in a sleight-of-hand by flouting the official Congress position without actually ever openly repudiating it.

All in all, Kumarappa's time on the NPC proved to be unfruitful in furthering the agenda of the AIVIA. But it did serve a useful purpose in pointing to the deep cleavage between Gandhi and the Congress on the question of economic growth and development in an independent India. The formation of the NPC clearly marked the emergence of the development modernists in Indian politics, who shed the pretence of commitment to official Congress resolutions that were shaped by Gandhi. However, instead of openly repudiating the Gandhian view, the strategy of Bose and Nehru was to deflect criticism by repeatedly claiming that their espousal of large-scale industrialization was not a contradiction of the Congress position. This strategy has paid rich dividends as reflected in much of the writing on Indian planning since. To take only one instance, a recent biography has argued that Subhas Bose was 'quite ecumenical in the composition' of the NPC and had 'also *accommodated*' a man like Kumarappa.[93]

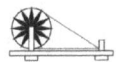

Till the time of the founding of the AIVIA, Kumarappa was chiefly known for his assessment of India's financial obligations as well as having been the editor of *Young India* during a time of national crisis. One of the few regions that offered early support for the AIVIA was Andhra which had an active Gandhian base during the Non-cooperation and Civil Disobedience years. In April 1935, Kumarappa travelled through the region lecturing on the AIVIA and its objectives. The speeches delivered by him covered the salient features of the association's agenda and were soon published as *Philosophy of*

[91] Chattopadhyay, 'The Idea of Planning in India, 1930–1951', p. 100.

[92] Chattopadhyay, 'The Idea of Planning in India, 1930–1951', p. 110.

[93] Sugata Bose, *His Majesty's Opponent: Subhas Chandra Bose and India's Struggle against Empire* (New Delhi: Allen Lane, 2011), p. 146; emphasis added.

the Village Movement.[94] Gandhi's keen espousal of village industries meant that this otherwise obscure volume was extensively reviewed in the national press. Most reviewers were agreed on the moral urgency of doing justice to India's farmers and artisans. Nevertheless, they were not very impressed by the philosophical foundation on which Kumarappa sought to build his argument for a decentralized village economy posited in opposition to both capitalism and communism. By August 1935, Kumarappa had repaired to Simla to recuperate and circumstantial evidence suggests that he might have spent his months there thinking through the ideas presented in Andhra as well as his public debate with JP. The result was edited and revised by Amrit Kaur into a more tightly argued exposition that appeared a year later as *Why the Village Movement?* Rejecting the conception of the 'Economic Man', Kumarappa 'sought to examine the chances of basing an economic order on cultural values and human needs which formed the foundation of the old Oriental Civilization'.[95]

Although it is hardly as well known as *Economy of Permanence,* as a well-argued Indian manifesto for economic decentralization *Why the Village Movement?* remains unsurpassed. If Gandhi's socialist critics thought of constructive work as a foolish and misguided effort by naive do-gooders, Kumarappa was now giving notice of a deeper normative agenda by propounding a theoretical basis for Gandhian economics as well as a programmatic translation through the AIVIA. The first edition of the book was subtitled as 'A Plea for a New Economic Order in India' but undoubtedly it was written keeping in mind the debate with JP. Apart from explaining Kumarappa's position, *Why the Village Movement?* was meant to be an ideological challenge to the ascendant creed of leftism in India. Indeed, Kumarappa's title is a clumsily worded reprise of JP's socialist screed against Gandhi, *Why Socialism?* which had just been published. When the third edition of *Why the Village Movement?* appeared in early 1939, it carried a new commendatory foreword by the Mahatma. By this time, Kumarappa had revised the subtitle as 'A Plea for a Village-Centred Economic Order in India'. The changed subtitle was not merely semantic

[94] J. C. Kumarappa, *Philosophy of the Village Movement.* In these speeches we can also see the development of Kumarappa's own rather specific interpretation of economic history.

[95] J. C. Kumarappa, 'Preface to the First Edition', *WVM.* About Amrit Kaur's work on the book, see Letter to Amrit Kaur, 14 November 1936, *CWMG.* Since we have already examined Kumarappa's economic philosophy earlier in the book, here we confine ourselves to recounting the history of this volume.

but, taken together with Gandhi's foreword, it indicated a sense of urgency. The formation of the NPC indicated that the balance of the debate on the economic future of India was heavily loaded against the Gandhian position. Indeed, Gandhi was himself responding with some urgency when he declaimed in his foreword that Kumarappa's book 'answers almost all the doubts that have been expressed about the necessity and feasibility of the movement'.[96] Gandhi must have had the NPC in mind when he added that the book was of no use to those determined to 'destroy the villages and dot India with a number of big cities with highly centralized industries'. By the end of the Second World War, Kumarappa was ready with a revised fourth edition. If in 1935 he was assailed for arguing that communism was a form of 'rationalised capitalism', he now felt vindicated by the events of the war. Of special interest was 'the alignment of Russia with the imperialistic forces of Great Britain and the United States' which proved that centralized industries were a detriment to the democratic decentralization of political power.[97]

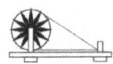

The Congress had purportedly entered office to further the Constructive Programme, but Gandhi was quite aware of the general disinterest towards his cause. Nevertheless, writing in *Harijan*, he evinced the hope that there would be a 'Minister whose sole business would be to look after khadi and village industries' and that the expertise of the AISA and the AIVIA would be utilized to prosecute such constructive work.[98] Gandhi's essay appeared around the time that the NPC was to commence its deliberations. Although many leaders were indifferent to Gandhi's proposal, there were some elements within the Congress that were sympathetic towards village industries. The Congress Government of the Central Provinces and Berar responded with alacrity. Within a week of the appearance of Gandhi's essay, it appointed an Industrial Survey Committee with Kumarappa as the chairman. Amongst its terms of reference, the committee was to visit villages to 'study their economic condition and examine the possibility of reviving cottage industries' as well as 'report on the industrial possibilities of the raw materials available' including 'forest and mineral resources'. Undoubtedly,

[96] M. K. Gandhi, 'Foreword', *WVM*, third edition, 2 February 1939.

[97] J. C. Kumarappa, 'Preface to the Fourth Edition', *WVM*, 1945.

[98] M. K. Gandhi, 'How to Popularize Khadi', 10 December 1938, *CWMG*.

the move to appoint this committee to conduct the survey (henceforth the CPB Survey) was a direct response to the formation of the NPC by Bose.[99]

As a reluctant member of the NPC, and about to embark on the CPB Survey, Kumarappa developed his position on the role of planning in a trenchant essay.[100] With his penchant for categories, he skewered many votaries of a variety of approaches to economic planning. Chief amongst them was the 'academic' type that approached the problem 'not with an open but with a blank mind'. For the sake of scientific accuracy, no amount of expenditure was spared by this type and 'eternity' was considered as 'the time limit for perfection'. As a result of such fidelity to truth, 'laborious enquiries will have to be made to be convinced that the villagers are starving'. The second category of surveyors whom he critiqued had 'propaganda' in mind and set out to gather evidence to prove preconceived theories. In a reflection of the debates of the time, for Kumarappa, illustrative of this approach was the exposition by Keynes on the exchange ratio in *Indian Currency and Finance*. The third approach he described was 'clinical', like that of a lecturing surgeon whose objective is not 'the patient but the study of the malady'. Here, the patient is only a 'convenient medium in order to focus attention'. In such an approach no fieldwork is necessary, and a 'library is the sole source of information'. Although propriety imposed some restrictions on Kumarappa, evidently he felt that different members of the NPC could be categorized according to these traits.

In contrast to such sterile methods, Kumarappa plumbed for a 'diagnostic survey' where 'the attention is not on the disease but on the patient', and all efforts are geared towards a quick remedy. The concept of a diagnostic survey originated in the work of the urban planner, Patrick Geddes, who had carried out a series of studies in India a few decades before Kumarappa. Kumarappa was certainly aware of the work of Geddes, and while in America had read the latter's *Cities in Evolution*. However, while Geddes had the Indian city in mind, Kumarappa creatively deployed the diagnostic approach towards the crisis in India's villages. In an indirect critique of the composition of the NPC, he argued against the expertise of

---

[99] J. C. Kumarappa (Chairman), *Report of the Industrial Survey Committee*, part 1, vol. 1 (Nagpur: Government of the Central Provinces and Berar, 1948), p. 1.

[100] J. C. Kumarappa, 'Economic Surveying and Planning', *Harijan*, 28 January 1939. This essay was published as a pamphlet along with some relevant Congress Working Committee resolutions as J. C. Kumarappa, *Economic Surveying and Planning* (Rajahmundry: Hindustan Publishing Co. Ltd., 1939).

academics who 'have no living touch with the people'. Instead of closeting themselves in meeting rooms, the planners 'must come into close contact with those whose condition the committee seeks to improve'. He opined that any plan prepared by the Congress had to reflect its ideals, and therefore it would need 'to co-ordinate the economic plan so as to enable the masses to strengthen their economic position'. While he was unable to get Nehru and others to change course with their planning exercise for India, the CPB Survey was conducted in accordance with Kumarappa's conception. Thus, over a mere two weeks in early 1939, multiple survey groups made up of student volunteers examined more than 600 villages covering a population of 15 lakhs.[101] In keeping with Kumarappa's philosophy, the costs were limited to under Rs 5 per village surveyed, which was a fraction of the original estimated expenditure.

The report went into much detail regarding the state of the villages surveyed and had many suggestions on specific industries based on the resources of the region. Since much of what the report said strongly reflected Kumarappa's philosophical position, we need not examine its details here.[102] In any event, by October 1939, the Congress governments had resigned, and the CPB Survey had no impact on state policy. However, as Gandhi pointed out, what stamped the survey as 'an original report' was its framing of general principles to be followed in economic planning. In particular, it presented a rare statement of the Gandhian conception of the role of the state in economic affairs, especially given the enthusiastic endorsement of Gandhi who serialized a summary of the report over six issues of *Harijan*.[103]

Much of the writing on Gandhi's understanding of the state has focused on a schematized reading of his early work, *Hind Swaraj*. Gandhi and Kumarappa had all along argued for economic decentralization, but it was by no means an unqualified position. Thus, although Kumarappa felt that the 'State should not interfere in more ways than it can help', it was not an anarchist position.[104] It was the responsibility of the state to reconcile the short-term needs of individuals with the long-term interests of society as a whole. Similarly, since social disparity is a reality of life, 'the

---

[101] *Report of the Industrial Survey Committee*, part 1, vol. 1, p. 9.

[102] There is also much in the survey that is ecologically sound and ahead of its time.

[103] The summary was titled 'An Original Report' and appeared between May and July 1939.

[104] *Report of the Industrial Survey Committee*, part 1, vol. 1, p. 1.

interests of the weak have to be protected by the State'. Given the scale of resources at its disposal, it is evident that 'the State can either create employment or unemployment by the mode of its expenditure'. This led Kumarappa to argue that while the state should exercise strict economy in its expenditures, this was not an absolute dictum. Since the colonial state spent its resources on purchasing British goods, Kumarappa argued that buying cheaper goods from abroad was not desirable if local expenditure by the state provided employment opportunities for those who paid the taxes that the state spent. Although, it called for a role for the state in the economy, the Gandhian approach differed from the socialist position. Given that taxation fell disproportionately on the poor, Kumarappa argued that the state should not capitalize its revenue since this would 'dam the current of circulation' of money within the economy. Clearly, the argument here was to use public revenues to bring more people into the economy rather than invest them into capital-intensive industries as conceived by the planned economic order being fashioned by the NPC.

Kumarappa also examined the deadening hand of bureaucracy and its impact on the village industries as well as the villagers themselves. In a tone with much contemporary resonance, the report said that 'no expert worth the name can be away from his field'.[105] Trusting the economy to desk-bound experts would be like being treated by a non-practising physician who possessed a medical degree. The living touch with the villages in the course of the survey offered some startling lessons. Most instructive were the findings of the committee that the ordinary villagers had an annual income of a mere Rs 12 per head, at a time when the national average was pegged at around Rs 65. Evidently, as Gandhi pointed out, the villages of the region were far poorer than was assumed by the 'arm-chair scientist who relies for his figures on books'.[106] Another telling fact was that of the revenues collected by the state, a mere 1.5 per cent was spent on the Department of Industries that was tasked with improving the economic productivity of the region.

The Provincial Government of the North-West Frontier Province (NWFP, now known as Khyber Pakhtunwa in Pakistan) was headed by Dr Khan Sahib, who was a member of the original board of the AIVIA. Consequently, Kumarappa was also asked to study the economic situation in NWFP and make recommendations. In early 1940, he travelled extensively through six districts of the province as well as the states of

[105] *Report of the Industrial Survey* Committee, part 1, vol. 1, p. 7.
[106] M. K. Gandhi, 'An Original Report', *Harijan*, 15 July 1939.

Dir, Swat, and Amb, and investigated the economic conditions in thirty-four villages spread across the region.[107] He organized his recommendations around the fact that the Government machinery was limited in this region compared to the rest of India. Consequently, he confined himself to recommending a working plan of 'a few industries which can be started immediately'.[108] As was the case with the CPB Survey, the NWFP report had no material impact for the Congress ministries had resigned and India was soon engulfed in a political conflagration. By the time the Interim Government took charge in 1946 much had changed and Kumarappa was once again requested to revisit his recommendations and modify them according to the new situation. In his supplementary report, he suggested an approach based on his idea of Balanced Cultivation wherein he drew up a plan for cultivation that addressed the needs of three million people, 'allowing the average citizen about 2800 calories per day and about 25 yards of cotton cloth per annum'.[109] While all of this did not have much impact, viewed from the perspective of the continuing chaos in Khyber Pakhtunwa, the idea of a survey for economic development of this region seems like a distant dream.

In his economic surveys, Kumarappa sought to strike a delicate balance between the individual and the state. The role of the state was a crucial issue in all conceptions of social ordering and Kumarappa's economic philosophy was no exception. Thus, while he disagreed with the NPC's inordinate focus on large-scale industrialization based on an urban economy, Kumarappa sought to channel the power and the resources garnered by the state to serve the needs of the rural Indian who was representative of the disadvantaged.[110] This fundamental contradiction was to persist when Kumarappa set out to examine the agrarian economy of independent India.

Despite the lukewarm attitude of the Congress, the provincial ministries were not entirely lacking in interest in the constructive programme. Some of them did solicit help from the AIVIA which, in

[107] J. C. Kumarappa, *A Plan for the Economic Development of the North-West Frontier Province* (Peshawar: n.p., 1940). The count of thirty-four villages is based on the travel map given in the report.

[108] J. C. Kumarappa, *A Plan for the Economic Development of the North-West Frontier Province*, p. 8.

[109] J. C. Kumarappa, *Supplement to the Report on the Economic Development of the North-West Frontier Province* (Peshawar: n.p., 1946), pp. 1–2.

[110] The problem of defining the precise role of the state in economic development remains an unresolved debate in economic thought.

turn, felt that the sudden expansion of its field of work left it 'with totally inadequate provision of men and materials to cope with the situation'.[111] By the end of 1938, the AIVIA's resources in Maganvadi were stretched to the limit to accommodate the additional trainees deputed by the various provincial governments.[112] But the experience of working in tandem with the government was a brief one. By October 1939, owing to the British attitude on India's role in the Second World War, all the seven Congress provincial governments had resigned. The new political developments led to 'uncertainty as to what the attitude of the Government will be to non-political constructive work' and the AIVIA was hesitant to 'launch on any new ventures'.[113] A stalemate prevailed with the government not withdrawing its co-operation but not offering it in a sustained manner either. It was under these circumstances that Kumarappa carried out his two pioneering economic surveys of the Central Provinces and Berar and the NWFP. While the cataclysmic events of the early 1940s ensured that the surveys did not have any impact in material terms, the surveys serve as exemplars of Kumarappa's economic philosophy deployed in the service of a large-scale transformation of society. Along with his pioneering study of Matar Taluka, they constitute the oeuvre of Gandhian surveying.

The wildly swinging political fortunes taught the AIVIA a valuable lesson to fend for itself as it had 'done formerly without looking to Government aid'.[114] Kumarappa remained a lone figure in drawing the appropriate lessons of self-reliance from the experience in dealing with government during the crucial period of 1937–9. The failure of the Gandhian leadership to recognize the consequences of depending on the state had a telling effect on the fate of khadi and village industries in independent India.

---

[111] *AIVIA Annual Report*, 1937, p. 1.

[112] *AIVIA Annual Report*, 1938, p. 1.

[113] *AIVIA Annual Report*, 1940, p. 1.

[114] *AIVIA Annual Report*, 1941, p. 2.

Figure 7 The Kumarappa brothers: Bharatan, J. T. Cornelius, Joseph, and J. M. Kumarappa. Probably taken in the early 1930s. *Photograph courtesy of Baryalai Shalizi.*

Figure 8 The nationalist at work, probably 1931. *Photograph courtesy of Magan Sangrahalaya Samiti, Wardha (Maharashtra).*

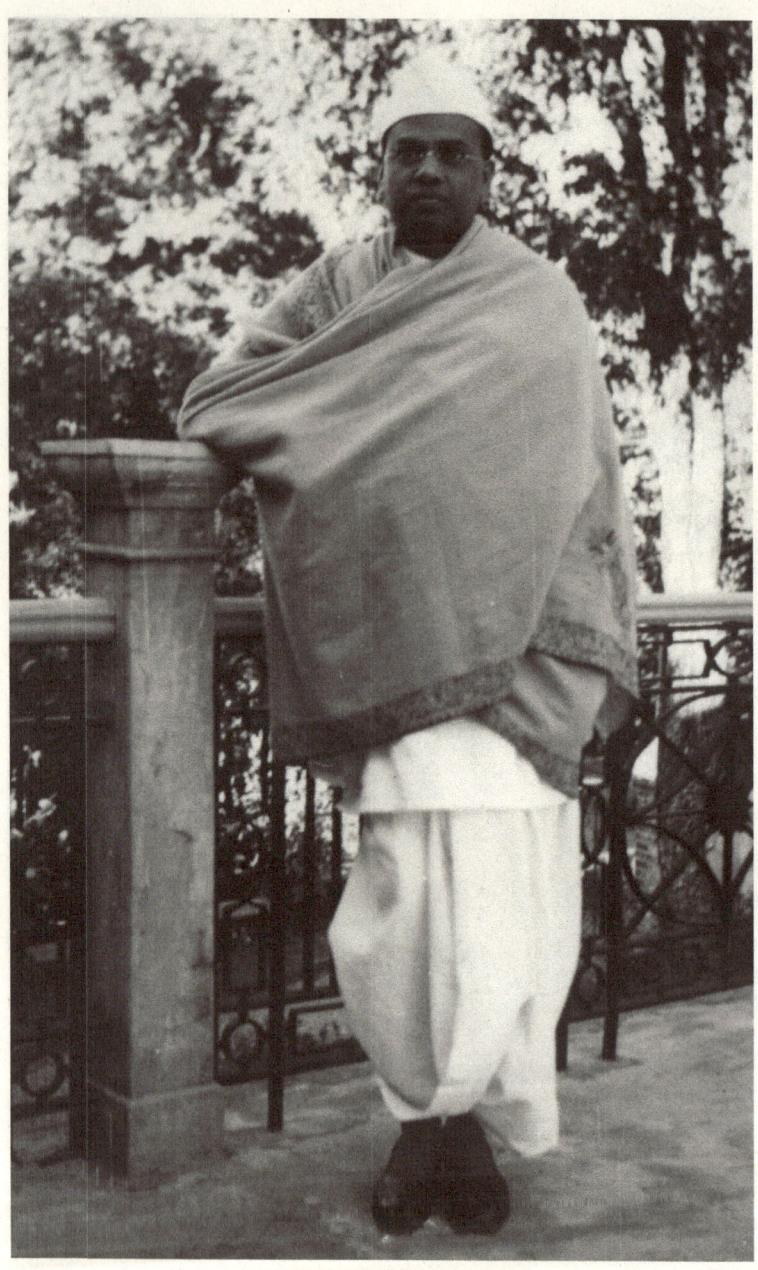

Figure 9 Kumarappa in Simla in the winter of 1935–6. *Photograph courtesy of Magan Sangrahalaya Samiti, Wardha (Maharashtra).*

Figure 10   This group portrait was very likely taken by Kumarappa in Simla. The individuals in the foreground are (left to right) Amrit Kaur, Kasturba, and Devadas Gandhi. The person in the background behind Amrit Kaur is Gandhi's secretary, Pyarelal. *Photograph courtesy of Magan Sangrahalaya Samiti, Wardha (Maharashtra).*

Figure 11   Crowd at the inauguration of the Magan Sangrahalaya in Wardha, 30 December 1938. *Photograph courtesy of Magan Sangrahalaya Samiti, Wardha (Maharashtra).*

Figure 12   Kumarappa and Gandhi at the inauguration of the Magan Sangrahalaya in Wardha, 30 December 1938. *Photograph courtesy of Magan Sangrahalaya Samiti, Wardha (Maharashtra).*

Figure 13   The Magan Sangrahalaya. *Photograph courtesy of Magan Sangrahalaya Samiti, Wardha (Maharashtra).*

Figure 14 Kumarappa lived in a small hut at Maganvadi for almost two decades. *Photograph courtesy of Magan Sangrahalaya Samiti, Wardha (Maharashtra).*

Figure 15 With two of his nieces. *Photograph courtesy of Magan Sangrahalaya Samiti, Wardha (Maharashtra).*

Figure 16 The hut has been carefully preserved to this day. *Photograph courtesy of Venu Madhav Govindu.*

10   Stone for Bread

The experiment of the provincial governments was always a tentative one and the political detente between the Raj and the Congress had an air of unreality to it. Events in faraway Europe would soon dramatically reinforce the fact that, as long as it was a colony, India's interests would always be subordinated to the needs of its colonizers. In September 1939, when Hitler invaded Poland, Britain was finally drawn into the global conflagration of the Second World War. Instinctively, without the pretence of consulting either the Executive Council or the Indian Legislative Assembly, Viceroy Linlithgow unilaterally joined India to the War. This act inaugurated a period of enormous strife and uncertainty in India that only came to an end after the assassination of the Mahatma in 1948. Of the many dynamic social and political forces unleashed during this period, three were of particular significance. While Quit India was the culmination of a series of Indian campaigns against foreign rule, the 1940s also saw the rapid consolidation and empowerment of the communal forces that led to Partition. From our vantage point, the third and most important factor operating in Indian life during this period was the economic exploitation of India during the Second World War.[1]

---

[1] Although the literature on Indian political affairs in this period is extensive, works that focus on the impact of the War are far fewer. A history of the 'high politics' of the period is available in Johannes H. Voigt, *India in the Second World War*

In the mid-eighteenth century, the economic exploitation of India by the British was symbolically inaugurated when Robert Clive had the loot from Bengal's treasures floated down the Ganga on barges. By the time of the Second World War, this exploitation had been perfected into a fine art. Wars have always had a ravenous appetite, and the British were determined to utilize the resources of India to the fullest for its larger objective of winning a global war. More than two million Indian men served as soldiers during the War years, and Britain also took advantage in commandeering India's natural resources. Enormous amounts of food, timber, and other *matériel* were taken out of India during the War. As a result of the extraordinary extraction of India's resources for the War effort, between 1940 and 1945, India was subjected to an unprecedented economic crisis. The result was widespread hardship to the poor including the death of at least three million people in the Bengal Famine of 1943.[2]

The consequences of India's subject status become clear when we contrast the agreements Britain entered into with the United States and India. If America provided a large supply of goods to Britain and the other Allies, these provisions were subjected to a Lend-Lease agreement. As a result of war production, the American economy received a fillip that finally ended the residual consequences of the Great Depression. In contrast to the agreement that the Americans set down as creditors, it was debtor Britain that laid down the terms of its financial agreement with India. Britain coveted India's resources and desperately wanted them to be deployed for its own use. However, it set about devising means to defer payment as well as leave the possibility of avoidance of payments in the future. Under normal circumstances such a financial scheme would be impossible, but as a colony India had no real say in the matter. Thus, instead of paying for the goods that it took out of India, Britain held the payments in reserve in London, with a promise to pay them in the future. Within India, however, the purchase of commodities had to be paid in real rupees. It is here

---

(New Delhi: Arnold-Heinemann, 1987). A more recent general narrative is Yasmin Khan, *The Raj at War: A People's History of India's Second World War* (New Delhi: Random House India), 2015. The most comprehensive history till date of India's War experience is Srinath Raghavan, *India's War: The Making of Modern South Asia, 1939–1945* (London: Allen Lane, 2016).

[2] Some estimates put this figure at a far higher level of five million or more.

that colonial monetary policy came to the rescue and resolved Britain's predicament. The result was the controversial affair variously known as the Sterling Credits or Sterling Balances or Sterling Securities.

The monetary origins of the Sterling Credits lay in the recommendations of a British commission on Indian currency and finance—also known as the Hilton Young Commission—in 1926 that pegged the Indian rupee to the pound at an artificially high price of 1s. 6d., with the consequences of reduced profits for Indian exports as well as increasing the value of British capital invested in India.[3] Another of the commission's recommendations resulted in the setting up of the Reserve Bank of India (RBI) in 1935. In the meanwhile, in 1931 Britain got off the gold standard and made its currency freely convertible. However, the rupee continued to be held at the artificial rate with enormous consequences for the Indian economy in the 1930s.[4] As they were no longer on the gold standard, in the framing of the Reserve Bank Act the British had left a loophole which 'conveniently provided for the forty percent backing of currency notes by bullion or Sterling Securities with the only condition that the bullion part is never below 40 crores'.[5] In other words, as long as 40 crores of bullion reserves were available, both the British pound and gold were on an equal footing. This left the RBI virtually free to print as much paper currency as it wished. Indeed, this was the mechanism adopted to 'finance' the British appetite for Indian goods during the War years. For the Indian public at large, the consequences were catastrophic.

Backed by the draconian Defence of India Act, as the War progressed so did the free export of food and other goods out of India to the Middle East and other regions where Britain was fighting the Axis forces. The purchase of these goods was done through the curious expedient outlined above. The debtor nation of Britain wrote out IOUs that it held with itself in London. Against such a vague promise of reimbursements in the future, the Government of India printed enormous amounts of rupees to pay for the purchases. The enormity of the volume of resources taken out of India can

---

[3] Till 1971, the British pound (£) was divided into 20 shillings (s.) or 240 pennies (d.).

[4] These consequences included the drain of massive amounts of gold that left Indian shores. With Britain off the gold standard, many colonies had to tie their currency to the pound sterling creating the economic bloc that came to known as the Sterling Area.

[5] J. C. Kumarappa, 'A Stone for Bread', *GUP*, December 1942. Also see B. R. Shenoy, *The Sterling Assets of the Reserve Bank of India* (New Delhi: Indian Council of World Affairs, 1946), p. 6.

be gauged by the changes reflected in the balance sheets. Although, as we have seen earlier, the Congress Select Committee on Financial Obligations had disputed the so-called public debt of India, by British reckoning in 1939, India's external sterling obligations stood at 350 million pounds. By the end of the War in 1945, this equation was quite the opposite as India's Sterling Balances were almost four times that amount.[6]

As most economic history narratives suggest, the War had made the debtor colony of India a creditor of Great Britain, which was an advantage for India's nascent process of industrialization after Independence.[7] However, this view does not account for the fact that the costs of effecting this transformation were inordinately borne by India's poor who suffered from the effects of high inflation, widespread scarcities and, of course, famine and its attendant grim harvest. To keep up with the demand for goods for the War effort, the RBI had resorted to massive printing of currency. Consequently, if on the eve of the War in 1939 there were 227 crores of rupees in circulation, by 1942 the currency in circulation had more than doubled to 525 crores. The result was a rapid inflation of prices. Compared to a base figure of 100 in August 1939 the wholesale price index in India rapidly rose to a peak of 353 in four years![8]

Lured by the high prices, Indian farmers parted with their produce that was bought out by the British companies set up for the purpose and shipped out of the country. Little did the peasants realize that the high returns were of no value in the face of galloping inflation and the sheer scarcity of goods for purchase.[9] Kumarappa was amongst the earliest to read the signs of things to come. By early 1941, he repeatedly called for the use of 'barter' to tide over the crisis that had come to grip the countryside.

[6] B. R. Tomlinson, 'Indo-British Relations in the Post-Colonial Era: The Sterling Balances Negotiations, 1947–49', *The Journal of Imperial and Commonwealth History*, vol. 13, no. 3 (1985): 142–62.

[7] An official history of the RBI titled the chapter corresponding to the liquidation of the Sterling Balances as 'The Problems of Plenty, 1947–56'; see G. Balachandran, *Reserve Bank of India, 1951–1967* (New Delhi: Oxford University Press, 1998), pp. 593–624.

[8] From the table in B. E. Dadachanji, *Monetary System of India* (Bombay: D. B. Taraporevala and Sons, 1947), p. 135.

[9] Some historians have argued that the experience was not uniformly negative and that some regions 'prospered' during this period. See Indivar Kamtekar, 'A Different War Dance: State and Class in India, 1939–1945', *Past and Present*, vol. 176, no. 1 (2002): 187–221. However, the evidence presented for this view is of a limited nature.

Though money as a medium of exchange 'undoubtedly has its place in our economic life', Kumarappa argued that monetizing every transaction obliterated human values.[10] While we have discussed his argument on these lines in an earlier chapter, it is important to recognize the proximate reason for such a view. The use of a barter system, Kumarappa argued, 'would have helped to make it impossible for Government to perpetuate the injustice of using India's reserves to the tune of crores in the London money market while our industries were starving for funds'.

The massive movement of goods and the development of Indian industries to meet the sudden demand has led some to argue that India was experiencing a war boom. As a colony at the exploited end of the equation, India had always had recurring export surpluses and a more appropriate view was that this 'export surplus of India was a measure of her economic backwardness'.[11] This problem was also reflected in the acute food crisis that was developing.[12] Indeed, Bharatan Kumarappa argued that India's balance of trade wherein its exports exceeded its imports could hardly be called a 'healthy' situation as 'a half-starved, ill-fed and under-nourished people can certainly not afford to send out food produce ... without sinking further into starvation and misery'.[13] Instead, India's farmers should be urged to grow for themselves and not for the export market as 'it is only by thus conserving our resources for our own people that we can rescue them from their present state of poverty and despair'. The acute shortages created due to the War policy forced the Government of India to reverse its policies. If it had encouraged farmers to produce cash crops for the factories, now with the shortage of shipping for export of non-essential commodities, and 'with the pressure of carrying food to Great Britain, the seeming solicitude for the villager vanishes and he is now asked to shift for himself and grow food crops or starve'.[14]

By 1942, rampant inflation had reduced the intrinsic value of the rupee. Setting out his explanation of how money lubricates the wheels of

[10] J. C. Kumarappa, 'Barter in Action', *GUP*, January 1941.

[11] Bimalendu Dhar, *The Sterling Balances of India* (Calcutta: Nababharat Publishers, 1956), pp. 3–4.

[12] As a historian of the Indian economy points out, Indian 'export of foodgrains was by no means an indication of a surplus ... [but] should be called a tribute exacted by the foreign rulers ... although the commodities themselves were not forcibly taken by the rulers who left it to the so-called free operation of the market and the Indian traders and moneylenders to do the work for them'; see Rothermund, *Government, Landlord and Peasant in India*, p. 28.

[13] Bharatan Kumarappa, 'Trade Balance and Our Poverty', *GUP*, May 1941.

[14] J. C. Kumarappa, 'Economic Self-Sufficiency', *GUP*, October 1941.

long-distance trade but leaves the poor vulnerable to shocks in different parts of the economy, Kumarappa argued for a creative solution using a 'people's mint' instead of the sovereign currency issued by the Government that had been so debased in recent years. The solution that provides 'a way to non-violent control of the market, to a distribution of wealth with the minimum of friction and to a mint under the control of the people' was available in Gandhi's idea of yarn currency, that is, the use of homespun khadi yarn as a medium of exchange.[15] Wishing to draw a large number of people into the economic web, this 'local currency' was 'calculated to give a hallmark to things that are running waste today', that is, the huge, untapped reservoirs of human labour, 'and bring them into the market of commodities'.

The Kumarappa brothers consistently argued that only by directing 'raw material production to meet local demand' could India ward off the evils of 'periodic depressions, unemployment and economic instability' that were attendant on global trade.[16] The acute economic crisis and shortage of goods made people turn towards the Gandhian idea of decentralized production and consumption as the only sound principle of economic organization. Kumarappa pointed out that if we do not wish 'the economic life of our villages to be tied to the chariot wheels of British imperialism', India's primary producers had to recognize the grave dangers of depending on trade for its basic needs. Such a dependence, he presciently argued, 'is gambling with life stakes'.[17] He was also bemused by the proclamation of the Atlantic Charter by 'the heads of Governments of two of the most industrialized and imperialistic nations of the world' enunciating principles that 'will lead humanity to a better future inaugurating a reign of peace'.[18] Such peace and amity, Kumarappa argued, could only be built on the bedrock of self-sufficiency and restriction of the industrial hunger for the raw materials of the colonies.

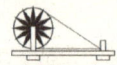

Although the colonial regime in India did not have any sympathy for the nationalist sentiment, the Viceroy and other administrators were

[15] J. C. Kumarappa, 'People's Mint', *GUP*, February 1942.

[16] Bharatan Kumarappa, 'Raw Material Production for Export', *GUP*, June 1941.

[17] J. C. Kumarappa, 'Economic Self-Sufficiency', *GUP*, October 1941.

[18] J. C. Kumarappa, '"V" for Village Industries', *GUP*, September 1941.

worried about having to deal with the severe political consequences of the growing crisis. In contrast, their London bosses, led by that inveterate imperialist Winston Churchill, remained quite unconcerned with the fate of millions of Indians and were unwilling to accept limits on the amount of resources they could continue to draw out of India. Having resigned from the provincial governments in protest against the Viceroy's declaration of India joining the War, the Congress could do little towards the abatement of the expropriation of India's food. By early 1942, the crisis in India took an even more serious and unexpected turn with the threat of war literally arriving on Indian shores. The steadily advancing Japanese army had occupied Burma and was threatening to overrun India. Once again, India's subservient position was clearly demonstrated. Although it contributed a large number of troops, while it 'lay exposed to a possible Japanese attack', the Indian divisions deployed in the Middle East were not brought back to defend the country, but continued to be used 'for the benefit of the defence of the Empire'.[19] It looked like the British obsession with the geopolitics of the Great Game had run aground and India was to pay a severe price for having its eastern shores fully exposed and underprotected.[20]

Apart from the direct threat of an invasion, the Japanese occupation of Burma had the immediate consequence of ending India's annual import of 1.5 million tonnes of Burmese rice which was about 5 per cent of India's annual rice consumption. By the middle of 1942, the *Gram Udyog Patrika* was reporting with concern on the severe shortages of food grains in the country.[21] Unlike the Government's impractical remedy of urging farmers to grow more food, the AIVIA averred that 'a more practical method within the reach of all is to stop eating polished rice and to insist on having unpolished rice'. It noted that polishing of rice entailed an enormous loss of the yield as well as removed the most nutritious part of the grain. Thus, if in 1942, India consumed about 27.2 million tonnes of rice per annum, the 10 per cent loss due to polishing of rice worked out to almost 3 million tonnes, that is, the loss due to mill polishing of rice was twice as much as the rice imports from Burma. Thus, the constructive workers argued that even in the adverse

[19] Voigt, *India in the Second World War*, p. 140.

[20] For a discussion of the Japanese invasion of India that never happened, see Indivar Kamtekar, 'The Shiver of 1942', *Studies in History*, vol. 18, no. 1 (2002): 81–102.

[21] 'Shortage of Rice', *GUP*, June 1942.

conditions of the time, self-sufficiency was within reach, if only Indian society had the will to execute it. As in the case of yarn currency, the eminently sensible proposal of using unpolished rice did not have a chance in the chaotic days of this period. Despite India being subjected to severe food shortages over the next decade, such proposals had no significant political support within the Congress or without.

By the end of 1941, the British had also adopted a 'scorched earth' policy that involved the destruction of infrastructure that an occupying Japanese force could potentially utilize. Thus, many villages in the coastal regions were forcibly evacuated and boats and vehicles were confiscated and destroyed. With the real threat of a Japanese invasion, Allied troops began arriving in large numbers in India and were moved to the eastern front further taxing the strained resources of the country. The possibility of a Japanese attack on India and the designed-for-rejection offer of Dominion Status by Stafford Cripps quickened the political pulse. Gandhi was alarmed at developments wherein he saw no preparation for Indian freedom that the Congress demanded; rather it was 'a preparation pure and simple for the defence of the British Empire'.[22] The situation in India had become intolerable and was crying out for resolution. As a way out of the explosive crisis that was building up, Gandhi demanded the 'orderly and timely withdrawal of the British from India'. If the British were desperate to save their Empire, Gandhi had concluded that if India was to be saved, Empire had to go. The result was the historic August 1942 demand of 'Quit India' and the Gandhi mantra of 'Do or Die'. The British response was swift and Linlithgow decided to use the mailed fist. The entire top leadership of the Congress was immediately arrested and there was a severe crackdown all over the country. Indians responded to the challenge with widespread protests and acts of sabotage thereby giving notice that the days of unbridled British power were finally over.

By late 1942, as Kumarappa recognized, there were 'unprecedented conditions when the nation is facing two fronts—the Britishers within and the Japanese without', both with the intent of 'exploitation of the people'.[23]

---

[22] M. K. Gandhi, 'Foreign Soldiers in India', *Harijan*, 26 April 1942.
[23] J. C. Kumarappa, 'Gandhi Jayanti', *GUP*, September 1942.

At such a time of grave political and economic crisis, with the leadership of the Congress behind bars, it was felt that the village constructive worker had the tremendous responsibility of providing correct guidance. It was also seen as a great opportunity to bring home the lessons of self-reliance and press for the development of a decentralized economy that could protect people from the vagaries of war and political events in faraway places across the world. Indeed, this was also the substance of the CWC resolution on Gandhi's Constructive Programme adopted in this period. However, given the devastating blow that the British dealt to the Congress leadership, the AIVIA found itself incapable of utilizing this opportunity to propagate its ideology. Soon, Kumarappa was himself put behind bars.

A large number of public figures including many Gandhians were caught up in the enormous ferment of the Quit India movement. Due to the limited nature of archival material available, it has not been possible to piece together the exact nature of Kumarappa's activities immediately preceding his arrest and eventual imprisonment. Nevertheless, a few valuable pointers including references in his own writings have provided us with a partial understanding.[24] With the entire CWC imprisoned, many of the younger leaders stepped in to fill the void. Unlike the previous mass campaigns, during Quit India the argument for ahimsa was a qualified one. Gandhi himself averred that 'everyone is free to go the fullest length under ahimsa'.[25] Most of the emergent leadership went underground to direct the operations against the government, and a new feature of Indian protests was the acceptability of sabotage of public infrastructure as long as it did not harm human life. One source has stated that Kumarappa had advocated sabotage activities and went to the extent of arguing that the arms of the police had to be snatched away.[26] This claim in an oral history seems far-fetched especially since, as a constructive worker, Kumarappa was pledged to not indulge in political activity. Moreover, in later years, Kumarappa proudly argued that he was jailed by the British even though 'he had never done an overt act or courted arrest' during his years in public life.[27] However, there is some evidence that suggests that in the latter half of 1942

---

[24] These include Vinaik's *Gandhian Crusader* and K. K. Chaudhari, *Quit India Revolution: The Ethos of Its Central Direction* (Mumbai: Popular Prakashan, 1996). However, it must be pointed out that the evidence is sketchy and incomplete and could possibly be incorrect in certain instances.

[25] 'Message to the Country', 9 August 1942, *CWMG*.

[26] Cited in Chaudhari, *Quit India Revolution*, p. 148.

[27] J. C. Kumarappa, 'Ends and Means in Bhoodan', *GUP*, June 1955.

he had gone underground. An intelligence report 'credits Kumarappa with directing the inter-Provincial underground activities'.[28] On one occasion, when Kumarappa was proceeding from Nagpur to Bombay by train, the police were on the lookout for him and planned on arresting him en route at Wardha. Kumarappa is said to have outwitted the police by sleeping on an upper berth in a third-class compartment while the police searched the first- and second-class coaches. Arriving in Bombay, he evaded arrest for a few more days by staying at a guest house owned by his friend, Shoorji Vallabhdas, at the hill station of Deolali. This was cocking a snook at the Raj, for Deolali had a major army encampment and 'was the last place for the police to search out a Congressman'.[29] Eventually, he was arrested in a major swoop in Bombay on 18 November 1942 along with a whole host of Congress leaders.[30]

There is some sparse but tantalizing indirect evidence of Kumarappa's activities between the August call for revolt and his eventual arrest in November. Although the *Gram Udyog Patrika* had always carried Kumarappa's writings since its inception, unusually the October and November 1942 issues did not carry any signed articles by him, suggesting that he was underground during this period. The other interesting source is a broadcast on the clandestine Congress Radio.[31] In an undated recording, Usha Mehta is heard reading an article on the 'waste paper' called Indian currency. By the end of 1942, there was acute scarcity all around the country and inflation was wreaking havoc. Although Kumarappa is not mentioned as the author of the article read on the Congress Radio, his imprint is unmistakable. Characterizing the British system of finance as 'large-scale pickpocketing' the broadcast warned Indians to beware of 'this high finance'. Instead of allowing India's grain harvests to be taken away, the broadcast urged farmers to stock grains for a year by putting them away 'in small quantities in remote villages unapproachable to quick moving vehicles and any sale in bulk should be objected to by the village'. The 'Quit India Sena' was urged to 'protect the masses against these international brigands and highway robbers with respectable top-hats and titles'. Interestingly enough,

---

[28] Chaudhari, *Quit India Revolution*, p. 158.

[29] Vinaik, *Gandhian Crusader*, p. 119.

[30] Chaudhari, *Quit India Revolution*, p. 157.

[31] Audio recording that was available at http://www.gandhiserve.org and is no longer online. Usha Mehta was arrested and the equipment for the Congress Radio seized on 12 November 1942, so this broadcast must have been done before this date.

although he was underground, an adapted version of the broadcast essay was published after his arrest in the December 1942 issue of the *Gram Udyog Patrika*. In a scathing indictment of the British Raj that he titled 'A Stone for Bread', Kumarappa laid bare the terrible injury being inflicted on India and its people. Unable to offer 'goods and services any longer in exchange for the commodities and the purchasing power she stands in need of so badly', Great Britain was offering India Sterling Securities.[32] If he had been arguing for some form of barter to be put in place to protect India's primary producers from the vagaries of the war, now Kumarappa approached the issue with great urgency. He was also keen to get people to recognize that the high prices being paid for the goods by the agencies of the government to be used towards the war effort were a dangerous trap. First, these were inflated prices and did not reflect the true value of the rupee. Further, if such sales were going to create acute scarcities, the poor would never be able to purchase goods for their basic needs and would face starvation. In such 'uncertain times' he advised the villagers 'not to part with their commodities for paper money, but to exchange it against goods only'. Appealing to the local shopkeepers to help handle the crisis, Kumarappa asked for some form of a barter economy to be created 'to relieve the situation'. In the end he warned the villagers to be prepared for the tough times ahead and advised them 'to store in their granaries foodstuffs needed for their household for at least two years'.

For Kumarappa this turn of events was the final proof of the dangers inherent in a money economy, and he approved of the sentiment in *Faust* when it attributed the creation of money to Mephistopheles, the devil.[33] In this period, the RBI had printed enormous amounts of currency against the Sterling Credits. Thus, while the currency in circulation in India more than doubled between 1939–40 and 1942, the concomitant bullion remained stable at 44 crores whereas the Sterling Credits had ballooned from 78 crores to 325 crores, that is, 'accounting practically in itself for the whole inflation of nearly 300 crores'. In fact, the problem would become even worse in subsequent years. If in 1942 Kumarappa had complained of the currency circulation growing to 525 crores, by 1945–6 it had increased to a massive 1,200 crores. As expected, this growth was based on the virtual soundness of the paper money of Sterling Securities, which had grown

[32] J. C. Kumarappa, 'A Stone for Bread', *GUP*, December 1942.
[33] J. C. Kumarappa, *Currency Inflation: Its Cause and Cure* (Wardha: The All-India Village Industries Association, 1949), p. 9.

to an incredible 1,550 crores.[34] Kumarappa calculated that if one only took the bullion backing as having real value, 'the proportion of assets to liabilities works out at 8.4% and not at 70.6% as the Reserve Bank' claimed. In other words, the value of the rupee had been reduced to about 1 anna, and while Great Britain obtained for its own use real goods worth 325 crores produced by 'the sweat of the brow of the masses', in return 'helpless India has been made to part with commodities to this extent and to hug useless paper securities in return'.[35] If it was bad enough that India's poor were made to part with their food against a promise of payments in the future, this scheme had a potential danger with devastating consequences. In 1942, with the Japanese forces making major advances across Southeast Asia, the fate of the global war was as yet undecided. Had Britain and its allies lost the war to the Axis forces, the Sterling Securities held in India's name would 'not be worth the paper they [were] printed on'. With Britain eventually winning the War, this dangerous possibility has been forgotten. As an aside one may add that although the description of the Cripps offer of Dominion Status as 'a post-dated cheque on a crashing bank' is often incorrectly attributed to Gandhi, this characterization was a perfect description of the Sterling Securities that Britain was offering India in lieu of *matériel*.[36]

Although they would not stop extracting unrequited goods from India, the British administration was increasingly worried about the ballooning size of their future sterling debts. In response they tried to mask the problem by forcible repatriation of sterling assets in India, that is, Britain unilaterally set about liquidating its debts 'by the use of India's sterling receipts to repatriate the Indian sterling debt bonds and railway annuities outstanding in the London market'.[37] However, by the middle of 1942 the problem could no longer be camouflaged in this manner as all of India's outstanding debt had been liquidated. Kumarappa was angered by this blatant manipulation that effectively paid off British investors in advance and made the Government of India take on the entire liabilities of the future. In the context of the ominous threat of a Japanese invasion,

---

[34] The figures have been rounded off and are for the period 1945–6; see Dadachandji, *Monetary System of India*, p. 27.

[35] J. C. Kumarappa, 'A Stone for Bread'.

[36] For a discussion of the origins of this description of the Cripps proposals, see J. N. Sahni, *The Lid Off: Fifty Years of Indian Politics, 1921–1971* (New Delhi: Allied Publishers, 1971), p. 166. Also see Gopalkrishna Gandhi (ed.), *The Oxford India Gandhi: Essential Writings* (New Delhi: Oxford University Press, 2008), p. 747.

[37] Tomlinson, 'Indo-British Relations in the Post-Colonial Era'.

to Kumarappa this debt liquidation was a hurried scraping off of the dish in preparation for the abandonment of India and he angrily denounced it as the 'spearhead of the financial scorched earth policy'. The *Harijan* had been suspended during this period, but Kumarappa's exposé of the financial shenanigans of the Government in the *GUP* worried an edgy administration. Indeed, although Kumarappa was not a political figure and was only interested 'to see social justice meted out to the helpless', it was inevitable that he would be incarcerated.[38] As he argued, a 'Government conceived in avarice ... hates to have its nefarious activities exposed to the limelight of public opinion'.

Although he was arrested in November 1942, Kumarappa was prosecuted in March 1943 for his article that had been published in the December 1942 issue. During the hearing of his case, the Sessions Judge asked as to what would have been the result had the advice tendered by Kumarappa been followed. The counsel for the defence jumped up to reply that had the farmers in Bengal followed Kumarappa's suggestion, lakhs of people would not have perished there. The judge replied that he was only concerned with the implications on the war effort and the relevance to the Defence of India Act, and sentenced Kumarappa to three simultaneous terms of two-and-a-half years of hard labour.[39] When the judge congratulated the public prosecutor 'on the able way he had handled a difficult case', the prosecutor interrupted him and informed the court that he was 'working under the instructions of the prisoner himself' as he had failed to obtain the advice of any other economist.[40] Kumarappa's statement in court that set out his analysis of the economic crisis in India was published later that year as *Currency Inflation: Its Cause and Cure* and remained banned till the advent of the Congress ministries in 1946.

The severe crackdown on the Congress had effectively suppressed the political challenge to the British handling of the political and economic crises of the times. However, an unlikely group of individuals courageously raised their voices against the wartime economic policy. In early 1943, the Bombay economist C. N. Vakil published a pamphlet titled *The Falling Rupee*

---

[38] J. C. Kumarappa, *Stone Walls and Iron Bars* (Allahabad: New Literature, 1946), p. 1.

[39] Vinaik, *Gandhian Crusader*, p. 120.

[40] Vinaik, *Gandhian* Crusader, p. 120.

176 / The Web of Freedom

that warned of the risks of runaway inflation that loomed on the horizon. The timing and relevance of Vakil's intervention ensured widespread publicity that effectively exposed the Government which was 'anxious to see that the inflation which they were practising was concealed as far as possible from the public'.[41] In fact, although Kumarappa's essay appeared prior to Vakil's intervention, during the trial Kumarappa quoted from *The Falling Rupee* to substantiate his arguments.[42] By April 1943, a group of eminent Indian economists had issued a manifesto calling attention to the fact that the price rise in India was not due to scarcity of commodities alone but was largely fuelled by the RBI's reckless printing of currency. In a virtual vindication of Kumarappa's position, they argued that the 1943 inflation in India was 'a deficit induced fiat-money inflation', that is, of the worst kind as it was 'the most inequitable way of distributing the war burden and usually involves large transfers of wealth from the poorer and the middle classes to the richer classes'.[43]

By the time Kumarappa began serving his sentence in Jabalpur Jail, the economic hardship of India was extremely serious. The Viceroy was informing London that while his Government had managed the supplies for the war effort and succeeded in 'holding the population quiescent', the situation was 'already strained almost to a breaking point'.[44] Linlithgow was worried that people at large would refuse to accept paper currency and demanded that Britain had to choose between 'utilizing India as a base for operations and utilizing India as a source of supply for overseas theatres and countries'. By this time the famine in Bengal had taken on serious proportions, but Britain would hardly countenance any change in policy. As has been pointed out in a recent indictment of Churchill's role in the making of the Bengal Famine, 'famine and sterling debt were two sides of the same coin'; between 1939–40 and 1942–3, the expenditure of the Government of India had increased tenfold, half of which was due to the sterling debt that Britain owed India.[45] However, instead of organizing relief

---

[41] C. N. Vakil, *War against Inflation: The Story of the Falling Rupee, 1943–77* (Delhi: Macmillan Company of India Ltd., 1978), p. 9.

[42] Vakil recalls this episode in his memoirs written in the 1970s, although he gets some details wrong. See *War against Inflation*, pp. 17–18.

[43] Reprinted as Appendix I of C. N. Vakil, *Financial Burden of the War on India* (Bombay: C. N. Vakil, July 1943).

[44] Quoted in Madhusree Mukherjee, *Churchill's Secret War: The British Empire and the Ravaging of India during World War II* (New Delhi: Tranquebar, 2010), p. 140.

[45] M. Mukherjee, *Churchill's Secret War*, p. 203.

efforts, the War Cabinet commanded New Delhi to carry out propaganda and curb inflation. At the same time, it set up a committee for 'finding ways to reduce the sterling debt'.[46] In other words, having obtained enormous amounts of material including food from India which had led to rampant inflation and famine, Britain was now planning to wriggle out of its debt obligations by repudiating it. A sense of the rather incredible nature of the British position can be had by considering the size of the debt it had piled up with India. By the end of the war in 1945, of the total external liabilities of Great Britain, a third was owed to India and this amount was about one and a half times the amount of the monies lent by the United States to Great Britain.[47] By 1947, India's Sterling Balances were 'estimated at 17 times the annual revenue of the Government of India and one-fifth of Britain's gross national product'.[48] As we will explain below, this figure is itself a severe underestimate since the Congress had disputed much of the public debt ascribed to India that the British had wiped out using the Sterling Credits. In 1875, at the high noon of Empire, the then Secretary of State for India, the Marquess of Salisbury, had with revealing honesty argued that 'as India must be bled, the lancet should be directed to the parts where blood is congested, or at least sufficient, not to those which are already enfeebled from want of it'.[49] Now in the last years of colonial rule, Salisbury's successors dispensed with his dictum of sparing the weak and drew upon India's resources in an indiscriminate and inhuman manner.

While in 1942 Gandhi and the Congress had held that the Japanese aggression was primarily due to the British presence in India, the politicians of Britain turned this argument on its head. They argued that Britain was not required to pay India back as 'it had been saved from Japanese aggression by Allied war efforts and it did not behove' India to make claims against Britain.[50] Expectedly, the leading proponent of this repudiationist school was Winston Churchill who, in his famed history of the Second World War, presented an argument that can only be described as a bare-faced lie.

---

[46] M. Mukherjee, *Churchill's Secret War*, p. 150.

[47] Aditya Mukherjee, *Imperialism, Nationalism and the Making of the Indian Capitalist Class, 1920–1947* (New Delhi: Sage Publications, 2002), p. 137.

[48] Estimate taken from B. R. Tomlinson, *The Political Economy of the Raj: 1914–47*, p. 140, quoted in A. Mukherjee, *Imperialism, Nationalism and the Making of the Indian Capitalist Class*, p. 134.

[49] Quoted in Reginald Reynolds, *The New Indian Rope Trick: Or What Became of the Debt?* (London: Indian Freedom Campaign, 1943), p. 13.

[50] Dhar, *The Sterling Balances of India*, p. 68.

Ignoring the millions who perished in Bengal as well as India's widespread and enormous hardship, Churchill wrote that 'no great portion of the world population was so effectively protected from the horrors and perils of the World War as were the people of Hindustan. They were carried through the struggle on the shoulders of our small island'.[51] Churchill's argument was a rather vulgar one and, in a 1950 debate in the House of Commons on the Sterling question, he was told that his attitude towards India was unrealistic and 'totally lacking in humanity'.[52] However, the repudiationist position was not confined to Churchill alone and the Labour Party also shared in this view. Speaking in 1947 as the British Chancellor of the Exchequer, Hugh Dalton argued that the 'vast accumulation of debt represents an unreal, unjust and unsupportable burden' and 'must be very substantially scaled down'.[53] Dalton argued that a sign of British strength 'must be refusal to take on fantastic commitments which are beyond her strength and beyond all limits of good sense and fair play'. In other words, paying India back what it was owed was just not cricket. It must be said that amidst this chorus for repudiation there were morally upright Britons like the Fabian G. D. H. Cole and the Quaker friend of India, Reginald Reynolds, who found the idea of Britain reneging on its debts to India to be morally repugnant. With his characteristic wit, Reynolds likened the whole affair of the sterling debts to the Indian rope trick, that is, the debts kept rising up till they suddenly disappeared.[54]

The repudiationist approach was an extreme form of moral hazard and was not confined to the politicians alone. It also found support from a pivotal figure in the economic discourse of the time, John Maynard Keynes. Keynes had been an important figure in the formulation of India's currency policy in the 1930s but in the aftermath of the War he played a far more important role on the international stage during the negotiations on a new international monetary regime at the Bretton Woods conference in 1944.[55]

[51] Winston Churchill, *The Hinge of Fate* (n.p.: Rossetta Books, 2002), p. 260.

[52] Quoted in Dhar, *The Sterling Balances of India*, p. 135.

[53] Quoted in J. C. Kumarappa, 'Using the Giant's Strength as a Giant', *Harijan*, 18 May 1947.

[54] Reynolds, *The New Indian Rope Trick*.

[55] The negotiations at Bretton Woods defined the post-war architecture of international finance which included the emergence of the US dollar as the reserve

Although Keynes and his American counterpart were eager to build a stable system that would rescue capitalism from the ashes of the War, they were equally keen to block any discussion of Britain's sterling obligations towards India, Egypt, and other creditors. While the Indian delegation 'found it difficult to understand how any scheme, which purported to regulate international monetary relations in the post-war world, could ignore so fundamental a question', all attempts by India to make Britain internationally accountable for its debts failed.[56] At Bretton Woods, Keynes argued that Britain's debts to India were a bilateral affair and could not be subjected to international scrutiny. However, Keynes was also the chief British negotiator on a loan from the United States under the post-war Anglo-American Financial Agreement wherein Britain undertook to speedily renegotiate its sterling obligations with India and other countries as well as 'scale down the size of the balances themselves'.[57] Thus, while India was blocked from making debts owed to it by Britain accountable to international agreements, it was subjected to the terms and conditions set by the emergent global power, the United States.

Kumarappa was released from prison in early 1945 and later that year, with the War over, he could finally take stock of the net worth of India's assets appropriated by Britain. About two million Indian soldiers had been deployed on various battlefronts, and it had cost Rs 1,300 crores; in addition the Indian administration had spent 1,200 crores. Moreover, using the paper backing of Sterling Securities, Great Britain had taken goods worth 1,500 crores out of India for their war effort. In effect, '4000 crores have been charged to India on account of this war which is to perpetuate Britain's stranglehold on our country', that is, 'we are made to pay for our own slavery'.[58] Thus, while Britain argued that it owed India around 1,600 crores, this figure could not be accepted at face value. Instead he argued that the 4,000 crores Britain had unilaterally written off by charging it to India under the various heads given above had to be scrutinized afresh, that is, instead of Britain's figure of 1,600 crores, Kumarappa argued that the

---

currency as well as the foundation of the International Monetary Fund (IMF) and the International Bank for Reconstruction and Development that came to be known as the World Bank.

[56] Dhar, *The Sterling Balances of India*, p. 92. At different stages, some of the Indian negotiators felt that it was better for India to withdraw from the Bretton Woods negotiations but this did not happen.

[57] Tomlinson, 'Indo-British Relations in the Post-Colonial Era'.

[58] J. C. Kumarappa, 'A Stolen Coconut for Ganesh', *GUP*, October 1945.

settlement should address itself to a total figure of 5,700 crores. Although colonial India's negotiators had failed to make Britain accountable on an international platform, on the eve of Independence, Kumarappa called for the institution of an impartial tribunal to 'prevent the debtor himself playing the role of the judge and the jury'.[59] After all, he remarked, 'what negotiation can a rat carry on with a cat?'[60]

Kumarappa was particularly exercised by the manner in which during the period of forcible repatriation of India's sterling debts, Britain had written off 1,700 crores as war costs to be paid by India and an additional 400 crores against past public debts. It may be recalled that Kumarappa was a crucial figure in the 1931 Congress Select Committee that had questioned the financial obligations of India towards Great Britain at a point when India was the debtor country. Curiously, much had changed in Indian politics between 1931 and 1947. If earlier a defiant Congress had challenged the 'public debts' incurred in India's name, by 1947 the Congress leadership had quite forgotten its earlier demands. Indeed, during the entire period of negotiations carried out on the settlement of the Sterling Credits question, Kumarappa remained a solitary figure in arguing against a premature conclusion of a settlement, and that 'free India has to have a voice in the matter and it should not be forestalled'.[61] By early 1947 the sterling negotiations were being carried out on the basis of the figure of 1,600 crores that was defined by Britain, and Kumarappa wished to make Britain's unilateral decisions subject to a fresh scrutiny and open negotiations on the entire figure of 5,700 crores. A month before Partition, he lobbied hard with Nehru to press for a solution that would make the question of the debts a part of the political settlement between India, Pakistan, and Britain. Kumarappa told Nehru that 'a judicial tribunal may be set up to fix the amount which would ultimately enter into Pakistan–India negotiations' and he also wanted Gandhi to put pressure on Nehru on this matter.[62]

[59] J. C. Kumarappa, 'Debtor, Judge and Jury', *Harijan*, 25 May 1947.

[60] J. C. Kumarappa, Preface to *Blood Money* (Wardha: The All-India Village Industries Association, 1948).

[61] J. C. Kumarappa, 'Who Should Call the Tune?', *GUP*, February 1947. It is rather remarkable that, despite its fundamental impact on Indian society, the entire episode of Sterling Credits is hardly ever represented in the historiography of India's decolonization and remains confined to specialist writings on economic history.

[62] Letter from J. C. Kumarappa to Jawaharlal Nehru, 5 July 1947, Correspondence Files, Kumarappa Papers. Also see 'Letter from J. C. Kumarappa to Mahatma Gandhi', 5 July 1947, S. N. 10197.

The significance of Kumarappa's suggestion on India's negotiating position stands out in relief when we consider the British view on this matter. Recognizing Britain's vulnerability on this count, in 1946, its Prime Minister Clement Attlee had explicitly instructed the Cabinet Mission to India that 'there could be no question of offering ... concessions on the financial side in order to secure a political settlement'.[63] When the negotiations between Great Britain and India had begun on the terms of settling the sterling debts, Kumarappa recognized that the old 1931 Congress challenge against British claims on India's public debts had been all but forgotten. Since the negotiations would effectively address the entire financial history of Britain's exploitation of India, he briefly recapitulated India's public debts and credits in a volume that he tellingly titled *Clive to Keynes*.[64]

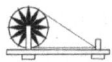

The history of India's economic exploitation under British rule is a long and complicated one. Nineteenth-century chroniclers such as Naoroji and Dutt played a key role in providing an economic basis for Indian nationalism and its critique of Empire. However, in the twentieth century, the British methods of resource extraction had become quite complex and sophisticated. As a result, knowledge of the mechanisms whereby Indian wealth was extracted during this period remains confined to a small tribe of economic historians. We will not discuss the specific financial content of Kumarappa's argument in *Clive to Keynes* as it is a reprise of the position taken in the Congress Select Committee report as well as the above discussion on the sterling controversy. However, its significance lies in the fact that it was written to be easily understood by the lay public. As a result, *Clive to Keynes* remains till date among the best exposés of the manner in which 'the stately homes of England are founded on the skeletons of India'.[65] Kumarappa argued that while the exploitation of India was 'inaugurated by the empire builder Clive with his bare-faced loot', it was commendable for its 'undisguised nature', but as the years progressed, his successors adopted methods of 'increased concealment'.[66] Clive's

[63] Quoted in Chattopadhyay, 'The Idea of Planning in India, 1930–1951', p. 245.

[64] J. C. Kumarappa, *Clive to Keynes: A Survey of the History of Our Public Debts and Credits* (Ahmedabad: Navajivan Publishing House, 1947).

[65] J. C. Kumarappa, *Clive to Keynes*, p. iv.

[66] J. C. Kumarappa, *Clive to Keynes*, p. 29.

methods were improved upon by 'the commercial dishonesty of the East India Company'.[67] By the Victorian era, Britain coveted India's resources but 'was anxious to appear honest and above board'. This predicament was resolved, Kumarappa argued, by 'wholesale falsification of accounts'.[68] By the time of the Second World War, this art was perfected into the method of Sterling Securities which was 'simplicity itself'.[69] Thus, Kumarappa argued that from the eighteenth century Company high priest, Clive, to 'the twentieth century financial high priest of the far-flung British Empire', Keynes, 'they have run through the whole gamut of financial crimes'.[70] If anything, Kumarappa argued, 'Clive was refreshing in his adventurous exploits, though he may have lacked the 'varsity accent' of his latter-day representative'.

In the contemporary context where Keynesian economics is posed as a counterfoil to the free market ideology of the Chicago School of economics, the clubbing of Keynes with the robber baron Clive might strike the reader as odd. However, as outlined above, while he was concerned with stabilizing the economy of the Western world, Keynes had no compunction in causing grave injustice to India by repeatedly and vigorously arguing for the scaling down of Britain's sterling obligations towards India as well as keeping this question outside the purview of international scrutiny. Indeed, as a distinguished biographer remarked, all through his life Keynes 'assumed the Empire as a fact of life and never showed the slightest interest in discarding it .... He never much deviated from the view that, all things being considered, it was better to have Englishmen running the world than foreigners'.[71] In this, he was following in 'the hallowed [Utilitarian] tradition set by Macaulay and the Mills in the nineteenth century', or, as Kumarappa would have it, in the unsavoury tradition of Robert Clive.[72]

Kumarappa was profoundly shaken by the Indian experience of the Second World War and the suffering endured by India's poor. Indeed,

[67] J. C. Kumarappa, *Clive to Keynes*, p. 13.

[68] J. C. Kumarappa, *Clive to Keynes*, p. 13.

[69] J. C. Kumarappa, *Clive to Keynes*, p. 29.

[70] J. C. Kumarappa, *Clive to Keynes*, p. 35.

[71] Robert Skidelsky, *John Maynard Keynes· Hope Betrayed, 1883–1920*, London: Macmillan Press, 1983, p. 91.

[72] Skidelsky, *John Maynard Keynes*, p. 176. For a full-length study of Keynes' India connection, see Anand Chandavarkar, *Keynes and India: A Study in Economics and Biography*, London: Macmillan Press, 1989. To put it mildly, our reading contradicts Chandavarkar's heroic image of Keynes.

much of his ecological and agrarian prescriptions stemmed from his understanding of the effects of rampant inflation and famine during the War era. Consequently, he argued that the large numbers of Indians who worked in the agrarian economy needed a currency run on a basis very different from that of industrialized countries. In particular, he was worried about the devastating impacts of inflation on the earnings of farmers who depended on the profits of seasonal harvests to tide over the intervening months. Thus, Kumarappa felt that currency should work more as a medium of exchange rather than as a storage of purchasing power. To achieve this objective, he argued that 'it was essential to maintain the intrinsic value of our currency by an adequate backing in gold' instead of 'a fiduciary issue of notes with great instability of purchasing power'.[73]

If Kumarappa had been critical of British callousness towards the welfare of ordinary Indians, soon he would realize that those negotiating on behalf of India were not very solicitous either. Indeed, a key figure in the negotiations was independent India's first finance minister, Shanmukham Chetty, who had a rather dubious public record and was 'widely criticized as having sold India to the interests of Britain' at the Imperial Economic Conference at Ottawa in 1932.[74] However, there were others who recognized the dangers inherent in the manner in which India was negotiating on its rights. The economist Manu Subedar was a member of India's negotiating team at Bretton Woods. Although Subedar was no radical, he found the official Indian position adopted by his colleagues distressing enough to send an anguished appeal to Sardar Patel for intervention. Subedar argued that India should stay out of the Bretton Woods negotiations, and 'should not miss this chance of exposing to the whole world the bad intentions of England towards us'.[75] 'If financial issues of this magnitude, which arise only once in a generation, are going to be settled in this slipshod way', Subedar argued, there was 'very little hope for the future of our country.'

Between 1947 and 1949, British and Indian teams met for five rounds of negotiations on the terms and conditions that would apply to India's utilization of its sterling reserves. Kumarappa was appalled at the settlement

[73] J. C. Kumarappa, *Clive to Keynes*, p. 34.

[74] Review of *Economic Ambassador: The Life and Work of Dr. Sir R. K. Shanmukham Chetty* by Nilkan Perumal, *Hindustan Times*, 1 May 1955, Press Clippings, Kumarappa Papers.

[75] Letter from Manu Subedar to Sardar Patel, 15 February 1946 in *Sardar Patel's Correspondence, 1945–50*, vol. 3, edited by Durga Das (Ahmedabad: Navajivan Publishing House, 1971), p. 211.

that Chetty agreed to in London in August 1948 on the terms of repayment of the Sterling Securities. Great Britain 'after making all manner of unilateral deduction from' India's credit had scaled down the outstanding dues to 1200 crores. Then, it 'successfully pleaded that it is impossible for her to pay, in the near future, the amount that she owes to India which is less than 1/6th of her annual income'.[76] Britain also managed to get India to accept conditions whereby the rate at which the sterling reserves could be drawn upon was severely restricted thereby denying India free use of its reserves. If the Indian negotiators were willing to forgo many of India's claims on the debts owed, Kumarappa would come to be further disappointed at the manner in which India would use the sterling reserves available. He had argued that it was India's villages that had paid the price of the War in India and the sterling reserves were built out of the exploitation of the rural poor. As a result, since 'our rural parts require a considerable amount to be spent on development', the sterling reserves ought to be spent for such purposes. However, in this he was to meet disappointment for, instead of spending the money accumulated on helping the desperately poor of India, the business class were 'anxious to lay their hands on this wealth so that their own programme of industrialization may be stepped up'. Thus, the tragedy of rural India was doubly compounded, as India's 'negotiators have been more than anxious to obtain capital goods for industrialists in India'. Indeed, as Subedar had told Patel, the dilution of India's position was done at the behest of 'big business, contrary to the real interests of Indian masses'.[77]

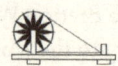

Arrested in Bombay in November 1942, Kumarappa spent about a year as an undertrial detainee in Bombay, Wardha, and Nagpur before being eventually sentenced to hard labour and transferred to Jabalpur Prison, probably in October 1943.[78] Unlike his previous term in Nasik, in Jabalpur, Kumarappa spent much of his prison time in isolation. He would have felt the absence of his brother Bharatan who was imprisoned in Nagpur

[76] J. C. Kumarappa, 'The Modern Debtor', *Harijan*, 15 August 1948.

[77] Telegram from Manu Subedar to Sardar Patel, 15 February 1946, in *Sardar Patel's Correspondence, 1945–50*.

[78] This guess of the date of sentencing is calculated on the basis of his comments in J. C. Kumarappa, *Practice and Precepts of Jesus* (henceforth *PPJ*) (Ahmedabad: Navajivan Publishing House, 1945), p. xi.

during this period.[79] It is during this period of isolation and loneliness that Kumarappa penned his most well-known book, *Economy of Permanence,* as well as his interpretation of his spiritual heritage in *Practice and Precepts of Jesus.* In Jabalpur Prison severe restrictions were imposed on him. Thus, while he was allowed a limited number of religious texts and conservative newspapers, the prison authorities went to the extent of disallowing Kumarappa access to copies of his own books, lest he 'should seduce himself'.[80] Kumarappa had suffered from various ailments for many years and after about fifteen months of imprisonment in Jabalpur, and with his kidneys in poor shape, his health rapidly deteriorated. His situation was so alarming that he left instructions with the jail authorities on the disposal of his body and personal effects after his death. The authorities were worried about his dying in prison and informed his family in Madras. A sister and nephew arrived at Jabalpur, not knowing whether they would be given his ashes or body, or be able to see him in flesh and blood.[81] Released on 2 January 1945, Kumarappa was taken to recuperate in the house of the only person his sister knew in town, an Indian Christian doctor in government service. But a rebellious Gandhian who had spent time in prison was hardly welcome in this household and, after wandering around with nowhere to go, Kumarappa eventually found a resting place. To everyone's surprise, the man who was given up for dead made a rapid recovery and was strong enough to travel back to Wardha in a few days. A worried Gandhi was glad to see Kumarappa emerge alive from prison and twitted him for having been 'naughty to be so ill'.[82]

Within a few months of Kumarappa's release, the first edition of *Economy of Permanence: A Quest for a Social Order Based on Non-violence* was published in 1945 with a foreword by Gandhi. Kumarappa suffered from very poor health during this period and the second part of the book, *Man in Gregation,* appeared as a separate volume only in 1948. Most subsequent reprints have combined the two parts into a single volume. Kumarappa's

---

[79] Bharatan was arrested and tried for his role as the publisher of *Gram Udyog Patrika* which carried J. C. Kumarappa's essay, 'A Stone for Bread'.

[80] J. C. Kumarappa, *Stone Walls and Iron Bars,* p. 8.

[81] J. C. Kumarappa, *Stone Walls and Iron Bars,* p. 16.

[82] Letter to J. C. Kumarappa, 5 January 1945, *CWMG.*

current reputation as an early preceptor of ecological thought is partly due to the resonance of the title *Economy of Permanence* with contemporary environmental concerns. However, *Economy of Permanence* is a philosophical exposition on human nature and its social implications. Perhaps due to his serious illness during its writing, the spiritual and philosophical ideas presented in *Economy of Permanence* are difficult to follow and, as the Mahatma politely observed in his foreword, the book 'needs careful reading twice or thrice if it is to be fully appreciated'.[83]

Earlier, Kumarappa had presented his two manuscripts to Gandhi and solicited forewords for them. Soon, Gandhi returned *Practice and Precepts of Jesus* with a commendatory foreword enclosed in an envelope addressed to 'Dr. Kumarappa, D. D.' Kumarappa took this to be an 'impish joke on a layman like him' writing on religion and let it pass.[84] By now he had become used to the unearned title of 'Dr' bestowed upon him. All three of his brothers had doctoral degrees, and as a result he was often mistakenly referred to as 'Dr Kumarappa'. Ever the stickler for correctness, in his early years of public life, Kumarappa diligently wrote to newspaper editors who had conferred the undeserved honour on him. Eventually he tired of this routine and 'left the sub-editors to their own devices'. In some time, Kumarappa received the foreword for his *Economy of Permanence*, this time with the degrees of 'Doctor of Divinity' and 'Doctor of Village Industries' bestowed upon him. While he took the joke, Kumarappa wrote back seeking Gandhi's permission to correct the reference to 'Dr Kumarappa' in the foreword and replace it by the more appropriate 'Prof. Kumarappa' by dint of his time spent at Gujarat Vidyapith. Gandhi refused to accept the change and was later challenged by Kumarappa on the Mahatma's arrogance in bestowing such degrees of his own making. Gandhi's jocular reply was that he could do so as the chancellor of the Gujarat Vidyapith.

Kumarappa had indeed proved his mettle as a constructive worker with an unparalleled understanding of the economic needs of the Indian village. But that insight and knowledge only meant that he would spend the rest of his life fighting a rearguard battle against the ideology of rapid industrialization that had little room in it for either the village or the villager.

[83] M. K. Gandhi, Foreword to *Economy of Permanence*, 20 August 1945, *CWMG*.

[84] J. C. Kumarappa, 'The Chancellor of Gujarat Vidyapith', in *Reminiscences of Gandhiji*, edited by Chandrashanker Shukla (Bombay: Vora and Co., 1951), p. 162.

11   The Spirit of Jesus

As was common among many nationalists of his time, Kumarappa's life was profoundly shaped by his spiritual beliefs without being burdened by theological dogma. His views on religion can be classified into two distinct phases. During the Civil Disobedience campaign, Kumarappa presented a critical attitude towards the organized Christianity of the Church and missionary activity. In the years that followed, he made a novel attempt to return to the original fount of the teachings of Jesus and apply them to contemporary questions.[1] Although he had begun questioning the nature of the Church during his time in England, in Bombay, Kumarappa remained an active member of his church. Thus, prior to his departure for the United States in 1927, Kumarappa was recommended as having a 'Christian character ... without reproach' and 'as a brother beloved and true yoke-fellow in the Gospel'.[2] However, during his time in Columbia, one can discern a significant change in his attitude.[3]

[1] J. C. Kumarappa, *Christianity: Its Economy and Way of Life* (henceforth *CEWL*), Preface (Ahmedabad: Navajivan Publishing House, 1945), p. iv.
[2] Letter of recommendation from William Carey, Missionary of the Baptist Missionary Society, 21 March 1927, Subject File, 1, Kumarappa Papers.
[3] This is evident from the notes he took during this period. For instance see the notes he took for a lecture delivered on women in India in 1928, Subject File, 4,

By the time he entered prison a few years later, Kumarappa's personal attitude to religion had been completely transformed.

Kumarappa's Christianity appeared in the public view during the Civil Disobedience campaign of 1930–1. His writings in *Young India* were filled with biblical quotations and allusions used to substantiate his position. Like many kindred spirits, he perceived the nationalist struggle in moral terms. But the choice of biblical terms was not one of personal proclivity alone. Rather, it was a response to the decidedly Christian vocabulary used by British opponents of Civil Disobedience. For many Englishmen, rallying under the banner of Christianity and fighting for the interests of Britain were the same and 'there was nothing new in considering the Viceroy as the representative of a Christian Empire'.[4] This was particularly true in the case of Viceroy Irwin, and the British made much of his devout Catholicism. In administering India, Irwin had emphasized his duties as a Christian. Nevertheless, as an astute observer remarked, 'the Viceroy in him had triumphed over the Christian'.[5]

As a rare Indian Christian in Gandhi's fold, Kumarappa was acutely aware of a burden of representation. Prior to the Matar Survey, some Christian friends tried to dissuade him from helping the 'heathen'. However, as the Christian life 'of his friends was not particularly elevating', Kumarappa did not share their revulsion towards the 'heathen' Mahatma.[6] During the Civil Disobedience movement, the government had unleashed severe violence on peaceful satyagrahis. Angered by such brutality, Kumarappa expected fellow Christians to remonstrate against the government's easy recourse to violence. However, the churches and many clergy openly supported the Raj. To Kumarappa's mind, this was an unpardonable act on part of those who were expected to do the most to uphold the values and ideals that Jesus represented. Nevertheless, his early writings on this matter demonstrated a rather uncharacteristic forbearance and Gandhian tolerance. In discussing police brutalities, Kumarappa called for the salve of love in

---

Kumarappa Papers. It is pertinent to note that it is around this time that his eldest brother published an essay which seems to have made a deep impression on Kumarappa. See J. J. Cornelius, 'An Oriental Looks at Christian Missions', *Harper's Monthly Magazine*, vol. 154, no. 3 (1927): 598–606.

[4] G. Studdert-Kennedy, *British Christians, Indian Nationalists and the Raj* (New Delhi: Oxford India Paperbacks, 1999), p. 162.

[5] D. F. Karaka, *Out of Dust* (Bombay: Thacker and Co. Ltd., 1940), p. 218.

[6] J. C. Kumarappa, Preface to *PPJ*, p. x.

response and titled his essay 'Father Forgive Them'.[7] During this period of political turmoil, the Archbishop of Canterbury issued a 'request for prayers for divine guidance for the Viceroy and all having responsibilities of rule and wielding public influence in India'.[8] While aware of the imputation here that the British in India were going through a period of trial, Kumarappa turned this appeal around and applied it to his fellow satyagrahis. For prayer to have meaning, he argued that it should be accompanied by a deep faith in God, 'ourselves and above all faith in our cause' and the requisite effort to 'translate our prayer into action'. However, once he realized the scale of brutality at places such as Dharasana and Peshawar, Kumarappa's dam of restraint broke. He launched a scathing attack on the position of missionaries and their avowed 'neutrality'.

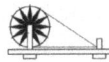

The spread of missionary activity in alliance with Western imperialism made Christianity suspect in the eyes of the majority of Indians. Indeed, 'the East has come to think of Christianity as part of the political game of the West'.[9] While most missionaries were at best indifferent to the nationalist cause, the few who wished to follow their conscience had a serious problem on hand. Church missions coming into India were allowed in on the sufferance of the colonial regime. Moreover, American missions had to sign an agreement that 'all due obedience and respect should be given to the lawfully constituted Government' and 'while carefully abstaining from political affairs', its missionaries would provide 'loyal co-operation with the Government'.[10] While under normal circumstances the relationship between the missions and the government was amicable and the former even received government monies for their work, the British were seldom shy in enforcing their own ideas on the neutrality of the missions. This arrangement came to be sorely tested during the Civil Disobedience campaign.

[7] J. C. Kumarappa, 'Father Forgive Them', *Young India*, 15 May 1930.

[8] J. C. Kumarappa, 'Lord in Mercy Hear Us', *Young India*, 22 May 1930.

[9] J. J. Cornelius, 'An Oriental Looks at Christian Missions'.

[10] Agreement between British Government and Foreign Missions Conference of North America quoted in J. J. Cornelius, 'An Oriental Looks at Christian Missions'.

As we have seen earlier, Reginald Reynolds had found it difficult to work at *Young India* and he decided to head back to England. En route to catching his ship in Colombo, Reynolds was entertained in Madurai by the American missionary, Ralph Richard Keithahn. For this 'political' act, Keithahn was packed off home by his mission even though the government had not demanded it.[11] This was particularly egregious since Reynolds 'was staying with Englishmen and English officials along the way'.[12] With this victory over an acquiescent mission, attempts were also made to threaten the English priest Verrier Elwin who was also a host to Reynolds.[13] Elwin's Ashram survived this crisis and in a few years Keithahn himself returned to work in India and became a close friend of Kumarappa.

In June 1930, the National Christian Council of India, Burma, and Ceylon issued a suggestion for a day of prayer for India. As in the case of the call for prayer from Canterbury, Kumarappa converted this thinly veiled sectarian appeal into a righteous call and endorsed it to his fellow satyagrahis who in their struggle 'have to wait in prayer constantly to obtain guidance and power'.[14] Kumarappa criticized the continued indifference of missionaries towards the suffering of non-violent protesters and challenged them to go beyond the futile repetition of 'beautiful words on bended knee, with firmly closed eyes and uplifted hands'. Pointing to the incongruity of the clergy picnicking at various waterfalls and 'spending a life of ease and pleasure at the Hill stations while our brethren are being done to death on the plains', he challenged them to come to the aid 'of all our brethren in distress'.[15]

Two months earlier, Kumarappa had written a pamphlet titled *An Appeal to All Christian Workers and Missionaries* and sent it to some 150 Christian leaders and missions.[16] In a historically accurate judgement,

[11] Reynolds, *A Quest for Gandhi*, pp. 78–80.

[12] 'Dr. Keithahn on Mission Work in India', *Indian Social Reformer*, 23 August 1930.

[13] Letter from Verrier Elwin to J. C. Kumarappa, 26 June 1930. Correspondence Files, Kumarappa Papers.

[14] J. C. Kumarappa, 'A Day of Prayer', *Young India*, 19 June 1930.

[15] Based on the references to various waterfalls, the hill station Kumarappa was alluding to was Kodaikanal, a base for many missions active in south India. As an affluent professional, Kumarappa himself used to holiday there and was familiar with both the terrain and its residents.

[16] Appeal dated 17 April 1930, reproduced in *Young India*, 26 June 1930. The count of 150 copies is from Kumarappa's letter to Verrier Elwin, 5 July 1930, Correspondence Files, Kumarappa Papers.

Kumarappa argued that the political situation was one of the greatest crises 'in India's long history' which would 'leave its mark not only on India but on humanity itself'. Gandhi had given the lead to the quest for the 'moral equivalent of warfare' and Kumarappa earnestly desired that fellow Christians would stand on the side of righteousness in this struggle. For those who 'profess to follow the Prince of Peace', this was both a moment of 'great responsibility' and 'an opportunity ... the like of which Christendom has never faced before'. Although quite aware that there were many Christians who had honest political differences with the freedom fighters, Kumarappa argued that there could be 'no difference of opinion regarding non-violence'. He hoped that despite their differing political positions, Christians would appeal to 'the Government to use humane methods' in dealing with the Civil Disobedience campaign.

Although Kumarappa's appeal fell on deaf ears, it elicited a controversial response from Foss Westcott, a man with the formidable title of Lord Bishop of Calcutta and Metropolitan of India. Enclosing a copy of his appeal, Kumarappa wrote an additional note to Westcott who as the head of the Anglican Church in India was a man of importance. Couched in an unusually respectful, almost deferential tone, Kumarappa pointed out to Westcott that it was a poor reflection of Christian values that the British Government 'should perpetuate such atrocities' which 'will do incalculable damage to the cause of the Christian Church in India'.[17] For Christians, non-violence was not a policy matter but a basic tenet that made it 'incumbent on the Church ... to propagate the principle' and desired 'a definite lead' from Westcott.

Westcott was himself an admirer of Gandhi's social agenda and was much moved as a witness to the Mahatma's 1924 fast for Hindu–Muslim unity in Delhi.[18] In his reply to Kumarappa, Westcott argued that he gave Gandhi 'whole-hearted support' in social reform since in this realm, Gandhi seemed 'to truly follow in the footsteps of Jesus Christ'.[19] However, he did not appreciate it when Gandhi 'identified himself with

[17] Letter from J. C. Kumarappa to Foss Westcott, 19 April 1930, reproduced in Young India, 26 June 1930.

[18] Foss Westcott, 'Gandhi's Fast for Hindu–Muslim Unity', in Mahatma Gandhi: Essays and Reflections on His Life and Work, edited by S. Radhakrishnan, second enlarged edition (London: George Allen and Unwin Ltd., 1949), pp. 310–13.

[19] Letter from Foss Westcott to J. C. Kumarappa, 24 April 1930, reproduced in Young India, 26 June 1930.

192 / The Web of Freedom

the political aspirations of the Nationalists'. Westcott argued that there was such a thing as Natural Law that was 'absolutely fixed and reliable' upon which depended the order of the universe. In other words, the civil disobedience challenge to the rule of the British was tantamount to violating the ordering of the universe established by God himself. Citing Jesus who asked that we 'render unto Caesar the things that are Caesar's', Westcott accused the satyagrahis of grave misconduct since they availed themselves of the safety and 'all the services' that a stable government provided, while thinking that one could 'at liberty violate its laws with impunity'. From this astonishing assertion, Westcott went on to decry Kumarappa's claim that 'the example of Jesus Christ gives any warrant for the practice of civil disobedience'.

Much surprised by the Bishop reading him 'a homily on civil disobedience', Kumarappa sent back a devastating reply.[20] He had not once mentioned civil disobedience in his letter and had not asked that Westcott 'support Gandhiji in his political campaign'. Rather he wanted Westcott to urge the use of non-violent means instead of the 'inhumane methods used by the Government'. The failure of the clergy to record their protest against such brutalities was 'tantamount to a denial of our Lord'. Although a layman, Kumarappa had a sound grasp of Christian doctrine and proceeded to demolish Westcott's 'misapplication of scripture incidents and partial quotations'. Westcott had quoted the scriptures to suggest that Jesus had urged his disciples to obey the Scribes and Pharisees. Kumarappa resented this 'partial quotation calculated to misinterpret Jesus' and went on to argue that Jesus had urged an obedience to 'a higher moral law' and not 'blind obedience' as evidenced by the rest of the chapter Westcott had quoted from. If Westcott's reasoning here was mangled, he was even more 'terribly confused' about the distinction between Natural Law and man-made ones. Unlike obedience to the higher law, Kumarappa argued that 'man-made laws are only rules laid down for the regulation of society' and need to be overturned when they were 'totally immoral or anti-social'. In his letter, Kumarappa deliberately used the salutation of 'Brother' and signed off 'Yours Fraternally'. By addressing the Metropolitan as a fellow brother, Kumarappa was insisting on his right as a conscientious Christian to meaningfully interpret the New Testament. He was also indirectly challenging the racial distinction that the missionaries maintained in their minds.

---

[20] Letter from J. C. Kumarappa to Foss Westcott, 2 May 1930, reproduced in *Young India*, 26 June 1930.

Kumarappa's original letter was a timely intervention as many Indian Christian youth were chafing at the limits placed on them by their respective churches. The Church tried to undermine the intellectual and emotional appeal of Kumarappa's argument. Westcott's response was reproduced in various diocesan magazines and his arguments were repeated in his Bishop's Letter in the *Calcutta Diocesan Record*.[21] But the Church chose to only publish the Bishop's letter and did not provide its readers with either Kumarappa's original appeal or his response to the Bishop's letter. This partial representation of the issue in the organ of the Church upset some priests like Verrier Elwin and those of the Christakula Ashram in Tirupattur whose residents endeavoured to identify themselves with the people of India. They urged Kumarappa to publish the entire correspondence in *Young India* in the interest of truth. The entire episode deeply wounded Kumarappa's sense of justice as the Church's attempts to mislead were an 'offence against all that is held sacred in human relationship'.[22] In his *Mandalay*, Rudyard Kipling had written of the desire of the Englishman to be 'East of Suez ... where there ain't no Ten Commandments'. Now, Kumarappa wondered if this also applied to the Bishops.

During this entire period, Kumarappa had carried out a mutually appreciative correspondence with the soon-to-be-renegade Christian missionary, Verrier Elwin. As someone who was himself threatened with deportation for his sympathies for the satyagrahis, Elwin recognized the constraints under which missionaries operated in India. Many were responsible for running hospitals and other charities and dared not run afoul of the government. Elwin agreed that 'a missionary today in India must witness to the Truth' but pointed out that many missionaries 'imagine Civil Disobedience to be forbidden by the Bible'.[23] Kumarappa retorted that this was not 'a Christian attitude' and gave the example of his own *Young India* which was willing to forfeit its expensive printing press rather than accept the limits placed

[21] Studdert-Kennedy, *British Christians, Indian Nationalists and the Raj*, p. 160.

[22] J. C. Kumarappa, 'When Angels Are Accursed', *Young India*, 26 June 1930.

[23] Letter from Verrier Elwin to J. C. Kumarappa, 7 July 1930, Correspondence Files, Kumarappa Papers. To counter this view and also answer the Metropolitan, Elwin wrote a pamphlet titled *Christ and Satyagraha* in which he laid out the conditions under which Civil Disobedience was acceptable to Christians.

on it by the government.[24] By the time Kumarappa was released from prison in March 1931, the role of missionaries in India had again become a subject of controversy. This time the initiative was taken by Manilal Parekh, a Gujarati Jain who had converted to the Anglican Church and had eventually become an independent evangelist.[25] Elwin edited the journal, *Christa Seva Sangh Review*, and having received an essay by Parekh on his conception of an 'ideal missionary', Elwin sought an article on similar lines from Kumarappa. The result was a renewed controversy, this time a private one between Kumarappa and Elwin.

Kumarappa's essay on 'Christian Ideals in a Free India' was already looking to an India that was to be rid of colonial domination and find its own bearings and be 'free to express her indigenous culture'.[26] Such an India, Kumarappa argued, 'will honour Christ and will receive Him with open arms'. This acceptance would be of 'the purest form of Christianity—the way Jesus lived'. In such a conception of religion there was no place for a Church since 'Christ never founded a church' like the 'one that masquerades under his name'. Kumarappa's position here was a radical one and obviously controversial. Rejecting both the significance of the Church and its claim of absolute revealed truth for Christianity over other religions, Kumarappa was opening up space for a far more syncretic approach towards spirituality.

Kumarappa argued that 'all true communion between God and man must be purely personal' and that 'neither in the rituals of one faith nor in the blind beliefs of another can we realize God'. People could work out their spiritual salvation only 'with the greatest sympathy and understanding' for each other. While the principle enunciated here was a general one for a society with many faiths, Kumarappa's specific targets were the rites of Baptism and the Holy Communion. The bread and wine used in the Communion to symbolize the flesh and blood of Jesus scandalized many Indians. Since 'the highest form of religion can offend nobody', Kumarappa argued against the continuation of such practices in a culture that found its symbolism abhorrent. For him, wearing khadi was 'nearer an observance of the spirit of Christ than partaking' in such sacraments. Elwin desired to omit

[24] Letter from J. C. Kumarappa to Verrier Elwin, 5 July 1930, Correspondence Files, Kumarappa Papers.

[25] 'Biographical Notes' in *An Indian Approach to India*, edited by Milton Stauffer (New York: Mission Education Movement of the United States and Canada, 1927), p. vii.

[26] J. C. Kumarappa, 'Christian Ideals in a Free India', May 1931, Speeches and Writings, 10, Kumarappa Papers.

the offending paragraph from Kumarappa's essay and publish the rest. This request was met with stubborn resistance from Kumarappa who refused to have the reference to the Sacraments removed and instead suggested that Elwin answer it elsewhere in the journal. Elwin refused to accept this proposition since the Mass was both intimate and holy to the Catholics. Moreover, Kumarappa levelled the accusation that Elwin was succumbing to the sentiments of his own Church. Elwin who was engaging Kumarappa with a true spirit of brotherhood termed this criticism as 'ill-informed, ill-mannered and abusive'.[27]

Kumarappa's denunciation of the rituals of the Catholic Church should not be misunderstood as the sectarian view of a Protestant. Ever the iconoclast, Kumarappa had no use for ritual practices if they were an impediment to brotherhood amongst people drawn from different communities. Although he was confirmed at the age of sixteen, Kumarappa had refused to participate in the Mass and disregarded his 'mother's entreaties' even as a boy.[28] Kumarappa was deeply upset with the indifference of his fellow Christians to the larger Indian predicament. Elwin's reticence in the matter of the Sacraments, he reckoned, was akin to preventing writing on birth control and sex lest it offend the 'susceptibilities of some old maid'.[29] Besides, he argued, while the Christians were sensitive in such matters, their churches were unconcerned with 'the sentiments of Hindus and Muslims'. The episode revealed a trait of Kumarappa that was both a strength and a weakness. Although his anger against the Church was justified, a quarrel with Elwin was unwarranted. Indeed, Elwin had been one of the few genuine advocates for India from within Western Christianity and did not deserve to be dragged into a controversy of this nature. In any event, to resolve the deadlock, Kumarappa made a proposal that was likely to be most agreeable to both parties. He wanted both of them to submit the entire matter to Gandhi for adjudication. Gandhi was in prison at this time and we do not know if he conjured up a resolution to this vexed dispute.

Kumarappa's alienation from institutional forms of religion had begun as early as his time in England. During his six years in London, he had

[27] Letter from Verrier Elwin to J. C. Kumarappa, 21 April 1931, S. N. 17054.
[28] Letter from J. C. Kumarappa to Mahatma Gandhi, 6 May 1931, S. N. 17044.
[29] Letter from J. C. Kumarappa to Verrier Elwin, 25 April 1931, S. N. 17055.

regularly attended 'all kinds of denominational services' during the period of the First World War.[30] He was offended by the singing of the hymn 'God Save the King' which was unchristian for its 'tribal appeals to destroy the enemy'.[31] Even worse, 'every pulpit [was] converted into a recruitment platform' during the First World War.[32] To Kumarappa's mind, the War had 'reduced to ashes all claims of universality of the Christian Church and brought down Christianity to the form of pure nationalism'.[33] In its pursuit of power, instead of owing allegiance to 'its lawful Master', Jesus Christ, the Church 'had become the mistress of the State' and supported 'it in all its exploits of violence and greed'.[34] Thus disillusioned, Kumarappa and his brothers came to share a belief that it was time to 'renounce our Christianity and follow Christ'.[35] Strikingly, for the rest of his life, Kumarappa lived by this personal conviction.

As with his dislike of the attitude of the Church and missionaries in India, Kumarappa was unhappy with the social and cultural separation of Indian Christians from mainstream Indian life.[36] Indeed, Indianizing his family name and arriving at the Gujarat Vidyapith robed in khadi were part of a deliberate exercise in overcoming this separation. Although the most visible Indian Christian nationalist in the early 1930s, Kumarappa was not alone in such sympathies. During this period, and certainly influenced by his example, many young Indian Christians had come to recognize that 'the Christian evangel could not function normally in India until it is rescued from the ecclesiastical overgrowth that has come from the West and is adapted to the great religious heritage of this ancient land of religions'.[37] These attempts to forsake European forms and ceremonies as inessential

[30] J. C. Kumarappa, 'On Churchianity', Letter to the Editor in *Hindustan Times*, 28 January 1936, Press Clippings, Kumarappa Papers.

[31] J. C. Kumarappa, *PPJ*, p. viii.

[32] J. C. Kumarappa, *CEWL*, p. 48.

[33] J. C. Kumarappa, Review of Vergilius Ferm (ed.), *Religion in Transition*, 1937, Speeches and Writings, 1, Kumarappa Papers.

[34] J. C. Kumarappa, 'Who Are My Brethren?', *Indian Social Reformer*, 27 December 1930.

[35] J. J. Cornelius, 'An Oriental Looks at Christian Missions'.

[36] J. C. Kumarappa, 'What Lack I?', n.d., Speeches and Writings, 10, Kumarappa Papers.

[37] Preface to G. V. Job, P. Chenchiah, V. Chakkarai, D. M. Devasahayam, S. Jesudasen, Eddy Asirvatham, and A. N. Sudarisanam, *Rethinking Christianity in India* (Madras: A. N. Sudarisanam, 1939).

to the belief and practice of Christianity were a serious challenge to the Church. However, there was an even greater challenge posed to institutional Christianity in India—the life of Mahatma Gandhi. Since his years in South Africa, many Christians recognized the greatness of Gandhi and attempts were made to convert him to Christianity. While Gandhi had gained immensely from the life and teachings of Jesus, in the ultimate analysis, he rejected the claim of Christianity as the sole path to truth and salvation. While this was a serious enough challenge to the dogma of the Church, some even went to the extent of arguing that 'a true Christian in India today must necessarily be a Gandhian' since the Mahatma was 'giving a practical demonstration of the applicability of the teachings of Jesus'.[38]

Kumarappa rejected the perception that Christ's teachings were to be limited to personal relationships and admired 'Gandhiji for revealing the all-pervading quality of religion and infusing spiritual life into the dry bones of politics'.[39] However, the radical, and dare we say, liberative nature of Kumarappa's views on the value and purpose of religion is strikingly visible on the vexed question of conversion. If in contemporary times, the debate on conversion is framed in terms of minority rights, during the colonial era it was inexorably tied to the critique of Empire. Although, he did not 'wish to belittle the services rendered by missions' in India and acknowledged their 'yeoman service in the past', Kumarappa did not accept the Church's definition of Christian faith.[40] In particular, he refuted the view that to be a 'brethren of Christ' it was necessary to be a member of a Church. While the ancient religions of Judaism and Hinduism called for elaborate ceremonies and rituals to provide order to the daily lives of the faithful, Kumarappa argued that Christianity did not fall under such a definition of religion. Consequently, 'while a person

[38] S. K. George, *Gandhi's Challenge to Christianity* (Ahmedabad: Navajivan Publishing House, 1947), p. x. While a tutor at the Bishop's College in Calcutta, George wrote to Westcott supporting Kumarappa's position in the Kumarappa–Westcott controversy. Eventually, owing to his nationalist leanings, George had to resign his position at the college and endured a life of much personal agony and material privation.

[39] J. C. Kumarappa, 'The Enemy: Ours and Theirs', *Young India*, 26 June 1930.

[40] J. C. Kumarappa, 'Who Are My Brethren?', part II of a talk published in *Indian Social Reformer*, 3 January 1931, Speeches and Writings, 4, Kumarappa Papers.

may be a good Hindu he may yet owe allegiance to Jesus' and 'as long as there is nothing repugnant in one religion to the tenets of another there is no cause for conversion'.[41]

Conversion was, and remains, a matter of serious contention in India. A key critique of Hinduism by the Church was the treatment of untouchables. The proponents of conversion held that the 'inequality of opportunity' would only be overcome by accepting 'the Christian teaching of the Divine Will of the Father'.[42] In reply, Kumarappa argued that 'denial of equality of opportunity [was] largely due to man-made institutions'. If a religion was 'to be judged by the conduct of its followers', Kumarappa asked, 'why not also Christianity for the grasping greed and blood thirstiness of Europe?' While indeed the caste system was evil, the solution did not lie in the act of conversion.[43] In a most damning indictment, Kumarappa argued that conversion 'is only a mode of increasing the adherents of an institutional religion called Christianity of which Jesus was neither the founder nor a member'.[44] Rather, the only meaningful conversion is 'to a field of service and not to any man-made fold'. Here, Kumarappa's position is similar to that of Gandhi who was opposed to conversion from one faith to another. Gandhi held that every religion had both a sound ethical doctrine and an encrustation of dogma and hypocrisy. One could accept and assimilate all that is of value from other faiths without any violence to one's own religion of birth. This was the reason for Gandhi's refusal to allow others who wished to leave their Christian faith to become Hindu.[45]

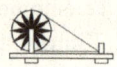

His sharp and biting criticism of the Church had angered many and consequently there have been no serious attempts to grapple with

[41] 'Methods of Missionaries Have No Sanction of Jesus', *Bombay Chronicle*, n.d., Press Clippings, Kumarappa Papers.

[42] Basil Mathews quoted in Kumarappa's review of *The Church Takes Root in India*, Speeches and Writings, 1, Kumarappa Papers.

[43] Kumarappa's review of *Christ and Communism* by E. Stanley Jones, Speeches and Writings, 1, Kumarappa Papers.

[44] J. C. Kumarappa, *CEWL*, p. 52.

[45] See comments of Verrier Elwin in Francis Watson (Script and Narration), *Talking of Gandhiji* (Bombay: Bharatiya Vidya Bhavan, 1965), p. 18.

Kumarappa's Christianity.[46] But he also presented a creative interpretation of Christianity in the Indian context which is far more valuable. As a Gandhian expositor of Christian values, Kumarappa attempted to demonstrate a 'close accord' between Indian tradition and 'the mind of the great Teacher of Nazareth'.[47] Attuned to the Indian idea of all religions being paths to the same Godhead, Kumarappa argued that if Jesus 'spoke as though he were God himself ... Krishna [also] speaks in that way in the Gita'.[48] This did not imply that each made exclusive claims and there was 'room to construe their claim to be merely a media for the word of God'. To the extent that this interpretation views Jesus as a son of God, it was unexceptionable to the Church. However, Kumarappa sought to radically undermine the Christian claims of exclusivity by viewing Krishna as another corporeal manifestation of the *same* God. Rebuking fellow Christians for whom 'belief in Christ has almost become an obsession', Kumarappa argued that it was not through adherence to form and ritual, but 'we shall know the brethren of Christ by their Christ-like actions'.[49] Kumarappa put forth a radical proposition by arguing that 'even an atheist or an agnostic' would be owned up by Christ 'if they are sincere in their views and follow their conscience'. By living by their ideals, such people would be doing 'the will of the Father in Heaven'.

The similarities of their views should not lead us to believe that Kumarappa was merely following Gandhi's ideas on religion. As with his economic thought, Kumarappa had independently arrived at his spiritual ideas that concurred with those of Gandhi.[50] The independent evolution of Kumarappa's thinking is clearly visible in a brief exchange that he had with Gandhi on the role of vows in a person's spiritual life. While incarcerated

---

[46] An important exception is Solomon Victus, *Jesus and Mother Economy: An Introduction to the Theology of J. C. Kumarappa* (Delhi: ISPCK, 2007). Also see R. S. Sugirtharajah, 'The Satyagrahi and His Scriptures: J. C. Kumarappa and His Bible during the Indian Independence Struggle', *Journal of Commonwealth and Postcolonial Studies*, vol. 15, no. 1 (2008): 162–78.

[47] 'Indian Christian Nationalists to the Fore', *Indian Social Reformer*, 2 August 1930, Printed Matter, Kumarappa Papers.

[48] J. C. Kumarappa, 'Who Are My Brethren?', part II.

[49] The same view is obtained in the hymn *Vaishnava Jana To* that was much loved by Gandhi.

[50] Within a year of arriving in Ahmedabad, Kumarappa was giving public lectures wherein he demonstrated a mature view on the purpose of spirituality and religion.

at Yeravda Jail in 1930, Gandhi wrote a series of weekly letters addressed to the inmates of Sabarmati Ashram in Ahmedabad. The letters briefly examined the principal ashram observances and were translated from the original Gujarati into English for wider dissemination.[51] In one such weekly address dealing with the 'importance of vows' in one's life, Gandhi said that a 'vow means unflinching determination, and helps us against temptations'.[52] Kumarappa took exception to this proposition and argued that all individuals were not alike in their moral and spiritual capacities.[53] While vows did help by preventing a weak mind from lapsing into old ways, they also quickly degenerated into a habit and 'in time our moral sense gets palsied'. In fact, Kumarappa went on to blame the taking of 'vows and blind obedience to custom and authority' for a fair share of 'the present degeneration in our country'. Gandhi recognized the problem posed by Kumarappa and pointed out that the original term he had used was *vrata* (व्रत) which had a different set of connotations than the English translation of 'vows' implied. What Gandhi had in mind was not 'publicly administered' vows but 'a promise made to oneself'. While he agreed with Kumarappa's assessment, Gandhi argued that vows were a concession to reality since the 'strongest men have been known at times to have become weak'. Kumarappa's subsequent responses and comments are unavailable, but if Gandhi's subsequent letters are any indicator, it appears that Kumarappa remained unconvinced of the Mahatma's arguments.

By the time he emerged from Nasik Jail in 1933, Kumarappa had clearly formulated his economic philosophy and also consolidated his views on religious matters. From then on, there is an increasing convergence of Kumarappa's economic philosophy and his spiritual orientation. His rejection of centralized economic production finds its counterpart in a rejection of the Church as a centralized entity. Curiously, with his penchant

---

[51] The English translations were subsequently published as a collection titled *From Yeravda Mandir: Ashram Observances* (Ahmedabad: Navajivan Publishing House, 1945).

[52] M. K. Gandhi, *From Yeravda Mandir*, p. 49.

[53] 'The Importance of Vows: A Correspondence', Correspondence between J. C. Kumarappa and Mahatma Gandhi reproduced in *Gandhi Marg*, vol. 3, no. 2 (April 1959): 127–31.

for categorization, during the period when he was forming his ideas on 'types of economies in nature', Kumarappa also obtained a similarly graded classification of various religions. The religions of the past could be termed authoritarian, militant, ethnical, and social. While, despite their defects, such approaches have had their value in the past, Kumarappa now argued for an entirely personal approach to religion, that is, a 'pure religion' as he termed it. This was a radical form of decentralization whereby 'religion is the relation that governs a man's personal attitude to God, to his ideals, to his fellow-man, to society and to the world'.[54]

This argument was framed by Kumarappa in an address titled 'Religion of Jesus' that he delivered at a parliament of religions in 1936. The choice of the name of Jesus instead of Christ was a careful and deliberate distancing from the sociological origins of Christianity in a much older Judaic practice. By a rejection of both the Hebraic roots and European rituals, Kumarappa was opening up space for his notion of 'pure religion' which sat at the pinnacle of his classification. Interestingly, this typology closely mirrors Kumarappa's 'types of economies in nature'. In particular, if an 'economy of service' represented the teleological outcome of man's quest for economic salvation, his 'pure religion' represented 'a personal spiritual union with God and the world'. In other words, in the spiritual realm, Kumarappa was calling for an extreme form of decentralization with no reference to custom and ritual practice.

As a hermeneutic manoeuvre, such an approach achieved many objectives. By delinking the spiritual import of the teachings of Jesus from social and cultural encrustations, Kumarappa brought Christianity in greater alignment with the ethos of India's religions. While conversion to institutional Christianity was unnecessary, there ought to be no objection to the acceptance of the teachings of Jesus. However, if in the 'economy of service', sentient beings had a moral obligation towards others, it could be no different in Kumarappa's definition of 'pure religion'. It is for this reason that while he argues for individual communion with God, he also imposes an obligation towards fellow beings in the world.

Like Gandhi, Kumarappa was less interested in the historical fact of Jesus, a view that scandalized many connected with the church. As one reviewer disapprovingly noted, he 'does not seem to attach any significance to the Cross or the person of Christ'.[55] Rather, he was more concerned

[54] J. C. Kumarappa, *CEWL*, p. 58.

[55] M. P. Job, in review of J. C. Kumarappa, 'Religion of Jesus', *National Christian Council Review*, November 1937, pp. 607–8.

with the spirit that Jesus embodied and what it meant for humanity. As a consequence, along with rejecting the sociological practices of Christianity, Kumarappa also disputed the finality of the revelation of Jesus. Instead he opined that 'Jesus was no static force'.[56] Rather, 'his was a dynamic personality' and 'growth is its essence'. Consequently, Kumarappa argued that the spirit of the teachings of Jesus allowed for the incorporation of such ideas without being tied down by dogmatism. Thus, while Jesus extended love to encompass all human beings, the Buddha had extended it to cover 'all sentient creatures'. Kumarappa's use of the example of the Buddha here is one with the idea of immanence, that is, the view that the presence of the divine is manifest in the material world. However, in Kumarappa's writings the idea of immanence is not in terms of compassion alone, rather there is an insistent demand that one's meaning in life be realized in terms of service to others. In his early days as a nationalist, Tagore's poetic expression served to mirror Kumarappa's views:

Leave this chanting and singing and telling of beads!
Whom dost thou worship in this lonely dark corner of a temple with doors all shut?
Open thine eyes and see thy God is not before thee!

He is there where the tiller is tilling the hard ground and where the pathmaker is breaking stones.
He is with them in sun and in shower, and his garment is covered with dust.
Put off thy holy mantle and even like him come down on the dusty soil![57]

As a constructive worker, Kumarappa persistently emphasized the ideal of *karma yoga*—although he did not use the term itself—and sought to locate it in the teachings of Jesus. Indeed, in the thick of the Civil Disobedience campaign, Kumarappa was arguing in *Young India* that 'God has no hands and feet but ours'.[58] Thus, he urged the use of the dictum laid down by Jesus that 'whosoever shall do the will of my Father ... the same is my brother'.[59] On a different occasion, Jesus pointed out that 'I was hungered and ye gave me meat. Verily I say unto you, inasmuch as

---

[56] J. C. Kumarappa, *PPJ*, p. 37.

[57] Rabindranath Tagore, *Gitanjali* (New York: The Macmillan Company, 1914), pp. 8–9.

[58] J. C. Kumarappa, 'Father Forgive Them', *Young India*, 15 May 1930.

[59] Quoted in J. C. Kumarappa, 'India's Challenge to Christian Youth', *The Guardian*, 11 December 1941, Speeches and Writings, 4, Kumarappa Papers.

ye have done it unto one of the least of these my brethren ye have done it unto me'. For Kumarappa, this meant that when 'our land is full of the hungry, the thirsty, the down-trodden', the 'duties devolving' on Christian youth were clear. He urged others to view their lives as 'a consecrated sacrifice for the benefit of the needy ones'.[60]

The ethical teachings of major religions have shared in the promotion of the common good and defining a moral basis of 'right living'. In addition to these values, Kumarappa very creatively integrated the teachings of Jesus with some of the central themes of his economic philosophy. His writings on religion are shot through with the necessity of decentralized economic production and the dignity and meaning of work. Arguing that 'man does not live by bread alone', Kumarappa pointed to the 'other standards of value' that ought to determine one's approach to life.[61] Thus, when a disciple asked Jesus, 'Whence should we have so much bread in the wilderness, as to fill so great a multitude?', he might as well have been wondering about the Indian situation. The answer, of course, lay in Gandhi's 'blueprint of the work before us'. Alluding to John Ruskin's famed *Unto This Last*, Kumarappa drew attention to the two parables used therein. In the 'parable of the vineyard', all workers were paid the same wages at the end of the day thereby teaching us that 'man is not a machine which [merely] works'.[62] Thus, instead of dealing with 'labour as a commercial commodity ... we have to reconsider the fundamental basis of our relations'. The commandment to 'love thy neighbour as thyself' could be seen as a plea for a decentralized economy whereby we purchase goods produced by our neighbour rather than from a far-off source.

Owing to a sense of propriety, Kumarappa refrained from criticizing Hindu practices whereas he often rebuked his fellow Christians for their failings. However, just as he did not hesitate to criticize the caste system of Hindu society, he felt no restraint when promoting the village economy. Thus, after a tour of south India, he deplored the 'repairs and remodelling of temples' done using 'unsightly concrete pillars and corrugated iron sheets for roofs'.[63] Such measures 'reflected the decayed state to which we have fallen'. Not only were such modern works 'alien to the spirit' of the

[60] J. C. Kumarappa, 'What Lack I?', n.d., Speeches and Writings, 10, Kumarappa Papers.

[61] Quoted in J. C. Kumarappa, 'India's Challenge to Christian Youth'.

[62] J. C. Kumarappa, 'Economics of Sharing', *GUP*, May 1955.

[63] 'Remodelling of Temples: Dr Kumarappa's Criticism', *The Hindu*, 31 August 1938, Press Clippings, Kumarappa Papers.

temples, they also deprived local artisans of their work. In the past, such temple complexes 'supported local industries and gave employment to the people of the locality'. Indeed, 'the temples were the centres which radiated life to the people around'. By failing to provide meaningful work to the local craftsmen and workers, the temples were not fulfilling their role as institutions of cultural and moral worth. By tying up his economic ideals with religious principles, Kumarappa suggests 'a new orientation of religion where worship is brought into the open air of everyday life'.[64] Indeed, 'one of the misfortunes of our age has been the segregation of religion from the everyday business of life'.[65] It is particularly noteworthy that in his comments on temples, Kumarappa's emphasis is not on charity, a role traditionally associated with Hindu religious institutions. Rather, he shifts it to the right to work and just wages.

Kumarappa had wished to refute the argument that it was 'not feasible to put the teachings of Jesus' into practice in modern times.[66] While the pressures of work prevented him from doing so, his term in Jabalpur Jail during the Quit India movement presented an opportunity. Thus, in June 1944, he set down his views on the teachings of Jesus and their relevance to contemporary lives. He tied the eternal teachings of Jesus to contemporary moral imperatives by considering the meaning of the lines of the Lord's Prayer, the three temptations presented to Jesus, and a critical examination of the Commandments. This interpretive work was published in 1945 as *Practice and Precepts of Jesus* with a foreword by Gandhi, who saw it as 'a revolutionary view of Jesus' that was worthy of study by people of all religions.[67] Although it had a message beyond the confines of India, Kumarappa's work provided a sound basis of interpretation of the Bible for Indian Christians. While rejecting the dross of the old ways, he threw light on those aspects of Indian life 'which are imperishable and worthy of being treasured'.

---

[64] J. C. Kumarappa, 'Religion and Politics', Speeches and Writings, 9, Kumarappa Papers.

[65] J. C. Kumarappa, 'The Price of Righteousness', *Indian Social Reformer*, 26 July 1930, Speeches and Writings, 4, Kumarappa Papers.

[66] J. C. Kumarappa, *PPJ*, p. ix.

[67] M. K. Gandhi, 'A Word', in J. C. Kumarappa, *PPJ*, p. iv.

Having learnt his Christian literature at his 'mother's knee', Kumarappa had no pretensions to being 'a philosopher or a scholar in Christian theology'.[68] However, he hoped that his thoughts would offer a measure of psychological help to 'some wandering soul' who was similarly placed. Stating his 'canons of interpretation', Kumarappa explained that to understand the message of Jesus, it was necessary to remove 'all Jewish theological phraseology and subjective literary gloss' and ignore 'signs and miracles'.[69] Arguing against a literalist reading, he reasoned that in addition to the teachings of Jesus, one should depend 'on the guidance of the Spirit of Truth'.[70] For him, the teachings of Jesus were contained in the four gospels of Matthew, Mark, Luke, and John 'which form some of the most human documents'.

Kumarappa's choice of the book title was, for those with the eyes to see it, a deliberate and provocative reference to a major controversy in the history of Christianity in India. The man at the centre of this episode was a key figure of nineteenth-century India, Raja Rammohan Roy. In 1820, Roy published a volume of extracts from the gospels that he titled *Precepts of Jesus*. The approach and intent of the volume was simply to 'expunge the gospel records of their historical incidents, miracle stories and doctrinal references, herd together the moral teachings of Jesus and portray him as a great ethical teacher'.[71] Instead, *Precepts of Jesus* was drawn into a furious sectarian controversy between Trinitarians and Unitarian believers in England resulting in a bitter attack against Roy by some Baptists that took on racial overtones.[72] Although this controversy was more than a century old by the time Kumarappa wrote his own volume, his use of Roy's title is laden with symbolic significance. While distancing himself from the missionary view of Hinduism, Kumarappa was also signalling an allegiance to a historical and cultural lineage in India that began with Roy's critical examination of Christianity. This was an assertion that Jesus was a teacher with a universal message that could not be confined to adherents of a

[68] J. C. Kumarappa, 'Preface', *PPJ*, p. vi. Kumarappa dedicated this book to his mother.

[69] J. C. Kumarappa, *PPJ*, p. 1.

[70] J. C. Kumarappa, 'Preface', *PPJ*, p. xi.

[71] R. S. Sugirtharajah, *The Bible and Empire: Postcolonial Explorations* (Cambridge: Cambridge University Press, 2005), p. 4.

[72] For a discussion of the nature of this controversy, see Lynn Zastoupil, *Rammohun Roy and the Making of Victorian Britain* (New York: Palgrave Macmillan, 2010).

Church with Western origins.[73] However, whereas Rammohan Roy was primarily concerned with excavating the Vedanta-like spiritual unity of the teachings of Jesus, as a Gandhian constructive worker, Kumarappa had other objectives in mind. An advocate of a life of service to one's fellow beings, Kumarappa wished to derive a moral basis for daily living from the spiritually laden teachings of Jesus. Hence the considered title *Practice and Precepts of Jesus*.

A principal objective of *Practice and Precepts of Jesus* was to establish the moral and spiritual sovereignty of each individual. In his reply to Kumarappa in 1930, Bishop Westcott had argued for the ideal of an obedient citizen of the state and upheld Paul as an exemplar. Now, Kumarappa felt it necessary to undermine such an 'upholder of Empire' and Paul comes in for much criticism for being influenced by 'the Aristotelian doctrine of the subordination of the individual to the State'.[74] However, despite the value the Church placed on Paul's example, for Kumarappa, Paul was no guide as his view was 'repugnant to Jesus' teaching of the freedom or sovereignty of the individual personality of the child of God'. Rather, the life of Jesus was a fight against authoritarian rule and 'a heroic attempt to assert the divinity of man and the absolute supremacy of the Spirit of Truth'.[75] A key insight introduced here is the enlargement of the precepts of Jesus to now encompass the idea of Truth itself. In other words, Kumarappa was arguing for the supreme value of one's own conscience that makes an individual answerable not to the punitive punishment of man-made laws but that of a higher, moral law. Indeed, one could argue that *Practice and Precepts* and *Economy of Permanence* are texts that respectively consider the spiritual and material implications of obedience to a higher moral law in our lives. This is no coincidence since Kumarappa wrote both the texts at the same time in Jabalpur Jail and indeed the ideas in the two works are often interpenetrated. Kumarappa did recognize that sometimes it becomes difficult to distinguish between a man-made law and a divine one. In such instances, he argued that 'the Spirit of Truth, our Comforter and Teacher, is the only reliable Guide at such times'.[76] This means of reckoning is strikingly similar to the

---

[73] Indeed, as Gandhi opined in his foreword, Kumarappa wrote with a 'confidence born of a living faith in the belief that the West, though nominally Christian, has not known the true Jesus of the Gospels'.

[74] J. C. Kumarappa, *PPJ*, p. 104.

[75] J. C. Kumarappa, *PPJ*, p. 107.

[76] J. C. Kumarappa, *PPJ*, p. 97. The influence of Gandhi's 'inner voice' as well as his definition of 'Truth is God' are quite evident in this argument.

'standard of value' proposed in the *Economy of Permanence*.[77] The way to achieve this sense of objectivity is to 'only strive to do the will of the Father and carry out our duties without reference to any rewards'.[78]

A substantial portion of *Practice and Precepts* is given over to a careful consideration of the familiar Lord's Prayer.[79] Whereas Kumarappa's exegesis considers at length each line of the Prayer, the imprint of the Gandhian primacy given to the dignity of human life and labour is evident. Thus in consideration of the line 'Give us today our bread for the morrow', Kumarappa deploys a variety of interpretive strategies to claim that this was not meant to be a mere supplication for food. Instead, the nutritive value of the bread when assimilated into our bodies was meant to signify the 'bread of life', that is, a complete assimilation of the teachings of Jesus. A similar understanding is obtained when considering the temptation presented to Jesus to satisfy his hunger by converting stones to bread. This Jesus refused and remarked: 'Man shall not live by bread alone, but by every word that proceedeth out of the mouth of God.'[80] For Kumarappa this signified that human beings ought not to live a 'narrow, self-centered' existence by choosing a well-paying career and satisfy their own personal hunger for material possessions.[81] Such lives ultimately bind down human beings by taking away their moral autonomy and converting them into 'well-provided pet dogs'.[82] Rather, the salvation of the individual lay in selfless service to suffering humanity with both dignity and humility. This was a hard challenge, 'The Acid Test' that determined those who were true followers of Jesus.

Perhaps surprisingly, the first edition of *Practice and Precepts* sold out quickly and Kumarappa noted with a hint of satisfaction that 'even orthodox Christians have welcomed it' and 'most of the reviews were appreciative'.[83] He ascribed the success of his book to the terrible ravages of the Second World War that was fought between Christian nations, prodding many to revisit their faith. However, his reputation as a fierce critic of the Church

---

[77] J. C. Kumarappa, *EOP*, p. 36. See p. 91 for the definition.

[78] J. C. Kumarappa, *PPJ*, p. 19. This is nothing but the central message of the *Gita*.

[79] The Lord's Prayer is a key prayer in Christianity and is recognizable from its beginning: 'Our Father in Heaven/hallowed be your name ...'.

[80] J. C. Kumarappa, *PPJ*, p. 59.

[81] J. C. Kumarappa, *PPJ*, p. 61.

[82] J. C. Kumarappa, *PPJ*, p. 62.

[83] J. C. Kumarappa, Preface to the Reprint of *PPJ*, p. xiii.

prevented many Christians from owning him as one of their community. In fact, there were some occasions when he was flatly denied access to churches. Soon after Independence Kumarappa was thought to harbour leftist sympathies, a no-go subject with the Church of that era.[84]

Apart from reinforcing our views on his personality, Kumarappa's Christianity is also a measure of the nature and influence of Christianity in the late colonial period in India. If Rammohan Roy's attempt at a moral view of Jesus met with fierce criticism from the doctrinal Church, a century later Kumarappa was fearlessly and openly denouncing officialdom and practices of the Church. Although he was amongst a few such critics, his move away from institutional Christianity represents the emergence of independent and critical thinking within Indian Christians. Not only was he able to debate the likes of Westcott on an equal footing, he also broke new ground with his interpretation of Christianity. In this matter, Kumarappa's writings and speeches on the teachings of Jesus are akin to Gandhi's views on the *Gita*. Although their approaches to these texts were humble, thoughtful, and respectful, neither gave way to dogmatic acceptance. Both were at home in their cultures and lived experience, and spoke with the authority that came with such rootedness. Moreover, each precept and moral dictum was thoroughly tested on the anvil of reason before being accepted. At all times, the Spirit of Truth, that is, satya as seen by one's conscience, was the moral compass with which to navigate through the difficult waters of human life.

At the same time, the acceptance of the teachings of Jesus would mean nothing without them being brought into action in one's own life. This demanded that people 'consecrate' their lives in service to others and devote themselves to tackling the urgent demands of contemporary problems and crises. Around the time the AIVIA was founded, Gandhi had said with reference to the Buddha, that 'if I had the good fortune to be face to face with one like him, I should not hesitate to ask him why he did not teach the gospel of work, in preference to one of contemplation'.[85] One suspects Kumarappa might have done likewise.

---

[84] During a trip to Vienna, he noted that the highlight was meeting Hewlett Johnson, the so-called 'Red Dean' of Canterbury who provoked much criticism for his sympathetic view of the Communist nations. See 'Kumarappaji in Vienna', *GUP*, January 1953.

[85] M. K. Gandhi, 'A Talk', *Harijan*, 2 November 1935.

12   The Light of Science

The value of Kumarappa's work lies in his ability to present an economic philosophy while working to improve village industries. Right at the inception of the AIVIA, Kumarappa was clear that while 'the industries that had long sustained millions' were languishing, if India 'was to progress economically and culturally it was imperative that the villages had to become centres of activity'.[1] If the villager had to have social and economic autonomy, the villages had to be made 'self-dependent, self-supporting and self-respecting'. An important, and often forgotten, aspect of this understanding was the emphasis that both Gandhi and Kumarappa laid on adapting and modifying the village economy 'to meet the present-day needs'. Kumarappa repeatedly emphasized that the entire effort of the AIVIA was 'to bring science and progress into the stagnant pools that are called "villages" today'.[2] The AIVIA intended to assemble and disseminate reliable and scientifically validated information on all aspects of village-based production as well as carry out research work on its own. But if science was to be brought to bear on the problems of the villages, the association needed trained workers. In a lament that is strikingly contemporary, Kumarappa pointed out that capable individuals

[1] *AIVIA Annual Report*, 1935, p. 1.
[2] J. C. Kumarappa, 'Scared of the Machine?', *GUP*, October 1949.

'end up in town in search of secure employment' and 'the artistically inclined deserted the indigenous art'. The cumulative impact of this process for many decades has only 'brought ruin and distress to our country-side'. Sapped of skill, energy and hope, the villagers had neither 'the enterprise … nor the resources to carry out experiments' towards improving their methods of production.[3]

The crux of the problem, as Kumarappa saw it, was the 'dearth of intelligent and venturesome persons' who would 'study the needs of the people and by *intensive experiment and research*' provide the ideas and knowledge needed to help organize the villages into self-sufficient groups. However, 'public opinion amongst the educated [was] either apathetic or definitely against' the AIVIA since 'even the most enlightened' felt that it was indulging in a futile exercise.[4] Kumarappa felt that the scientifically trained individuals were most culpable. Instead of serving the needs of the masses, scientists were poor trustees of their knowledge which they placed 'outside the reach of the villagers' and sold 'their services to the highest bidder'.[5] The lack of well-trained workers was only one of many constraints that affected the AIVIA during its entire period of existence. The other chief problem was that while there were many village industries, till then 'no organized effort or scientific knowledge has been directed' towards the village economy, making the AIVIA a pioneering effort.[6]

For Gandhi, both khadi and village industries were essential to breathe life into the village economy. However, in comparison with khadi, the constructive work carried out by Kumarappa and the AIVIA has received scant scholarly attention. The reasons for this neglect are twofold. First, Gandhi relied upon Kumarappa to develop the AIVIA. Much of the village movement discourse of Kumarappa and his colleagues appeared in the *Gram Udyog Patrika* and has been ignored by scholarly work that largely relies on *The Collected Works of Mahatma Gandhi*.[7] The second and more significant reason was the changed circumstances under which the AIVIA

---

[3] 'A Catechism on the All-India Village Industries Association', *Contemporary India*, 29 June 1935, Speeches and Writings, 2, Kumarappa Papers.

[4] *AIVIA Annual Report*, 1939, p. 1.

[5] J. C. Kumarappa, 'Science and Industrial Development', Speeches and Writings, 9, Kumarappa Papers.

[6] *AIVIA Annual Report*, 1935, p. 1.

[7] For this biography, it has taken many years to assemble the primary archival material from diverse sources. Nevertheless, to the best of our knowledge, a full set of issues of the *Gram Udyog Patrika* does not exist.

was founded and operated in. Arising out of the indifference of the Congress leadership towards constructive work, Gandhi had chosen to delink the activities of the AIVIA from Congress politics. This, coupled with a growing faith in the modern industrial economy, led the Indian intelligentsia away from Gandhian constructive work, including village industries.[8]

In its early years, the AIVIA concentrated its efforts on improving villages through an emphasis on rationalizing the available diet, improving village industries, and tackling that most obdurate of Indian problems, sanitation. Cleanliness was a personal obsession with Gandhi and it was made a central agenda of the association. However, inducing caste-ridden village India to shed its prejudices was another matter.[9] While the AIVIA enthusiastically took up sanitation work, there was 'little co-operation' from the villagers owing to, as the AIVIA euphemistically put it, 'traditional sentiment'.[10] At the Haripura session of the Congress in 1938, Kumarappa had noted with satisfaction that the success of the volunteers in keeping the environs clean 'demonstrated beyond all doubt how effectively this dire problem of India can be solved if every person will give half a minute's thought every day to cover up dirt'.[11] This was indeed wishful thinking as Kumarappa himself noted that 'scavenging work has been the hardest for village workers' who faced ostracism by the villagers, leading the AIVIA to doubt the idea that practice was better than precept.[12] After five years of failed attempts, in 1940 the AIVIA was sorrowfully reporting that with regard to sanitation its 'scattered efforts have proved too feeble for the task'.[13]

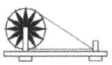

In economic terms, Gandhi spoke of the exploitation of villages as 'organized violence' which could only be countered by the revival and

---

[8] It may be said that the same is true of later scholarship where the interest in khadi has been largely due to its political and semiotic significance rather than its role in political economy as a means of socio-economic reconstruction.

[9] For an episode recounting the difficulty of demonstrating the importance of sanitation, see Narayan Desai, *Bliss Was It to Be Young with Gandhi* (Bombay: Bharatiya Vidya Bhavan, 1988), pp. 34–6.

[10] *AIVIA Annual Report*, 1935, p. 8.

[11] J. C. Kumarappa, 'Lessons from Haripura', *GUP*, March 1938.

[12] *AIVIA Annual Report*, 1936, pp. 5–6.

[13] *AIVIA Annual Report*, 1940, p. 6.

patronage of village industries 'in place of things produced in city factories, foreign or indigenous'.[14] For Kumarappa, the remedy to the problems of village industries was not in their abandonment but to 'bring the light of science' to them.[15] Modernizing village industries was central to the challenge of stemming the outflow of raw material—as well as people— from the villages. The challenge was to enable the village to make best use of its own resources and such self-help had to address the diet available to the villager. While improving the quality and quantity of food was a task of fundamental importance, Kumarappa's work linked the nutritional needs of the villages to questions of deeper significance—political economy and state policy as well as the ecological web that sustained life. It is through a critique of public policy, both before and after Independence, and his own prescriptions that Kumarappa's 'green' ideas emerge. Thus, humble items of food become key modes of grappling with larger questions. During the early years of the AIVIA's existence, the issues of *Harijan* were filled with notes on the nutritional value of a variety of food items. Indeed, the AIVIA workers had taken Gandhi's complaint on the lack of basic nutritional information to heart. Soon the organization had accumulated enough scientific knowledge to issue thorough but simply written monographs on a variety of foodstuffs like jaggery, rice, and oilseeds. By 1941 it had published a *Table of Indian Food Values and Nutrition* as well as a popular volume on *What Shall We Eat?* which were pioneering efforts in the scientific tabulation of Indian nutrition and exposition on dietetics respectively.[16]

In addition to addressing the question of diet and nutrition, the AIVIA made considerable efforts to assemble, systematize, and disseminate scientifically validated knowledge and information in an easily accessible manner. It published a series of pamphlets and guides—in Hindi, Marathi, and English—on a variety of small-scale industries like bee-keeping, paper-making, and so on, that were designed to help the poor villager make full use of available natural resources with a minimal amount of capital. These early efforts at acquiring and disseminating information were only a first step towards understanding and addressing the needs of India's village

---

[14] M. K. Gandhi, 'Why Only Khadi?', *Harijan*, 20 January 1940.

[15] J. C. Kumarappa, *WVM*, p. 110.

[16] Interestingly enough, these Gandhian publications also provided information on the nutritional content of beef and human milk. Similarly, in the pages of the *Gram Udyog Patrika* there was also much discussion on the nutritional value of eggs and fish.

industries. While the scope of such industries on the national scale was enormous, the AIVIA necessarily focused on areas of work where it could make a useful contribution. Although it is not possible for us to summarize the entire body of research and experimental work carried out at Maganvadi and elsewhere, here we seek to illustrate the nature of the exercises carried out under Kumarappa's supervision.[17]

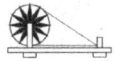

A specific area of early interest was that of the palm *gur* or jaggery industry. If Gandhi's question on the composition of gur went unanswered by India's scientists in 1934, within a year the AIVIA was able to provide an authoritative reply based on its own chemical analysis. However, there were weightier reasons than satisfying Gandhi's curiosity for Kumarappa and his colleagues to be interested in the fate of the humble palm. The AIVIA did not limit itself to the analysis of palm gur, but comprehensively advocated its development as the 'only rational source of sugar in India'.[18] While sugar was a key component of a healthy diet, it was increasingly being obtained from sugarcane processed in centralized factories with serious implications. Industrially manufactured sugar is nutritionally inferior to jaggery which is rich in a variety of minerals. Although the sap of the palm was made into alcoholic toddy in most regions, it was converted into jaggery only in some parts of India. The AIVIA sought to propagate this latter use of palm gur on a national scale and set about training workers for the task. It was also able to carry out a painstaking comparative economic assessment of the industry in regions as far-flung as UP, Madras, and Bengal.[19] Traditionally the tapper castes held a ritually low status and were ranked amongst the poorest of Indians. With the collapse of the traditional palm gur industry and Gandhi's advocacy of prohibition, the AIVIA sought to provide a sustained means of livelihood to the tappers. Such advocacy was not based on mere surmise. Rather, by maintaining a detailed record at one of its production centres, the AIVIA

---

[17] It would be fitting to mention some of the constructive workers who carried out the extensive experimentation at Maganvadi, that is, Gajanan Naik (palm jaggery), Jhaverbhai Patel and Devendra Gupta (oilseeds), and K. B. Joshi (paper). Needless to say, this list is merely illustrative and not exhaustive.

[18] G. Ramachandran, 'The Romance of Palm Gur', *GUP*, April 1950.

[19] Gajanan Naik, 'Palmyra-Gur Economics', *GUP*, October 1940.

was able to conclude that the manufacture of palm gur could provide adequate employment to a family for eight months a year.[20] Through its experiments in Maganvadi, the AIVIA also developed a cheaper substitute to the expensive centrifugal machines used in sugar manufacture that were beyond the reach of the ordinary villagers. This made it possible for sugar manufacture to be carried out as a small-scale industry.[21]

If the use of white sugar deprived the individual user of nutritional value, growing sugarcane diverted scarce resources of land and water that could be used to produce much-needed food grains. In contrast, the palm easily grew on scrub land that was otherwise unsuitable for cultivation. Based on the experience garnered and its own statistical analysis, the AIVIA argued that substituting sugarcane with palm gur would result in the release of some 200,000 acres from sugarcane cultivation.[22] The profligate nature of growing sugarcane was easily recognized in that it used large tracts of irrigated land whereas only a fifth of the viable palms were being tapped in India.[23] However, much of this discourse was a plaintive cry that fell on deaf ears and India's sugar mills continued to grow in strength.[24] As we shall see later, Kumarappa had to perforce aid protests directed against the powerful sugar mill owners of Madurai district.

Decades later, that towering moral figure of independent India, Baba Amte, recalled Gandhi's proposal that Amte make palm gur his life's mission. Having witnessed the ravages of large dams and irrigation projects and the baneful influence of the sugar lobby on India's politics, an older and wiser Amte came to recognize the wisdom of the Mahatma's simple proposition.[25]

Along with its mission to propagate palm gur, the AIVIA also mounted a rearguard attempt to rescue another age-old village industry from the

[20] Gajanan Naik, 'Palm Gur and Living Wage', *GUP*, May 1940.

[21] 'Sugar Making', *GUP*, February 1938.

[22] Gajanan Naik, 'Palm Gur in Food Economy', *GUP*, January 1946.

[23] D. K. Gupta, 'The Sugar Coated Food Shortage', *GUP*, June 1949.

[24] For an examination of India's sugar mill industry, see Sanjaya Baru, *The Political Economy of Indian Sugar: State Intervention and Structural Change* (New Delhi: Oxford University Press, 1990).

[25] Rajni Bakshi, *Bapu Kuti: Journeys in Rediscovery of Gandhi* (New Delhi: Penguin Books, 1998), p. 193.

ravages of industrialization, the traditional oil press or *ghani*. The decline of the ghani is a prime exemplar of the manner in which the intricate web of social and ecological relationships within the village were sundered by industrialization in the context of a colonial economy. At the same time, the AIVIA's work on the problem of oil presses illustrates the novel manner in which Gandhi and Kumarappa sought to reconstitute a new economic order based on village industries. While today's Indian elite are beginning to recognize the virtues of cold-pressed cooking oil, Kumarappa and his colleagues were a tiny minority of constructive workers who relentlessly—and with little effect—argued against the licensing of oil mills. Along with the reduced nutritional value of oil pressed using industrial extraction methods, every mill deprived many oil-pressers of a legitimate livelihood which, in turn, rendered idle the bullocks used in traditional oil presses. Unable to afford tractors for ploughing their fragmented landholdings, most Indian farmers necessarily had to maintain bullocks to provide the motive power required in their fields. Since ploughing was a seasonal activity, without the work of the oil press or for pulling bullock carts, most communities found it economically unviable to maintain their animals.[26] While the modernists viewed the use of bullocks in the fields and for oil presses as quaint and outmoded, Kumarappa perceptively recognized that with the limited capital available in the hands of Indian farmers, neither the bullocks nor the ghani could be dispensed with. Having recognized the indispensability of the traditional ghani, he and his colleagues set about improving their designs to make them cheaper and more efficient. The Maganvadi team carefully studied many traditional designs from around the country and settled on a simplified design that was christened the *Magan ghani* and was adjudged the best design in the country.[27]

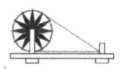

The constructive workers at Maganvadi set out to adapt traditional village industries to a modern context. Unlike large-scale industries that were

[26] Indeed, the use of bullock carts for transportation was the subject of an extended discussion in the pages of *Harijan* and *Gram Udyog Patrika*.

[27] Vinaik, 'Maganvadi Ghani Wins the Prize', *GUP*, January 1954. Also see K. T. Achaya, *Ghani: The Traditional Oilmill of India* (Kemblesville: Olearius Editions, 1993), for a discussion on the design principles of the Magan ghani.

backed by the deep pockets of the capitalists and the resources of the state, the poor farmer or individual producer could scarcely afford the time or the resources required to carry out experimentation and research. In the absence of an organized effort, improvements would be sporadic. Besides, it was scarcely possible for such innovations to be transmitted beyond a limited group. In such a scenario, simple as they were, the research and experiments carried out by the AIVIA had the potential to at once affect the 'lives of millions of people'.[28] The association consistently sought to develop village industries—'pluck them from the laboratory and transplant them in thousands of places in the country'. For instance, from its early experiments the AIVIA concluded that the *til* or sesame seeds from Bengal yielded far less oil than those grown in Bombay Presidency.[29] Such an observation made it feasible to improve the yields across the provinces. Similarly, the AIVIA found that the traditional ghani often caused injury to the bullock's neck, resulting in lost work because the animal had to be periodically rested. The AIVIA took the lighter load-beam design used in the Gujarat region and 'adopted it with necessary modifications'.[30] In a similar vein, workers at the AIVIA modified the traditional method of hand pounding of rice by modifying the curvature of the mortar and finning it thereby preventing grain from being pushed out. The result of this simple expedient was that the new design could be used by a single operator as opposed to two people required for the traditional version.[31]

In our discussion here, we have only briefly alluded to a few elements of the extensive work of the AIVIA. A comprehensive study of the work of the AIVIA, in conjunction with that of technical innovation in khadi, promises to be a rewarding exercise. If approached without the contemporary gestures towards semiotic and cultural interpretations, such a study will afford us a deeper understanding of Gandhian science and technology and its interplay with the wider political economy.[32] We may parenthetically remark here on the term 'appropriate or intermediate technology' popularized by the economic seer E. F. Schumacher and his

[28] G. Ramachandran, 'The Romance of Palm Gur', *GUP*, April 1950.

[29] *AIVIA Annual Report*, 1935, p. 18.

[30] *AIVIA Annual Report*, 1942–3, p. 8.

[31] *AIVIA Annual Report*, 1941, p. 10.

[32] An important beginning of first-rate importance has been made in the case of khadi in C. Shambu Prasad, 'Exploring Gandhian Science: A Case Study of the Khadi Movement' (PhD dissertation, Indian Institute of Technology, Delhi, 2001); and R. Ramagundam, *Gandhi's Khadi: A History of Contention and Conciliation* (New Delhi: Orient Longman, 2008).

followers. These terms have on occasion been applied to describe the work of Gandhi, Kumarappa, and the AIVIA. While Schumacher's coinage of the 1960s is of vital significance and has many similarities with the work at Maganvadi, a retrospective application of the term obscures more than it illuminates. Schumacher's ideas were developed in the context of the European disillusionment with positivism following the destruction wrought by the Second World War. The decades of the 1960s and 1970s were marked by the politics of 'development' in the context of the Cold War. Ever since its coinage, appropriate technology has tended to encompass a wider variety of meanings than was perhaps intended. The context for the work of Kumarappa and his colleagues was different from that of Schumacher and his followers. The AIVIA operated amidst a society's political battle for freedom when the future of India's economy was deeply contested. Although useful in some respects, describing the village industries experiments of the AIVIA as appropriate technology strips it of historical specificity, not to speak of the agency of a colonized people to define their desired destiny. Most importantly, it must not be forgotten that Gandhi and Kumarappa conceived the AIVIA's work as key elements of a non-violent economic order, not merely as appropriate technical innovation.

The wide variety of village industries, public indifference, and the political storm of the 1940s meant that in comparison with the khadi movement, the AIVIA never managed to garner a true foothold for its work. But Gandhi's seriousness of intent was evident when in early 1942, upon the completion of seven years of the AIVIA, its constitution was modified and he took upon himself the presidentship of the association. Although there could have been some satisfaction at the achievements in the face of adverse circumstances, Kumarappa was rather measured in his assessment. 'In these seven years,' he argued, 'we have cultivated a nodding acquaintance with a few village industries, have begun to recognize the rudiments of village economics, carried on a few experiments in the processes, and attempted a reorganisation of some industries.'[33]

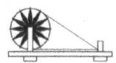

To counter the perception that village industries had no relevance in a modernizing economy, Kumarappa and his colleagues endeavoured to

[33] J. C. Kumarappa, 'Passing of the First Stage of the AIVIA', *Harijan*, 22 February 1942.

demonstrate that the inefficiency of village industries was not due to their intrinsic nature. Rather, it was a reflection of wider factors in the political economy, especially state policy. Kumarappa argued that much of the efficiency of large-scale industries stems from the favours granted to them by the state. For instance, state-sponsored agricultural research was focused on the improvement of cash crops meant for industries such as long-staple cotton suitable for making mill yarn, thick-rind sugarcane that could withstand bruising during transportation to the mills, and tobacco.[34] This bias was felt to be particularly egregious at a time when the country was faced with enormous food shortages. Similarly, India was a major exporter of raw materials and imported many finished goods, all of which benefited the British economy. Britain's priorities were reflected in the railway tariff policy of the colonial state, whereby it was cheaper to transport goods to the port city of Bombay than to India's interior.[35]

As we have seen, the commandeering of India's resources during the Second World War resulted in enormous hardship for many Indians, including the catastrophic Bengal Famine of 1943. Even the Congress that was politely indifferent to Gandhi's advocacy of the village economy had to reckon with the demands of the situation. In early 1942, with the severe dislocation of transportation and the looming possibility of a Japanese invasion, the CWC exhorted its workers that 'village and cottage industries afford a solution desirable in itself and more particularly suited to the needs of the moment'.[36] Consequent on the crisis, 'people tried to produce what they could for their own needs and the needs of their neighbours with the limited resources available to them'.[37] In the face of the severe food shortages, the AIVIA would have appeared to be prescient in its focus. However, it was cruelly ironic that while there was a growing recognition of the value and resilience of a localized economy, many of the association's workers, including Kumarappa, were arrested and its efforts were completely disrupted. The British repression of the Quit India agitation all but destroyed the AIVIA as an organization.

In the early 1950s, Kumarappa and his colleagues demonstrated that the power efficiency of bullock-driven ghanis was comparable to that of

[34] J. C. Kumarappa, 'These Agricultural Colleges', GUP, October 1946.

[35] J. C. Kumarappa, 'Public Costs of Centralised Production', GUP, August 1941.

[36] Quoted in Bharatan Kumarappa, 'Congress and Village Industries', GUP, January 1942.

[37] AIVIA Annual Report, 1944, p. 2.

the oil presses run in mills using electricity.[38] Similarly, by comparing the relative productivity of machines and labourers in relation to daily wages and the cost of electricity, Kumarappa argued that the electricity supplied to industries was enormously subsidized.[39] The policy bias against the village economy became more pronounced during the War years. With adequate shipping unavailable for imports, there was a severe shortfall of manufactured goods.[40] The exigencies of fighting a global war eventually forced the Raj to allow for the development of Indian industry which, in turn, strengthened the hands of Indian capital. In the aftermath of the War, indigenous capitalists were able to exert significant influence on government policy in a manner that flew in the face of logic or fair play. Thus, while the railways transported mill-oil, it refused to allocate wagons to transport oilseeds for ghanis thereby making ghani oil expensive. In situations where such discrimination was not enough, the objectives of the mill-owners were achieved by enforcing administrative fiat. Thus, many provincial governments were prevailed upon to issue orders banning the manufacture of sugarcane jaggery in the vicinity of sugar factories.[41] The result was a pincer move meant to 'deprive the peasants of their birthright to manufacture gur'. Such ordinances were 'on a par with the crippling of the spinners and weavers of muslin' in eighteenth-century India. Along with such state policies, representative of a gross abuse of power, the AIVIA's work was also severely affected by continued scarcity of natural resources after the War. Thus, despite the demand for its ghanis, the AIVIA had to contend with the 'difficulty of obtaining wood of proper girth, due to the deforestation that had taken place by the requirements of Military Departments being met by indiscriminate cutting down of trees'.[42]

With regard to village industries, there was a continuity between the policies of the colonial state and that of newly independent India. The India that emerged from the War period, including the Congress which would soon hold political office, finally turned away from Gandhi and the social and economic order that he had cherished. Indeed, many of

[38] D. K. Gupta, 'Efficiency of Power Driven Oil Mills and Bullock Ghanis', *GUP*, June 1953.

[39] J. C. Kumarappa, '"Cheap" Power', *GUP*, July 1954.

[40] For a discussion of the impact of colonial obduracy on the famine situation in India, see Madhusree Mukherjee, *Churchill's Secret War.*

[41] Gajanan Naik, 'Ban on Gur Making', *GUP*, February 1946.

[42] *AIVIA Annual Report*, 1946, p. 1. Till date, a comprehensive ecological history of India during the Second World War is not available.

the orders prohibiting village industries from manufacturing goods were passed after the Congress took over the reins of power in 1946. If the fate and use of India's wartime Sterling Balances disturbed Kumarappa, such abuse of policy was a turning point since, 'such orders are in keeping with imperialism and not with Popular Ministries'.[43] From now on, the AIVIA's struggle for economic justice and to place India's villages at the heart of the economy was to be waged against erstwhile comrades in the Congress and other fellow Indians. As early as 1948, the AIVIA was 'greatly disappointed' with the lack of 'attention and help from the National Government'.[44] Nehru's government had failed to reform India's colonial bureaucracy and 'left much of the administration in the hands of the old services with the result that [the AIVIA] was left high and dry as under the previous regime'.

Kumarappa was far-sighted with regard to the relationship between human activity and the environment. Amongst the earliest of thinkers to clearly distinguish between finite resources and renewable ones in nature, his was a lone voice ranged against the enthusiastic advocates of large-scale industrialization. In his own lifetime there was little recognition of these views as our contemporary ecological crises were far into the future. In more recent times, Kumarappa has been correctly identified as an early preceptor of environmental thought in India. Now that many of the problems he had warned against have come to pass, there is far greater acceptance of the wisdom in Kumarappa's views. However, his ecological insight and attendant prescriptions are only one manifestation of a deep and original philosophical vision that translated the moral basis of ahimsa into a decentralized economic order. To put it differently, Kumarappa's environmentalism was a logical *derivative* of his universal touchstone, the Natural Order. Thus, as early as 1930, he argued that

[i]n studying human institutions we should never lose sight of that great teacher, Mother Nature. Anything that we may devise if it is contrary to her ways, she will ruthlessly annihilate sooner or later. Everything in nature seems to follow a cyclic movement. Water from the sea rises as vapour and falls on land in refreshing showers and returns back to the sea again. All

---

[43] J. C. Kumarappa, 'Village Industries Be Hanged', *GUP*, October 1946.
[44] *AIVIA Annual Report*, 1947–8, p. 1.

creatures consume inorganic substances and by the process of nutrition build their organic bodies out of them. But by death, disintegration and dissimilation such organic matter is returned to the inorganic world again. A nation that forgets or ignores this fundamental process in forming its institutions will disintegrate. Our economic situation in India today is largely due to the absence of this natural order.[45]

Kumarappa held that the scientific character of any course of human action was to be judged by the extent to which it conformed to nature and 'where we deviate from nature, to that extent we are unscientific'.[46] As a result, he argued that 'the real producers of wealth are those who co-operate with nature and through the operation of natural forces' produce things for human use.[47] Viewed from this vantage point, Kumarappa's ideas do not appear as stand-alone ecological prescriptions. They remain firmly embedded in a context of a rich interplay of philosophical ideas, political economy, and painstaking experimentation. Consequently, it would be incorrect to conflate his ecological vision with the instrumental calculus of 'green' public policy and advocacy that one encounters in our contemporary times. At the same time, one may not divorce the ecological truth of Kumarappa from his concern with the fate of the individual. Specifically, Kumarappa's ecological thought did not view the natural environment as devoid of human intervention. Thus, he argued that India's developmental 'projects have to be scientific in the sense that the needs of our people and the resources at our disposal should be co-ordinated with restrictions under which nature has placed us'.[48] Indeed, this is also the burden of an influential argument on the typological differences between different modes of the global environmental discourse.[49]

This intricate interplay of ideas, values, and material considerations can be best seen by examining one of the village industries we have considered above, that is, oilseeds. Kumarappa's espousal of the oil presses in the village was not due to their employment potential alone. If growing sugarcane instead of obtaining sugar from palm trees was profligate, the industrial crushing of oilseeds was a far worse form of

[45] J. C. Kumarappa, 'Rebuilding India'.

[46] J. C. Kumarappa, 'What Is Progress?', *Harijan*, 13 April 1947.

[47] J. C. Kumarappa, 'The Down-Trodden', *GUP*, February 1949. As remarked earlier this is also the basis of Kumarappa's theory of economic value.

[48] J. C. Kumarappa, 'Our Guides', *GUP*, December 1953.

[49] Ramachandra Guha and J. Martinez-Alier, *Varieties of Environmentalism: Essays North and South* (New Delhi: Oxford University Press, 1998).

ecological damage. Not only did the installation of an oil mill create unemployment in the village by using up all locally available oilseeds, it did far greater harm by removing essential nutrients from the ecological cycle. Throughout his public life, Kumarappa devoted enormous attention to the maintenance of soil fertility. Indeed, this was the central ecological concern that he related to social well-being as well since, 'in the final analysis, fertility of the soil is the fountainhead from which springs all nourishment'.[50] He recognized that both the residual nutrient-rich oil cake after crushing and manure from cattle dung were essential to closing the nutrient cycle. Once oilseeds were sent to the mills for crushing, in most instances the oil cake never returned to the village. In colonial times, along with manure and bonemeal, oil cake was exported out of the country. This practice was only temporarily stopped during the war years due to the non-availability of ships for such export.[51]

With the advent of independence, Kumarappa evinced unhappiness with the thoughtless adoption of American-style industrial methods of agriculture without considering their validity under Indian circumstances.[52] With their abundance of land, Americans were 'wasteful in their agricultural methods' with nary a consideration for 'the loss in fertility of the soil'. India, Kumarappa argued, could not afford to be so profligate since mechanized agriculture did not allow the limited amounts of cultivable Indian land to recuperate, and soon enough 'we shall be reaching the stage of exhaustion' of its productive capacities. In other words, 'there is a world of difference in the principles governing Agriculture as an industry and Agriculture as an occupation'.[53] Kumarappa went on to argue that the Indian method of agriculture 'has been a co-ordinated cycle of the earth, animal, and man and our needs were produced by these means'.[54] Indeed, the Indian 'conception of Dharma relates us to the animal kingdom and to vegetation and to the soil' and 'brings in considerations of moral values in our everyday

[50] J. C. Kumarappa, *A Plan for Rural Development* (Nagpur: The All-India Village Industries Association, 1946), p. 23.

[51] J. P. Patel, 'The Problem of Oil Cake', *GUP*, November 1941.

[52] J. C. Kumarappa, 'Adaptability', *Harijan*, 27 March 1949.

[53] J. C. Kumarappa, 'Boyd Orr, Dodd and Ourselves', *GUP*, July 1949.

[54] J. C. Kumarappa, 'Our Guides', *GUP*, December 1953.

dealing'. 'Bereft of such relation and holding to material considerations only', Kumarappa pointed to the fact that 'man in America stands as an outside exploiter of the rest of his fellow creatures sentient or otherwise'. Of course, since Kumarappa's time, Indian agriculture has increasingly attempted industrial methods of cultivation with its attendant consequences.

If the large-scale mechanization of agriculture in America was necessitated by the relative scarcity of labour in that country, it was rather dangerous to 'import capitalistic principles where capital is scarce and labour is in abundance', that is, to view farming through the industrial lens. A corollary of the destruction of the ghani was the replacement of bullocks by tractors for ploughing. Such a move towards mechanization of agriculture was, in the vivid phrase of one constructive worker, an act of 'thwarting nature'.[55] For the AIVIA, the protection of the cow in the village economy was not due to popular Hindu sentiment. Caught between the fanaticism of 'different sections of the population centered around cow slaughter', Kumarappa sought to focus the debate on the indispensable role of animals in the village economy.[56] If an artisan depended on his tools for his livelihood, so did the Indian farmer on the cow. In Kumarappa's view, it was the recognition of this role that led to the conferring of a status of 'divinity on the cow and the raising of cow slaughter to the level of a religious question'. As Kumarappa recognized, 'the cow symbolises a way of economic life just as much as the internal combustion engine and the lorry typifies another way of economic life'.[57] He argued that the transition of the Western economy from horse power to coal and eventually to petroleum entailed increasing levels of economic violence. The breakdown of the agrarian economy in which the cow was a central part, Kumarappa asserted, was a much more serious problem 'than the mere slaughter of the four-legged and two-horned animal'; he wondered if those 'who stand up against cow slaughter can show their hands clean of bovine blood from this higher interpretation of cow protection'.[58]

Kumarappa also argued for retaining the great diversity of local cattle breeds available in India. By the time of Independence, there were two worrying problems. While the large-scale slaughter of cattle for the Allied war effort had created a severe shortage of milk, the trend of replacing

[55] V. L. Mehta, 'Thwarting Nature', *GUP*, February 1946.

[56] J. C. Kumarappa, 'The Cow Economy', *GUP*, October 1947.

[57] J. C. Kumarappa and others, *The Cow in Our Economy* (Kashi: Akhil Bharat Sarva Seva Sangh, 1958), p. 12.

[58] J. C. Kumarappa and others, *The Cow in Our Economy*, p. 15.

these hardy varieties by the larger British breeds was increasingly taking hold.[59] If the constructive workers understood that a farmer with a small landholding needed a smaller bullock that consumed less fodder, there was also a recognition that despite the pitiable state of Indian cattle, 'centuries of careful breeding' made the Indian cow superior to its Western cousin.[60] The local breeds could live on meagre fodder as well as 'resist disease and withstand the tropical heat much better than the British cow' whereas the cross-breeds had 'proved disastrous'. The wisdom in this observation has been ignored by the state policy of independent India with devastating effect, while the value of preserving native breeds continues to be rediscovered by private individuals to this day.[61]

At a time when the modernists argued for abandoning the cow in favour of the tractor, the AIVIA's workers recognized that this was neither feasible nor desirable when many Indian farmers could hardly even afford to maintain large bullocks. Similarly, although Kumarappa agreed that Indian farmers used 'simple and comparatively primitive' implements with a 'considerable scope for improvement', he keenly defended them against an oft-repeated charge of failure to adopt other modern agricultural practices.[62] In particular, Kumarappa was exasperated by armchair experts who criticized the Indian farmer for the insufficient manuring and shallow ploughing of his fields. For Kumarappa, in a country 'where the monsoon is a gamble', it was 'the height of stupidity to ask the farmer to sink more capital in the form of manure on the off-chance of a good monsoon'.[63] Apart from such economic considerations, the use of tractors was undesirable as

---

[59] Kumarappa also noted that shortly after the War, in Orissa many ghanis were idle as the cattle were sold off to the government to supply meat to the Allied Forces who poured in to fight against a potential Japanese invasion. Without the animal motive power, the oilseeds had to be sent to places as far as Kanpur for pressing. See J. C. Kumarappa, *A Plan for Rural Development*, p. 6.

[60] Bharatan Kumarappa, 'Why Gandhiji Fusses Over the Cow?' in *The Cow in Our Economy*, p. 27.

[61] On the tragicomedy of the Khariar bull, see P. Sainath, *Everybody Loves a Good Drought: Stories from India's Poorest Districts* (New Delhi: Penguin Books India, 1996), pp. 3–9. For a recent citizens' initiative on local cattle, see Sainath's newspaper columns 'Holy Cow! Small Is Beautiful' and 'Cattle Class: Native vs Exotic' in *The Hindu*, 5 and 6 January 2012 respectively.

[62] J. C. Kumarappa, 'Balanced Cultivation as a Basis for Self-Sufficient Villages', *GUP*, April 1951.

[63] J. C. Kumarappa, 'Rebuilding India'.

they did not 'make any contribution to the maintenance of soil fertility'.[64] In contrast, the 'urine and dung that the plough animals yield are invaluable constituents of the farmyard manure which, more than any other single factor, is essential for keeping up the fertility of the soil'. Mechanization of agriculture meant that along with importing petrol, Indian agriculture increasingly depended on the inferior aid of artificial fertilizers.

With regard to fertilizers, Kumarappa used a homely metaphor and distinguished between the human use of food and medical drugs. While the bulk of human nutrition should be derived from wholesome food, drugs should be used in a controlled and limited fashion to remedy a problem. Analogously, Kumarappa argued that artificial fertilizers are 'not plant food but they are medicines to the soil'.[65] Therefore he contended that artificial fertilizers should not be used in an indiscriminate manner but should be prescribed 'where the mineral contents of the soil may be deficient'. In other words, fertilizers were subject to the toxicological dictum, the dose makes the poison. The determination of the need for such a calibrated application of fertilizers was to be done by trained soil chemists, as rampant use of artificial inputs was akin to a 'layman administering medicines to a patient and it may be equally tragic in its results'. Kumarappa also pointed out that nothing was more important than 'the work done by the earthworm ... in fertilising the soil, and helping the recuperative process'.[66] This aid of the earthworm was lost when organic manure was replaced by artificial fertilizers and consequently the soil needed to be broken up by tractors. Although the use of chemical fertilizers led to 'immediate bumper crops, in the end [it] brings about a corresponding exhaustion of the land'.[67] Kumarappa also recognized that 'behind the specious pleading for the chemical fertilizers lies the anxiety of the fertilizer factory owners to push for the sale of their products'.[68] It is with these issues in mind that he opposed the opening of fertilizer factories like the one at Sindri.[69] As in the case of cattle breeds, contemporary India continues to suffer from the devastating impact of indiscriminate use of fertilizers in a context of diminishing yields.

[64] J. C. Kumarappa, 'Balanced Cultivation as a Basis for Self-Sufficient Villages'.

[65] J. C. Kumarappa, 'Soil Food vs Drug', *GUP*, September 1947.

[66] J. C. Kumarappa, *Gandhian Economic Thought* (Bombay: Vora and Co., 1951), p. 26.

[67] J. C. Kumarappa, *An Overall Plan for Rural Development* (Wardha: The All-India Village Industries Association, 1948), p. 45.

[68] J. C. Kumarappa, *An Overall Plan for Rural Development*.

[69] J. C. Kumarappa, 'Is It Too Late?', *GUP*, February 1948.

Flowing from his understanding of the Natural Order, the central question that Kumarappa identified in agriculture was the restoration and maintenance of soil fertility. Indeed, both his critique of modern industrial modes of agricultural production based on artificial fertilizers, mechanized farming, and so on, and the body of ecological insights based on the agrarian economy radiate from the central precept of the health of the natural environment, that is, soil. Readers may recognize the parallel between Kumarappa's obsession with soil fertility and Marx's insight on the ecological degradation attendant on capitalist production.[70] Kumarappa had indeed read parts of *Capital* while at Columbia, but his intellectual debt to Marx on this question is of a limited nature. In particular, Kumarappa's own creative contribution was in relating the issue of soil fertility to two other vital questions, that is, the survival of village industries against the hammer blows of industrialization and the degree of economic autonomy to be available to villagers working these traditional industries. Certainly, the fundamental break from Marx would be in his measuring these issues on a scale of values determined by the Natural Order and man's place in it.

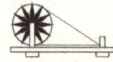

Along with maintaining the continual flow of ecological dependence within the agrarian economy, Kumarappa called for ecological prudence to dictate India's mineral policy. India's finite reserves of minerals were 'the treasure trove of a nation' as they represented a 'source of employment' and it was the birthright of Indian artisans to make best use of them.[71] An early preceptor of what is now known as inter-generational equity, he argued against export of minerals which was 'doing a disservice to the generations yet to be born'. Although the reserves might seem large enough, he held that since they represent 'the rights of our future generations we have to deal with them with a full sense of responsibility'. As far as minerals were concerned, the only sensible policy was that of conservation and

[70] This degradation, labelled 'metabolic rift' by later scholars, pointed to the disjunction between town and countryside that arose out of industrial capitalism. For more details see John Bellamy Foster, *Marx's Ecology: Materialism and Nature* (New York: Monthly Review Press, 2000).

[71] J. C. Kumarappa, 'Our Mineral Policy', *GUP*, January 1947.

Kumarappa argued that it would be appropriate to designate the head of the Minerals Department as 'the Conservator' of minerals.[72] As India was not yet ready to make best use of its minerals, 'nothing is lost by letting them rest where they are', to be 'held in trust for generations to come'. Only after India has addressed its primary needs, Kumarappa argued, should it turn to 'investigate our mineral possibilities by scientific prospecting' and it was 'not wise to merely dig up the ores and send them abroad. Such a course is equivalent to the action of a prodigal who sells his patrimony so as to live on it'.[73] Needless to say, India's recent experience of rampant illegal mining and its baleful influence on our political system bears out Kumarappa's foresight and wisdom.

If Kumarappa was critical of the irresponsible use of India's minerals, he was distressed even more by the reckless mining of a far more precious resource, the limited reserves of India's groundwater. Although he was deeply sympathetic to the farmer's predicament of being dependent on a fickle monsoon, Kumarappa was highly critical of the use of electric pumps for extracting groundwater for irrigation. Since 'in most parts of the country the water level is already low', the use of pumps meant that the poorer sections lost out first as their wells and tanks dried up before the limited reserves of groundwater are severely depleted, foreshadowing 'ruin and desolation to the countryside'.[74] Instead of such profligacy with precious resources, Kumarappa argued that 'we require *small* dams put across streams, rivulets and rivers to hold back *some* of nature's gifts in store'.[75] Arguing against the 'grandiose schemes ... for raising big dams and river control', in the 1951 *Draft Outline of the First Five Year Plan*, Kumarappa reasoned that it was far more important to address the continual problem of soil erosion and felt that 'there should be innumerable schemes for bunding nallas and hill streams at short intervals'.[76] Not only would this address the problem of erosion but it would help conserve water for

[72] *Report of the Industrial Survey Committee*, part 2, vol. 1, p. 2.

[73] J. C. Kumarappa, 'Our Mineral Policy', GUP, January 1947. In his biography *The Gandhian Crusader* (p. 110), M. Vinaik states that Kumarappa omitted discussion of manganese and coal in the CP and Berar survey to conserve them for future use, but the Government redeemed this lacuna by promptly appointing another committee.

[74] J. C. Kumarappa, 'Adaptability', *Harijan*, 27 March 1949.

[75] J. C. Kumarappa, 'Adaptability'; emphasis added.

[76] J. C. Kumarappa, 'Remarks on the Five Year Plan', GUP, August 1951.

local use by raising the water table. We may parenthetically remark that Kumarappa recognized the potential for conflict over water resources in the years to come. Since India was severely dependent on seasonal rains, he argued that instead of basing the reorganization of states on linguistic grounds, 'our states should follow river valleys' so as to 'be able to control our resources without coming into conflict' with each other.[77]

Kumarappa's extensive travels throughout the country in 1946 and later while working on the Agrarian Reforms Committee had alerted him to the fact that the key to increasing the prospects for wet cultivation was the maintenance and expansion of minor irrigation works. India's extensive system of tanks had silted up due to 'long neglect over decades' and Kumarappa argued that a serious effort to dredge them would yield both silt for the fields and allow for greater storage of the monsoon rainwater.[78] Indeed, he hoped in vain that India's Sterling Credits would be used for such purposes. Kumarappa also clearly anticipated an ecological issue that has come to be recognized in recent times as 'virtual water', that is, the effective transfer of the utility value of precious water that occurs when a society exports commodities that consume significant amounts of water. Writing in 1951, a full four decades before the idea was introduced into Western scholarship, Kumarappa could, arguably, be credited with coining the term.[79] Contesting the assumption that electrification was an unqualified good, Kumarappa illustrated his view with the example of the introduction of electric pumps in South Arcot district of Tamil Nadu. In areas where crops like jowar that consumed little water were grown, one now had fruit farming. This 'eventually resulted in the water from the villages being *virtually exported* to places like Madras, Bombay, Bangalore and other cities in the form of fruits and the villagers being left without the water'.[80] In a similar vein, Kumarappa pointed out that the projected electric power produced at the Damodar Valley Corporation was equivalent to the manual labour of eight million workers. Consequently, introduction of modern technology without consideration of its social and human costs

---

[77] J. C. Kumarappa, 'The Reorganisation of States', *GUP*, November 1955.

[78] J. C. Kumarappa, 'The Draft 2nd Five Year Plan', *GUP*, March 1956.

[79] The British geographer Tony Allan is credited with the concept and with propagating its use. Allan had originally used the term 'embedded water' that was later replaced by the catchy coinage 'virtual water'. For a popular introduction, see Tony Allan, *Virtual Water: Tackling the Threat to Our Planet's Most Precious Resource* (New York: I. B. Tauris, 2011).

[80] J. C. Kumarappa, *Gandhian Economic Thought*, p. 50; emphasis added.

that would be borne by India's poor was akin to snatching away the straw that a drowning man was desperately trying to grasp.[81]

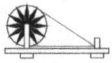

In independent India, a significant consideration in the debate on the use and abuse of the environment has centred on forests. Although in Kumarappa's lifetime the extraction of forest resources had picked up pace especially during the Second World War, its severity was even greater in later decades. Consequently most of his ecological concerns have been focused on agrarian issues, soil fertility in particular. Nevertheless, he did have a keen understanding of the history of forest use in colonial India. Amongst the earliest of Indian critics, he recognized that the colonial 'forest policy was dictated by the needs of revenue of a top-heavy administration'.[82] Kumarappa also pointed to the intimate connection between social welfare and careful forest utilization. Although he was against the indiscriminate and large-scale felling of timber during the War years, Kumarappa established the connection between people and forests at two distinct levels. In the first instance, he recognized that many village and cottage industries had evolved on the basis of utilizing forest resources. Under the colonial dispensation, these collections were subjected to duties by either the forest department or, as in the case of the Central Provinces, by the *malguzar* collectors. Kumarappa argued that in combination 'these exactions work harshly on the villagers and handicap their productivity' as the minor forest produce was either made unavailable or became prohibitively expensive.[83] As a remedy, he called for necessary 'legislative action to safeguard the welfare of the people'. During the public debate on the First Five-Year Plan, Kumarappa called for a redefinition of the role of the forest department which viewed the forests as sources of revenue. In particular, he emphasized the importance of 'minor forest products which form an important source of raw material for many industries of importance'.[84]

The second, and more significant, relationship that Kumarappa understood was the intimate link between forest policy and soil fertility

---

[81] J. C. Kumarappa, 'Snatching Away the Straw', *GUP*, November 1954.

[82] J. C. Kumarappa, *Our Food Problem* (Wardha: The All-India Village Industries Association, 1949), p. 2.

[83] *Report of the Industrial Survey Committee*, part 1, vol. 1, p. 5.

[84] J. C. Kumarappa, 'Remarks on The Five-Year Plan', *GUP*, August 1951.

through a chain of causal relations. The colonial forest policy had made it increasingly difficult for villagers to procure firewood or forest manure for their own use. By the time of the Second World War, massive timber extraction from India as well as the shortage of imported coal due to the non-availability of shipping created a widespread fuel famine. In combination, fuel scarcity and the lack of access to forest compost had a telling effect on 'the proper maintenance of the fertility of the soil' on Indian farms.[85] Thus, Kumarappa was among the few to recognize that the agrarian problem could not be divorced from India's colonial forest policy.

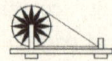

The colonial and independent Indian governments shaped their policy to aid the proliferation of many mills and factories. Upon the transfer of power into Indian hands in 1947, the depth of the colonial state was clearly demonstrated in the form of bureaucratic powers and a control regime that were systematically deployed in favour of the industrial capitalist at the cost of the small producer. Congress ministers extolled the contributions of large-scale industries to India's economy and happily went about inaugurating mills for making sugar, polishing rice, and manufacturing partially hydrogenated oil that came to be known as *vanaspati ghee*. The Gandhians were dismayed by this betrayal of the public cause and over the years the *Gram Udyog Patrika* and *Harijan* consistently published a large number of articles decrying the abuse of executive power but to no avail.[86] To aid the mills in procuring raw materials, a rash of executive orders was issued all over India that either banned or placed severe controls on traditional village industries like jaggery making or oil pressing by ghanis. The *Gram Udyog Patrika* presents a persuasive case that the death of many of India's village industries did not happen due to the natural superiority of industrial manufacture. Rather they were systematically and deliberately killed off by the use of massive doses of state power. This was nothing but a speeded-up reprise of the well-known story of the death of Indian textiles in the colonial era, except that the perpetrators were working in the name of the various governments of independent India.

---

[85] J. C. Kumarappa, *Our Food Problem*, p. 2.

[86] See, for instance, K. G. Mashruwala, 'A Minister's "Good Fortune"', *Harijan*, 27 March 1949.

If Kumarappa was unhappy with the colonial regime spending public money on agricultural research on cash crops, he was now furious with the indiscriminate opening of mills and factories which would monopolize production of the very same items that the village industries were manufacturing. He was irked by the consistent propaganda made by the mill owners that their methods of production were 'scientific' and superior to the traditional ones. India seemed to him to be 'possessed with a mania to destroy all nutrition provided by nature by the use of mills—white rice, white sugar, hydrogenated oils'.[87] Although India was a major producer of rice, in many regions rice was replaced by cash crops. For instance, in Bihar, sugarcane took over much of the traditionally rice-growing lands as did the farming of coconuts for soap manufacture in the Malabar region. As a result of this shift towards cash crops, the rice trade involved long-distance transportation and indeed India imported rice from Burma and sometimes from places as far away as Brazil. Traditionally, when locally produced and consumed, rice was dehusked only when the need arose. With the long-distance transportation of rice, it was necessary to reduce its weight by removing the husk. Consequently, rice also had to be polished to rid it of the nutritious and fibre-rich pericarp that would have been attacked by insects and worms. The result was polished, white rice which the insects left alone while humans 'discarded the nutritious pericarp and took the pure unhealthy starch themselves'.[88] While it helped fill the bank balances of sugar and soap manufacturers, substituting wholesome unpolished rice with the imported, polished variety in the diet of the wider population did not seem to Kumarappa to be a 'scientific choice'.

Kumarappa was amongst the earliest thinkers to argue that the value of food had to be reckoned in terms of its total nutritional content rather than merely by counting calories. Decades later, this is a lesson that remains largely outside the purview of the endless public policy debates on feeding India's populace. To justify their existence, the mill owners carried out propaganda that made claims on the virtues of their manufacturing processes. If Kumarappa had to counter the publicity of rice mills by arguing that rice 'bran is food for human beings' and not just cattle, his greatest ire was reserved for a growth industry of the time, hydrogenated oil made into a solid cooking medium known as vanaspati ghee and colloquially

[87] J. C. Kumarappa, 'Science Runs Amuck', *Harijan*, 27 April 1947.
[88] J. C. Kumarappa, 'Science and Industrial Development', *Speeches and Writings*, 9, Kumarappa Papers.

referred to by a popular brand name, Dalda. Along with other Gandhians, he repeatedly pointed out the social and health costs of substituting ghani-pressed cooking oil with this unhealthy product that he christened as *nakali* or fake *ghee*. Arguing that hydrogenated oil was harmful to human health and was tantamount to cheating the public, Kumarappa demanded that the vanaspati mills be banned as they were detrimental to public welfare.[89]

In recent years, trans-fats in hydrogenated oil products have been implicated in increased heart disease, and vanaspati ghee has all but disappeared from the kitchens of middle-class and affluent Indians. Instead, health conscious and savvy consumers have become familiar with a rich vocabulary of terms such as organic, cold-pressed, extra virgin, and even ghani. Of course, all of these terms apply to healthy, nutritious products that now occupy a niche, premium market that is out of the reach of the ordinary consumer. It bears repeating that the oil produced by the bullock-driven ghani that the AIVIA made a futile attempt to protect had all the attributes that India's elite have come to swear by. Indeed, this seems to have been the story of the modernization of India's food industry. Since Independence, large-scale industrial methods displaced many village and small-scale industries along with the people who depended on them for a livelihood. Although many of the virtues of these traditional practices have been rediscovered, they have now reappeared in the newly packaged form of 'health foods'. In the process, neither can India's farmers profit from this growing market nor can they even dream of using such products themselves.[90]

Kumarappa was angered by the bias towards industrialization and remarked that 'science is being prostituted [as] its use has been denied to the masses'.[91] However, he and his colleagues at the AIVIA did not limit themselves to decrying the abuse of state power and the mendacity of India's industrialists. Despite having 'no eminent scientists to boast of' and

---

[89] See J. C. Kumarappa, 'Nakali Ghee', *Harijan*, 25 May 1947, as well as 'For Sale—A Pacifier!', *Harijan*, 26 January 1947.

[90] A similar crisis grips the handloom sector where spinners and weavers cannot afford to wear the cloth they painstakingly manufacture.

[91] J. C. Kumarappa, 'Science and Industrial Development', Speeches and Writings, 9, Kumarappa Papers.

using an 'ill-equipped small laboratory', the AIVIA workers attempted to address the problems of the village industries themselves. To be effective, their solutions needed to address the social, economic, and ecological dimensions of the village economy. Of the many experiments carried out at Maganvadi, we examine one that stands out for its ability to reflect all of these concerns in a microcosm.

By 1942, the severe shortages created by the Second World War were a painful reminder of India's vulnerability due to its dependence on imported goods. In the chaos of the period, the AIVIA saw the opportunity to impress upon the general populace the lesson that self-reliance was 'the only true basis of independence'.[92] Thus, while the country erupted in the revolt of Quit India, the August 1942 issue of *Gram Udyog Patrika* was entirely devoted to a single problem far removed from political turbulence. It was on the everyday necessity of lighting. In an era when electricity was not available in most Indian villages, artificial lighting was only possible using lanterns. While India was the world's largest producer of oilseeds, it was ironic that 'even the remotest village is dependent on imported kerosene oil for lighting purposes'. The AIVIA had been working on the design of a lantern fuelled by non-edible vegetable oil. Now, with the uncertainty of the political crisis and the severe shortages on hand, Kumarappa released the design of the lantern that was named the *Magan Dipa*.[93] It provided a solution that can only be described by that much misused term, holistic. In its design and deployment of this lantern, the AIVIA demonstrated significant creativity in addressing technical considerations while being mindful of the constraints of cost. However, the greater value of their solution lay in that their lantern also addressed itself to the wider economic and ecological imperatives that were the mandate of the AIVIA.

The use of non-edible vegetable oil for lighting posed a technical challenge since oil is thicker than kerosene and does not rise up a wick with ease. To obtain a steady flame with low soot required a design that could easily regulate a steady supply of the heavier oil. Although this problem could be solved by the chemical thinning of oil, the AIVIA was mindful of the increased costs involved. Instead, its design solved the problem by drawing on a well-known principle based on gravitational force, that is, Hero's fountain. As raw material such as tin sheets required to make new lanterns were unavailable, the AIVIA resorted to modifying existing kerosene lanterns which would also amount to savings for the customer.

---

[92] Bharatan Kumarappa, 'Independence', *GUP*, March 1942.
[93] J. C. Kumarappa, 'The Magan Dipa', *GUP*, August 1942.

However, given the severe shortage of resources and driven by their desire to help as large a section of the population as possible, the *Magan Dipa* issue of the *GUP* provided an elaborate set of technical drawings and instructions so that anyone with a modicum of skill could carry out the modifications.

The use of conventional kerosene lanterns affected India's resources in two complementary ways. While the import of fuel and lanterns resulted in an annual economic drain of Rs 20 crores, the irony was that India was at the same time a major exporter of edible and non-edible oilseeds to the West. The loss here was not merely economic but also had social and ecological costs as the export of oilseeds out of the village deprived the agrarian economy of a highly valuable by-product, that is, the residual oil cake that was traditionally used both as cattle feed and soil nutrient. Kumarappa's calculations showed that apart from saving Rs 20 crores of revenue in kerosene imports, the oil cake would yield revenue of Rs 7.5 crores while providing employment to as many as a quarter million people nationwide. In addition, the manufacture of Indian lanterns would itself generate Rs 20 crores of annual business for Indian craftsmen. Thus, local pressing of oilseeds was a vital link in forming a tightly coupled system where the needs of the farmers and oil pressers, the cultivable land and cattle would be simultaneously addressed. In contrast, the export of oilseeds out of the village led to unemployment within the village and accentuated the problem of India's 'ill-fed cattle and exhausted land'. It may also be noted that as far as the needs of agrarian India were concerned, there was nothing to distinguish between the export of oilseeds out of the country or their use in India's own oil mills.

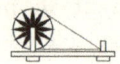

Kumarappa was deeply shaken by the severe food shortages and famine conditions that India had experienced during the War years and later. He was particularly struck by the fact that India was utterly vulnerable to disruption of food imports and the ease with which a callous Raj diverted internal supplies and left the general population to starve. The basic cause of food shortage, he argued, was 'the departure from the village economy of self-sufficiency'.[94] With the increasing monetization of the economy, 'even the growing of cereals has become a money crop'. The result was

[94] J. C. Kumarappa, 'Balanced Cultivation', *GUP*, June 1946.

that instead of saving their food for themselves, farmers 'hoarded their notes which could not command foreign market in grains with the result that we now face famines every year'. Even as he wrote the essay, 'A Stone for Bread' in late 1942, Kumarappa recognized that India's economy was exceedingly vulnerable and 'warned that the result will be that there will be famines not only next year, but year after year'.[95] In Jabalpur Jail, he spent much time thinking about how to avoid such famines and concluded that 'food must be our first care'.

The only remedy was a back-to-basics approach where each region resorted to Balanced Cultivation of land with an aim of self-sufficiency.[96] Ordinarily, self-sufficiency in food has come to mean adequate production of cereals. Kumarappa argued that if the focus is on the overall physical well-being of a person, one needed a broader appreciation of nutritional self-sufficiency that included protein, vitamins, minerals, and trace elements. He argued that while the food crisis of the 1940s affected caloric availability, the lack of adequate nutritional elements in the Indian diet was a long-standing problem. This more wholesome view of the thali meant that planners ought to move beyond thinking of grains to include fruit and vegetables, milk, gur, oilseeds, and other produce that 'supplies the body with all its requirements in their correct proportions so as to keep it fit and healthy'. Such needs of the individual had to find reflection in the agrarian economy as Balanced Cultivation. Kumarappa calculated that, in his time, the per capita land availability for food cultivation was 0.7 acres which was inadequate 'according to the present distribution of cultivation'. Instead, he proposed a schematic plan that would achieve sufficiency in a 're-ordered system of agriculture'. The Balanced Cultivation scheme called for a planned use of available land to grow cereals, pulses, oilseeds, cotton, and a variety of other crops to provide for a diet yielding about 3000 calories per day while addressing the need for other nutritional elements like minerals, vitamins, and indeed roughage. In addition, Kumarappa's scheme also provided for a per capita annual yield of cotton equivalent to 25 yards of cloth.[97] His critics viewed his advocacy of self-sufficiency as

[95] J. C. Kumarappa, *A Plan for Rural Development*, p. 7.

[96] J. C. Kumarappa, 'Balanced Cultivation', *GUP*, June 1946.

[97] In the 1950s, Kumarappa pursued this theme by examining data collected by the Agrarian Reforms Committee (ARC) as well as pre-Independence Government records and the 1941 Census. The resulting statistical analysis was published as *A Note on Balanced Cultivation* (New Delhi: All-India Congress Committee, 1951).

a narrow-minded and parochial solution out of tune with the demands of a globally integrated world. But, for Kumarappa, self-sufficiency did not 'mean that each individual will be producing everything he needs'.[98] Nor did it imply that the village was to be economically cut off from the rest of the world and remain mired in backwardness. In fact, the basic unit that he assumed for Balanced Cultivation was a population of one lakh that denoted a region and not an individual village. While he agreed that every village had to carry out trade to obtain commodities that it could not produce, Kumarappa argued that such trade should only be in surpluses. A village should have first right to use its own products before others could lay a claim on them.

The subjugation of Indian agriculture to colonial needs and the increased significance of cash crops had deeply worried Kumarappa as this combination had broken through the 'rampart of safety' provided by traditional modes of self-sufficient farming.[99] While there was no going back to the outmoded methods of the past, he was convinced that reconstituting Indian agriculture on the basis of local self-sufficiency was a matter of utmost priority. The metaphor he used was of the ocean liners of old that could be easily torpedoed. Having travelled on them during his days in the West, Kumarappa knew that the modern designs 'divided the hull into several watertight compartments' that provided for improved safety. Since 'the human race has not developed the far-sightedness' of true brotherhood, he argued that the only way to ensure the protection of people was by the approach of self-sufficiency that he advocated.[100] In the early years after Independence, Kumarappa continued to develop this theme of Balanced Cultivation as a means to protect the fundamental needs of the Indian villager.

[98] J. C. Kumarappa, 'Self-Sufficiency', *GUP*, June 1950.

[99] J. C. Kumarappa, 'Balanced Cultivation', *GUP*, June 1946.

[100] J. C. Kumarappa, 'Is It Narrow and Self-Centred?', *GUP*, August 1946.

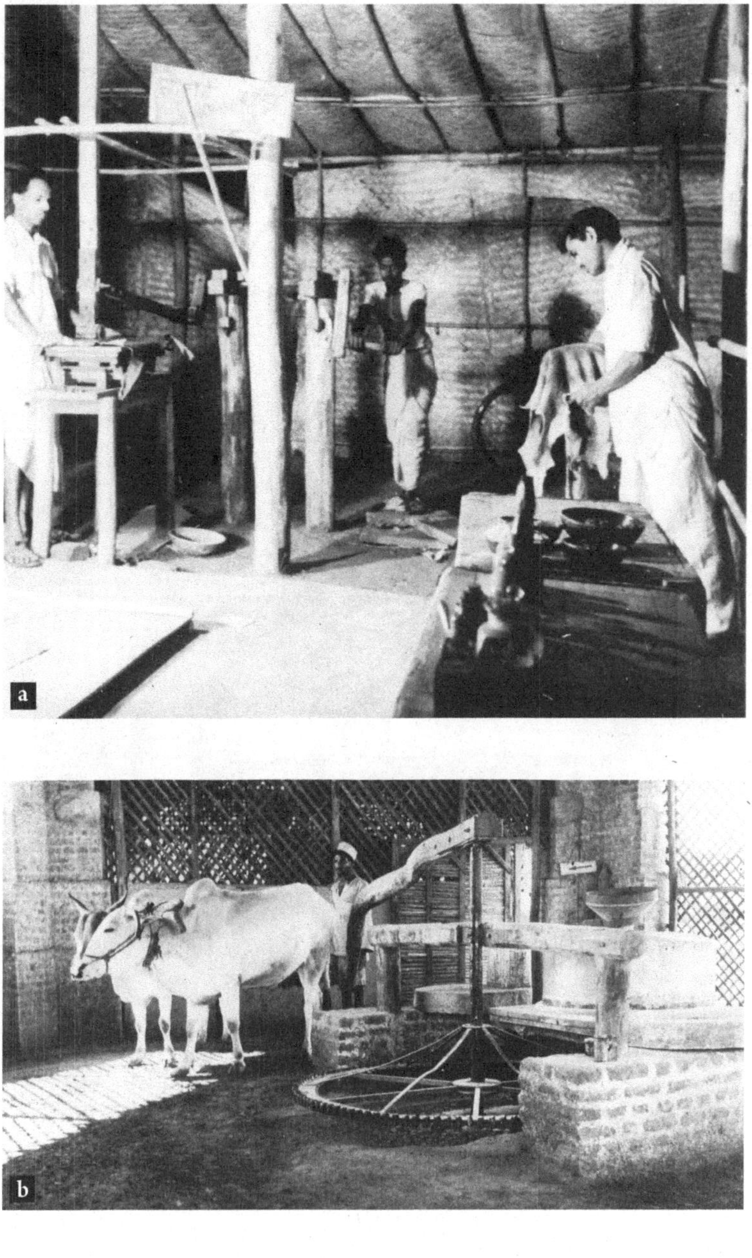

Figure 17 Village industries: (*a*) processing of leather, (*b*) extraction of oil using a *ghani*,

(*c*) manufacture of handmade paper, (*d*) laboratory work,

(e) library, and (f) exhibit of *charkhas* and *khadi*. *Photographs courtesy of Magan Sangrahalaya Samiti, Wardha (Maharashtra).*

13   Whither Sarvodaya?

B y 1946, the AIVIA had resumed work but continued to be plagued by the problems inherited from the Quit India period. While the 'Provincial Governments were still busy with their politics' and hardly paid 'any thought to the economic programme', Kumarappa was invited 'to study their provinces and give them a scheme'.[1] Consequently, he travelled extensively around the country and also spent some time in Ceylon (now Sri Lanka) advising people's organizations there. In that year, he had maintained excellent health despite travelling over 20,000 miles 'from Colombo to Kabul and Kathiawad to Cuttack'.[2] These travels gave him direct exposure to the multitude of crises that gripped the country. If chronic shortage of food was a major cause for worry, with the devolution of power to the Interim Government, there were rapid political developments with serious implications. Kumarappa's engagement with these problems is reflected in his poignant, thoughtful, and often harshly critical articles in the *Gram Udyog Patrika*. In early 1947, amidst the deepest turmoil of his own life, Gandhi wrote a touching letter to Kumarappa from Noakhali. In his letter, Gandhi was earnestly solicitous

[1] *AIVIA Annual Report*, 1946, p. 1.
[2] Letter from J. C. Kumarappa to Mahatma Gandhi, 1 February 1947, S. N. 32146.

of the AIVIA's work and Kumarappa's personal well-being.[3] Kumarappa wrote that he had not been in touch with the Mahatma, since 'it is a sin to bother you and so I never write to add to your labours'.[4] Answering Gandhi's queries, he complained that most of the Congress governments 'seem to be concerned with vote-catching programmes and schemes rather than real, solid, constructive work'.

Kumarappa's travels were not limited to within the subcontinent. In the middle of 1947, he played an unusual cameo role on a trip to England. With the coming transfer of power, a conference between Indian and British interests was organized in London in July 1947 to negotiate on the future of Indian shipping. Under British rule, the bulk of the international trade with India was carried out by British shipping agencies, and the implicit assumption of the conference was to arrive at a more equitable sharing of the shipping trade. Shoorji Vallabhdas, a member of the AIVIA's board and Kumarappa's friend, was a member of this delegation. In order to keep some of the shipping magnates from pushing their own personal interests at the conference, Vallabhdas persuaded Kumarappa to join the delegation as an economic adviser.[5] Three decades had passed since Kumarappa's time in London, and he was eager to use this opportunity to visit and understand the post-war situation. Although the London conference ended in a fiasco, for Kumarappa it was not an entirely wasted effort as it provided him a first-hand experience of post-war England and also enabled contact with some important Pacifists.

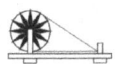

As in the political sphere, the divergence between the Congress and Gandhi on economic questions became increasingly apparent during this period. Although the constructive organizations worked with the official sanction of the Congress, the relationship between khadi and village industries and Congress politics was always a tenuous one. Now, in the face of real political power passing into the hands of the Congress, this

---

[3] Letter to J. C. Kumarappa, 26 January 1947, *CWMG*.

[4] Letter from J. C. Kumarappa to Mahatma Gandhi, 1 February 1947, S. N. 32146.

[5] Letter from Shoorji Vallabhdas to J. C. Kumarappa, 12 June 1947, Subject File, Loose, Kumarappa Papers. Vallabhdas believed that the presence of a confidant of Gandhi would act as a deterrent.

polite fiction was given a quick burial. The policies followed in the case of khadi and village industries were a direct repudiation of the stated position of the Congress during the long decades it waged the struggle for freedom. The decades of slow and hard work of the constructive workers towards building local self-sufficiency was being unravelled by the Congress itself.

Soon, a familiar pattern established itself and Kumarappa would spar with many provincial governments on their industrial policies. At the end of August 1946, a conference of industries ministers was organized in Poona 'to consider a common course of action on an agreed programme'.[6] With Gandhi in attendance and urged by the AIVIA, the conference resolved that 'plans for economic development should centre round the farmer and agriculture', and it briefly revived Kumarappa's hopes.[7] Eventually, nothing came out of such declarations, as the 'ministers were prevailed upon by various interests to compromise' on the programme suggested by the AIVIA.[8] An exception to the rule was the Madras Government under Tanguturi Prakasam that declared a policy against the setting up of new textile mills in favour of khadi. This resulted in a furore and some hostile news reports attributed the new policy to the handiwork of Kumarappa.[9] The textile policy was in fact Prakasam's own, but Kumarappa did have a hand in the framing of a broad plan for rural development for the Madras Province, the Firka Development Scheme.[10] However, this scheme never had a reasonable chance with the resignation of the Prakasam ministry. In the meanwhile, there arose a brief possibility of Kumarappa having a direct hand in shaping policy at the national level.

In the middle of 1946, the battle was well and truly joined with the election of Acharya Kripalani as Congress President. Kripalani's election was perceived as a morale booster to constructive work, and

[6] *AIVIA Annual Report*, 1946, p. 2.

[7] J. C. Kumarappa, 'A Village Centred Plan', *GUP*, September 1946.

[8] *AIVIA Annual Report*, 1946, p. 2.

[9] J. C. Kumarappa, 'Greatness Thrust upon Us', *GUP*, January 1947.

[10] In the Madras Province, a district was divided into talukas which were, in turn, sub-divided into *firkas*. Along with his associates, G. Ramachandran, R. R. Keithahn, and G. Venkatachalapathi, Kumarappa was a member of the Select Committee that framed the scheme for development work and also a programme for the training of workers. The Committee's report is reproduced in Tenneti Viswanatham, supplement to *The Journey of My Life: An Autobiography by Tanguturi Prakasam*, translated by I. V. Chalapathi (Hyderabad: Prakasam Institute of Development Studies, 1992), pp. 363–7.

when Jayaprakash Narayan resigned from the CWC, Kripalani offered the position to Kumarappa. Kumarappa, in turn, pointed out the AIVIA rule that prevented constructive workers from entering office. Keenly desirous of having another Gandhian in the CWC, Kripalani argued that the AIVIA's rules needed to be 'modified to suit the changing needs of the times' and that Kumarappa's word would have more weight with the various Congress ministries if he was on the CWC.[11] Kumarappa himself recognized that India had reached 'a stage when economic reconstruction occupies a central stage in the political set-up'.[12] Pressurized by others to take up the offer, he wrote to Gandhi laying out the problem with the AIVIA rules.[13]

In the meanwhile, based on rumours reported in the newspapers, Gandhi wrote saying he would 'watch [Kumarappa's] career with considerable interest' and that there was 'much to be cleaned in those stables' of the CWC.[14] But on receipt of Kumarappa's letter, Gandhi recognized his error and corrected himself by saying that 'the healthy rule which prevents the members of constructive organizations from becoming members of the Working Committee should not be tampered with however tempting a particular offer may be'.[15] Thus ended Kumarappa's brief involvement in the mainstream politics of the Congress. As an aside, we note that this was a reiteration of an earlier position on constructive workers that arose in 1937 when the Congress provincial governments were formed and Kumarappa was offered the position of a minister by Vallabhbhai Patel. With Gandhi's concurrence, Kumarappa declined the offer since he was committed to the AIVIA and its agenda.[16] Within Gandhian circles, there exists folklore to the effect that Gandhi desired that Kumarappa be made the first finance minister of independent India.[17] On a related note, one source states that he had suggested to Nehru in 1951 that there should be a separate ministry for village and cottage industries in the central

[11] Letter from J. C. Kumarappa to Mahatma Gandhi, 22 March 1947, S. N. 32148.

[12] 'J. C. Kumarappa for Congress Cabinet: Awaiting Gandhiji's Formal Approval', *Indian Express*, 24 March 1947, Press Clippings, Kumarappa Papers.

[13] Letter from J. C. Kumarappa to G. Ramachandran, 28 March 1947, S. N. 32150.

[14] Letter to J. C. Kumarappa, 16 March 1947, *CWMG*.

[15] Letter to J. C. Kumarappa, 29 March 1947, *CWMG*.

[16] Vinaik, *Quest*, p. 117.

[17] Although this is quite plausible, there is no conclusive evidence available in this regard. For a version of this view passed on orally, see Lindley, *Gandhi's Economist*, p. 47.

government with Kumarappa in charge. Nehru is said to have refused on the grounds that he did not agree with Kumarappa's views.[18]

Although he did not join the CWC, Kumarappa sought to influence government policy through the formation of a Constructive Programme Committee of the Congress. Kumarappa had long felt the need for such a committee to advise the various Congress governments on rural development. Without official sanction, he was 'unable to interfere in the government plan'.[19] In a remarkably perceptive article written in March 1947, Kumarappa argued that during the recent 'decades the Congress [had] been a fighting organization' dedicated to ending British rule.[20] Consequently, the task of constructive work was left to associations like the AISA and AIVIA that carried on 'their allotted duty without interfering or taking part in any belligerent activities' against the colonial government. Now that the Interim Government was in place with the Congress leaders at the helm, it was necessary to 'make the whole Congress organization into a constructive body'. Thus, Kumarappa argued, having 'freed [the people] from political bondage', it was time for the Congress 'to take upon itself the feeding, clothing, and the providing of shelter to the masses', that is, work 'towards the economic Swaraj of the people'. Using a metaphor rich in biblical overtones, Kumarappa argued that it was time to convert 'swords into ploughshares'. It is this argument for a radical transformation of the Congress that Gandhi was to later convert into his proposal for a Lok Sevak Sangh.

As a Congress president who was a keen advocate of constructive work, Kripalani was an exception that proved the rule. By and large, the Congress pursued policies that went against the interests of the village economy. This was most clearly visible in the response to the food crisis that had gripped the country. During the Second World War, the diversion of massive quantities of food and other goods to the war theatre had precipitated starvation on an unprecedented scale in the countryside. The attendant inflation was sought to be artificially controlled by rationing of goods and the control of their prices. The scarcity of food was widespread and the crisis was worsened by the colonial Government's policy of diverting material away from the village industries to be utilized by mills

---

[18] Pandit Sunderlal, 'Dr. J. C. Kumarappa as I Knew Him', *Asian Reader*, vol. 1, no. 4 (1968): 20.

[19] Letter from J. C. Kumarappa to Mahatma Gandhi, 1 February 1947. S. N. 32146.

[20] J. C. Kumarappa, 'Swords into Ploughshares', *Harijan*, 9 March 1947.

and factories. If such troubles could be ascribed to the colonial hand in India, the welfare of the masses fared no better under the provincial governments that passed into Congress control. If 'controls were a vicious legacy of the war', the Congress ministers were hardly willing to part with the power they offered.[21] The *Gram Udyog Patrika* reported with dismay the number of ways the 'popular ministries' were 'killing village industries by their indiscriminate use of price controls'.[22] Upon arriving in strife-ridden Delhi in late 1947, Gandhi himself joined the battle for decontrol since he felt that such policies gave rise to 'fraud, suppression of truth, intensification of the black market and to artificial scarcity'.[23] Above all, Gandhi argued, such a policy killed the initiative of people and undid 'the teaching of self-help they have been learning for a generation'. He asked if 'the voice of the people [should] be drowned by the noise of the pundits who claim to know all about the virtue of controls'.[24] By December 1947, owing to his relentless pressure, sugar was decontrolled. Gandhi and other constructive workers were not naive in believing that decontrol would not have any attendant problems. But the imposition of price control and rationing in India was already attendant with corruption and fraud and was rather ineffective. Kumarappa viewed control as a complete failure as it did not seriously address the need to increase production, that is, address the supply end of the equation. Instead, 'the mere rationing of existing stocks ... places an undue strain on the distributing mechanism and encourages black-marketing'.[25]

Deeply unhappy with the turn of events, Kumarappa filled the pages of *Harijan* and the *Gram Udyog Patrika* detailing the manner in which the newly installed governments were setting out policies that were nothing but a blatant repudiation of the ideals of swadeshi and were sure to strangle the nascent village industries that the AISA and AIVIA had carefully nurtured over the years. For instance, as part of exacting war reparations against Japan, in direct repudiation of the Congress commitment to khadi,

[21] Pyarelal, *Mahatma Gandhi: The Last Phase*, part 2, reprint of 1958 edition (Ahmedabad: Navajivan Publishing House, 1997), p. 650.

[22] J. C. Kumarappa, 'Controls and Controls', *GUP*, July 1946. It was also as a response to the crisis that during this period Kumarappa began to formulate his approach of Balanced Cultivation.

[23] Speech at Prayer Meeting, 3 November 1947, *CWMG*.

[24] Speech at Prayer Meeting, 17 November 1947, *CWMG*.

[25] J. C. Kumarappa, 'What Needs Controls and How', *GUP*, December 1952. In contrast to this position, the received wisdom holds that decontrol leads to severe price rises.

the Government of India imported Japanese cloth and yarn through commercial firms. Apart from the damage to khadi, Kumarappa was incensed at India staking claim to 18 per cent of the total items to be repatriated from Japan on moral grounds. 'It is a tragedy', he argued, 'that our springs of Swaraj should be polluted at the start' by exacting 'blood money' reparations from defeated Japan.[26]

The anguish of constructive workers at the collapse of their ideals is best captured in a letter to Gandhi by the veteran constructive worker from Andhra, Gollapudi Sitarama Sastri, or as he was popularly known, Swami Sitaram.[27] It 'passes my comprehension', Sastri said, how the 'Union Government manned by such stalwart men, pillars of the Congress' like Nehru, Patel, Rajendra Prasad, Rajaji, and Azad 'should be silent parties to such action evidently opposed to the Congress tradition' of the past four decades. Sastri pointed out that he could 'visualise the agony' that Gandhi must feel 'at the strange developments' that were taking place and was 'conscious of the immeasurable generosity with which [Gandhi was] helping these lifelong co-workers, in spite of their deviation from and disclaimer of [his] ideals and methods'. Articulating the question utmost on the minds of the public as to what the Mahatma's position was on such developments, Sastri beseeched him to tackle the 'fissiparous tendencies that have already set in and arrest the decay of the movement' for swadeshi and sarvodaya. While he was deeply involved in dousing the flames of communal hatred, Gandhi was scarcely unaware of this deep chasm that lay between the Congress of the day and the social and political order that he had presented as an ideal to the nation for the past three decades. He articulated his disapproval of the working of the Government in clear but measured words during the course of his daily prayer meetings in Delhi. But if he had to take on the task of challenging the political Congress, he needed to first set in order the constructive organizations themselves.

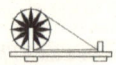

In early 1945, Gandhi was seized with the idea of merging the constructive organizations thereby creating a countervailing force to that of state

---

[26] J. C. Kumarappa, 'Blood Money', *Harijan*, 22 June 1947. Also see J. C. Kumarappa, 'The International Chore-Bazar', *Harijan*, 1 June 1947.

[27] Copy of Letter from Gollapudi Sitarama Sastri to Mahatma Gandhi, 20 June 1947, Correspondence Files, Kumarappa Papers.

power that the Congress was increasingly eager to wield. This attempt at reorganization floundered and he was drawn into the maelstrom of communal conflict. Finally, in December 1947, he revisited the idea of merging the various constructive organizations. In a meeting in Delhi, Gandhi articulated his position on constructive work and its relationship to political power. In discussing a letter that pointed out that the Constitution being shaped in Delhi had no mention of the *gram panchayat* that had always been considered 'the foundation of our future polity', Gandhi asked his audience to recognize that the 'social order of our dreams cannot come through the Congress of today'.[28] He was, as yet, unwilling to publicly criticize his political colleagues. Instead, he urged constructive workers to look within to understand why there was 'already a slackness in constructive efforts'. But his views on the nature of political power were categorical. Gandhi was asked if constructive workers should form 'themselves into a separate body and [go] into Government for the furtherance' of their agenda. Sensing the seductive allure of political power that tugged at the heart of this question, Gandhi said that constructive workers ought to keep out of politics that had become so corrupt that 'anyone who goes into [it] gets contaminated'. Tellingly he reminded his fellow workers:

> The objective of the constructive works organizations is to generate political power. But if we say that political power having come, it must be ours as a price for our labours, it would degrade us and spell our ruin.

If the constructive workers were to act as an alternative locus of moral and political power, Gandhi reasoned it was necessary 'to set our own house in order' and the constructive organizations ought to 'work unitedly and in co-operation'. If there was resistance to Gandhi's radical ideas amidst the politicians, it was no less so amongst some of the constructive workers themselves. There were some constructive workers who indirectly opposed the merger as it would reduce their powers and influence.[29] While Gandhi had urged constructive workers to look within for reasons of their failure, it was not as if he was unconcerned with the state of affairs within the Congress proper. The Congress had repudiated its moral inheritance of constructive work and sacrifice during the freedom movement and was now enjoying the fruits of power. If the Congress stalwarts treated him with respect but

[28] Discussion at Constructive Works Committee Meeting, 11/12 December 1947, *CWMG*.

[29] For some of the details on attempts to stall the merger, see Pyarelal, *Mahatma Gandhi*, p. 669.

regarded him as a spent force, Gandhi was reaching deep within himself to devise a strategy that would once again foreground satya, ahimsa, and sarvodaya. In a bold bid to purge the Congress, Gandhi sought to have the popular and unimpeachable Jayaprakash Narayan elected as president in place of Kripalani who found himself unable to obtain the co-operation of Nehru's government.[30] The failure of this attempt inexorably led Gandhi to believe that 'no patchwork treatment can save the Congress', and it was best to dissolve it 'before the rot sets in further'.[31]

While Gandhi believed that such a radical move would 'purify the political climate of the country' he knew that he could carry nobody on this matter. However, such lack of enthusiasm was seldom a deterrent to Gandhi and, as is well known, days before his assassination he drafted a radical proposal that since the Congress had 'attained political independence' for India, its current form 'as a propaganda vehicle and parliamentary machine' had 'outlived its use'.[32] If the Constitution that was being drafted had no place for a gram panchayat in it, Gandhi wanted the Congress to rebuild itself from the bottom-up into a Lok Sevak Sangh. Echoing Kumarappa's arguments that we have seen earlier, Gandhi envisaged that the new organization would take up the unfinished task of the Congress, that is, India's 'social, moral and economic independence in terms of its seven hundred thousand villages as distinguished from its cities and towns'.

While counterfactual history is fraught with risk, Gandhi was, arguably, readying himself to mount yet another moral challenge to the state and its edifice of power. This time the opponents were not colonial masters but compatriots he had worked with and moulded for many decades. While the Congress rejected his proposal as outlandish, it may be argued that Gandhi's assassination saved them the embarrassment of openly disowning the man who had created the mighty edifice of the party. Had Gandhi lived a while longer, India's 'tryst with destiny' might have been an altogether different one.

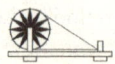

Despite the pressing demands on him to tackle the communal question in Delhi and Punjab, a meeting to discuss the reorganization of constructive

[30] Rajmohan Gandhi, *Mohandas: A True Story of a Man, His People and an Empire* (New Delhi: Viking, 2006), p. 657.

[31] Pyarelal, *Mahatma Gandhi*, p. 676.

[32] Draft Constitution of the Congress, 29 January 1948, *CWMG*.

work was scheduled for early February of 1948 at Sevagram, and Kumarappa was tasked with organizing it.[33] Having met Gandhi on 27 January 1948, he returned to Wardha to prepare for the meeting scheduled for 3 February 1948.[34] However, with Gandhi's assassination on 30 January 1948, the entire scenario changed. The assassination was a cataclysmic event and Kumarappa's mind inevitably turned to a similar event in the historical past, that is, the crucifixion of Jesus. In an article published in the *Harijan* that was penned the day after the assassination, Kumarappa urged the readers, 'Let not your heart be troubled'.[35] Quoting extensively from the Gospel of John, he pointed out that 'the words spoken [by Jesus], when he was about to be tortured to death, have a special significance for us today'. Arguing that 'things unseen are more real than the things seen', Kumarappa was nevertheless acutely aware that the 'attainment of Gandhiji's ideals' was in the spiritual and material welfare of his fellow men. In a call to the faithful, Kumarappa urged that 'we wipe away our tears and gird our loins and face the task before us with unrelenting faith in God and man'.

The meeting planned for February was confined to the administrators of constructive organizations. However, under the circumstances created by Gandhi's assassination, the wider family of his compatriots was invited to Sevagram in March.[36] Reflecting the changed circumstances since their polemical debate in 1935, Jayaprakash Narayan was invited to the meeting at the express request of Kumarappa.[37] Seeking to keep the focus of the discussions on Gandhi's original agenda, prior to the meeting, Kumarappa circulated a proposal outlining the process of merging the constructive

[33] *AIVIA Annual Report,* January 1947 to June 1948, p. 3.

[34] On Kumarappa meeting Gandhi on 27 January, see Interview to Kingsley Martin, 27 January 1948, *CWMG.* On Gandhi's proposed visit to Sevagram, see Letter to Kishorelal Mashruwala, 29 January 1948, *CWMG.*

[35] J. C. Kumarappa, 'Let Not Your Heart Be Troubled', *Harijan,* 8 February 1948.

[36] The preliminary discussions and the conference proper were held between 11 and 15 March 1948. The deliberations of these meetings were published in Hindustani as *Rachnatmak Karyakarta–Sammelan ka Vivaran* (रचनात्मक कार्यकर्ता-सम्मेलन का विवरण) (Sevagram: R. S. Dhotre, 1949). We are grateful to Atmaram Saraogi and Gopalkrishna Gandhi for making a copy of this rare document available to us. A condensed English translation is available as Gopalkrishna Gandhi (ed.), *Gandhi Is Gone: Who Will Guide Us Now?* (New Delhi: Permanent Black, 2007).

[37] Letter from R. S. Dhotre to J. C. Kumarappa, 28 February 1948, Subject File, 18, Kumarappa Papers.

organizations. However, the overwhelming majority of participants at the Sevagram meeting had little to do with the operational specifics of these organizations. Consequently, they dwelt on their relationship with Gandhi and also on the many crises that had gripped independent India's polity and society. In the process of these wider deliberations, many fine distinctions that Gandhi had himself maintained were easily transgressed. Consequently, the Sevagram meeting led to a radical reconstitution of Gandhi's legacy. While a detailed analysis is beyond our scope here, two specific issues merit consideration.

First, Gandhi had become increasingly aware of the need to challenge the Congress in power and insisted on maintaining the distinction between the political Congress and the constructive workers. However, other than Kumarappa, this distinction was lost even on the constructive workers who organized the Sevagram meeting. Thus, the curious spectacle of Jawaharlal Nehru inaugurating the meeting. Nehru's arrival at the meeting led to 'uniformed police with fixed bayonets ... and barbed wire all around' the Sevagram ashram.[38] While Kripalani voiced his protest at such a violation of the ethos of the place, Kumarappa was upset enough to entirely boycott Nehru's visit. Fighting the many fires that raged all around, Nehru spoke feelingly about India's predicament and the danger of the country being torn asunder. In itself this was unexceptionable. However, in a strange move, the organizers made the various representatives of constructive work organizations 'place before Panditji details of their functioning and their difficulties'.[39] Evidently, it did not matter that the Congress had rejected Gandhi's call to disband itself. Moreover, Nehru had made no secret of his contempt for constructive work and its value. Thus, in reply to Jhaverbhai Patel's representation on behalf of the AIVIA, Nehru questioned the very value of the economy that Gandhi and Kumarappa were trying to build. While this was an honest difference of opinion, Nehru also lectured his audience to focus on Gandhi's fundamental ideas. Take 'away khadi and village industries and all those other things', he argued, 'and Bapuji's fundamental ideas still remain intact'![40] At a meeting that was centred on reorganizing Gandhi's constructive work organizations, this was a strange affair.

[38] G. Gandhi, *Gandhi Is Gone*, p. 53.

[39] G. Gandhi, *Gandhi Is Gone*, p. 54.

[40] G. Gandhi, *Gandhi Is Gone*, p. 60. Here, the phrase 'village industries' replaces the translation used, 'cottage industries'. The original phrase used by Nehru is 'gram udyog'.

The second significant fact of the Sevagram meeting was the anointment of Vinoba Bhave as heir to Gandhi's constructive work legacy. While his moral worth was beyond question, Vinoba was in many ways constituted differently from the Mahatma. If Gandhi was a supremely gifted builder of organizational capacities, Vinoba was quite the opposite with anarchist sensibilities. Thus, instead of the discussion focusing on how best to merge Gandhi's constructive organizations, Vinoba objected to the very idea of any form of organization as he had 'always been rather opposed to the fetters of institutions'.[41] Instead, he plumped for a 'fraternal brotherhood'. To be fair to him, at this point in time, Vinoba was deeply worried about the danger of a cult being formed around the late Mahatma. However, in the process, Vinoba created enormous confusion by pushing forward the idea of an amorphous brotherhood with no constraints or rules. This flew in the face of Gandhi's lawyer-like meticulous attention to the nuts and bolts of organizational planning. Kumarappa recognized the danger inherent in Vinoba's proposition and pointed out that 'a loose-hanging and flabby organization will do nothing' and end up harming the constructive work agenda.[42] In a plaintive note, Kumarappa rued the fact that after Gandhi's death, they were 'groping for the light that will tell us what is to be done with Swaraj'.[43] This was the time to 'derive a new inspiration from constructive activities'. Recognizing the blurring of the lines between the Congress and constructive work, Kumarappa reiterated Gandhi's views from the December 1947 meeting in Delhi. He argued that

> [d]emocracy means decentralization of political power. We do not want to enter government. Let the government come to us. And let the government ask us for guidance. Let government ask us, constructive workers, to empower it. The entire Cabinet sought sanctuary at Gandhiji's feet. Let us also, with our limited strength, aim at acquiring an inner energy.

The Sevagram meeting was probably cathartic to many of Gandhi's stunned followers. However, by failing to grapple with key questions at this crucial meeting, the cause of constructive work was inadvertently dealt a severe blow. In a sense, the eventual decline of the Sarvodaya ideal in the public realm can be traced back to all that did not transpire at the Sevagram meeting. Vinoba's ideas resulted in the formation of a separate organization known as the Sarvodaya Samaj which created enormous confusion.

[41] G. Gandhi, *Gandhi Is Gone*, p. 31.
[42] G. Gandhi, *Gandhi Is Gone*, p. 39.
[43] G. Gandhi, *Gandhi Is Gone*, p. 93.

A distraught Kumarappa was given the onerous task of merging the constructive organizations in the face of 'much opposition from influential quarters'.[44] The elisions were not lost on the wider public. An angry worker commiserated with Kumarappa and wrote that the 'Sarvodaya Conference at Wardha has betrayed its weakness in not having the courage to ask the constructive field workers never to enter [the] parliamentary field'.[45] Instead of concrete ideas, he argued, 'the Wardha Conference ended in mere verbosity'. In 1949, the Sarva Seva Sangh was created and various constructive work organizations, including the AIVIA, were merged into it.

Another element in the reconstitution of Gandhi's constructive work legacy was the institution of the Gandhi Smarak Nidhi—or the Gandhi National Memorial Fund—with an intent for the funds to be 'utilized largely for furthering the manifold constructive activities in which Gandhiji was interested'.[46] Rajendra Prasad was elected president of the fund with Kripalani and Kumarappa as secretaries. Arguing against raising funds for a physical memorial, Kumarappa pointed out that Gandhi's programmes never lacked in finances but the 'one great difficulty has always been the lack of the human element'.[47] Kumarappa put forth a bold demand for apostles who would through their 'devotion and renunciation' embody the ideals of the Mahatma and would in turn 'radiate the light that characterized Gandhiji'. Apart from the sheer waste of money on statues, pillars, and the like, Kumarappa's argument was also an expression of a more pressing concern. For a while, many amongst the Gandhian fold had been disturbed by the ability of the Rashtriya Swayamsevak Sangh to attract the youth to its divisive programme. The fact that the Gandhian community was no longer able to inspire such youth to dedicate themselves to more worthy causes was utmost in many minds. Turning the light inwards, Kumarappa said that 'if thousands of our young men have been similarly misguided into paths of violence, the fault lies with us for not having brought the way

[44] Letter from J. C. Kumarappa to P. K. Salve, 28 March 1948, Correspondence Files, Kumarappa Papers.

[45] Letter from R. Mandreswara Rao to J. C. Kumarappa, 7 April 1948, Subject File, 18, Kumarappa Papers.

[46] Rajendra Prasad, 'Two Resolutions', *Harijan*, 15 February 1948.

[47] J. C. Kumarappa, 'Gandhi Pillars', *GUP*, March 1948.

of non-violence to them'. Thus instead of 'merely banning the institutions', it was necessary to channel such idealism 'into constructive ways'. Many agreed that the communal virus had to be condemned, but Kumarappa was also highly critical of the national leadership. He pointed to the acute irony when 'even before the warmth of [Gandhiji's] body was gone' it was decided to accord him 'a state funeral ... with salutes from guns!'[48] If anything, it 'seemed as though organised violence' was 'gloating over the passing away of its inveterate enemy'.

Based substantially on donations from a few industrialists, the *nidhi* rapidly grew in size to a corpus of Rs 13 crores.[49] The outspoken Kumarappa characterized the 'memorial fund [as] just conscience money screwed out of stained hands'.[50] Eventually he resigned his 'secretaryship of the Memorial Fund and declined to serve on their Board of Trustees ... made up of twenty-two politicians and industrialists' as against two constructive workers. In contrast to the nidhi, Kumarappa proposed that a 'fund' of one lakh volunteers be raised to carry forward Gandhi's agenda. Asked how he would administer it, Kumarappa called for the first three donations—Pandit Nehru to rally the youth, Amrit Kaur to raise a women volunteer corps, and Sardar Patel to apply his administrative acumen to the task.[51] While this was obviously a rhetorical flourish, the point about the fall from Gandhi's idealism was made.

[48] J. C. Kumarappa, 'Memorials', *GUP*, March 1948.

[49] Vinaik, *Gandhian Crusader*, p. 149.

[50] Letter from J. C. Kumarappa to Dwarka Nath Bhargava, 21 April 1949, Correspondence Files, Kumarappa Papers.

[51] Vinaik, *Quest*, p. 122.

14   Land to the Tiller

During the decades leading up to freedom, a most crucial issue that emerged was the future of India's agrarian economy. The question of social and economic justice in independent India was decidedly tied to the fate of the vast numbers of peasants, sharecroppers, and agricultural labourers who formed the bulk of India's population. In the years immediately following Independence, Kumarappa attempted to foreground the concerns of the agrarian economy and India's farmers. With the benefit of hindsight, we know that independent India failed to render justice in the fullest measure to the agrarian economy and to farmers. Insight into the nature of this failure can be obtained by considering Kumarappa's dogged attempts to highlight the concerns of the millions of lives that depended on the agrarian economy.

To a significant extent, the vexed nature of India's agrarian crisis has its origins in the land and taxation policy adopted by Britain since the inception of its rule over India. The colonial policy, both under the East India Company and the British Crown, was largely shaped by its need for a reliable and substantial source of revenue. In an agrarian economy, these revenue demands translated into an extractive and exploitative system of taxation on landownership and agricultural production. In pre-colonial India, ownership and cultivation rights in land were not identical and a whole variety of customary practices and social relations had evolved in the different regions of the subcontinent.[1] Over a period of time, the British carried out a massive re-engineering of both the legal basis of land rights and the concomitant social equations through the institution of systems of *zamindari* such as the Permanent Settlement of Bengal as well as taxation policies in the ryotwari areas of southern and western India. The outcome was a transformation, whereby the 'Indian peasantry became a tenantry under British rule'.[2] The result was devastating, and when the traditional caste-based inequalities were compounded with the economic demands of colonial rule, life for the Indian peasant became intolerable. As one commentator remarked, 'two centuries of British rule had thrown the entire peasant economy of India into a period of permanent and acute crisis'.[3]

If British dominion over India resulted in an exploitative equation between the metropole and the colony, the land revenue policies of zamindari created a homologous relationship between the landlord and the peasant. Indeed, India's *zamindars* 'functioned economically as the native garrisons of an alien imperialism'.[4] The conditions created by these multiple layers of exploitation would come to inform the defining characteristic of Indian nationalism, that is, the simultaneous struggle for political freedom from the British and social emancipation from the inequalities inherent in Indian society.[5] A striking feature of the early Indian indictment of British rule had been its economic critique of colonialism. From the early 1920s, Indian nationalists also adopted an increasingly strident tone against the economic divide that existed *within* Indian society. A central premise of this critique was that the Permanent Settlement in Bengal and zamindari

[1] These economic relations were highly unequal and reflected the social inequalities of Indian society.

[2] Rothermund, *Government, Landlord and Peasant*, p. 86. Using available evidence, Rothermund concluded that 'Indian feudalism had the rights of the peasant at its base and that the rights of superior tenure holders were a superstructure built upon this solid foundation, whereas English law took the right of the lord as its point of departure and then constructed its various limitations in terms of rights encroaching on that fundamental right' (p. 88).

[3] H. D. Malaviya, *Land Reforms in India*, second edition (New Delhi: All-India Congress Committee, 1955), p. 8.

[4] H. D. Malaviya, *Land Reforms in India*, p. 46.

[5] Gandhi's historical role was to embody leadership on both of these central problems. From its earlier avatar of representing elite interests, Gandhi had transformed the staid Congress into an inclusive platform and thereby significantly modified its class character. Starting with the novel use of satyagraha in Champaran in 1917, the masses were increasingly drawn into the political campaign for freedom.

and ryotwari taxation were the bedrock of the inequity of colonial rule. Throughout the 1930s and 1940s along with the struggle against British rule, national politics saw the emergence of a demand for justice for the exploited peasantry. As a result of both its opening up to encompass multiple class interests, and steady challenges of militant peasant protests from outside, the Congress had to perforce respond to these demands. Since the Lahore and Karachi sessions of 1929 and 1931 respectively, the Congress increasingly committed itself to delivering tangible relief to India's farmers.

In the early 1930s, the Congress led campaigns against agricultural rent and taxation, but within a decade it was clear that radical land reforms were necessary. Although land reform could not be achieved without independence, the Congress was pressed to clarify its position. Given its rather egregious nature, there was widespread acceptance within the Congress leadership that the system of zamindari had to be abolished. However, on the question of appropriate compensation there was far less clarity or consensus and the Congress found itself in a quandary. In fighting the British, the Congress sought to present a united front of different segments of society. As a result, the simple expedient of expropriating the assets of the powerful zamindars seemed politically infeasible. By the mid-1930s, the abolition of zamindari was tied to the idea of 'reasonable compensation'.[6] Although the vexed question of compensation continued to exercise the Congress leadership, Gandhi arrived at a clear position. Asked for his views by the American journalist Louis Fischer in June 1942, Gandhi had no hesitation in arguing that land had to be confiscated without compensation as 'it would be financially impossible for anyone to compensate the landlords'.[7] While being held in the Aga Khan Palace, Gandhi had told Mirabehn that the land would be owned by the state and if it was not given willingly, the zamindars 'will have to do so under legislation'.[8]

While the Congress was radicalized to an extent, the British position was far less amenable to change. With no popular mandate, the Raj needed the propertied classes to back their presence in India. In 1928, the Royal Commission on Agriculture in India had carried out a massive and detailed inquiry into the possibilities of improving food production in India. The commission was expressly prohibited from looking into the question of

[6] H. D. Malaviya, *Land Reforms in India*, p. 59.

[7] Louis Fischer, *A Week with Gandhi* (Bombay: International Book House Ltd., 1944), p. 73.

[8] 'Bapu on Land Distribution', *Harijan*, 29 December 1951.

either landownership or tenancy. The severe agrarian crisis during the War years and the devastating Bengal Famine of 1943 finally forced the Raj to consider these issues. The Famine Inquiry Commission report of 1945 carried out the first systematic official study of the countrywide land tenure system.[9] But, as a dissenting member argued, the Famine Inquiry Commission failed to address 'wider issues such as the moral implications of the system, its inequitable basis, and the degenerating influence it exercises on the vast population under it.'[10] In the aftermath of the War crisis, the Congress view also gained clarity, although it was decidedly less radical than expropriation. In its election manifesto of 1946, the Congress articulated its position that was to become crucial in the rapidly evolving political situation and have a telling impact on the long-term prospects for land reform in India. Although it averred that 'the reform of the land system ... involves the removal of intermediaries between the peasant and the State', it also declared that these intermediary rights should 'be acquired on payment of equitable compensation'.[11]

After these elections, many Congress-led provincial governments had set in motion steps towards tackling the question of land reform, most notably in the case of the UP Zamindari Abolition Committee that covered the infamous landed gentry of Awadh. Now that the reins of power were finally in its hands, the Congress was increasingly called upon to address the issue of agrarian land utilization. For a long time, both the colonial regime and many nationalists had believed that India's agricultural land had come to be exceedingly fragmented resulting in greatly diminished yields. In particular, given the grave food crisis that gripped the country at the time, it was believed that agriculture had to be reorganized to take advantage of modern technologies that could only be economically viable on a minimum scale. With a view to increased productivity of the land, the Congress argued that 'while individualist farming or peasant proprietorship should continue, progressive agriculture as well as the creation of new social values and incentives require some system of cooperative farming suited to Indian conditions'. These ideas on land reform and agriculture came to

[9] Relevant sections on land tenures were issued as a separate volume, *Land Tenures in India*.

[10] 'Minute of Dissent by Manilal B. Nanavati', in *The Famine Inquiry Commission: Final Report*, Madras: Manager of Publications, 1945, p. 348. Nanavati also pointed out that the Floud Commission appointed by the Bengal Provincial Government in 1938 had definitely called for the abolition of zamindari.

[11] Quoted in H. D. Malaviya, *Land Reforms in India*, p. 75.

be reasserted in the formulation of the economic policy of the Congress in the influential *Report of the Economic Programme Committee* written under Nehru's chairmanship with Kumarappa as a member.

By the time the central leadership of the Congress began to devote attention to agrarian questions in late 1947, the provincial governments had already undertaken measures towards abolishing intermediaries in their own land revenue systems. Given these circumstances, and the varied histories and specificities of each region, it was argued that the individual states 'should be free to deal with the question of abolition of the system in accordance with their peculiar circumstances'.[12] While indeed this argument had much merit, it also allowed the landed classes to assert a degree of local control over the legislation on land reform. At a conference of revenue ministers, it was agreed that while land reform could proceed in a piecemeal fashion, it was both desirable and possible to have a common basis of concerted action in the post-abolition era on a variety of questions of importance to the agrarian economy. Consequently, Rajendra Prasad, as the president of the Congress, appointed the Congress Agrarian Reforms Committee (ARC) with Kumarappa as its chairman.

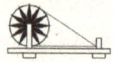

Before we proceed to examine the work of the ARC, it is instructive to consider its terms of reference:

> The Committee will have to examine and make recommendations about agrarian reforms arising out of the abolition of zamindari system in the light of conditions prevailing in the different provinces. The Committee will consider and report on co-operative farming and methods of improving agricultural production, position of small holdings, sub-tenants, landless labourers and generally on improving the conditions of agricultural rural population.[13]

---

[12] H. D. Malaviya, *Land Reforms in India*, p. 82.

[13] J. C. Kumarappa (chairman), *Report of the Congress Agrarian Reforms Committee*, (henceforth *ARC Report*) (New Delhi: All-India Congress Committee, 1949), pp. 3–4. The other members of the committee were the economist M. L. Dantwala; S. Das Gupta of the Government of West Bengal; T. V. Raghavulu who represented agricultural labour and later became the minister for education in Andhra Pradesh; O. P. Ramaswamy Reddiar, the Premier of Madras Presidency for most of the tenure of the committee; the well-known *kisan* leader and organizer

Although these terms of reference did not expressly prohibit the ARC from considering questions of land reform, they were framed with a view to defining policy *after* land reforms were carried out. The terms of reference were also muddled as they explicitly defined the ARC's remit as dealing with the zamindari areas and did not mention the ryotwari regions which had entirely different conditions. In any event, the emphasis was not on a radical solution to the landownership question but 'co-operative farming and methods of improving agricultural production'.

The committee first drew up a questionnaire that was sent to the provincial governments, provincial Congress committees and others with expertise in agrarian issues. An examination of the 182 responses received led the committee to conclude that it was difficult to formulate 'an overall approach to the agrarian problem of the country' using the replies alone, as they did not provide insights into local variations. Instead, Kumarappa decided that the committee should travel extensively across the country to 'collect data first-hand by local enquiry' as well as 'get the reactions of the peasants to the proposed scheme of agrarian reforms'.[14] Despite his very poor health, between June 1948 and January 1949, Kumarappa travelled more than 14,000 miles and visited the provinces of CP and Berar, Bombay, Assam, West Bengal, Orissa, Bihar, Madras, and the United Provinces. These ARC visits offered Kumarappa an unparalleled, if depressing, understanding of the ground realities of agrarian India. During these travels, the committee examined more than 250 expert witnesses, received a variety of notes and memoranda and visited many villages to get first-hand knowledge of agrarian conditions. Based on the extensive regional and local evidence thus gathered, the *ARC Report* was prepared and submitted to the Congress in July 1949.[15] However, owing to the unsettled political situation in the country, the committee could not visit the important Punjab region or any of the princely states.

N. G. Ranga; Ameer Raza who served as the Secretary of the UP Zamindari Abolition Committee; Phulan Prasad Verma who worked at the Damodar Valley Corporation; and K. Mitra of the AICC who acted as the secretary of the committee.

[14] *ARC Report*, p. 4.

[15] The ARC recommendations addressed the issues of land reforms, the pattern of agrarian economy, the role of co-operative farming as well as the appropriate bureaucratic mechanism of land management. In addition, it also addressed the problems of agricultural indebtedness, rural finance and marketing, as also the concerns of landless labourers and the way to promote agricultural improvements and agro-industries.

The ARC began with the assumption that no lasting improvement in production and efficiency was possible without 'comprehensive reforms in the country's land system'.[16] It reiterated the Congress position that 'in the agrarian economy of India there is no place for intermediaries and land must belong to the tiller'. However, as the ARC emphatically argued, the issue of agrarian reform was greater than land reform and had to address a large variety of complex and differentiated problems that went far beyond the conceptual simplicity of zamindari abolition. For, 'even after the abolition of zamindari, there would remain a large element of non-cultivating interests in the land'. To address this vexed problem of ownership rights, the ARC recommended that, with some exceptions, subletting was to be prohibited and that anyone cultivating for a continuous period of six years automatically gained full occupancy rights. While allowing for the possibility of owners resuming cultivation to be able to retain their land rights, the ARC called for a strict definition of ownership rights based on personal cultivation, that is, 'only those who put in a minimum amount of physical labour and participate in actual agricultural operations would be deemed to cultivate land personally'. Although a 'one size fits all' solution was undesirable, to achieve coherence in its recommendations—'variety in form' with 'unity in idea'—the ARC laid out its normative objectives. It sought to provide an opportunity for the development of the farmer's personality, to eliminate any scope for exploitation, to achieve maximal efficiency of production as well as design schemes that are practicable.[17]

The ARC had to strive hard to reconcile the objectives of providing 'a reasonable standard of living to the cultivator' while improving the overall efficiency of agricultural production. The key conceptual idea that the committee evolved to address these two criteria was three different norms for landholdings, that is, Basic, Economic, and Optimum. An Economic holding was one which could afford a reasonable standard of living to the farmer.[18] It is here that Kumarappa's personal imprint and his concern with the larger social and ecological objectives become apparent as the Economic holding had to also 'provide full employment to a family of normal size and at least to a pair of bullocks'. Contradicting the modernist view, it

[16] ARC Report, p. 7.
[17] ARC Report, p. 8.
[18] The definition of an Economic holding did not specify a fixed size of landholding as the amount of land required to afford a decent living would show great variation across the country. The Optimum holding was specified as being three times the size of an Economic holding.

argued that 'for a good long time Indian agriculture is not going to be mechanised because no substantial portion of the population employed in agriculture can be taken to any alternative employment through industrial development'.[19] The other controversial proposal of the *ARC Report* was the introduction of 'a ceiling to the size of holdings which any one farmer should own and cultivate'.[20] Given the fundamental objective of reducing social inequity and the limited availability of land, the ARC argued that it would be 'irrational and unjust' not to put a ceiling. The committee went a step further and argued that analogous to their recommended ceiling on land holdings, the Congress should endeavour to fix 'the maximum limits of income in other sectors of our economic life'.[21] Evidently, the contemporary debates on caps on corporate salaries have precedents at least as far back as 1949.

The *ARC Report* was the first significant Congress document that unambiguously specified a ceiling on landholdings. However, much of the subsequent state legislation parried the question of fixing a ceiling. The inability and unwillingness of the Congress to seriously follow through on land ceilings was the chief reason for the failure of land reforms in independent India. By this time, India's farming land had become exceedingly fragmented to the point that apart from satisfying psychological land hunger, the tiny or small fragments of lands held by the majority of farmers were neither economically viable nor efficient. In a frank assessment of the practical limits to agrarian reform, the ARC recognized that rehabilitating these land fragments was 'beyond the organisational competence of the State'.[22] However, it argued that in between these unviable sizes and that of the Economic holding, there was a broad spectrum that the committee termed as a Basic holding. Such holdings were 'not palpably uneconomic and would be capable of being built up' by viable measures into an Economic holding.[23]

Before we examine the recommended farming practices, it is important to understand the notion of land rights that the ARC recognized. The British destruction of the fabric of Indian economic life was achieved by two interlocking measures. Along with the destruction of the artisanal economy, especially that of handlooms, the zamindari and ryotwari systems

[19] *ARC Report*, p. 44.
[20] *ARC Report*, p. 9.
[21] *ARC Report*, p. 22.
[22] *ARC Report*, p. 9.
[23] *ARC Report*, p. 22.

of landownership and tenancy resulted in an unequal relationship between the peasants on the one hand and the landlords and the state on the other. Although the ARC recognized that scholarly opinion was divided on the exact nature of the proprietary rights in land prior to the advent of the East India Company, it had no hesitation in agreeing with Marx's characterization of British land management in India as 'a string of unsuccessful and really absurd experiments in economics'.[24] While recognizing that there was an entire legal tradition in India in land rights, the ARC maintained that it was far more concerned with redeeming the situation as obtained upon Independence, since 'in defining the new scheme of rights we should look forward'.[25] The ARC argued that the actual cultivator should have 'permanent and heritable right of cultivation in land'.[26] However, in seeking to reconstitute the vitality of the village community, the ARC inflected the argument on property rights by opining that rights in the land 'should be shared between the community and the tiller'.[27] In particular, it argued for the strict prohibition of subtenancy as the entire rationale for land reform was to remove the non-cultivating interests that had interceded in the relationship between the peasant and the state.

Although it is not explicitly stated in the *ARC Report*, one may be sure of the two key motivations for Kumarappa here. First, he recognized the complex circumstances within which the rights of the tiller would be operationalized. Even under the most radical dispensation of land reform, due to the exceedingly large number of claimants over the land most tenants would not be able to make ends meet with the little land that they might be able to lay claim to. Under such circumstances, it was quite likely that over a period of time, this land would get alienated again. Second, under the pressures of an increasingly monetized economy, peasants were likely to move towards cash crops. As we have seen earlier, the War years had taught Kumarappa that self-sufficiency in food ought to be the fundamental guiding precept for agrarian reform. It is with such exigencies in mind that the ARC sought to strike a balance between individual property rights and

[24] Quoted in *ARC Report*, p. 34.
[25] *ARC Report*, p. 35. A recent assessment of Kautilya's *Arthashastra* argues that the colonial stereotype of the Oriental Despot who held sway over all the land is incorrect. Both the sovereign and the tiller customarily shared rights. See Thomas R. Trautmann, *Arthashastra: The Science of Wealth* (New Delhi: Allen Lane, 2012), p. 121.
[26] *ARC Report*, p. 35.
[27] *ARC Report*, p. 10.

the far more complex social and economic context within which a peasant lived and worked. Thus, in a delicate balancing act, it was argued that neither did property rights imply that the owner was free to use or misuse the land as he wished, nor did it mean that 'the State should assume all the rights and authority leaving no scope' for the cultivator. The solution to this conundrum lay in administering the requisite social control in the hands of 'a decentralised machinery, namely, the Village Community'.[28] This view stemmed from the belief that unlike the alien power of a distant state, the peasant could exercise some control and influence over the village community. Written at a time when the legal framework of the Indian Constitution was not yet in place, the ARC was necessarily vague in defining this 'village community'. In any event, the village panchayat did not even figure as an institution in the Constitution that was adopted and the ARC's land rights recommendations remained an academic endeavour.

Apart from the redistribution of land rights, the ARC also concerned itself with the modes of farming appropriate for the different types of holdings it proposed. In the main, the committee was concerned with the modus operandi to be adopted with respect to the vast number of fragmented landholdings that were smaller than the Basic one. It was not possible to achieve any improvement of productivity without enforcing some sort of co-operative effort between the individual landholders. As in the case of rights over land, once again we witness the contradictory forces in the complicated suggestions of the ARC. The ARC evinced a distaste for the 'odium of coercion', but strove hard to evolve a mechanism whereby it would be possible for marginal farmers to pool their resources into a co-operative society.[29] However, it also recognized that 'co-operation does not work in the midst of utter poverty and destitution'.[30] The mechanism proposed by the ARC was an elaborate and unconvincing argument for multipurpose co-operative societies that would somehow reconcile these contrarian impulses as well as take the edge off the coercive powers of the state.[31] The ARC was far clearer in proposing the use of collective farming efforts on reclaimed waste land. It argued that by organizing landless labourers into such collective farms, it would be possible for the state to

[28] *ARC Report*, p. 36.

[29] *ARC Report*, p. 26.

[30] *ARC Report*, p. 25.

[31] The ARC also dwelt at length on the nature of the multipurpose co-operative societies it advocated, the forms of finance and market as well as issues of concern such as agricultural indebtedness, and the promotion of agro-industries.

satisfy the 'land hunger' of the poor as well as work out the mechanisms of collective farming. It is likely that these arguments arose out of the collective views of the committee and were not necessarily Kumarappa's personal views. Despite plumbing for co-operative endeavours in farming, the ARC was quite clear that the small holdings 'may not be pooled into a single giant farm but may be allowed voluntarily to join in any co-operative joint farm', that is, the ARC argued for a fair amount of flexibility and freedom of choice for individual farmers to organize themselves into a variety of scales of operation.[32] However, in later years, when placed in less sympathetic hands, the idea of co-operative farming took on a far more bureaucratic and coercive form leading to vigorous opposition from various quarters.[33]

The *ARC Report* was a key document on agrarian reform at a crucial juncture of India's political evolution, but its recommendations were far from unanimous. The two important political leaders on the committee, namely O. P. Ramaswamy Reddiar and N. G. Ranga, disagreed with the majority opinion and wrote their own 'Minute of Dissent'.[34] With an eye to the availability of mechanized power, Reddiar and Ranga held that it was inappropriate to tie the notion of an Economic holding to 'the maintenance of or work for a pair of bullocks' or fix on a formula for the size of holdings.[35] Their dissent hinged on two crucial issues. First, although they believed that help from the state had to be provided, Reddiar and Ranga were opposed to any form of compulsion in making co-operative farming possible. Second, they correctly argued that many of the questions surrounding land rights in the zamindari areas ought not to inform land rights policy in the ryotwari areas of southern India that the duo hailed from. They argued that unlike the zamindars the south Indian 'peasants possess both the ownership and cultivation rights' and while they ploughed their profits back into improving the land, for such a peasant 'any idea of paying compensation to only one of these two great components of his rights over land becomes incomprehensible and goes against his fundamental conception of social justice'.[36]

---

[32] *ARC Report*, p. 26.

[33] A prime critic of an authoritarian form of co-operative farming was the farmer leader and future prime minister, Charan Singh. See Charan Singh, *India's Poverty and Its Solution* (Bombay: Asia Publishing House, 1964). An earlier version of this book was published under the title *Joint Farming X-Rayed: The Problem and Its Solution*.

[34] A third member, T. V. Raghavulu, did not sign the final report.

[35] *ARC Report*, p. 191.

[36] *ARC Report*, p. 201.

Kumarappa argued that the dissenting note was 'rather academic' as Reddiar and Ranga had failed to participate in the extensive travels of the committee.[37] Kumarappa's complaint might appear to be the peevish response of a committee chairman unable to deal with dissent. However, it was indeed the case that apart from attending meetings held in southern India, neither Reddiar nor Ranga spared any time to travel with the committee to either examine any of the witnesses or gather first-hand knowledge. If Reddiar was busy administering the Madras Province as its premier, for most of the duration of the ARC's term, Ranga was travelling in England and the United States.[38] In fact, except for Kumarappa, none of the other members put in any significant effort in touring the country to obtain evidence. Although he did not explicitly say so, in Kumarappa's eyes this betrayed a lack of seriousness in engaging with the vital questions surrounding the agrarian economy.

Some of the problems with the ARC Report lay in its very terms of reference. Designing agrarian policy for the entire country in the context of the abolition of zamindari was a contradiction that could hardly be overcome. As a result, in trying to formulate a single framework, the ARC Report is shot through with inadequate attempts to reconcile multiple issues of great complexity. Admittedly, the rather explicit views on land ceilings and other issues made the ARC Report a document with radical potential. Indeed, a leading scholar of India's political economy sees it as 'the first major product of socialist–Gandhian collaboration on an outstanding public issue after Independence'.[39] However, it is hard to agree with such an interpretation unless one assumes that the socialist and Gandhian ideologies were simultaneously embodied in the persona of Kumarappa. The composition of the committee and its attempts to reconcile many contrarian impulses militated against a clear line of argument. Indeed, given our understanding of Kumarappa's personality it is rather surprising that he agreed to chair such a committee in the first place. One may surmise that it was the significance of the problem of agrarian reform that made Kumarappa agreeable to take on the chairmanship of the ARC. This interpretation is based on the fact that many of the recommendations of the ARC Report do not fit well with Kumarappa's own sensibilities. Indeed,

[37] ARC Report, p. 2.
[38] For one side of the exchange between Ranga and Kumarappa, see N. G. Ranga, Agony and Solace: Correspondence, Statements, Speeches etc. 1936–1974 (Nidubrolu: Kisan Publications, 1974), pp. 156–9.
[39] Francine Frankel, India's Political Economy 1947–2004: The Gradual Revolution, second edition (New Delhi: Oxford University Press, 2004), p. 67.

despite his sharp and angular personality, the contents of the *ARC Report* suggest that at a crucial juncture, Kumarappa did accede to the Gandhian principle of compromising on specifics without prejudice to one's own fundamental beliefs.

In any event, the recommendations of the *ARC Report* floundered on the rocks of realpolitik. For entirely valid reasons of protecting individual rights, the framers of the Constitution provided for due process and 'sought to protect the individual's personal liberty against prejudicial action by an arbitrary Executive'.[40] Consequently, the process of expropriation of zamindari land was delayed due to legal challenges in the courts till Nehru's government was forced to amend the Constitution. The other factor that militated against significant land reforms was that the cash-strapped state governments could not mobilize finances to compensate for the acquired land. To make matters worse, the central government told the states not to expect help in this regard and the RBI refused to float bonds on the grounds that it would undermine international confidence in the rupee.[41] It is an important question to ask as to why part of the Sterling Balances were not used towards zamindari abolition, especially since a significant part of the credit was built out of agricultural produce appropriated by the British during the War years. Of all such factors, the most significant development was the relegation of the institution of the village panchayat to the doghouse of Directive Principles. Without an adequate framework of legal enforcement of political decentralization, the possibility of significant progressive legislation on land reform was foreclosed.

In the long run, the *ARC Report* had limited influence on the course of Indian agrarian reforms. Consequently, much of the literature on the politics around land reform in independent India deals with the report in a rather perfunctory manner. In a few instances, scholars have failed to recognize the precise nature of the relationship of the report with the larger context of political bargaining in the early years of Independence. This gap in understanding has led to gross misinterpretations of both the basis *and* consequences of the ARC report. Thus, one writer declared

---

[40] Granville Austin, *The Indian Constitution: Cornerstone of a Nation* (New Delhi: Oxford University Press, 1999), pp. 105–6.

[41] For instance see Jawaharlal Nehru, *Letters to Chief Ministers: 1947–1964*, volume 1, edited by G. Parthasarathy (New Delhi: Oxford University Press, 1985), p. 190. This position is explicitly spelt out in Letter from Jawaharlal Nehru to O. P. Ramaswamy Reddiar, 9 September 1948, O. P. Ramaswamy Reddiar Papers, NMML.

that it 'failed to provide a solid, analytical, factual base for agrarian reform and land reform'.[42] Instead, its recommendations reflected 'nationalist polemics ... golden age myths ... the misinterpretation of economic precepts ... and ideological dogma'. This denunciation traces the subsequent failure of India's agrarian reforms to the purported failures of the *ARC Report*. However, a more attentive examination of the context within which the report came to be written may lead to more tenable conclusions.

The work of the ARC was carried out in the interstitial period between the end of colonial rule and the promulgation of the Constitution, that is, it was shaped in the context of an information vacuum as to the normative legal framework that would render its recommendations into concrete action. Indeed, the omissions and commissions in India's Constitution played a far more significant role in the failure of land reforms. Another noteworthy feature of the ARC was that it was a committee constituted by the Congress and not by the Government of India. Admittedly, for many, in these early years of freedom there was not much of a distinction between the Congress party and the government. However, by conflating the party with the state we ignore the variegated nature of political opinion within the Congress. As far as executive power was concerned, it was really the Congress-as-the-state that carried the day. Therefore, the ARC recommendations lacked the necessary official imprimatur and were easily ignored. In making its large body of complex recommendations, the *ARC Report* called for the setting up of a vast organization tasked with placing the agrarian sector at the heart of the national economy. In the event, this place at the 'commanding heights' came to be occupied by the Planning Commission with priorities that militated against the needs of agrarian India.

Kumarappa insisted that a clear understanding of the agrarian problems could only be had by the ARC travelling extensively to take direct evidence 'by visiting rural areas and meeting the man behind the plough' and not limit itself to the evidence taken in the cities.[43] Although most of the other

[42] F. Tomasson Jannuzi, *India's Persistent Dilemma: The Political Economy of Agrarian Reform* (Boulder: Westview Press, 1994), p. 66.

[43] 'Congress Inquiry into Agrarian Reforms: Report Expected To Be Ready in November Next', *Times of India*, 7 July 1948, Press Clippings, Kumarappa Papers.

members did not spend much time travelling, Kumarappa himself ranged across the length and breadth of the country and saw the pernicious effects of the caste order in rural India. Throughout India he witnessed different forms of agrestic serfdom where, for all practical purposes, 'field labourers are slaves bought at nominal cost by the land owners', although in legal terms they were debtors and not slaves.[44] An experience in the district of Gorakhpur deeply disturbed Kumarappa. Here, he learnt, members of the ritually and socially oppressed *chamar* caste were allowed the 'privilege' of collecting undigested grain from cow dung.

Kumarappa repeatedly denounced such social degradation that was the lot of landless labourers and inevitably the weight of his criticism resulted in a controversy. While taking evidence in Kozhayur, a village near Mayiladuthurai in present-day Nagapattinam district, the ARC noticed that many houses had been destroyed by the henchmen of the *mirasdar* landowners of the area. The committee was told that this fate was meted out to the labourers 'as a reprisal against their demand for higher wages' and it also heard stories of physical violence in all the villages of the region.[45] The rank exploitation of the labourers by the landowners of the region had been a serious and persistent problem. Kumarappa's public comments on this matter forced the Madras Government to institute an enquiry into the violence in Kozhayur. Eventually, the influence of the landlords prevailed and the immediate controversy was defused by the government which indulged in much dissimulation in the Legislative Assembly on the correctness of Kumarappa's statements.[46]

His travels on the ARC reinforced Kumarappa's views on the utilization of land. He had argued that to achieve local self-sufficiency in food and other necessities, the available land had to be utilized for Balanced Cultivation. Now he was worried by the serious incursion of the profit motive into agriculture that viewed land as an instrument of financial investment. The changed role of land 'from being a granary' into an investment 'resulted

[44] J. C. Kumarappa, 'The Down-Trodden', *GUP*, February 1949.

[45] *ARC Report*, p. 134.

[46] The relations between the landowners and the labourers in the region remained iniquitous and tense. In 1968, this problem erupted when many Dalits were burnt alive in the village of Keezhavenmani.

in tremendous deterioration in the relation of the various factors' that constituted a healthy agrarian economy.[47] Kumarappa argued vigorously against landlords who were 'parasites on land' as they took too large a share of the agricultural wealth produced by the farmer, leaving the latter impoverished. Kumarappa recognized that while in the immediate sense it was not possible to 'achieve the ideal of expropriating the owners of land', at the very least the landlord's profits must be limited. If some argued that agriculture does not pay, Kumarappa's retort was that no industry would be profitable if the owner demanded the lion's share of the profits.[48] However, unlike the rather straightforward solution of investing property rights in the hands of the tiller, Kumarappa was developing a far more complex view on the issue of land rights when he argued that 'land must be the common property of society to feed itself' which meant that 'no proprietory right can be recognised in land'.[49] Kumarappa also extended this argument in more radical directions when he asked:

> How much of the sunlight belongs to a man? We cannot have ownership in sunlight, air, water, etc. In the same way there can be no more possession in land, which is God-given social property. It is to be used for the benefit of the whole society. Just as sunlight, water, air, etc., belong to the community, so also land must belong to the community.[50]

Here, Kumarappa was creatively marrying decidedly modern values with ideas with deep traditional roots. Specifically, by categorizing land with natural resources such as sunlight, water, and air, he presented a viewpoint that has come to be recognized as the ecological principle of a 'land ethic'.[51]

However, if land was to be viewed through the prism of an ecological ethic, its use also had to serve a multitude of social and economic purposes, in particular that of the welfare of agricultural workers including the landless

[47] J. C. Kumarappa, 'Land—Its Use', *GUP*, July 1951. Amongst the various factors that Kumarappa had recognized was what Marx had called 'commodity fetishism' whereby social relationships were mediated through commodities and money.

[48] J. C. Kumarappa, 'Minimum Wages and Democracy', *GUP*, August 1950.

[49] J. C. Kumarappa, 'The Parasites on Land', *GUP*, June 1950.

[50] J. C. Kumarappa, *Gandhian Economic Thought*, p. 32.

[51] The term 'land ethic' was coined by the American pioneer of environmental ethics, Aldo Leopold in his *A Sand County Almanac and Sketches Here and There*, illustrated by Charles W. Schwartz, published in 1949 (New York: Oxford University Press).

labourer. By dint of the importance of his labour, the agriculturalist should naturally be entitled to 'a position of advantage amongst wealth producers', that is, the labouring classes. Instead, Kumarappa found that despite their hard work, the farmers and agricultural labourers were worse off even when compared to industrial workers.[52] And amongst those who worked in the fields 'the real result of exploitation dribbles down to the level of landless labour'. By 1951, it was evident that reconstruction of the rural economy was not a priority for the rulers of independent India. If the Congress in power had failed to provide the lead on meaningful land reform, the recommendations of the ARC were also given a quiet burial. The systemic bias against the agriculturalist also found expression at the highest levels of the state. Thus, while Gandhi had held that the agriculture portfolio 'should be the birth-right of the Premier as it provides the very sap for the nation's existence', Kumarappa found that in the Union Cabinet, the Food and Agriculture portfolio was an 'unwanted baby' that was often given to a newcomer.[53] Under these disappointing circumstances, the work of reconstructing Indian society, he argued, could not be done by appeal to the government and its institutions but had to be undertaken 'by those of us who are strong by standing by those who are weak and taking upon ourselves the duty of sponsoring the cause of the underdog'.[54] By this endeavour 'we shall build our new-born nation on a firm social foundation of equality and self-respect restoring to everyone the dignity of a human being—a temple of Gods'. Kumarappa found that there were very few who were willing to share in such a programme in the first flush of Independence. Although many workers had valiantly fought against the British, once freedom arrived they were 'searching the debris for the spoils rather than continue the work that they were doing formerly'. If his attempt to influence state policy through the *ARC Report* had failed, Kumarappa was also increasingly at odds with fellow Gandhians at Wardha.

Undeterred by this lack of interest, he sought to demonstrate the feasibility of local self-sufficiency by reorganizing the agrarian economy. In May 1951, Kumarappa published a slim booklet titled *The Unitary Basis for a Non-violent Democracy* that laid out his normative argument for social

[52] J. C. Kumarappa, 'Balanced Cultivation as a Basis for Self-Sufficient Villages', *GUP*, April 1951.

[53] J. C. Kumarappa, 'A Blue-Print for the Ministry for Food and Agriculture', *GUP*, September 1950.

[54] J. C. Kumarappa, 'The Down-Trodden', *GUP*, February 1949.

reconstruction on an agrarian basis.[55] While social equality and justice were essential, Kumarappa argued that it should also 'prevail in the economic field as that is of the most universal interest'.[56] He asserted that 'democracy cannot exist where there is starvation, nakedness and poverty alongside of glut and glamorous living which condition indicates exploitation of the weak by the strong'. However, unlike the prevailing view calling for a significant role for the state in the economy, he argued that the 'unitary basis' for reconciling the twin goals of economic justice and the autonomy of the peasant community lay in a different realm. It required the creation of largely self-sufficient, local economies centred on Balanced Cultivation that would provide for the fundamental needs of a community.

Kumarappa recognized that the efficacy of this argument was not to be established under the controlled conditions of a laboratory, but 'in the area of everyday village life'.[57] His experiment would not be merely a technical one but was meant 'to provide the basis for a country-wide self-sufficient programme of rural reconstruction'. Thus, in 1951, a year shy of the age of sixty, a very ill Kumarappa left Maganvadi to embark on a bold and ambitious experiment to 'get a complete picture of a non-violent community life'.[58] It was time to start work on a new experiment that was the natural culmination of the trajectory of Gandhian experimentation towards social reconstruction that began at Sabarmati with khadi, was enlarged to village industries at Maganvadi, and now had to address 'all activities of a society—economic, social and political'.

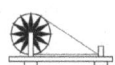

A key element for demonstrating the viability of a healthy community was the execution of Kumarappa's theoretical argument for Balanced Cultivation. With this in mind, along with some associates, he scouted the area around Wardha for a suitable location. Eventually, they settled on the village of Seldoh that lay some 20 miles from Wardha where a 16-acre plot of largely

[55] J. C. Kumarappa, *The Unitary Basis for a Non-violent Democracy* (Wardha: The All-India Village Industries Association, 1951).

[56] J. C. Kumarappa, *The Unitary Basis for a Non-violent Democracy*, p. 1.

[57] J. C. Kumarappa, 'Balanced Cultivation as a Basis for Self-Sufficient Villages', *GUP*, April 1951.

[58] J. C. Kumarappa, 'Pannai Ashram', *GUP*, December 1954.

barren land was acquired at a price of Rs 2000.[59] On 17 May 1951, the Pannai Ashram was inaugurated at Seldoh by Kumarappa's friend and compatriot, Acharya Kripalani. The work was eventually extended to cover 185 acres of which 85 were acquired from absentee landlords and the rest were provided by the government.[60] Kumarappa's choice of the Tamil word *pannai*, meaning agriculture, as the name for an ashram in central India was a curious one. One may conjecture that this was the riposte by a Tamilian unhappy at the insular turn towards Hindi that was evident in Gandhian circles since the demise of the Mahatma.

Kumarappa was clear from the outset that the success of his experiment depended on obtaining the co-operation of the villagers. The opportunity for breaking social barriers and establishing a rapport with the people presented itself soon on his arrival in Seldoh. An early attempt to dig a well yielded sweet water and Kumarappa used the occasion to break the traditional caste hierarchy by serving a feast to the children of the lower castes. He made a further impression on the community when he 'resolved to have his abode in the most backward area of the village', that is, amongst the Gond *adivasis* of the region.[61] Despite his illness during this period, Kumarappa moved into a corner of a 'small and dilapidated house in Gondvadi' and lived there for a year. To develop a clear understanding of the specific requirements and constraints of the village economy, Kumarappa and student volunteers from the AIVIA training programme spent time surveying the village. Besides conducting surveys, the early months were spent tackling the coupled question of sanitation and soil fertility. Kumarappa saw the use of dry latrines as not only an affront to human dignity but also an ecological travesty. The team of workers constructed a few trench latrines and also spent much time collecting waste and refuse from around the village to be converted into useful manure. This was an attempt to teach by example, and on the farm he devised a carefully controlled experiment to test the actual value of cow dung and human manure in increasing productivity. In an attempt to practically demonstrate the efficacy of manuring, various experimental plots 'under different crops and manures such as from night-soil, cow dung, village silt and sullage etc., were laid out' and contrasted with plots that did not get any manure.

[59] *Pannai Ashram, Seldoh: Development Report from Its Foundation 17th May 1951 to 31st May 1953*, Bound Volume, 25, Kumarappa Papers.

[60] J. C. Kumarappa, 'Pannai Ashram', *GUP*, December 1954.

[61] *Pannai Ashram.*

With the first general elections in the offing, Seldoh was not immune to the influence of party politics and caste groupings. Kumarappa had no doubt that in a modern, mass democracy there was a need for 'organising the kisans' in political terms.[62] However, he felt that the communist approach that replicated the methods of mobilizing industrial workers was ill-suited to rural conditions and militated against attempts to build a non-violent social order. Moreover, he argued that such mobilization was not entirely 'selfless as a good deal of party interest' played a major role in the communist strategy. Indeed, while fighting against injustice and exploitation, Kumarappa felt that India had to undertake the challenge of presenting an alternative to 'the Soviet programme in co-operation and communal living that is now based on violence'.[63] The solution lay in developing the other dimensions of Kumarappa's 'unitary basis', that is, community participation in direct democracy. While the Constitution of India had bypassed the panchayat as an institution, he recognized that a coherent plan for the development of the village was contingent on participatory democracy taking roots in the village. Within a few weeks of arriving at Seldoh, he constituted the *aam sabha* or a general assembly of all adults in the village. The Seldoh aam sabha met every fortnight to elect a 'cabinet' with at least one woman member. This cabinet was tasked with carrying out the necessary work that had to be undertaken in the ensuing two weeks.

Kumarappa utilized every public occasion to present his worldview to the village community. When a land dispute arose, he presented a solution that justly distributed land rights between the individual and the community and was based on his argument that the productive value of land was a social good. On this occasion there were three claimants to a piece of land: a widow, her adult daughter, and an occasional tenant. As he had argued in the abstract setting of the *ARC Report*, in this dispute Kumarappa reasoned that justice will be done only when the 'interest of the land' is held paramount and that it 'must go to one who can take best care of it'.[64] Accordingly, he concluded that while the old widow would not be able to cultivate the land, the occasional tenant had no incentive to maintain its fertility. However, while awarding it to the daughter, Kumarappa also ensured that both the mother and the tenant retained some rights to the

[62] J. C. Kumarappa, 'Organising the Kisans', Speeches and Writings, Loose, Kumarappa Papers.

[63] J. C. Kumarappa, 'Pannai Ashram', *GUP*, December 1954.

[64] *Pannai Ashram*.

produce of the land. Thus, his solution of distributing the ownership and cultivation rights was in line with traditional Indian practices in the husbanding of land. But at the same time, by enforcing mutual rights and obligations he emphasized the reciprocity of relationships that form the web of life.

The experiment of social reconstruction through the Pannai Ashram at Seldoh was highly ambitious in scope and even under very favourable circumstances would have required a reasonable duration of time to achieve a measure of success in its objectives. However, right from its inception the Pannai experiment was hobbled by multiple constraints. The close co-operation with the villagers that existed in the early days was weakened once the workers moved into newly built ashram huts. The animosity that had developed between Kumarappa and other Gandhians was reflected in the obstacles placed in the way of the project. The work at Seldoh was to be funded by the Sarva Seva Sangh—into which the AIVIA had merged—but the release of money was delayed on bureaucratic grounds leading an angry Kumarappa to explain that he could not be 'party to the Pannai Ashram being placed on an imprest basis'.[65] Also, there were constant demands on Kumarappa's time including travel outside India. However, the main problem was his own poor health. While he had suffered from problems due to high blood pressure ever since he joined Gandhi in 1929, within two years of moving to Seldoh Kumarappa's health had considerably deteriorated. By late 1954 Kumarappa's dilated heart made all work infeasible and 'with very great reluctance and regret' he handed over the Pannai Ashram to the Sarva Seva Sangh.[66]

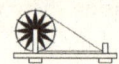

Around the time Kumarappa moved to Seldoh, the despairing Gandhian movement received a fillip, when a landlord in the strife-ridden Telangana responded to Vinoba Bhave's moral appeal and donated some of his land. The Bhoodan movement was born. Posited against the bloody revolution advocated by the communists, Vinoba's method succeeded in gathering voluntary donations of land to be redistributed to landless peasants.

[65] Letter from J. C. Kumarappa to Secretary, Sarva Seva Sangh, 17 September 1951, Subject File, 22, Kumarappa Papers.
[66] J. C. Kumarappa, 'Pannai Ashram'.

Despite their strident advocacy of land reform during British rule, the Congress leaders in power failed to address this fundamental problem of the countryside. As a result, while Indian public life was dominated by a variety of modernist opinion, it was the saintly, impractical, and reclusive Vinoba who forcefully brought the land question to national attention. This new-found opportunity to tackle the problem of public welfare galvanized many veteran and novice workers to plunge into Bhoodan work. In these early days of heady enthusiasm, Kumarappa was one of the few voices to point to the dangers inherent in the headlong rush to build a nationwide movement. With Gandhi gone, Kumarappa was amongst the few constructive workers with extensive experience and a serious understanding of the rather complex problem of land. He recognized that Bhoodan was serving the important purpose of 'long-needed reforms in the distribution of land to the tiller'.[67] However, he was probably the first notable individual to warn that merely transferring property rights without addressing the larger social purpose would create its own problems.

Many of the considerations that animated his recommendations as the head of the ARC now informed his critique of Bhoodan. In particular, Kumarappa was worried that allowing the new landowners to use their property to grow remunerative cash crops would contribute nothing to tackling the food crisis. Over the first few years of Bhoodan, there was a tremendous response and much land was collected. However, Kumarappa argued that if land had to be used to further the welfare of society and not individual interests, Bhoodan had a huge responsibility in building a balanced, self-sufficient, agrarian economy. He argued that the Bhoodan movement ought to pause and reorganize itself by paying careful attention to the correct utilization of the donated land. In particular, he wished that prior to Bhoodan, Vinoba and his team had built 'a cadre of men who would be trained and equipped with information and materials to enable them to handle the situation masterfully'.[68] Although such planning was not carried out, he argued that the situation could be redeemed by the organization of an agrarian college and many demonstration centres that could provide intensive training on the lines of the AIVIA's courses at Maganvadi. Recognizing that the best way to teach was to practise one's own precepts, he suggested that the land could be organized as model farms 'which will demonstrate the manner in which we want the land tenures to

[67] J. C. Kumarappa, 'After Bhoodan?', *GUP*, March 1953.
[68] J. C. Kumarappa, 'Agrarian Colleges' *GUP*, May 1955.

be worked out ... in a self-sufficient, self-controlled economy developing as far as practicable on Sarvodaya lines'.[69]

Kumarappa felt that the transformation sought by the Bhoodan idealists was impossible without understanding India's exceedingly complex and variegated agrarian problems. He felt that without trained personnel, 'we shall be merely playing with the problems that we open up with the Bhoodan movement that snatches away the land from a well-organized group of land holders [and hands it over] to an amateurish and purely idealistic group, which has no knowledge as to how to grapple with the problems placed before them'.[70] In a hard-hitting letter to Vinoba, Kumarappa pointed out that the problems of Bhoodan arose due to the enthusiasm for the fixing of targets which 'have emphasised the end and the means are very destructive'.[71] If Kumarappa wanted a careful consideration of the problems he had identified with the modus operandi of Bhoodan, Vinoba was spectacularly unmatched to the task. Although he was Gandhi's supposed 'spiritual' successor, Vinoba's impracticality and anarchist sensibilities meant that Kumarappa's Cassandra-like warnings went unheeded. Instead of responding to the substance of the criticism, Vinoba dismissed it by claiming that 'little do I like to enter into discussion' and instead advised Kumarappa to 'avoid harsh language' in his writings.[72] Many of the leaders of the Sangh were acolytes of Vinoba and Kumarappa's argument failed to garner any serious support.[73] By 1955, much land had been collected but there were no adequate plans to distribute it. Indeed, Kumarappa's warnings against an amateurish attempt 'to disturb a settled order while unprepared to properly organise the new set-up' had come to pass.[74] Many Gandhians were also evincing their concerns about the manner in which the movement was being conducted. Writing in a newspaper from her quiet perch in the Himalayas, Mirabehn echoed Kumarappa's worries and recalled Gandhi's reply on why he did

---

[69] J. C. Kumarappa, 'Demonstration Centres', *GUP*, May 1955.

[70] J. C. Kumarappa, 'Agrarian Colleges', *GUP*, May 1955.

[71] Letter from J. C. Kumarappa to Vinoba Bhave, 27 April 1955; reproduced in *Rajendra Prasad: Correspondence and Select Documents*, vol. 17, edited by Valmiki Choudhary (New Delhi: Allied Publishers, 1984), p. 285.

[72] Translation of Hindi letter from Vinoba to J. C. Kumarappa, 20 June 1955, Subject File, 31, Kumarappa Papers.

[73] See Subject File, 31, Kumarappa Papers, for his correspondence with Vinoba on Bhoodan.

[74] J. C. Kumarappa, 'Agrarian Colleges', *GUP*, May 1955.

not include agriculture in his constructive programme. 'I don't know enough about it myself,' Gandhi said, 'and I do not like to take up things with which I am not thoroughly conversant'.[75] She argued that just as Gandhi ensured that constructive workers themselves took up spinning, Bhoodan volunteers should also take up farming.

The problems created by Bhoodan were not limited to donated land. In his enthusiasm to build a movement, Vinoba called for Gandhi's constructive organizations to be closed down and the workers to be brought into Bhoodan![76] Workers at Maganvadi wrote plaintively to Kumarappa to complain about the manner in which seasoned workers engaged in their tasks were being pulled out and sent off to do Bhoodan work. Kumarappa was angered by this turn of events and argued that Vinoba's zeal for one programme 'should not destroy the work so far built up at the cost of tremendous pain, and infinite human effort over decades'.[77] When the Gandhian educationist Ashadevi Aryanayakam responded to the call of *jivandan* or donation of one's life to Bhoodan, Kumarappa was incensed enough to publicly criticize her decision. Although Ashadevi 'nobly came forward to dedicate her services to Bhoodan', Kumarappa argued that this was not a laudable move.[78] As a key Basic Education worker, Kumarappa felt that her life was already dedicated and 'abandoning Basic Education and taking to Bhoodan is definitely a retrograde step'. Recalling the approach of the Mahatma, Kumarappa pointed out that on every occasion of impending political upheaval, Gandhi gave explicit instructions to constructive workers like Kumarappa not to abandon their work. Worried about the consequences of Vinoba's actions, Kumarappa repeatedly emphasized that Bhoodan needed to create its own cadre of workers instead of drawing on those dedicated to working on the other aspects of the Sarvodaya Order. In a searching self-assessment of constructive work, he argued that

> [i]t is easier to destroy than to create. In all conscience our constructive work has been slow and has meant a great deal to build up even the present momentum. Are we to disband all this? A non-violent order needs

[75] Mirabehn, 'Some Reflections on the Bhoodan Movement', *GUP*, January 1956.

[76] Letter from Amrit Kaur to J. C. Kumarappa, 18 May 1955, Correspondence Files, Kumarappa Papers.

[77] Letter from J. C. Kumarappa to Vinoba Bhave, 27 April 1955.

[78] J. C. Kumarappa, 'Ends and Means in Bhoodan', *GUP*, June 1955.

these other factors no less. We cannot lightheartedly abandon the results of decades of concentrated struggle and work. Once we disband existing institutions we shall find it almost impossible to gather that amount of momentum again.[79]

Kumarappa's criticism of Bhoodan did not go down well amongst many of his fellow constructive workers. Many of the concerns he had voiced have since transpired and despite its undoubted significance, Bhoodan remained mired in messy controversy and failed to deliver on its possibilities. However, Vinoba and his colleagues paid no heed to Kumarappa's warnings and probably attributed them to his characteristic acerbity. Although it failed to invoke any introspection, Kumarappa's criticism of Bhoodan hardened the attitude of the new dispensation at Wardha towards him. While there was no public acrimony, with the Sarva Seva Sangh refusing to convert Pannai Ashram into the agrarian college he had desired, Kumarappa's break with his life in Wardha was now complete.

[79] Letter from J. C. Kumarappa to Vinoba Bhave, 27 April 1955.

15 India Adrift

The achievement of political freedom was accompanied by grave disappointment for those who recognized that economic justice was not in sight. While economic planning aimed for a high-growth pattern, the imprint of the moneyed and powerful on government policy was very clear. The legacy of the War years was also in evidence—a grave food crisis, all-round political chaos, and the growing clout of Indian capital. The dream of freedom had soured for the common people. By the time he submitted the *ARC Report*, Kumarappa was distressed with the policies of the Congress government. If, as he had written to Gandhi in Noakhali in 1947, the interim governments were merely following colonial policy, the situation in the 1950s looked even worse. He felt that the Congress and the government were both increasingly failing to redeem the promises of the past, and indulging in policies favouring the powerful at the expense of the welfare of the masses. Lacking the political stature of a Gandhi, Kumarappa found himself angrily denouncing the state of affairs and spent the last decade of his life in deep and profound disillusionment.

A key indictment of the Raj was its lavish and ostentatious living at the expense of the poor Indian peasant. Therefore, Kumarappa was incensed with Nehru's defence of Vijayalakshmi Pandit who as India's ambassador in communist Moscow felt it necessary to import expensive furniture from Stockholm.[1] Detailing the enormous expenditure incurred in maintaining the Governor-General of free India in pomp and splendour, Kumarappa likened India's situation to that of a 'beggar in tattered garments with an empty stomach, sporting a carnation in his button-hole'.[2] Warning that 'imperial splendour' coexisting with 'dire need and poverty' is the 'stuff that revolutions are made of', Kumarappa felt that fundamental changes were urgently called for. Neither arresting communists and socialists nor shibboleths like 'Mahatma Gandhi ki jai' were a cure for the 'intense acromegaly in the body politic'.

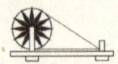

To tackle the widespread scarcities during the Second World War, the Raj had introduced rationing of food and had increased its control over food production and sale by creating 'a formidable interventionist machinery'.[3] This arrangement endowed administrators with sweeping powers that were often abused. In one instance, the District Magistrate of Anand in present-day Gujarat passed orders that milk in the district could only be sold to a certain European firm and milk producers were enjoined not to convert their milk into ghee for sale. Pointing to such blatant abuse of power, Kumarappa argued that 'big business is becoming greater than the Great Moghuls in our country'.[4] If the exigencies of War led the British to rule India by administrative fiat, the Congress-led Interim Government did very little to dismantle this regime. The central and provincial governments across the country did not hesitate to use the provisions of the War period to further the interests of businessmen. In November 1946, the central government instructed the provinces to discourage hand-processed sugar in favour of the nutritionally inferior factory-made white sugar.[5] Upon assuming power, India's rulers had asked people to be patient

---

[1] J. C. Kumarappa, 'Wanted a Philosophy', *GUP*, November 1947. For Nehru's explanation of this episode to Gandhi, see *Together They Fought*, p. 505 and p. 508.

[2] J. C. Kumarappa, 'Portents of a Revolution', *GUP*, June 1949.

[3] Rothermund, *An Economic History of India*, p. 119.

[4] 'Mills Should Quit India: Kumarappa's Plea for Decentralised Industry', *Indian Express*, 12 December 1945, Press Clippings, Kumarappa Papers.

[5] J. C. Kumarappa, 'Science Runs Amuck', *Harijan*, 27 April 1947.

and appealed that 'in the country's interest [they] desist from criticism'.[6] But during his extensive travels, Kumarappa was witness to the distress in the Indian countryside, and was angered by the political indifference to the plight of the cultivator. It was inevitable that the endurance of the rural areas was to be taxed by the abuse of state power in democratic India. For Kumarappa, the crisis came to a head in the winter of 1949–50 in the Nilakottai taluka of Madurai district.[7]

The farmers of the region typically grew sugarcane on a fourth of their landholdings and made gur or jaggery that was sold in the Madurai markets for a small margin of profit. By early 1950, a newly established sugar mill in the region had failed to procure enough cane for its requirements. By this time, central legislation had mandated that the local governments were duty-bound to procure the requisite sugarcane for mills in their region. The Madras government was induced to pass an order that required farmers of 122 villages within a 20-mile radius of the mill to obtain a licence to make gur. Without a duly issued licence that was practically impossible to procure, the farmer was forced to sell his cane to the mill at a low rate set by the government. The net effect was to deprive the farmers of their right to make gur using sugarcane grown on their *own* fields. Perversely enough, the order was timed to be passed when farm labour had been brought into the district and much of the cane had been harvested. Kumarappa calculated that by forcing the farmers to sell their harvested cane to the mills at the low controlled rates, the government was causing a loss of Rs 12 lakhs to the farmers of the district. Moreover, it also deprived thousands of labourers engaged in gur manufacture of their employment. Kumarappa argued that the use of the power of law 'to ride roughshod over the interests of the agriculturists' was 'a living disgrace to any society which claims to be democratic'.[8] Having spent years as a participant in India's struggle for freedom, an incensed Kumarappa declared that he was 'ashamed to be a citizen of this land where such a law can prevail with the so called National Government at the top'.[9]

Although the Madurai executive order on gur licensing was only one of many such examples, fortuitously there was one Gandhian worker in the region who took it upon himself to challenge it. Thirty-seven-year-old

---

[6] J. C. Kumarappa, 'Slavery under The Law', *GUP*, February 1950.

[7] This area is in present-day Dindigul district that was created in 1985.

[8] J. C. Kumarappa, 'Swaraj or Tyranny?', *GUP*, February 1950.

[9] 'Views on Private Property in Land', *Madras Mail*, 17 February 1950, Press Clippings, Kumarappa Papers.

Sankaralingam Jagannathan had recently moved to the area and had set up a modest 'Workers Home' in collaboration with Keithahn and Dr T. S. Soundaram, a constructive worker and wife of Kumarappa's associate, G. Ramachandran.[10] Owing to his relationship with Keithahn and Ramachandran, Kumarappa had visited this Home and helped train the workers. Jagannathan had come to recognize the centrality of the land problem and wished to find a non-violent solution. In order to understand life in the villages of the region, he took to walking around when he learnt of the licensing order. With advice from Keithahn and Kumarappa, he offered to organize the people against the 'slavish order [that was] similar to the British tax on salt'.[11] Soon police were deployed to confiscate the crushers and pans that farmers used for converting their cane into gur. One evening, when a police van having confiscated equipment got ready to leave, Jagannathan, in a fit of inspiration, lay down on the road blocking the exit. His action led many onlookers to follow suit and the van was immobilized. The police demanded to know how Gandhians could disobey the order of a national government, whereupon the response was that it was a slavish order not befitting the government of a free people. By midnight, some three thousand people had arrived from the surrounding villages, and on instructions from the government a tense stand-off was defused by the policemen returning the equipment and leaving the scene. The next day, a minister arrived and negotiated with Kumarappa and Soundaram. Eventually a compromise was reached that the government would not force the farmers on the sale of cane, while the Gandhians would not press for a boycott of the mill.

Jagannathan's action was that of an inspired and fearless man who by the power of his action broke through a web of deceit and intrigue. It is almost surely the first instance of an agrarian satyagraha carried out by free Indians against the injustices of their own democratic government. While

[10] Jagannathan went on to be recognized as a radical Gandhian activist and together with his wife, Krishnammal Jagannathan, fought many a battle on behalf of the poor, especially on distributing land to landless labourers and against the ecologically destructive prawn farming in the coastal regions of Tamil Nadu. For 'two long lifetimes of work dedicated to realising in practice the Gandhian vision of social justice and sustainable human development', the Jagannathans were awarded the Right Livelihood Award in 2008. For a biographical account of their work, see Laura Coppo, *The Color of Freedom: Overcoming Colonialism and Multinationals in India* (Monroe, Maine: Common Courage Press, 2005).

[11] Coppo, *The Color of Freedom*, p. 68.

the immediate consequences were that of forcing the state to back down, eventually using its influence, the government managed to get a third of the cane to be sold to the mill.[12] Jagannathan and his colleagues also paid a heavy price for his act of conscience. Many of the wealthy investors in the sugar mills were donors to the Workers Home, and after the satyagraha these donations dried up.[13]

While Congress politicians had learnt to ignore Kumarappa as an irritant, amongst the public at large the perception was quite different. As a Gandhian of unimpeachable integrity, he commanded a high degree of respect for speaking on behalf of the oppressed. Kumarappa's support for the sugarcane farmers angered the landlords of Madurai who were even more incensed when he bluntly told them in a meeting that 'the time has come when private property in land as a means of investment would be looked upon as a crime'.[14] The angry landlords accused Kumarappa of being a communist. His strident criticism was so worrying to India's new rulers that the Madras government even considered banning his activities in the region. As Jagannathan described it later, 'it would be a sad day for our country if justice and Communism became the same things in the minds of the people'.[15] But it would be even more astounding 'if a Congress Government had compelled Kumarappa to court imprisonment'. His challenge to erstwhile freedom fighters was so embarrassing that a member of Nehru's cabinet even wondered 'how it was possible for any Government to allow Kumarappa to go on in this way'.[16] The threat of Kumarappa's arrest passed, but not before he had driven home the point that while India had achieved political freedom, the struggle for economic justice had just about begun. As he put it, without a 'living union between the Government and the people', Indian democracy would remain formal but would lack in dharma.[17]

Despite the policy bias in favour of large-scale industries, there was much that commended the gur industry in terms of the economy and

[12] J. C. Kumarappa, 'Slavery under the Law', *GUP*, February 1950.

[13] A similar example of the price of obeying one's conscience is the case of the drop in donations to Baba Amte's Anandwan after he lent his unstinted support to the cause of the oustees of the Sardar Sarovar dam and their organization, the Narmada Bachao Andolan.

[14] G. Ramachandran and M. Vinaik, 'Rebel Still', in *Economics of Peace*, p. 28.

[15] S. Jagannathan, 'Worker among Workers', in *Economics of Peace*, p. 375.

[16] G. Ramachandran and M. Vinaik, 'Rebel Still', in *Economics of Peace*, p. 29.

[17] J. C. Kumarappa, 'Democracy—Formal or Dharmic?', *GUP*, March 1950.

employment potential. Even a few years after the Madurai satyagraha, the nationwide output of the gur industry was about three to four times that of sugar and provided employment to millions. Most crucially, in terms of the ratio of value of fixed capital to gross annual output, making gur was at least eleven times more efficient.[18] In other words, in comparison with sugar mills, the decentralized gur industry provided employment to millions at a far lower level of capital investment while producing a nutritionally superior source of sugar. Nevertheless, the powerful influence of big business ensured that state policy was consistently wielded in their favour. Thus, for instance, when in 1948 the government considered moves to combat high inflation, it contemplated reducing the controlled price of sugar. But, as Kumarappa observed, 'lest it should tell on the fat profits of the mills', the government planned on reducing the procurement price of sugarcane to achieve its objective.[19] In this manner, state power was used to create huge disincentives for the making of gur and over a period of time destroyed this village industry.

Similarly, to Kumarappa's mind, the policy of the government to procure food grains at a low rate from the farmers and sell them at a higher rate in the market smacked of brigandage. Forcible procurement, carried out with the backing of the police, was particularly infuriating since the government was doing little to help the farmers produce the food grains in the first place. The discontent with state policy was not limited to the likes of Kumarappa alone. In 1947, he had criticized his friend, the constructive worker Prafulla Chandra Ghosh who served as the first chief minister of West Bengal, for allowing sugar mills to be set up in his province. Now, disillusioned with the Congress, even Ghosh was angered by the Madurai gur order and called it a 'shameless alliance with the capitalists'.[20] Ghosh and Kumarappa were earlier at the centre of a related controversy. They had presided over a meeting of cultivators where government procurement of rice was discussed. Since the procurement price that the government offered did not even cover the costs of production, Kumarappa said that it would be understandable if the peasants disposed of their grains in other ways. This position was misrepresented in a media report as advocating a 'scorched earth' policy to prevent government procurement. While Kumarappa had not made such a statement, his view that the cultivators

---

[18] 'Some Indian Cottage Industries', *Economic Weekly*, 1 January 1955.

[19] J. C. Kumarappa, 'The Haves Have It', *GUP*, November 1948.

[20] Letter from P. C. Ghosh to J. C. Kumarappa, 23 November 1950, Correspondence Files, Kumarappa Papers.

had no obligation whatsoever to help the government in the matter was no less controversial. The result was a sharp indictment of Kumarappa by his compatriot, the Gandhian thinker K. G. Mashruwala in the pages of the *Harijan*.[21] While Mashruwala publicly criticized Kumarappa for his statement, Nehru complained in private to Rajendra Prasad and bemoaned that 'some of our older colleagues in the Congress have become more bitter than even avowed enemies'.[22] Strangely enough, Nehru believed that the fierce denunciation of government procurement policy by Kumarappa and Ghosh was 'just to create more trouble for the governments and bring them down'. Kumarappa and Ghosh were certainly not conspirators plotting the downfall of governments in power, but were only giving public expression to the 'exasperation prevalent throughout the country'.[23]

With the food crisis becoming serious and upon reports of police firing in Cooch Behar and hunger marches in Bihar, Kumarappa was livid. Ordinarily, he argued, such mismanagement would lead to calls for the ousting of the government. However, he rued the fact that Nehru's popularity was used as 'the instrument for white-washing the scandal occasioned by bad administration'.[24] In turn, Kumarappa argued that 'such popular persons should be in the opposition to command respect with the administrators' and thereby put moral pressure on them to do the right thing. Admittedly Nehru was plagued with innumerable administrative and political problems, but his uncharitable analysis of Kumarappa's speech was symptomatic of the deep malaise within the Congress. While Nehru seemed to expect constructive workers to demonstrate allegiance to the Congress party, he thought nothing of his government undermining the principles of constructive work itself. More significantly, the Congress was unable to either curb the growing selfishness and corruption within its ranks or profit from the advice and warnings from workers like Kumarappa who were tuned into the public sentiment. For many nationalists who had spent the best part of their life fighting for freedom, the downward spiral of the Congress was a grave situation. Soon this began to have major political implications, most notably the abandonment of the Congress by

[21] See K. G. Mashruwala, 'Unfortunate' and 'A Brother's Indictment', *Harijan*, 1 and 22 January 1950 respectively.

[22] Letter from Jawaharlal Nehru to Rajendra Prasad, 8 December 1949, published in *Dr. Rajendra Prasad: Correspondence and Selected Documents*, vol. 11, edited by Valmiki Choudhary (New Delhi: Allied Publishers, 1988), pp. 185–8.

[23] K. G. Mashruwala, 'A Brother's Indictment'.

[24] J. C. Kumarappa, 'Lack of Any Policy', *GUP*, May 1951.

some stalwarts who felt they had no meaningful role to play within the party. Acharya Kripalani was the first senior leader to leave in June 1951 when he founded the Kisan Mazdoor Praja Party (KMPP) to contest the first general election.

Given Kumarappa's strident criticism of the Congress, there was a fair bit of speculation on his political motives. Consequently, it was considered 'significant that the first public function undertaken by Acharya J. B. Kripalani after his resignation from the Congress' was the inauguration of Kumarappa's Pannai Ashram.[25] Indeed, Kripalani himself wanted Kumarappa's advice and desired his participation in the deliberations on the formation of the KMPP.[26] Kumarappa did participate but felt that while the KMPP's policy statement was 'unexceptionable' what was needed was 'an organisation to effectively implement it'.[27] The attribution of straightforward political meaning to Kumarappa's public pronouncements was a gross misreading. As someone deeply committed to Gandhi's vision of society, Kumarappa was uninterested in politics in the limited sense of elections and parliamentary democracy. Thus, he urged Kripalani to think of the spirit of Gandhi's suggestion of the Lok Sevak Sangh and 'modify it to suit the conditions today'. In Kumarappa's opinion this could be carried out not by forming another party, but by forming 'a Political and Parliamentary department' within the Sarva Seva Sangh. Although nothing came of it, Kumarappa's proposal was a bold one, laden with theoretical and political implications for both constructive work and the practice of politics. If we cut through the bitterness of his intellectual anger, this fleeting suggestion serves as a pointer to the timbre of Kumarappa's character. Unmoved by the lure of political office or lucre, Kumarappa's proposal was sarvodaya redux for the post-Gandhi era. The next year, India witnessed the successful holding of its first general election whereby the Congress was firmly installed in power. But many constructive workers had been agitated by the 'condition of the masses' that 'had gone from bad to worse' with no help from the national government.[28] The crisis led Kumarappa to join hands with the atheist activist Gora to

[25] 'Inauguration of Research Centre by Acharya Kripalani', *Nagpur Times*, 26 May 1951, Press Clippings, Kumarappa Papers.

[26] Letter from J. B. Kripalani to J. C. Kumarappa, 29 May 1951, Correspondence Files, Kumarappa Papers.

[27] Letter from J. C. Kumarappa to J. B. Kripalani, 6 June 1951. Correspondence Files, Kumarappa Papers.

[28] J. C. Kumarappa, 'Arthik Samata Mandal', *GUP*, July 1952.

form the Arthik Samata Mandal with a view to 'collect together patriots from all schools of thought to steadfastly work for the emancipation of the people from economic thraldom'.[29] A key issue that Kumarappa identified was that rural India sorely lacked social leadership since 'persons who would have been rural leaders have run away to cities to seek their fortunes as circumstances were not conducive to eke out a living in the village under the modern economic competitive order introduced from elsewhere'. The solution to this problem did not lie in pious exhortations to 'educated young men' to go to the villages since one could only offer them 'the prospect of semi-starvation [which was] the present lot of landless labour'.[30] Rather the remedy lay in paying adequate prices for agricultural products and making working in the agrarian economy an attractive proposition.

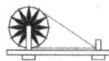

The official attitude towards the poor was brought home in an episode involving Kumarappa in Delhi. As a representative of constructive organizations, he participated in meetings of the Planning Commission Advisory Board at the Rashtrapati Bhavan. On one such visit, when he arrived in a horse-drawn *tonga*, Kumarappa was imperiously ordered off the road. On Kumarappa's insistence on his right to proceed on a public road, he was offered the justification that the road had to be cleared to allow Pandit Nehru to pass through. By the time he argued his way through to the portals of the erstwhile Viceregal Lodge, Kumarappa had been blocked four times. Despite his protest, this pattern was repeated the next day whereupon the exasperated Kumarappa 'threatened to arrive the next day ... in a bullock cart'.[31] At the meeting, invited to present his views, Kumarappa related the episode and insisted that 'a bullock cart driver in a democracy was as good a citizen as the Prime Minister himself'. Although Nehru agreed

[29] This exercise was largely ineffective, thereby illustrating the failure of constructive workers to organize themselves as political actors. The present-day Arthik Samata Mandal carries out important community work.

[30] J. C. Kumarappa, 'Unemployment and Swadeshi', *GUP*, August 1953. On a related note, Kumarappa presents an interesting argument that peasants cannot be organized along the same lines as industrial workers. For his line of reasoning, see 'Work among Kisans', *GUP*, June 1950.

[31] J. C. Kumarappa, 'Bullock Carts Not Allowed', *GUP*, September 1951.

with the proposition he submitted that Kumarappa had misinterpreted the purpose of such restrictions which were 'placed in the interest of the bullock cart drivers themselves as those roads were frequented by military lorry drivers' and in the event of an accident, it was the cart that would suffer. Kumarappa retorted that this was a lawyer's 'special pleading'. To his lay mind, it would seem that if one person was a threat to the safety of another, the restrictions ought to be placed on the former. Amidst peals of laughter, Kumarappa quipped that he would have put a notice declaiming 'Motor cars and lorries not allowed'.[32]

To Kumarappa's mind this episode revealed the perpetuation of injustice in India and reminded him of the old British argument of Trusteeship. Bearing witness to the plight of the peasant, he was also upset with India's leaders who 'in season and out of season ... never tired of telling the people ... to work hard, produce more and increase the standard of living'.[33] India's farmers were continually exhorted to 'Grow More Food', but there was scant attention paid to either the necessary rural investments or an adequate remuneration for their efforts. Denouncing this 'counsel of perfection' he defended the Indian peasant and argued that it was pointless to preach to the unfortunate the dignity of labour. Kumarappa's ire was not merely a reaction to urban indifference. With the government pushing for state-sponsored industrialization, the deep-rooted agrarian problems that had their origins in the colonial era received scant attention. As we have seen earlier, to Kumarappa's mind, the negotiations by the government on the utilization of the Sterling Balances held by India for industrialization represented a double betrayal. For the government, determined to modernize its industries, this was a natural choice, whereas for Kumarappa it flew in the face of natural justice.

In late 1952, he was asked to immediately visit Gorakhpur district 'to enquire into the famine conditions there'.[34] Having travelled some 350 miles and covered a population of 75,000, he found a distressing situation. With the failure of three consecutive crops, 'a large number

[32] The tonga episode did not end there. A government official attempted a justification that was promptly dealt with by Kumarappa in the January 1952 issue of the *GUP*. Due to the persistent effort of Gajanan Naik—an old colleague from Maganvadi who was now stationed at Delhi—space was allocated for tongas on the premises of the Rashtrapati Bhavan.

[33] J. C. Kumarappa, 'Work Hard', *GUP*, July 1950.

[34] Pandit Sunderlal and J. C. Kumarappa, 'Joint Statement on Gorakhpur Famine', 6 September 1952. Speeches and Writings, Loose, Kumarappa Papers.

had lived for a long period on grass seeds' and village after village looked like 'a house in mourning'. While the government had put in place some measures of relief work, it proved hardly adequate to tackle the problem. Kumarappa's observations during his trip have striking resonance with contemporary practices of relief work grudgingly undertaken by the government. Lamenting that 'the bureaucratic system of the British empire has not given way to real democracy', Kumarappa argued that a starving population should not be asked to take up strenuous relief work such as building roads.[35] The relief measures allowed for only one member of each family to be employed and the wages given were inadequate to stave off hunger. In many instances, the starving worker had to walk several miles to the work site. Such official indifference was made even worse with the tampering of public records whereby the cause of death was often put down to various diseases to provide deniability. Responding to the official position on starvation, Kumarappa retorted that 'the distress of the people does not require much statistical evidence and calls for only that much mathematical ability to be able to count their ribs and bones!' To Kumarappa's mind, the crisis in Gorakhpur was the result of a twofold problem. Much of the land was being farmed for sugarcane for the mills thereby leaving the population vulnerable during food crises. Moreover, there was 'absolutely no second line of defence against poverty ... in the form of agro-industries or other handicrafts'.[36] When the crops failed, the consequences of monoculture were devastating.

While castigating the government for its failure, Kumarappa was equally upset that there was no effort from 'the general public to meet the situation' and 'erstwhile constructive workers were apathetic or cared little'.[37] Strikingly, he pointed out that 'people seemed to be much more politically conscious than socially sympathetic'. Kumarappa's press statements on Gorakhpur and the photographs he took of the pitiable conditions there resulted in much controversy. Under pressure from the UP Government, many press agencies refused to carry the statements, forcing Kumarappa to call on Nehru to apprise him of the grim situation in the Gorakhpur countryside. Soon there were the inevitable denials with the chief minister arguing that Kumarappa's 'enquiry was partial' and

[35] J. C. Kumarappa, 'Gorakhpur Famine', GUP, October 1952.
[36] Pandit Sunderlal and J. C. Kumarappa, 'Joint Statement on Gorakhpur Famine'.
[37] J. C. Kumarappa, 'Gorakhpur Famine', GUP, October 1952.

that 'nobody died of starvation'.[38] The dissimulation got worse with the suggestion that Kumarappa's grasp of Hindi was inadequate for him to ascertain the true causes of deaths.

Meanwhile, the Constitution of India that was promulgated disappointed many constructive workers. On its release, the veteran constructive worker from Andhra, Swami Sitaram drew attention to the fact that in the past 'Gandhiji preached and the Congress accepted the idea of a decentralised administration based on village autonomy'.[39] Now, with political power in hand, 'the Constituent Assembly has practically given the go-bye [sic] to this Gandhian ideal'. Kumarappa, however, was not a man to pull his punches. The Constitution, he argued, had failed to 'lay down the respective duties of the citizen and the Government and correlate them'.[40] To begin with, the 'members of the Constituent Assembly were not truly representative' as they were 'more or less nominated, not elected by adult franchise'. He argued that the 'constitution must be written out of the real facts of life', that is, 'our own life-blood' which was not reflected in the final document produced. Indeed, in a constitution replete with clauses borrowed from all over the world, 'the thought and the culture of the people was not represented'.

Since the 1930s, while Gandhi's economic thought had no support from the political classes, the air was thick with the 'idea of planning'.[41] For a long while, nationalist opinion had already been arraigned against economic laissez faire. By 1944, even the Raj had come to think of post-war plans that called for state intervention. The apparent success of planning in the Soviet Union and the work of the Congress NPC also helped build a climate of favourable public opinion. With Independence on the horizon, many were anxious to shape the future economy of India. One of the earliest moves was by a group of influential industrialists and businessmen who drew up the Bombay Plan. Since there were several limiting constraints on economic

---

[38] J. C. Kumarappa, 'Plenty in Gorakhpur', *Blitz*, 20 September 1952, Press Clippings, Kumarappa Papers.

[39] G. Sitaram Sastry, 'Constitution of Independent India', *GUP*, April 1950.

[40] J. C. Kumarappa, 'Democracy—Formal or Dharmic?', *GUP*, March 1950.

[41] For a historical survey of this view, see Chattopadhyay, 'The Idea of Planning in India, 1930–1950'.

growth in this period, even these capitalists called for a significant amount of public investment towards a planned economy. For Kumarappa, planning was not about managing natural resources to derive the greatest material benefit. Rather, if a plan had to be 'worth the sacrifices' entailed, it had to address life as a whole and provide for 'the development of all the faculties of man'.[42] Viewed from this perspective, the Bombay Plan 'puts the cart before the horse' as it 'plans for materials and not for the people'.

In this atmosphere there was 'much curiosity about the idea of planning entertained by Gandhiji'.[43] Although the public demand was satisfied by a breezily assembled reply in the form of Shriman Narayan's *The Gandhian Plan of Economic Development for India*, in Kumarappa's opinion the answer lay in an examination of 'the genesis, structure and methods of working' of the many constructive organizations founded by Gandhi. While these constructive organizations did emphasize increasing the material productivity of the people, Kumarappa argued that their ultimate goal was to address the all-round development of man. Prior to his assassination, Gandhi had concluded that the Congress was incapable of rendering justice to the masses. However, in his absence, the constructive workers failed to provide the necessary political challenge and corrective. The March 1948 meeting in Sevagram proved ineffective in providing a fresh direction to constructive work. Therefore, in late 1949, the Gandhians made a brief renewed attempt to tackle 'the feeling of frustration all round', by formulating a plan 'to meet the present crisis in the country, as well as to build a permanent socio-economic order'.[44] The 'Sarvodaya Plan', intended to be 'implemented by the constructive organizations and accepted by the Congress', bore a strong imprint of Kumarappa's views on decentralized village industries, land reform, and Balanced Cultivation.[45] While acknowledging the tremendous challenges to India's political integrity in the wake of Partition, the Gandhians warned against the rather overt tendency to consolidate powers in the hands of the state. If the government fails to provide true freedom and 'does not harness the

[42] J. C. Kumarappa, 'An Iron Image with Feet of Clay', *GUP*, November 1945.

[43] J. C. Kumarappa, 'Planning for India', *GUP*, May 1945.

[44] *Principles of Sarvodaya Plan* (New Delhi: Sarvodaya Planning Committee, New Delhi, 1950), pp. 32–3.

[45] The one significant difference in emphasis is that the Sarvodaya Plan stressed the importance of political decentralization to a greater degree than can be seen in Kumarappa's writings which were often focused on the economic and agrarian dimensions of Indian life.

initiative of the common man', it would never play a vital role in the 'social efforts of the teeming millions', that is, it would never be truly democratic.[46]

The Gandhians carried moral weight but had limited influence on the policy-making of the Indian state. Nevertheless, at least one scholar of Indian planning has argued that the formulation of a Sarvodaya Plan exerted pressure on the Congress to respond. The result was the setting up of a planning commission by the Government of India.[47] While the constructive workers may have exerted some moral pressure on this count, ironically, their fear of increased centralization of powers did come to pass with the Planning Commission eventually becoming the controlling agency of the economy. At the same time, the composition of the Planning Commission made it clear that sarvodaya ideals would not exert any influence on its deliberations. Two conspicuous exclusions from the newly constituted Planning Commission—K. T. Shah and Kumarappa—'gave rise to some strong criticism in the Parliament'.[48] Shah was a left-leaning economist who had enthusiastically served as the Secretary of the pre-Independence NPC, but had lost caste with the new power hierarchy when he contested as the socialist candidate against Rajendra Prasad for the post of the president of India. Kumarappa had resigned from the NPC due to ideological differences, and it was hardly expected that Nehru's regime would take kindly to his caustic criticism and appoint him to the Planning Commission.[49]

The Planning Commission presented a draft of the First Five-Year Plan which was widely criticized for being an assorted grab bag of earlier British plans for post-war reconstruction. Kumarappa argued that any plan must be driven by a 'definite goal based on a view of life, be it material, moral, social or spiritual'.[50] To his mind, not only did the First Plan lack a coherent goal, it failed to tackle the serious issue of land distribution and the uplift of landless labour.[51] The absence of any real sense of purpose was also remarked upon by mainstream economists who criticized the First Plan for sloppily attempting to increase material production rather

[46] *Principles of Sarvodaya Plan*, pp. 27–8.

[47] Chattopadhyay, 'The Idea of Planning in India, 1930–1951', pp. 318–21.

[48] Chattopadhyay, 'The Idea of Planning in India, 1930–1951', p. 322.

[49] However, as noted earlier, he was appointed to the less influential National Planning Advisory Board to give representation to the views of Gandhian constructive workers in the process of national planning.

[50] J. C. Kumarappa, 'Plans or Projects?', *GUP*, August 1951.

[51] See J. C. Kumarappa, 'The Five Year Plan', *GUP*, December 1952.

than worry about 'better adjustment of the agents of production to secure better income distribution'.[52] By this time, it was quite apparent that Nehru's government had no intention to implement the rather radical proposals of the Kumarappa-led ARC. The Planning Commission's failure to seriously address the agrarian crisis did not escape public attention. Indeed, a leading journal was 'surprised at the mildness of [Kumarappa's] protest' against this aspect of the Plan.[53]

By the end of 1955, Kumarappa felt that there was a dim acknowledgement by the 'planners in their armchairs' that their urge to industrialize would fail to translate into employment.[54] Nevertheless, by the time the draft outline of the momentous Second Plan was issued, it was evident that the planners were still betting on manufacturing industries relieving the pressure on the land. With a lifetime of experience, Kumarappa persistently argued that it was only with village industries that one could meet the needs of employment. He also found much evidence of the craving for foreign exchange that was sought to be met by an 'all absorbing solicitude for the expansion of exports'.[55] Arguing that the masses did not need the foreign exchange that India's capitalist class so keenly desired, Kumarappa felt that instead of exporting raw materials, India needed to 'be courageous if we mean to practise self-sufficiency and rebuild our countryside' and enable Indian villages to retain the raw materials to be converted into consumer goods for their own use.

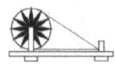

Arguing in 1946 that India's planners should be mindful of its poverty, Kumarappa illustrated his case by recounting a 1939 encounter with rank destitution that had affected him deeply. Travelling between villages one night during the survey of CP and Berar, he and his team of students spied a crouching figure trying to hide amidst some shrubs. On closer inspection, the huddled creature turned out to be an old woman dressed in rags. Driven by hunger and fearful of forest guards, she had come at night to collect grass seeds to boil into a gruel. Kumarappa argued against the focus on the 'miles of cement roads or tons of steel', as the people who required such industrial

[52] 'Five-Year Plan under Fire', *Economic Weekly*, 24 November 1951.

[53] 'Weekly Notes: The Attack from Wardha', *Economic Weekly*, 4 August 1951.

[54] J. C. Kumarappa, 'Is It the Dawn at Last?', *GUP*, October 1955.

[55] J. C. Kumarappa, 'The Draft 2nd Five Year Plan', *GUP*, March 1956.

facilities 'have the capacity to look after themselves'.[56] If India's planners wished to look after the needs of anyone, he said, 'look after this woman'.

It was due to this sensibility that Kumarappa had opposed a blanket approach to nationalization of private enterprises in the name of public interest. For instance, in 1947 he argued against the nationalization of India's various private airline companies as such a move could hardly help the poor of the country who have no use for air travel. Pleading for the public funds to 'be earmarked for the provision of facilities for the masses', Kumarappa felt that India's airlines were best left to their own devices as they were quite capable of taking care of themselves.[57] Throughout the 1950s, the half-hearted gestures towards socialism meant that many of the promises the Congress had made in earlier times remained unfulfilled. The radical thrust towards tackling deep-rooted and systemic inequalities was successfully parried under the guise of pragmatism and the limitations imposed by democratic governance. The inability and unwillingness of the Congress in power to come to grips with the problems on hand was most evident in the Avadi Resolution of the Congress in 1955 on adopting a 'Socialistic Pattern of Society'. This, Kumarappa argued, was neither fish nor fowl and attempted to give a 'newly coined phrase to a policy that the Congress Government has all along been pursuing and wishes to continue by lulling the general public to sleep by rhetorical flourishes'.[58]

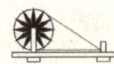

Kumarappa was not alone amongst the Gandhians to express dismay and disillusionment with the turn of events. His compatriot, G. Ramachandran, presented a masterly assessment of the crisis for the sarvodaya ideal when he asked, 'Whither Constructive Work?'[59] 'Constructive workers,' Ramachandran argued, 'will not break their hearts if their erstwhile

[56] J. C. Kumarappa, *A Plan for Rural Development*, p. 2.

[57] J. C. Kumarappa, 'Nationalization', *Harijan*, 5 January 1947. India did go ahead with nationalizing its airlines and the consequences of such decisions made in the name of socialism continue to reverberate in our decidedly capitalist times.

[58] J. C. Kumarappa, 'Neither Fish Nor Flesh', *GUP*, February 1955.

[59] G. Ramachandran, *Whither Constructive Work?* (Wardha: The All-India Village Industries Association, 1951). The essay was first serialized between July and December of 1950 in the *GUP*.

comrades, who have become the rulers of India, repudiate the constructive programme.'[60] Rather, it would only be good as it would 'put them on their test'. In a devastating indictment that is worth quoting at length, he pointed out:

> What is heart-breaking, however, is the lack of clarity in the situation for the common man. The common man who worships Gandhiji is misled into the idea that the Central and State Governments are dedicated to carry out Gandhian programmes. Why should not our leaders come out openly and declare that the Gandhian constructive programme with the villager at the centre is impossible, that khadi and village industries cannot occupy the centre of national economic reconstruction.... The painful tragedy is that our Governments wish to keep alive the false idea that they are carrying out the Gandhian programmes, while at the same time they are doing most things contrary.

Indeed, while the government had implicitly repudiated the entire Gandhian programme, 'ministers and leaders scrupulously put on khadi and often ask people to do Constructive Work, and at the same time do everything which makes khadi and Constructive Work look ridiculous and unwanted'.[61] Ramachandran argued that what was needed was 'the immediate escape from this contradiction'. But the events that would soon transpire would take a turn for the worse. If it was bad enough for Nehru's Congress to consistently mock and undermine the ideals and values of constructive work while claiming to follow Gandhi, soon Americans would join in on the game. For Kumarappa, a distressing situation was turning into an intolerable one.

---

[60] Ramachandran, *Whither Constructive Work?*, p. 2.
[61] Ramachandran, *Whither Constructive Work?*, p. 5.

16   The Spreading Chill

lthough the shipping conference in London in July 1947 was a
non-starter, Kumarappa had his own reasons to make the trip
three decades after he had left England. Apart from acquiring a
first-hand experience of post-war England, he spent his time there lobbying
politicians like Stafford Cripps and George Schuster on the question of
Sterling Securities and England's debt to India.[1] As a champion of village
reconstruction, it was natural that he would also make a trip to Leonard
Elmhirst's Dartington Trust.[2] But the more important relationship that
he established during this visit was with the Pacifists who played a
significant, if limited, role in an atmosphere of belligerence during the
war years in Europe. This brief contact resulted in an interview that is
a biographer's delight. While Kumarappa's public engagements in India
were as an expositor of a non-violent economic order, in this interview
he demonstrated a sound grasp of Indian and global politics. Asked if

[1] Vinaik, *Quest*, p. 161.
[2] Elmhirst was a confidant of Rabindranath Tagore and helped found the
poet's project for rural reconstruction named Sriniketan. As an aside, for Elmhirst's
views on the importance of soil fertility that mirror those of Kumarappa, see
Leonard K. Elmhirst, *Poet and Plowman* (Calcutta: Visva-Bharati, 1975).

Gandhi's ideals were accepted by the masses and the leaders, Kumarappa responded in the negative. Rather, he argued, that 'the evidence is that the Congress Indians will out-British the British. Our own capitalism will be as rapacious as yours'.[3] The credulous interviewer asked Kumarappa if he really believed that the British desired to create Pakistan. If in replying to Jayaprakash Narayan in 1935 Kumarappa's analysis of the nature of the Soviet state was accurate, his answer here was no less precise in foretelling future events:

> I am certain of it. Why, through the influence they will retain over a Moslem buffer-state, they will be able both to affect the policies of the Arab League countries, in which their oil interests are vitally involved, and to resist Russian penetration of the Near and Middle East. Remember, Russian ambitions are reflected in the new territorial demands of Afghanistan.

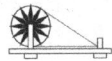

India's independence in 1947 had heralded a wave of decolonization across Asia and Africa. But that process was hardly a smooth affair. In a world that seemed to have learnt nothing from the ravages of the Second World War, decolonized nations were seen as mere pawns in the contest for global supremacy. Far from finding their hard-won independence secure, India and other Asian nations were confronted with the prospect of being drawn into the Cold War that showed all the signs of turning into a hot one. Having emerged from the Second World War as a global power, the United States sought to draw India into its own 'sphere of influence'. In this political atmosphere, Nehru's delicate position of neutralism was a continual source of irritation to the American establishment that disliked India's independent line on the Korean War. In the meanwhile, arising out of a complex set of circumstances that included the expropriation of its resources during the War years, India was gripped by a food shortage. Tentative negotiations took place for the provision of American wheat to help India tide over its crisis. Some hardliners wished to punish India for its lack of enthusiasm for American hegemony in Asia. But others in the Truman administration advocated the grant of the wheat loan to endear

---

[3] 'India's Path to Freedom: J. C. Kumarappa Interviewed in London', *Peace News*, 1 August 1947.

itself to India and address an anxiety that plagued Americans—a possible Communist takeover of India.[4]

In an America gripped by a paranoia of a 'Red under every bed', a most unlikely Indian became the target of harsh criticism. That man was the likable, mild-mannered Bharatan Kumarappa. By 1950, Bharatan was in the United States as an Indian diplomat at the United Nations Social Commission and decided to spend the winter of 1950–1 delivering lectures 'by way of Public Relations'.[5] The lecture tour was sponsored by the American Friends Services Committee, a Quaker organization that had won the Nobel Peace Prize in 1947. While Bharatan's intent was to explain India's neutral position to his audiences, a speech delivered in Texas caused a political furore. Thanks to the controversy it generated, a verbatim transcript of Bharatan's speech is available.[6] For sure, we may take Bharatan's arguments here to be also reflective of J. C. Kumarappa's viewpoint on the matter. Bharatan sought to explain to his audience as to why India had adopted a neutral course in the conflict between the Russians and the Americans. He argued that 'non-violence, liberty from foreign rule, and a desire to increase our standard of living' were the things uppermost in Indian minds. In particular, to understand India's point of view, it was necessary to recognize that it has been 'subject to foreign rule, and many ... have had several years of imprisonment ... [and] have lived for nothing else than the independence' of India. In discussing Russia, Bharatan argued that while the goal of Communism was a state where there was 'no room for exploitation or for suppression of the weak by the strong ... the methods that Russia has unfortunately adopted towards realizing this goal are violent, and the most violent imaginable, because we find that Russia has no scruples, has no religion, has no morality, and is prepared to throw everything to the winds when it comes to seeking its goal'. 'Russia in order to achieve her

---

[4] Robert J. McMahon, 'Food as a Diplomatic Weapon: The India Wheat Loan of 1951', *The Pacific Historical Review*, vol. 56, no. 3 (1987): 349–77. For a broader analysis of American foreign policy in South Asia during this period, see Robert J. McMahon, *The Cold War on the Periphery: The United States, India and Pakistan* (New York: Columbia University Press, 1994); and Dennis Merrill, *Bread and the Ballot: The United States and India's Economic Development, 1947–1963* (Chapel Hill: University of North Carolina Press, 1990).

[5] Letter from Bharatan Kumarappa, 10 January 1950, External Affairs, UNI Branch, F5(125) - UNI 49, National Archives of India.

[6] 'India and the Power Struggle', transcript of speech by Bharatan Kumarappa on 25 February 1951, Box 82, John M. Vorys Papers, Ohio Historical Society.

goal, has adopted totalitarianism' resulting in a 'complete suppression of liberty of thought and expression'. Therefore, India 'turns away in great disappointment from Russia'. While there was much to commend in the American way of life, American militarism and belligerence made India 'adopt a more hesitant attitude'. In a frank assessment, he pointed out that the American arming of the 'French against the independence movement in Indo-China' was 'an unpardonable sin' in Indian eyes, 'because of our desire first and foremost to be done with European imperialism in Asia'. Summarizing his views, Bharatan argued that while India rejected communism and the Russian approach, 'our first enemy is imperialism in Asia'. India desired 'peace and non-violence [but] not at the cost of sacrificing liberty'.

Bharatan's friendly criticism did not go down well with those who believed in American exceptionalism. Houston newspapers drummed up opposition that forced local universities and organizations to cancel the speeches they had invited Bharatan to deliver.[7] The controversy was a perfect foil for hard-line legislators who objected to the speech and also insisted that India be forced to repay the wheat loan in strategic materials like thorium.[8] In itself, Bharatan's views were unexceptionable. During his maiden tour of the United States in 1949, Nehru had insisted that 'colonialism, not communism, was the gravest danger to world peace'.[9] However, the Indian government 'expressed keen regret' on the reported remarks attributed to Bharatan.[10] While, perhaps in the interest of realpolitik, the Indian government did not attempt to defend its envoy against a gross misrepresentation, it fell to a *Washington Post* editorial column to make the case that Bharatan was 'quoted out of context' and point out that he had made a 'considerable point of distrust of Russian totalitarianism' and his speech was 'more a restatement of the neutralist position than criticism of the United States'.[11] Although the wheat loan was eventually approved, tainted by American hubris and manipulation, it failed to help the American position in India. Unusually, J. C. Kumarappa did not make a public comment on the wheat loan. Perhaps his silence stemmed from

---

[7] '2 Speeches Canceled for India's Delegate' and '3 Houston Talks Dropped', *New York Times*, 25 and 28 February 1951 respectively.

[8] 'Make It a Gift', *The Washington Post*, 15 March 1951.

[9] McMahon, 'Food as a Diplomatic Weapon: The India Wheat Loan of 1951'.

[10] 'India Regrets Talks in U.S. by Her Envoy', *New York Times*, 10 March 1951.

[11] 'Make It a Gift', *Washington Post*, 15 March 1951. Some individuals who had attended Bharatan's talks also came out in his defence.

a sense of decorum, since his brother had been dragged into an unseemly controversy. However, this episode would have angered J. C. Kumarappa who had consistently argued that the grim food situation needed a clear policy answer, not the promotion of cash crops on the one hand and import of American wheat on the other. The failure of the Indian government to defend Bharatan would have also hurt J. C. Kumarappa.

A year later, despite US Congressional hostility, the American government was offering economic assistance to India. The primary proponent of such aid was a Madison Avenue advertiser who had recently lost a re-election bid as governor of Connecticut, Chester Bowles. By late 1951, Bowles was appointed as the American ambassador to New Delhi and fancied himself as bringing the New Deal to India. Bowles conceived of massive economic aid to India as a bulwark against that scourge of American ambitions in Asia, communism. The Republicans holding the American purse strings were unimpressed with their envoy's strategy and the eventual assistance sanctioned was whittled down to 50 million dollars.[12] Although this was a fraction of what Bowles had desired, he quickly set about fashioning it in the manner of 'an imaginative and effective program of village development' that was attempted in nationalist China under Chiang Kai-Shek.[13] Apart from his personal rapport with the designer of the China plan, the inspiration here was clear. The 'loss' of China to Mao and his Red Army had led to much hand-wringing and acrimony in Washington. If this bitter experience was to be avoided with India, Bowles imagined, an integrated rural development plan was urgently required. What the Kuomintang (spelt Guomindang in Pinyin transliteration) failed to do in China, Americans would achieve in India.

Bowles wrote up an unofficial proposal for a scheme of village development that would lead to 'a nation-wide plan of village development' and presented it to Nehru.[14] He emphasized that the assistance came with 'no strings, economic, political or otherwise' and believed that Nehru had accepted 'at face value' the assertion that American aid 'was not a bribe

---

[12] For details, see chapter 3 of McMahon, *The Cold War on the Periphery*.

[13] Chester Bowles, *Ambassador's Report* (New York: Harper and Brothers, 1954), p. 196.

[14] Bowles, *Ambassador's Report*, p. 199.

designed to buy India's allegiance'. A two-hour conversation ensued and soon, in January 1952, India and the United States signed a Technical Cooperation Agreement whereby the United States granted aid with the intent of 'promoting and accelerating the integrated development of India'.[15] Successful advertiser that he was, Bowles sought wide publicity for the agreement and got it.[16] With typical bluster, he claimed that 'editorial comment was extravagantly generous'. In reality this was hardly the case. If the leftist critics could be dismissed for being pathologically anti-American, a much wider spectrum of public opinion also remained unconvinced. The *Economic Weekly* editorialized that in pushing economic assistance in India, Bowles was seeking an outlet for the 'colossal volume of industrial production' in the United States.[17]

The implications of the agreement were not lost on J. C. Kumarappa either. In an article, provocatively titled 'The Noose?', he warned of the tentacles of 'the American speciality [of] financial imperialism'.[18] Kumarappa worried that 'American penetration' in the form of such aid would bring in its agricultural practices that relied heavily on crude oil and machinery. Such dependence on imported materials was suicidal as it would be easy for the Americans to dictate terms in the future by merely stopping the supply of crude oil so that India would be 'starved into subjection' which 'will deliver us body, soul and spirit into American hands'. As regards the aid, although there were no overt conditionalities, the American hope was that India's 'tongue will be tied by moral obligations of one who has eaten American salt'. If that did not work, Kumarappa argued, 'the Atom bomb pile is always there'.[19] This sharp reaction did not go unnoticed and Bowles remarked that Kumarappa was 'a foolish man', but 'would like to argue it out' with him.[20] Interestingly enough, a meeting was arranged between the two men. While recognizing that Bowles was 'well intentioned', Kumarappa walked away unimpressed with the man who 'speaks too much for a diplomat but is good for an advertiser'.[21]

[15] 'Indo-US Technical Cooperation Agreement', reproduced as Appendix 1 in L. Natarajan, *American Shadow over India* (Bombay: People's Publishing House, 1952), pp. 299–304.

[16] Bowles, *Ambassador's Report*, p. 200.

[17] 'A New Deal in Mutual Aid', *Economic Weekly*, 1 March 1952.

[18] J. C. Kumarappa, 'The Noose?', *GUP*, February 1952.

[19] J. C. Kumarappa, 'The Almighty Dollar', *GUP*, March 1952.

[20] Reported in *Bombay Chronicle*, 26 February 1952.

[21] Letter from J. C. Kumarappa to Evelyn Hershey, 21 March 1952, Subject File, 26, Kumarappa Papers.

If American solicitude for India's villages raised eyebrows, the terms of the agreement disturbed many self-respecting Indians. According to the agreement, the American staff administering the funds 'shall share fully in the privileges and immunities' of diplomats, including 'immunity from suit in the courts of India'.[22] An incensed Kumarappa pointed out that this was 'unworthy of any self-respecting, independent country, as it confers diplomatic immunity to private foreign citizens working in our country'.[23] For a generation that had fought against colonization, such feelings were hardly surprising. Even the mild-mannered Mashruwala, who often rebuked Kumarappa for his intemperate writings, saw historical déjà vu in an agreement that was 'virtually a charter to U. S. to establish herself in India, first as a trading concern, and then as India's political boss'. It hurt that the 'Government of India has agreed to place at the disposal of U.S. all its administrative machinery and to become her advertising agency'.[24]

While Nehru's distaste for domineering Americans and his non-aligned approach is widely recognized, his choice to accept the Bowles proposal merits examination. For three decades Nehru had expressed disdain for Gandhi's constructive work programme for the revival of Indian villages. Instead, as at the time of the formation of the AIVIA, he had plumbed for radical land reforms and an industrial road to development. However, although the power of the Indian state was now in hand, there was little progress on land reform. Ironically, it was left to Gandhians like Kumarappa and Vinoba to raise this crucial question in the *ARC Report* and through the Bhoodan movement respectively. It was bad enough that the rural masses were not to get their share in the fruits of freedom as the focus was on rapid and massive industrialization. It was doubly ironic and unjust that Nehru would proceed to completely ignore the wealth of experience garnered by the constructive workers and put his faith in the hands of Americans who had not a clue about India and its complex problems.

The quixotic and haphazard nature of Nehru's interest in rural development did not begin with the Bowles proposal. In fact, before approaching Nehru with the funding for integrated development projects in rural India, Bowles had done some breezy homework. Although his inspiration sprang from the failed Chinese experiment, Bowles had to find an Indian exemplar as a suitable template. The model had to be both acceptable

[22] 'Indo-US Technical Cooperation Agreement'.
[23] J. C. Kumarappa, 'Community Projects', *GUP*, September 1952.
[24] K. G. Mashruwala, 'Indo-USA Technical Co-operation Agreement', *Harijan*, 18 October 1952.

to Nehru and also fit American sensibilities and strategic needs. Fortuitously, for Bowles, an American experiment in rural uplift that had begun some years earlier with Nehru's explicit and enthusiastic blessings was readily available for use. That experiment was the brainchild of an American urban planner, Albert Mayer, and was known as the Etawah Project.

Mayer's expertise was in urban planning in America and he had no experience or understanding of the rural problem in India. This fact, however, did not seem to be a deterrent either for him or Nehru. Presumably, Mayer's ample enthusiasm was deemed sufficient to entrust him with a major exercise. The lack of experience and understanding showed in Mayer's original proposal that consisted of 'a program of architectural and physical planning for villages'. Soon, this idea had to be drastically revised with the realization that 'thorough rural socioeconomic development' was the need of the hour.[25] By late 1948, Mayer was installed as the head of a 'pilot project' in Etawah. The 'pilot project' had begun with sixty-four villages which in three years had expanded to encompass some three hundred villages.[26] It was designed to address the improvement of seed and livestock, health and sanitation, and co-operative services. This, it was believed, would lead to an all-round improvement of the villages and yield valuable answers on how much 'productive social improvement' was possible and 'how quickly those results may be attainable'.[27] The Etawah exercise demonstrated an unyielding faith in the ability of modern technological and managerial approaches to work miracles. Brimming with optimism, Mayer set out to derive generalizable methods of rural improvement that could be rapidly replicated all over the country. His ignorance of the work at Maganvadi did not prevent Mayer from claiming that the Gandhians knew nothing of rigorous methodology, that Gandhi's approach was archaic, and that Indian villages needed 'a series of drastic remedies'.[28] That an American urban planner could presume to solve rural India's problems can only be explained as hubris. While Mayer's work was

---

[25] Albert Mayer and associates, *Pilot Project, India: The Story of Rural Development at Etawah, Uttar Pradesh* (Berkeley: University of California Press, 1959), p. 23.

[26] Preface by G. B. Pant, in Albert Mayer and associates, *Pilot Project, India: The Story of Rural Development at Etawah, Uttar Pradesh*, p. xi.

[27] Mayer and associates, *Pilot Project, India: The Story of Rural Development at Etawah, Uttar Pradesh*, p. 37.

[28] Mayer and associates, *Pilot Project, India: The Story of Rural Development at Etawah, Uttar Pradesh*, p. 21.

hardly radical, it held many attractions for Nehru. Along with a shared faith in technological modernity, Mayer's 'solution' came without the uncomfortable questions that Gandhians like Kumarappa and socialists and ex-Congressmen like JP and Kripalani relentlessly posed to Nehru and his government. Working under Nehru's patronage, Mayer was neither inclined to nor capable of posing such challenges.

Etawah did not address any of the serious questions of land reform or the building of a viable agrarian economy in the context of massive inequalities. However, it is precisely because of its anodyne nature that Etawah drew much attention from funders like the Ford Foundation and visiting American notables like Eleanor Roosevelt and Chester Bowles. When Bowles proposed to Nehru that the Etawah model be replicated on a national scale, Nehru felt it to be impractical. It was impossible to find enough educated workers sufficiently interested in village work. Bowles evinced surprise that Nehru with his 'commitment both to democratic economic progress and to young people' would react in this manner.[29] This was 'Cold War hardball' and eventually Nehru acceded to the American pressure. Thus was born the first major American intervention in India, the Community Development Project.[30] The man chosen to head it was Sushil Kumar Dey, an engineer educated in America, who had made his name in building the township of Nilokheri that resettled some eight thousand refugees.[31] Given his own views, Nehru made no attempts to harness the rich Gandhian experience in addressing rural concerns. However, despite clear indications to the contrary, others had no qualms in invoking Gandhi's name to suit their purpose. Bowles described the Etawah project as a combination of 'the Gandhian program of village development with the extension service techniques of the U.S. Department of Agriculture'.[32] He further went on to claim that 'Gandhi's concept of a balanced village ... is incorporated as the goal of every Community Development Project'.[33]

---

[29] Bowles quoted in Bret Wallach, *Losing Asia: Modernization and the Culture of Development* (Baltimore: Johns Hopkins University Press, 1996), p. 151.

[30] For a history of Community Development, see Daniel Immerwahr, *Thinking Small: The United States and the Lure of Community Development* (Cambridge, MA: Harvard University Press, 2015). For a review of this book, see Venu Madhav Govindu, 'A Palimpsest for Development', *Economic and Political Weekly*, vol. 50, no. 30 (25 July 2015).

[31] Bowles, *Ambassador's Report*, p. 201.

[32] Bowles, *Ambassador's Report*, pp. 228–9.

[33] Bowles, *Ambassador's Report*, p. 239.

The first phase of the Community Development Project was set to be implemented in fifty-five areas, each consisting of about three hundred villages thus encompassing about a crore of Indians within its scope. Although the project was envisaged on an ambitious scale, Kumarappa pointed out that its draft outline was 'so scanty that no detailed study can be made of the plans'.[34] He objected to the lack of 'an intimate knowledge of the human element' in the exercise. Since 'the Americans know no more about us than we do of the Eskimos', Kumarappa wondered what gave them any 'qualification to teach us'. In the compass of a few lines, he penetrated to the heart of the problem. The American-inspired scheme sought to 'bypass the fundamental rural question—Land Reform' and did not envisage 'regional self-sufficiency in food' and would eventually fail to provide adequate food security. Kumarappa argued that it was essential to rebuild rural India by promoting 'self-government and self-sufficiency' which was the only way to provide it an enduring basis. The approach adopted, however, would convert the village into 'a factory to produce goods that perish in time'.[35] Kumarappa was amongst the earliest to recognize that the approach to development adopted in the 1950s would eventually only focus on merely increasing net agricultural output and thereby fail to address the social needs of man. Therefore, he argued that 'we are launching on the greatest blunder when we turn for guidance towards America for our developmental schemes.... The sooner India turns to her own genius and relies on her own strength and resources for development the better it will be for herself and her message of peace to the world'.[36]

Despite having no clear sense of what Community Development was setting out to achieve, the nationwide project was set to be inaugurated by President Rajendra Prasad on 2 October 1952, the birth anniversary of Gandhi. The glib invocation of Gandhi's name in the context of an American-inspired project infuriated many village workers who appealed to Prasad not to inaugurate the project on Gandhi Jayanti. Kumarappa agreed that it was 'not in good taste that this ignoble Project should be inaugurated on Gandhiji's birthday'.[37] The appeal fell on deaf ears and, in his address, Rajendra Prasad said that it was 'a happy idea to inaugurate

[34] J. C. Kumarappa, 'Community Projects', GUP, September 1952.

[35] Evidently, Kumarappa was replying to the notions of 'development' and 'economic growth' that were crystallizing in this period.

[36] J. C. Kumarappa, 'Our Guides', GUP, December 1953.

[37] Letter from J. C. Kumarappa to R. V. Ramani, 24 September 1952, Correspondence Files, Kumarappa Papers.

the Community Development Programme on [Gandhi's] birthday'.[38] In a particularly egregious interpretation of the fundamental impulse of Gandhi's constructive work, Prasad went on to claim that despite 'the large amount of selfless work' done by Gandhiji's followers, its impact was limited due to lack of 'both money and technical personnel'. The agreement with the Americans, he was happy to note, remedied the situation and 'opened up new possibilities of advance along these lines'. Here, he was not speaking as Gandhi's comrade in Champaran but as the first citizen of a modern republic.

While the invocation of Gandhi's name was a self-serving gesture, Kumarappa was more deeply disturbed by the free hand the Americans were being given in running the entire project. If providing diplomatic immunity to Americans involved in the project was bad enough, it was galling that they were 'given a controlling voice in the affairs of the Community Projects' since they had an effective veto on any aspect of the project.[39] If the Americans contributed only one-sixth of the money, he wondered why it was necessary to accept it and start fifty-five projects. Instead, Kumarappa argued, India could have started work on forty-eight projects and preserved its self-respect. In a damning indictment of Nehru he argued:

> The whole scheme reflects an amazing lack of confidence on the part of the Prime Minister in the ability of his colleagues that he should bow so low to invite foreigners to rebuild the countryside. It is dangerous to hand over parts of the country to be experimented upon by foreigners. If the country is so bankrupt of capacity to solve its problems and rebuild the nation, it confesses its unfitness for Swaraj.

Given the 'danger in falling prey to the American block [sic]' in the Cold War, Kumarappa argued that 'those of us, who are committed to non-violence, cannot be associated with this scheme'. Fearing that the Community Development Project was 'the thin end of the wedge of the era of American Financial Imperialism ... on the wake of the departure of British Political Imperialism', with 'brutal frankness' he accused those cooperating with the project of being quislings.

Kumarappa's harsh comments on Community Projects, as they came to be called, were occasioned by Dey who sent him the draft outline for

---

[38] 'Integrated Development of Indian Villages', in *Speeches of Dr. Rajendra Prasad: President of India, 13th May 1951–31st December 1954* (New Delhi: President's Press, 1956), p. 31.

[39] J. C. Kumarappa, 'Community Projects', *GUP*, September 1952.

the project and was 'naturally anxious to have [Kumarappa's] opinion'.[40] In March 1948, upon assessing the Kurukshetra refugee camp, Kumarappa felt that the visit was 'a painful experience'.[41] However the one thing that impressed him was 'the little spot of vocational training imparted by Sri S. K. Dey and his band of devoted workers'. Kumarappa's outspoken criticism offended many, but Dey was cut from a different cloth. Upon meeting Dey, Kumarappa's associate, G. Ramachandran, 'felt attracted by [Dey's] vigorous personality, [and] his readiness to understand other points of view and his outspoken humility'.[42] Ramachandran invited Dey to Wardha where he had many meetings with constructive workers, including Kumarappa, and was vigorously challenged by the Gandhians in a jam-packed public meeting.

In the meeting, Dey had claimed that the project was 'planned in India by Indians for Indians' and 'would not admit that Americans inspired or controlled the Projects'. However, in taking a constructive approach towards Kumarappa's harsh criticism, he displayed remarkable forbearance and a sense of humility and purpose. Having risen to a position of considerable power, Dey took it upon himself to never forget that he was a 'farmer's son'.[43] He hoped to compete with Kumarappa in 'honest loyalty to India'.[44] More than any of Kumarappa's old colleagues in Wardha and Delhi, it was Dey who grasped his true nature. If Kumarappa's criticism was often harsh and unpalatable, Dey argued it was because Kumarappa was one of a 'rare tribe' that had Gandhi's 'baptismal fire intact'.[45] Although appreciative of Kumarappa's misgivings, Dey did not take him 'literally in the totally pessimistic view of the future'. Kumarappa, in turn, appreciated Dey's

[40] Letter from S. K. Dey to J. C. Kumarappa, 7 July 1952, Subject File, 20, Kumarappa Papers.

[41] Letter from J. C. Kumarappa to Mehr Chand Khanna, 30 March 1948, Subject File, 20, Kumarappa Papers.

[42] G. Ramachandran, 'The Maganvadi Study Circle', GUP, September 1952.

[43] Similar to Nehru's famed self-critical essay in Modern Review under the pseudonym of Chanakya, Dey, as the head of the Community Project, penned a reflective article in the project's journal Kurukshetra with the byline 'From a Farmer's Son', 'Destination Man—Some Implications', Kurukshetra, 26 January 1954, reproduced in Kurukshetra: A Symposium on Community Development in India (1952–1955) (New Delhi: Publications Division, 1955), pp. 20–3.

[44] Letter from S. K. Dey to J. C. Kumarappa, 15 December 1955, Subject File, 20, Kumarappa Papers.

[45] Letter from S. K. Dey to J. C. Kumarappa, 5 January 1956, Subject File, 20, Kumarappa Papers.

'willingness evinced to take the stick' and, despite his rapidly deteriorating health, was willing to help Dey with his work.[46] The friendship between the two deepened and as an occasional guest of the Dey household in Delhi, Kumarappa endeared himself to the entire family who 'never had a guest' like him.[47]

By 1956, the programme had grown at a fast pace and had a presence in 235,000 villages encompassing some 130 million rural Indians within its scope.[48] The rapid growth of coverage and number of schemes meant that its impact would be weak. Kumarappa was troubled by Nehru's statement in London expressing satisfaction with the high standards of work achieved under the Community Projects. Distressed at the prime minister's modest expectations, Kumarappa wondered if 'Shri Nehru would himself care to live under the prevailing conditions in these villages even for a few days'.[49] And then, speaking as a man who had spent the last twenty years in a small hut, he added for good measure, 'we would not'. In any event, there was a fundamental problem with the entire conception of the Community Projects. It was rather optimistic to presume that a bureaucracy that was crafted under an iniquitous colonial regime could be suddenly made to exert itself on behalf of poor villagers. Thus, while the Kumarappa–Dey friendship was maturing, the Community Projects were themselves mired in problems.

Soon after their inauguration, by the middle of 1953, the nature of Community Projects was changed. In combination with the Grow More Food campaign it was slowly, but inexorably, transformed into an All-India Extension Service. From now on, the focus of policy was on providing agricultural inputs without touching upon the fundamental problems of the agrarian economy. The bureaucracy that had been fretting at the potential loss of control could now breathe easy. As one editorial wryly put it, with the growing influence of the Planning Commission run by colonial-era bureaucrats, especially with 'V. T. Krishnamachari at the helm of affairs ... the benevolent District Magistrate is not likely to lose his pivotal position'.[50]

[46] Letter from J. C. Kumarappa to S. K. Dey, 22 October 1956, Subject File, 20, Kumarappa Papers.

[47] Letter from S. K. Dey to J. C. Kumarappa, 1 October 1956, Subject File, 20, Kumarappa Papers.

[48] Report: 1956–57 (New Delhi: Ministry of Community Development, 1957).

[49] J. C. Kumarappa, 'Wishful Thinking by Jawaharlalji', GUP, July 1956.

[50] 'Metamorphosis of Community Projects', Economic Weekly, 9 May 1953.

Indeed, the framing and execution of Community Development took place in the context of a 'deficit of democracy in the countryside'.[51] With the village panchayat being given short shrift in the Constitution, the problem became one of inducing the participation of the peasant without giving him any control over the planning of projects.

S. K. Dey was himself acutely aware of the difficulty in whipping a moribund system into action. At the same time, especially given his keen interaction with Kumarappa, he had a growing realization that the rural problem needed a solution vastly different from the current one of providing technical inputs. Given his training as an engineer, Dey confessed that he 'got naturally biased towards industrialization in a big way in the first flush of contact with the civilization of the West'.[52] Now, there was a growing realization that the immediate task was to organize and promote 'village and small industries planned within certain limits on the basis of regional self-sufficiency'. As the head of the Community Projects, Dey underwent a rapid education in the problem of rural reconstruction. In an essay published in the *Economic Weekly*, Dey developed a rationale for focussing on the needs of the villager as an individual rather than on increased agricultural yield alone. In the context of the decay of economic forces in Indian society, the different components of the economy had become indistinguishable. Hence, the only solution was to address the totality of the situation, that is, 'there is no scope for economic planning, only for social planning'.[53] Dey argued that while the obvious solution was for the poor with few resources to band together, it was not so easily apparent to the poor themselves since 'reason is at a low ebb in the mind of the villager at the moment'. In this context, he felt that the rallying cry of Indian planning, 'co-operation', slowly metamorphosed into a form of coercion of individuals into groups. Thus, while 'the growth of the individual should be the final objective of all action', eliciting the urge to grow from within was the key challenge.

Coming from a man who headed the Community Projects, this was a remarkable statement. And it would be no disservice to Dey to say

[51] Nick Cullather, *The Hungry World: America's Cold War Battle against Poverty in Asia* (Cambridge, MA: Harvard University Press, 2010), p. 86.

[52] Letter from S. K. Dey to J. C. Kumarappa, 21 November 1956, Subject File, 20, Kumarappa Papers.

[53] S. K. Dey, 'The Unit and the Individual', *Economic Weekly*, 5 November 1953.

that the impress of Kumarappa's thinking is also quite visible here. Dey's remark on the Indian villager could as well have come from Kumarappa or Gandhi:

> The primitive quality of our villager is not authentic. He is not primitive by original right. He has only relapsed to a primitive state.... The urge to grow throbs faintly. It is still there, else there would be no question of development any more but it has to be rediscovered from under an accumulating crust of degradation and despair. The first task in rural rehabilitation is to persuade the villager that it lies within his power to rise above his present condition through his own exertion.

Dey was also deeply troubled by the complacency that was setting in amongst the workers of the Community Projects, a primary reason being 'the spot compliments which we receive from foreign visitors to our programme after their casual observation of our work'.[54] By this time Kumarappa had moved and settled down in an ashram in Madurai district. To counter the tendency of complacency amongst workers, Dey struck upon the idea to have Kumarappa visit some projects and provide a 'detailed criticism', which would be carried in the in-house journal of the Community Projects, *Kurukshetra*. Dey hoped that such criticism by a man of Kumarappa's stature would 'give a shake-up' to the workers. However, the government employees involved were not too keen on being shaken out of their complacency, and they withheld their co-operation.

Over a week's time in January 1956, despite his failing health, Kumarappa travelled extensively in the T. Kallupatti block and visited twenty-seven villages, spread over 65 square miles with a combined population of about thirty-five thousand people.[55] While the tour notes were marked by Kumarappa's familiar imprint of precise surveys of the villages, the accompanying report is of much greater value. With regard to the work carried out by the government agencies, Kumarappa felt that most of it was non-productive in the form of welfare schemes and expensive public works. The nexus between public works and the contractors was very evident in the great emphasis on expensive building and road construction that did not necessarily address the more acute needs of the villages. With his emphasis on self-help, Kumarappa criticized such spending as it was

[54] Letter from S. K. Dey to J. C. Kumarappa, 15 December 1955, Subject File, 20, Kumarappa Papers.

[55] Tour Notes of J. C. Kumarappa in T. Kallupatti National Extension Service Block, Subject File, 20, Kumarappa Papers.

both extravagant and also not amenable to repair and maintenance by the villagers themselves. This, he argued, would only 'result in dilapidated buildings in a few years'. Echoing the observations made by Gandhian visitors to Etawah in 1952, even here in the deep south, Kumarappa found that the programme was largely benefiting the 'moneyed and influential' in the village.[56] The lower castes 'who are notoriously neglected still remain uncared for' and 'are still standing apart suspiciously'.

Kumarappa's harshest criticism was reserved for the moribund and thoroughly inappropriate nature of government intervention in Indian agriculture. He argued that while rural development must be 'the basis of all planning ... at present it appears as a spasmodic effort at decoration'. As always, he repeated his warnings against rampant use of artificial fertilizers with no consideration for the actual deficits of the soil, since there were no facilities available for any soil or water analysis. He warned that 'the Government seems more anxious to dispose of their fertilisers than to observe the ill effects of their use in the course of years of indiscriminate use on all kinds of fields'. However, the worst symptoms of this problem were the agricultural demonstration centres that could not justify their existence. Kumarappa felt that the selection of employees based on their holding of degrees was a mockery of the true need of a demonstrator to be able to lead by example. He argued that if the government was sincere in its purpose, it would provide the demonstrator with no means beyond those already available to an ordinary farmer. There would be no greater salutary lesson than if this employee proved in practice that one could support a family through superior agricultural methods. If the key problem was to motivate the people to improve their lives, the demonstrator had to set an example to ordinary farmers 'as to what they themselves can do on the same footing'. Instead, Kumarappa angrily declaimed, the 'salaried Agricultural Demonstrator ... is a standing monument of a parasite' as the only thing he succeeds in demonstrating is 'how a man can live comfortably on an unearned income'.

While Rajendra Prasad had claimed that the problem of resources and personnel would be solved with the American intervention, the reality was quite different. Despite a measure of work being faithfully carried out,

[56] J. C. Kumarappa, 'Report on Rural Development Work in Madurai District', Subject File, 20, Kumarappa Papers. For Gandhian critiques of Mayer's Etawah project, see Thakurdas Bang and Suresh Ramabhai, 'The Truth about Etawah', *Economic Weekly*, 3 May 1952; and S. N. Agarwal, 'Truth about the Etawah Project', *Modern Review*, September 1952.

all that 'these programmes have provided is an opening for the educated unemployed' who did not love rural India but were there for 'their own employment and advancement'. Thus, despite the immense possibilities one could have imagined, without co-ordinated planning or suitably motivated personnel, the Community Projects exercise 'languishes for want of a goal and purpose'.

17   Seeing Red

In the early 1950s, Indian sentiment against Western hegemony also led to an interest in China. Kumarappa soon became party to a complicated and acrimonious debate on his views on Chinese and Russian communism. In late 1951, he had barely settled down at Pannai Ashram when he received an invitation to join a group of Indians on a 'goodwill mission' to China, in time for the second anniversary celebrations of the People's Republic of China. Although he was initially reluctant to leave his work, Kumarappa was persuaded by co-workers to avail himself of the opportunity to study the situation in China.[1] We know much about Kumarappa's trip to China and Japan as he wrote regular letters to colleagues back in Wardha, extracts of which appeared in the *Gram Udyog Patrika* and were later assembled in a book, *People's China: What I Saw and Learnt There* (Wardha: The All-India Village Industries Association, 1952). Despite the language barrier and the conducted nature of his trip, the five weeks spent in China provided Kumarappa much to ponder over and gave a distinct shape to his public engagement and advocacy.[2] Pointing to the Chinese 'leaders who share the life of the

---

[1] G. Ramachandran, 'Kumarappaji in China', *GUP*, October 1951.

[2] Kumarappa travelled extensively in China between 23 September and 1 November 1951, see *Gandhian Crusader*, p. 124.

people', Kumarappa contrasted the self-indulgence and corruption of the Congress politicians.[3] Deeply impressed by the discipline of the people and their 'singleness of purpose and an iron determination', he likened it to the spirit that pervaded India during the Civil Disobedience campaign of the 1930s. While he was aware of the deeply authoritarian nature of government in China, Kumarappa chose to focus attention instead on elements of Chinese life that he felt would be instructive for Indians. In particular, he was struck by the determined manner in which the Chinese were tackling the agrarian problems and the material needs of the people. The situation at home compared unfavourably with the urgency he sensed in the Chinese countryside.

Although highly unusual coming from a Gandhian, Kumarappa was not alone in praising Maoist China. The disillusionment of 1962 was a good decade into the future and, during this period, Nehru was himself advocating a greater role for China in world affairs. Despite the reservations they had against violent revolutions, for a fairly wide spectrum of intelligent Indian opinion, there were many admirable aspects of the new China. If for Kumarappa the clincher was the attention paid to China's peasants under Mao, for others it was China's single-minded pursuit of material development. Consequently, in contrast with the Western perception of China, Indian opinion was quite favourable during this period. If the Americans saw the fall of the Guomindang as a disaster, Kumarappa saw it as the removal of a corrupt regime. Kumarappa also admired China's ability to build a *cordon sanitaire* and insulate itself from Western meddling at a time of growing American influence in Indian affairs.

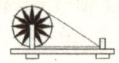

From China, on a request by the Indian government, Kumarappa flew to Japan in November 1951 and spent six weeks studying its industrial experience.[4] Japan was still under Allied occupation, and his encounters with racist discrimination against the Japanese in their own country, and Japan's rapid Americanization sharply contrasted with the experience in China. In Tokyo, Kumarappa addressed some councillors and

[3] G. Ramachandran, 'Kumarappaji in China, II', *GUP*, November 1951.
[4] Letter from J. C. Kumarappa to V. P. Iyadurai, 1 November 1951, Correspondence Files, Kumarappa Papers.

representatives of the Japanese parliament, the Diet. Asked to address the question of which is the leading nation in the world today', Kumarappa provided an analysis that applied the *triguna* theory of individual nature to interpret the characteristics of national cultures.[5] Accordingly, national life is largely defined by three principles, that is, material, social, and moral or spiritual. While no single factor exists by itself, 'by a cultural process these principles are developed finally into national ways of life'. Parsed through this typology, the Western powers were seen to be driven largely by material considerations whereas Soviet Russia's was an attempt to build a society on a 'social and economic basis'. While this was an advancement over the West, nevertheless 'omission of moral and spiritual values undermined [Russia's] strength'. Similarly, while he applauded the Chinese spirit of self-improvement, Kumarappa warned that China was 'in danger of throwing overboard the ancient culture she had depended upon all these ages to steady her. Permanent moral values are yielding place to expediencies'. If Kumarappa was critical of the West, he was equally unsparing of his hosts, arguing that by their wholesale adoption of the American way of life, the Japanese had thrown 'overboard their cultural and emotional life and expression'. As long as Japan aspired to the goals defined by the West, it would only play a secondary role in world affairs. Thus, while no nation had as yet adopted 'moral values as its ultimate criterion', Kumarappa argued that each nation had to aspire to evolve its own culture and leadership rather than imitate other exemplars.

While we do not know what his hosts made of this admonishment, Kumarappa's remarks were certainly shaped by the very purpose of his visit to Japan. If China was politically appealing to many Indians hankering for a revolution in their midst, for others, Japan was no less an example worth emulating. Kumarappa was asked to visit Japan with the explicit purpose of studying its agriculture and cottage and small-scale industries. In India there was 'a wave of thought' that keenly desired to imitate the Japanese form of industrial techniques and economic organization in the belief that such practices had 'led to the general apparent prosperity' of Japan.[6] Not only was this view widespread, such Indian admiration for Japan also

[5] J. C. Kumarappa, 'Leadership among Nations', *GUP*, January 1952. In Indic thought, beings or entities are primarily constituted of the three *gunas* or qualities of *satva*, *rajas*, and *tamas* in different proportions.

[6] J. C. Kumarappa, Introduction in *Report on Agriculture and Cottage and Small-Scale Industries in Japan* (New Delhi: Ministry of Commerce and Industry, Government of India, 1952).

had a long history.[7] Japan was considered a model for industrialization, whereby many industrial processes were carried out at the small-scale level. To many industrialists in India, such 'dispersed industrialization' was an attractive proposition, since it seemed to answer the need for generating employment in the rural areas without sacrificing modern technologies of production. In Kumarappa's view, such dispersal was hardly the answer as it retained all the attendant ills of large-scale industrialization and could not be considered true decentralization in spirit.

On his return, he wrote a report of his study of Japan that was published by the Indian government. Although he was deputed by the government to study Japan's cottage and small-scale industries, there was no meeting ground between Kumarappa's philosophy and the official view. In this report, he closely examined the various Japanese industries and the allied demand for their goods. While the official mandate was to study how cottage and small-scale industries could 'serve as feeders to large-scale industrial units', Kumarappa went on to demolish this premise. Without the necessary social demand for cottage-industry goods, he argued, it was futile to carry out a 'superficial reproduction of Japanese conditions' in India.

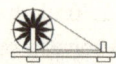

While Kumarappa was travelling in China and Japan, preparations were underway at Maganvadi to celebrate his sixtieth birthday on 4 January 1952. Kumarappa himself was reluctant to have a public celebration of such 'petty affairs' and wanted it moved to 'a day other than the birthday'.[8] Eventually he found it difficult to refuse his friends and returned from Japan just in time for the birthday celebrations. The public meeting held at Maganvadi was presided over by Kaka Kalelkar and one can get a sense of Kumarappa's immense local popularity from the fact that some three thousand people were in attendance.[9] The Gandhian touch was evident when four hundred students and workers offered gifts 'of hanks of self-spun yarn'. Of more enduring value for us is the Festschrift presented to Kumarappa on the occasion. Edited by two confidants, S. K. George and G. Ramachandran,

---

[7] See for instance, Meghnad Saha, 'The Philosophy of Industrialization'.

[8] Letter from J. C. Kumarappa to G. Ramachandran, 24 November 1951, Subject File, 23, Kumarappa Papers.

[9] G. Ramachandran, 'Shri Kumarappa's 60th Birthday', *GUP*, January 1952.

The Economics of Peace: The Cause and the Man is a faithful reflection of Kumarappa and the cause of constructive work that he made his own. Apart from extracts from his writings, the Festschrift also has valuable biographical sketches and anecdotes.[10] Reflecting the issues and concerns of the times, the rest of the contributions addressed themselves to interpreting a wide variety of problems and the Gandhian responses. While the Congress had drifted away far from its earlier social concerns, for the small circle of unreconstructed Gandhians, this was an occasion for shared communion and a time to reflect on Gandhi's unfinished task.[11] His sixtieth birthday, spent amongst friends and comrades, would have been a moment of quiet satisfaction for Kumarappa as he reflected on two decades in public service. However, any sense of peace was momentary.

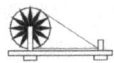

Kumarappa's commendation of China filled many with a sense of disquiet. The deep unease was centred around the role of violence in the Chinese Revolution and the subsequent communist state. Here, Kumarappa's AIVIA colleagues were inadvertently responsible for the confusion as they published extracts from his letters from China as articles in the *Gram Udyog Patrika*. When Kumarappa wrote these letters they were meant to address a select few in Maganvadi and did not carry any prefatory remarks. Consequently, these verbatim extracts raised as many questions as they answered. But, for now, Kumarappa's position was quite clear. Asked in an interview about how to counter the 'Communist Menace', his answer was categorical. On 'the true rock bottom' of genuine grievances of the people, the communists wished to 'build their structure of discontent and violence'.[12] However their emphasis on the material welfare of man was inadequate and Kumarappa argued that 'we have to use a stronger adhesive power in the form of moral and spiritual values'. He argued that India

[10] The extracts of Kumarappa's writings were assembled by S. K. George and the young Gandhian, Ravindra Varma. Many of the biographical sketches served as material for Vinaik's biography, *J. C. Kumarappa and His Quest for World Peace*.

[11] The fact that many stalwarts of constructive work were missing from the list of contributors tells an interesting story of the post-Gandhi era. While some had passed away or were alienated by Kumarappa's strong denunciations, many others had succumbed to the fish and loaves of office.

[12] 'Pannai Ashram Notes: IV', *GUP*, January 1952.

should learn the lesson of self-reliance from China but solve its problems using 'the powerful flashlight of Non-violence and Truth provided by Gandhiji'.[13]

The controversy over his China visit was only a prelude to a veritable storm that Kumarappa would generate on his visit to Russia. Within three months of returning from Japan, Kumarappa left for Moscow as a delegate to a big international economic conference that was attended by about 500 delegates from forty-nine countries over a fortnight in April 1952.[14] Conceived by the communist-sponsored World Peace Council and backed by the Soviet government, the conference was purportedly held to promote 'the peaceful co-operation of different countries and different systems and through the development of economic relations between all countries'. The ideological barrier deterred many from travelling to Moscow, but the unofficial representatives who made it were of no mean distinction.[15] Aside from quite open and extensive discussions, the conference also resulted in a number of unofficial business agreements between groups representing both sides of the Cold War divide.

In Moscow, amidst all the snow, Kumarappa's sartorial invention, the 'dhotijama attracted much attention and people were much concerned' that he would be unable to stand the cold weather.[16] Kumarappa's retort that the women standing around had even less protective clothing drew much laughter. At the conference itself, Kumarappa did not have much of a role to play. Although he presented two resolutions on 'planned international trade' and 'promotion of cottage industries', out of complicated considerations, no resolutions were eventually adopted.[17] If the non-partisan approach of the Russians was unusual, they had also taken the rare step of imposing 'absolutely no restrictions ... and many of the delegates took the

[13] J. C. Kumarappa, 'The Chinese "Sarvodaya"', GUP, February 1952.

[14] Alec Cairncross, 'The Moscow Economic Conference', Soviet Studies, vol. 4, no. 2 (October 1952): 113–32.

[15] Amongst the Westerners present were the left-leaning economists Joan Robinson, Maurice Dobb, Oskar Lange, and Piero Sraffa. Apart from Kumarappa, the Indian delegation of thirty-five individuals also included the planner P. C. Mahalanobis, economist Gyan Chand, and the sociologist, D. P. Mukerji. Communist leader, S. A. Dange, however, was refused a passport by the Indian government. See 'No Prominent Indians on List', New York Times, 1 April 1952.

[16] G. Ramachandran, 'Kumarappaji in Russia-I', GUP, May 1952.

[17] Cairncross, 'The Moscow Economic Conference'.

opportunity of travelling widely in many parts of the Soviet Union'.[18] Kumarappa himself travelled 'about 12,000 miles by air and about 2000 miles by railways' and visited many places, including Leningrad, Ferghana, Tashkent, and Stalingrad.[19]

If Kumarappa benefited from this rare opportunity to travel unhindered in Russia, the time spent together in China and Russia also widened his network of Indian contacts. In turn, his enunciation of economic principles seems to have made an impression on his fellow delegates. The Lucknow sociologist Dhurjati Prasad Mukerji published a report that, with a bit of hyperbole, described the Moscow conference as deriving from an 'Economics of Peace'.[20] Kumarappa himself set out his views and experiences in a lengthy article aptly titled 'A Peep behind the Iron Curtain'.[21] Russia was attempting to 'usher in an equalitarian society' and while it had not produced an ideal scenario, its progress was significant enough to cause 'consternation in the imperialist camp'. He went on to argue that the Iron Curtain was necessary to 'keep out the foreigners who will interfere and ruin the experiment which is going on there for the social reconstruction of Russia'.

Kumarappa also argued that India had its own 'iron curtain', between the government and the governed, which could not be removed till the existing economic and social inequalities were squarely addressed. As with China, Russia too compared favourably with India due to its emphasis on self-sufficiency and fairer distribution of income. Again, India compared poorly as 'our village people are being exploited as they cannot even get the proper price for their production'. However, he was not naive about the implications of the Russian approach, and his long-term diagnosis was extraordinarily accurate when he argued that

[i]n a family of nations we cannot always live with permanent iron curtains built up with suspicion and hatred. The maintenance charges of such iron curtains swallow up all advantages of technological advances and leaves [sic] the masses in comparative poverty still. The competitive race in armaments leads us to destruction.... Notwithstanding the undoubtedly great achievements to her credit, Russia is in a precarious unstable equilibrium no

[18] 'Moscow Conference', *Economic Weekly*, 26 April 1952.

[19] J. C. Kumarappa, 'A Peep behind the Iron Curtain', *GUP*, June 1952.

[20] D. P. Mukerji, 'International Economic Conference: Part I', *Economic Weekly*, 12 July 1952.

[21] J. C. Kumarappa, 'A Peep behind the Iron Curtain', *GUP*, June 1952.

less than America. Both need for their very existence enormous buttresses of violence. With such an order neither of them can contribute to the peace and goodwill in the comity of nations.

As he did with China, Kumarappa argued against adopting Russian methods which were unsuitable for India since 'we do not have the same history and disciplined behaviour pattern'. Besides, he argued, 'unlimited centralized and standardized production is based on regimentation, which ultimately leads to violence and disruption of society'. Instead, he felt that India would do well to take up Russia's 'patriotic fervour and spirit of self-sufficiency and swadeshi'.

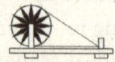

By now, Kumarappa's pronouncements had endeared himself to the left in India and in July 1952, he travelled to Berlin to attend an extraordinary meeting of the World Peace Council. The meeting was convened 'to consider the situation that has arisen out of the development of germ warfare in Korea, and the rearmament of Germany and Japan'.[22] The question of whether the Americans had used germ warfare in Korea became a major international controversy and till date it remains largely unresolved. Kumarappa was deeply perturbed by the evidence for germ warfare presented at the meeting and proposed a 'world-wide economic boycott against American goods until the United States stops its aggression on various fronts'.[23]

The Korean War and American ingress into newly independent India in the form of the Community Development Projects distressed Kumarappa. He explained that if Indians were 'rather inclined to appreciate imperialistic U.S.A. and Great Britain than Socialist Russia or China', he himself was less forgiving of the Americans.[24] By now Kumarappa's position on the two parties to the Cold War had developed into a full-fledged controversy. If such controversy arose out of Kumarappa's failure to qualify his position on communism, he was also responsible for exacerbating the problem. During his trip to China, he struck up a rather unusual relationship with a pioneer of muckraking tabloid journalism in

---

[22] J. C. Kumarappa, 'The World Peace Council Meeting', GUP, August 1952.

[23] 'Indian at Red Council Urges Boycott of U.S.', New York Times, 6 July 1952.

[24] 'Kumarappaji in Vienna', GUP, January 1953.

India, R. K. Karanjia of the *Blitz*. Apart from a shared dislike for Nehru's Congress and America, there was little else in common between the two men. Nevertheless, Kumarappa plied a receptive Karanjia with material to publish in the *Blitz*. Karanjia was much given to flamboyance and felt no compunctions in embroidering his stories. If Kumarappa's articles were angry and critical of the Indian government and American ambitions, Karanjia published them with lurid and scandalous headlines, and was not above putting words into Kumarappa's mouth. In one instance, the *Blitz* version of a Kumarappa article had a section titled 'Russia and China Nearer to Gandhism!', a suggestion that had no support in the essay itself.[25] Inevitably, such thunderous pronouncements generated much anger that was directed against Kumarappa. But the attempts to appropriate Kumarappa's name were not confined to the left alone. In the chilling atmosphere of the Cold War, American media was also paying close attention to public opinion in India and twisting it to suit its own purpose. Thus, in reporting on the Moscow Economic Conference, the *New York Times* opined that the Indian delegation, Kumarappa included, did not have any prominent personalities.[26] Yet, within weeks, the same paper felt it important enough to carry a mangled and incorrect report of a Kumarappa interview purportedly critical of the Soviets.[27]

This situation created much confusion and anguish amongst many in India who looked to Kumarappa as a moral exemplar and a true legatee of Gandhi. The criticism of Kumarappa's position was severe enough and there is evidence in his later writings that he had taken note of the problem. However, he had a streak of stubbornness that prevented him from owning up his own responsibility in creating the confusion. Asked for a clarification, instead of accepting a share of the blame, Kumarappa claimed helplessness since 'not only the Communists but also the Capitalist press use my remarks for their own purpose'.[28] Certainly, a part of the problem was the highly polarized debate on the role of leftist ideology in Indian society. But, in allowing his articles to be mixed up with Karanjia's distasteful attacks on Nehru and others, Kumarappa displayed a lack of judgement that seriously undermined his message.

[25] 'Prof J. C. Kumarappa Answers His Critics', *Blitz*, 5 July 1952, Miscellaneous Press Clippings, Kumarappa Papers.

[26] 'No Prominent Indians on List', *New York Times*, 1 April 1952.

[27] 'Indian Bars Soviet Ideas', *New York Times*, 15 May 1952.

[28] Letter from J. C. Kumarappa to Bhowani Prasad Chatterjee, 20 March 1953, Correspondence Files, Kumarappa Papers.

It was only some years later that Kumarappa explained the basis for his commendation of the communist countries he had visited. He argued that while both China and Russia had their flaws, he had no desire to do a 'Miss Mayo [who] came to look for the dirty things in India and found them'.[29] Instead he wanted 'to look at Russia from the point of view from which we may derive some benefit for ourselves'. However, during this period, his failure to adequately critique Russia's violent and totalitarian regime continued to generate controversy. Many, including his compatriots like Kripalani and Mashruwala, wondered how a staunch Gandhian could have turned into a communist. Kumarappa replied, rather unconvincingly, that he saw 'no contradiction in expressing admiration for China' for its seriousness in tackling 'poverty and starvation while holding to non-violence'.[30] After all, he argued, there was no such thing as absolute non-violence; much of life was a matter of minimizing violence. Indeed, 'under conditions of absolute non-violence none of us live or even die'. However, the criticism persisted and Kumarappa felt it 'necessary to reiterate [the] obvious faiths and tenets' that it was 'only under a decentralized economy that we can develop a universal brotherhood working on non-violence'.[31] All he had done was to appreciate the 'self-denying spirit ... [and] devotion to the cause of the masses' and singleness of purpose of the Russians. Besides, Kumarappa retorted, India need not adopt a 'holier than thou' approach when it was committing the sin of 'full cooperation with the users of Atom and Napalm bombs'.

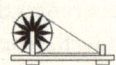

With the Community Development Projects slated to be inaugurated in October 1952, an Indian leftist press published a polemical exposé, *American Shadow over India*. By considering economic, political, agricultural, cultural and intelligence operations, the book presented an exhaustive indictment of American interests in India. A notable aspect of the book was a foreword contributed by Kumarappa. While the British presence in India had been a deterrent, Kumarappa argued, now that the 'protecting fence has been disbanded ... India presents an open field of

[29] J. C. Kumarappa, 'Some Lessons from Russia', *GUP*, December 1954.

[30] Letter from J. C. Kumarappa to Tejaswini Shukla, 4 February 1952, Subject File, 12, Kumarappa Papers.

[31] J. C. Kumarappa, 'Russia and China', *GUP*, July 1952.

ruthless exploitation'.[32] He warned against the loss of India's hard-earned freedom, since the American methods were not 'calculated to liberate its victims but to carry on its nefarious purpose like the spider'. When compared to Kumarappa's oeuvre laden with insight and wisdom, this foreword is a mere trifle. However, perhaps in a commentary on American intellectual preoccupations during the Cold War, it was reproduced in the two-volume *Sources of Indian Tradition* as an example of non-communist sentiment against America. While in itself, *American Shadow* consisted largely of data assembled without much discrimination, the sheer weight of its three hundred-odd pages of evidence provided some substance to the Indian fear of American hegemony. Bowles tried to diminish the significance of *American Shadow* by correctly describing it as 'Communist-inspired', but the Americans were quite worried about its impact.[33] Their paranoia against communists was so strong that *American Shadow* was subjected to a scrutiny by officials in the US Department of State. Characterizing the book as 'written to do harm to American interests in India', it was judged to have 'been extremely successful in this regard' which led to an unfortunate consequence. In his preface, the author of *American Shadow* had acknowledged his 'debt to an American friend ... who wishes to remain anonymous'.[34] In a curious case of textual forensics, the scrutinizing official opined that the 'meticulous indexing, use of footnotes and heavy economic approach' pointed the finger of suspicion at the agrarian economist and historian, Daniel Thorner.[35] Thorner had no acquaintance with either Natarajan or Kumarappa, but since he was already marked out for his leftist leanings, the purported association with *American Shadow* added to his travails with the American government.

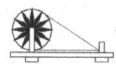

Owing to the politics of the Cold War, Kumarappa increasingly tied up the objectives of the so-called Peace movement of the leftists with his ideas on economic decentralization as a basis for enduring peace. In December 1952,

[32] J. C. Kumarappa, Foreword in L. Natarajan, *American Shadow over India*.

[33] Bowles, *Ambassador's Report*, p. 204.

[34] Natarajan, *American Shadow over India*, p. xvii.

[35] Alice Thorner, 'Excerpts from an FBI File', *Economic and Political Weekly*, vol. 17, no. 21 (22 May 1982): 878–84. The excerpts are from the FBI file on Daniel Thorner.

Kumarappa left for yet another trip to attend a World Congress for Peace in Vienna followed by a visit to Russia. While he was quite aware of the communist-sponsored propagandist nature of the trip, he increasingly saw the Soviet Bloc as a necessary evil, a counterweight to American aspirations of hegemony over the newly decolonized societies of Asia.[36] Despite such new-found leanings, Kumarappa's speech in Vienna on 'the Gandhian approach to World Peace' was a clear-eyed statement of the Mahatma's vision applied to the problem of ending international strife.

Gandhi's philosophy of truth and non-violence, Kumarappa argued, had to been seen in the context of the ancient formulation of dharma. Dharma was 'neither Religion nor Duty as is often indifferently translated'.[37] Rather, it 'is the purpose of existence of man'. If the basis of international warfare was to be traced to the modern outlook that 'turned man into an economic animal', the remedy lay in turning away from 'centralized and standardised methods' towards a decentralized mode of production. In light of this position, while Russia's state control of foreign trade was 'a healthy move' it came in for criticism by Kumarappa for continuing to adhere to 'centralized methods of production which is also basically a cause of conflict'. Arguing against the strategy of an arms race, Kumarappa felt that American aggression could not be countered by 'a mere threat of armed might [which] will only challenge them to a greater and more rapid production of armaments'. Instead, he advocated the Gandhian way of non-violent non-cooperation which, applied to the problem, implied an economic boycott of America to bring it to its senses.

Kumarappa identified the source of the spirit of violence that led to global wars in the very economic organization of the world where one nation coveted the resources and markets of the other. Hence, despite vast ideological differences, he saw the Russian attempt at self-sufficiency worthy of study and adaptation to Indian conditions. By placing his views

[36] For instance, Kumarappa saw the Moscow Economic Conference as Russia's attempt 'to divert American and British attention and energy from the huge production of war materials to the production of producer and consumer goods. By entering the world markets, Russia would compel the United States and Britain to compete with her in supplying goods to under-developed countries and thereby cut down their production for war and destruction ...' ('Dr J. C. Kumarappa Gives "All Your Answers" on Sovietland', *Blitz*, 17 May 1952, Miscellaneous Press Clippings, Kumarappa Papers).

[37] J. C. Kumarappa, 'The Gandhian Approach to World Peace', *GUP*, January 1953.

on Russia in front of the Indian public, he wanted to make the case that the 'conditions of social justice' were 'practicable in this hedonistic world of ours' and also to answer criticism that 'Gandhian conceptions are merely utopian and not practicable'.[38] Indeed, he was of the view that one aspect of the Russian economy that 'approximated in certain respects to Gandhian ideals was the price economy'.[39] While he recognized that the Russian approach of fixing wages was done under compulsion, Kumarappa felt that its effect of reducing inequality in wealth was quite attractive given the gross inequalities that haunted Indian society. A key question that was posed to Kumarappa was on the nature and role of violence in the Russian experience that he so appreciated. Despite his praise of Russia, Kumarappa clearly recognized that 'violent means can never solve any problems' and while it produced results in the short run its 'cost in human values is terrific' and always engendered 'an unstable equilibrium to be supported by counter-violence'.[40] He elucidated on the nature of the Russian situation using an analogy of vultures around a carcass. The Russian approach was 'to stand by the carcass with a stick in hand and drive away the vultures and continue to keep a constant watch'.[41] While this is 'successful in driving away the vultures of exploitation by violent force ... to maintain this state they have to keep the rod always in hand'. The non-violent alternative, Kumarappa argued, was to bury the carcass which could only be achieved by removing the scope for economic exploitation in society.

By 1954, Kumarappa's health was failing. Nevertheless, over three months between May and August of that year, he made a final trip to Europe. During this trip, Kumarappa travelled extensively across Germany and England, with visits to Bulgaria, Sweden, and France in between. Although he once again attended the communist-sponsored World Peace Council meetings in Berlin, much of his time during this trip was taken up in engaging another constituency that he had older links with—the Pacifists of Europe.[42]

---

[38] J. C. Kumarappa, 'Social Justice', *GUP*, May 1953.

[39] D. K. Gupta, 'Kumarappa and USSR', *GUP*, June 1953.

[40] J. C. Kumarappa, 'Social Justice', *GUP*, May 1953.

[41] D. K. Gupta, 'Kumarappa and USSR', *GUP*, June 1953.

[42] This included a week at the triennial conference of the Pacifist War Resisters International (WRI) held in Paris. Kumarappa had also addressed the Shrewsbury Conference of the WRI in 1948.

By the end of this trip, Kumarappa had decidedly toned down his position on Russian Socialism. The idea of war had become even more horrific with the development of H-bombs. While he continued to hold that the United States carried the larger share of blame, Kumarappa recognized that both 'the USA and the USSR have abandoned all peaceful methods of settling disputes as a foregone cause and are resorting to violence'.[43]

For Kumarappa, the three years that began with his visit to China in 1951 had been very eventful but unsatisfactory. His extended engagement with the left in India and his many visits abroad must be understood in light of his deep disillusionment with the evolution of the Congress in power, the compromised positions of many fellow constructive workers, as well as the rise of American hegemony backed with lethal military power. While he lacked political influence, Kumarappa carried considerable moral authority amongst the Indian public. Therefore, when Congressmen countered his criticism by accusing him of 'hobnobbing with Communists', it smacked of selfish motivations.[44] In turn, Kumarappa demanded that such politicians stand on their own merits instead of banking on the sacrifices of the freedom fighters of yesteryear. In a defiant response he savaged the self-serving Congressmen in power and remarked that 'a Communist saving a drowning child is much more praiseworthy than ten Congressmen with folded hands deploring it as the act of a Communist'! [45]

Although Kumarappa's writings and utterances during this period were both polemical and intemperate, it is most fruitful to view the entire episode as a Socratic debate. By adopting a sharply delineated position, Kumarappa was posing fundamental questions on political and economic issues and demanding to know what India's rulers were doing about them. If his views on China and Russia gave provocation, the subsequent criticism did have an effect on his writings. It led Kumarappa to clarify his position and, as was his wont, raise further provocative questions. Although he refused to admit it, it is evident that Kumarappa eventually recognized the problem with his unqualified statements on Russia and began to provide the necessary clarifications that were missing in his earlier declarations.

Notwithstanding the public controversy, his close associates were able to excavate the truth behind the confusion on Kumarappa's view. When

---

[43] J. C. Kumarappa, 'Fear Complex and a Ray of Hope', *GUP*, April 1955.

[44] J. C. Kumarappa, 'My "Retirement"', *GUP*, July 1953.

[45] J. C. Kumarappa, 'My "Retirement"'.

someone remarked that Kumarappa had come back from Europe with 'a double red cap' on his head, G. Ramachandran had a good laugh and wrote to Kumarappa:

> I know that not only your cap but your soul will remain as white as ever. What a fraud you are, pretending to be a Bolshie! There is no more fanatic devotee of non-violence than you are in the whole of India. You will either convert the Communist to non-violence or they will shoot you in the attempt. Let us see which of these happens. I hope for the first. There are others looking out for the second.[46]

[46] Letter from G. Ramachandran to J. C. Kumarappa, 4 February 1953, Correspondence Files, Kumarappa Papers.

Figure 18 Kumarappa travelled extensively for his work: (*a*) At the cattle farm of the Pattagarar of Palayamkottai in Tiruppur district of Tamil Nadu. The farm was well known as a breeding station for the Kangayam bull.
(*b*) Coppersmith's Bazar, Peshawar, taken in late 1939.

(*c*) Visiting the Summer Palace in present-day Beijing, 1951. Kumarappa is second from left. (*d*) The ruins of Hiroshima, 1951. In front of the Hiroshima Peace Memorial, Kumarappa is second from left.

(*e*) At the Zwinger Palace, Dresden, Germany, May 1954. Kumarappa is the figure in the middle, dressed in white *khadi* and wearing a Gandhi cap.

(*f*) Addressing a meeting of the War Resisters International in Paris, July 1954. The person seated on the left is Horace Alexander, a Quaker and campaigner for India's freedom. (*g*) With Fenner Brockway in August 1954. Brockway was an anti-war campaigner and a British MP. *Photographs courtesy of Magan Sangrahalaya Samiti, Wardha (Maharashtra).*

18 The Lion in His Winter

S ince his time in Nasik Jail in 1933, Kumarappa had been plagued by health problems stemming from high levels of blood pressure. Despite this handicap, over the years he managed to put in ten to twelve hours of daily work by leading a disciplined life and perhaps through sheer willpower. All through the period of travel in 1946 and later when he was on the Agrarian Reforms Committee, Kumarappa suffered from poor health, and the heavy workload eventually took its toll. In January 1951, he underwent a thorough medical examination that yielded alarming results. Owing to the many years of high blood pressure, his heart was dilated, arteries had thickened, and his kidneys were functioning at half of their capacity.[1] While he was 'ordered to retire from active work and settle down to a quiet life', in direct contradiction of such advice, in a few months he moved to Seldoh to found the Pannai Ashram. As we have noted in the previous chapter, it is in such poor health that Kumarappa travelled to China, Japan, as well as Russia and other European countries. In May 1953, he suffered a stroke and was forced to withdraw from active work and give up the Pannai experiment.

---

[1] Letter from J. C. Kumarappa to Mirabehn, 15 January 1951, Correspondence Files, Kumarappa Papers.

All through these years he had never publicly hinted at his poor health and his putting in his papers led to much media speculation. By now it was public knowledge that Kumarappa was at loggerheads with Vinoba and his followers. These problems as well as the controversy over his pronouncements on communism led many to believe that retirement on health grounds was 'a cloak for some internal differences of opinion'.[2] 'Amazed at the amount of public interest in the scrappy news' of his retirement, Kumarappa sought to publicly paper over the differences and argued that none were serious enough to lead to dissociation. Notwithstanding such public bravado, after two decades of service to the cause of the village movement, he had arrived at an ironic juncture in his life. In 1933, he had refused Bharatan's suggestion to move to south India since he had cast his life with the Gandhian cause. Now, with Gandhi gone, his health broken, and cold-shouldered by his colleagues, he set out to uproot himself one last time. In the autumn of his life, Kumarappa moved down south.

By this time, in addition to his health concerns, Kumarappa was also beset with financial problems. In the 1920s, he had aspired to earn a four-figure monthly income before marrying 'but Gandhi snared him before he reached that goal'.[3] However, those material ambitions belonged to a different past and now Kumarappa had no assets to speak of. When the Pune-based nature cure expert Dinshaw Mehta offered to treat him with a flexible financial scheme, Kumarappa's reply was poignantly sharp. The charge of Rs 600 for a nine-month period made Kumarappa think that he may be 'more valuable dead than alive'.[4] Such expensive nature cure, Kumarappa pointed out was 'beyond the reach of such of us who had made paupers of ourselves in the country's cause'. Having decided to spend his life in the public cause, his principles would have prevented Kumarappa from living with members of his extended and prosperous family. At the same time, he declined to accept the invitation to settle down at Gandhigram, the settlement founded by G. Ramachandran and T. S. Soundaram.[5] Eventually, he chose to make

[2] J. C. Kumarappa, 'My "Retirement"', GUP, July 1953.

[3] G. Ramachandran, 'The Man', in Economics of Peace, p. 36.

[4] Letter from J. C. Kumarappa to Dinshaw K. Mehta, 31 May 1955, Correspondence Files, Kumarappa Papers.

[5] Letter from J. C. Kumarappa to G. Ramachandran, 25 July 1953, Correspondence Files, Kumarappa Papers.

his home at the Gandhi Niketan Ashram in T. Kallupatti, located some 40 kilometres southwest of Madurai.[6]

Although he was gravely ill, Kumarappa was hardly the sort to repair to a quiet corner of the country and rest. In late 1953, he moved to the ashram of a friend in the Jaffna region of erstwhile Ceylon and underwent Ayurvedic treatment. Soon he was on the move again and in May 1954, Kumarappa went on a final trip to Europe. By December 1954, unable to carry on in this fashion anymore, Kumarappa reluctantly handed over the working of the Pannai Ashram to the Sarva Seva Sangh.[7] Using some of his money that had been left untouched for decades in an England bank, a small hut was constructed at Gandhi Niketan and Kumarappa moved into it in May 1955. However, he hardly had an opportunity to settle down before he had to be moved to a hospital in Madurai with exceedingly high blood pressure.[8] Not one to give up on his old ways of working, when his health showed some signs of improvement, he travelled for a month in far-off Assam in February 1956 providing advice to workers in the region.

In these final years of his life, Kumarappa's travels were related to his fundamental concerns. Disillusioned with the state of affairs in India, he continued to forcefully advocate adherence to Gandhi's fundamental tenets. A decade of India's experience with self-rule had proved deeply unsatisfactory and had clarified the distinction between the roles of the state and that of the moral exemplars in society. Kumarappa felt that constructive workers had grievously compromised their ideology by engaging with a state that was uninterested in building a non-violent social order. Speaking about the Second Five-Year Plan, he forcefully reiterated the responsibility of constructive workers:

> Those who wish to usher in a Sarvodaya order should not sit idle but actively work vigorously to achieve their goal. Such a programme will include non-violent non-cooperation with the Government in all its attempts to opiate the

[6] This ashram was founded in 1940 by G. Venkatachalapathy, a constructive worker who collaborated with Kumarappa on the formulation of the Firka Development Scheme and went on to work in various capacities in the government of the Madras state. In Tamil, 'kallupatti' means a 'quarry' and since there were many quarries in the area, this location was identified by its proximity to the Thevankurichi temple that lent the initial 'T'.

[7] J. C. Kumarappa, 'Pannai Ashram', *GUP*, December 1954.

[8] During this period, Kumarappa's blood pressure was registered at a dangerously high level of 180/110. Letter from J. C. Kumarappa to Amrit Kaur, 22 May 1955, Correspondence Files, Kumarappa Papers.

masses with superficial schemes which do not aim at stabilising village and small industries along with concentrated help to place agriculture on a firm basis. Window dressing and palliatives will not be of any use in promoting the Sarvodaya order but instead will prolong or perhaps defeat us in our struggle towards our goal.[9]

Under these despairing circumstances, Kumarappa moved closer to Gandhi's vision than ever before. For instance, while the idea of trusteeship seldom appears in Kumarappa's earlier writings, by this time he had come around to recognizing it as a fundamental organizational principle for society. With regard to the land problem Kumarappa recognized that the state had a role in enforcing the rights of the tiller. However, he felt that Bhoodan was misconceived as it was 'not duty based but centered on rights'. Arguing that the provisioning of land rights was within the sphere of the State or law, he felt that constructive workers should confine themselves to 'the development of duty mindedness' amidst the landowners. 'Any other course,' he asserted, 'will definitely lead us to violence ultimately.'

By this time, Kumarappa's break with the Wardha leadership was complete. When a co-worker wrote from Pannai, Kumarappa pointed out that 'it is no good claiming to be my man. It will only discredit you as they have no use for me too!'[10] Under such circumstances, Kumarappa did not participate in the 1956 Sarvodaya conference held at Kanchipuram. Once again his actions gave rise to commentary in the press which forced him to clarify his position. Kumarappa did not participate in the Kanchipuram meet as he felt that the fundamental principles of sarvodaya had been abandoned. He probably felt vindicated in his stand when some constructive workers reported back their observations of the meet. Unlike earlier times, the Kanchipuram event made special distinctions between important personalities and ordinary workers thereby vitiating the atmosphere. In particular, Kumarappa was upset with the lavish expenditure in providing air-conditioning and decoration of a bungalow that hosted President Rajendra Prasad 'at a cost of several thousand rupees for a stay of a few days, taking about 4 to 6 months in the preparation'.[11] Nor did he like the fact that ordinary village workers

[9] J. C. Kumarappa, 'Our Plans and Programmes', *GUP*, April 1956.

[10] Letter from J. C. Kumarappa to S. J. Pannase, 17 April 1956, Correspondence Files, Kumarappa Papers.

[11] J. C. Kumarappa, 'The Sarvodaya Camp at Kanjeepuram', *GUP*, July 1956.

were not allowed to meet Vinoba and 'only important leaders were granted that privilege'.[12]

In this mood of despondency, the one bond of camaraderie for Kumarappa was his relationship with S. K. Dey. As we saw earlier, upon Dey's request, the gravely ill Kumarappa had undertaken to inspect Community Development work in Madurai district in 1956.[13] Soon, in August 1956, Kumarappa suffered from a cardiac induced asthmatic attack and was once again hospitalized. He was repeatedly advised by his physicians to give up work and rest, which Kumarappa deemed a terrible prospect. However much he disliked to 'vegetate', as he put it, Kumarappa was forced to recognize that he had been 'discharged from the hospital with a life sentence hanging round his neck'.[14] The December 1956 issue of *Gram Udyog Patrika* was the last to be published, thus ending two decades of creative, insightful, and forceful advocacy of the cause of village industries and the concerns of rural India.

Within two months he was back in hospital, but Kumarappa was hardly one to resign himself to his fate. Although the body no longer complied, the fire in Kumarappa's belly was far from extinguished. His widespread contacts in the West also brought him abreast of the all-enveloping sense of violence on many fronts. When Britain tested the H-bomb, he felt that world peace was not achievable through 'resolutions and pious opinions'. It was time to offer satyagraha and, along with Western Pacifists, he 'offered to go to Christmas Islands to have my head presented as a target for the British'![15] On 25 June 1957, Bharatan Kumarappa, who was working in Delhi as the first editor-in-chief of the monumental *Collected Works of Mahatma Gandhi* died of cerebral haemorrhage. The unexpected loss of his younger brother and comrade-in-arms was a severe shock for Kumarappa and he was back in hospital in 'a serious condition and remained there for six weeks'.[16] With no improvement in his health, Kumarappa was eventually

---

[12] Kumarappa also expressed displeasure at the increasing dominance of Hindi in the working of sarvodaya institutions. Following Gandhi's death, the earlier practice of publishing in both English and Hindi was abandoned in favour of the latter. Kumarappa felt that sarvodaya work had to adapt to local needs and not demand the enforcement of Hindi.

[13] Kumarappa's Madurai report was the last in a series of economic surveys and studies that began in Matar in 1930.

[14] J. C. Kumarappa, 'Personal', *GUP*, November 1956.

[15] Vinaik, *Gandhian Crusader*, p. 203.

[16] Vinaik, *Gandhian Crusader*, p. 204.

moved to the Government General Hospital in Madras for better care in August 1957. In October that year, he suffered another setback when his eldest brother, J. M. Kumarappa, also succumbed to health problems. By this time, Kumarappa had been to the hospital on five occasions in the past three years and would spend the remainder of his life mostly at the General Hospital.

Kumarappa hated being confined to a bed and got out of the hospital as often as he could. He also chafed at the restrictions imposed upon him. His closest associate and devoted disciple, M. Vinaik, was often at the receiving end of Kumarappa's mercurial anger. Anxious about Kumarappa's rapidly deteriorating health, G. Ramachandran and other associates decided to celebrate his birthday on 4 January 1960. On that day, Kumarappa felt well enough to attend the public celebrations in Madras that were presided over by the chief minister, Kamaraj. After this event, his improved health led his associates to believe that he was out of the woods and they made plans to found a new ashram to house him upon his recovery. However, Kumarappa's health soon deteriorated further, his kidneys failed to function adequately and he needed spells of oxygen intake to cope with his congested lungs. On 26 January 1960, Kumarappa suffered a paralytic stroke and collapsed on the floor. In a few days it looked like he was recovering and some of his associates hoped he would be able to address a public meeting to commemorate Gandhi's martyrdom. On 30 January 1960, a gravely ill Kumarappa remained in a pensive mood all day as he contemplated the failed dreams of the Mahatma. That evening, at 9:25 p.m., Joseph Cornelius Kumarappa breathed his last. He was sixty-eight years old.[17]

---

[17] Many of the details of Kumarappa's last days are available in a note penned by N. Sivaramakrishnan, a young associate who nursed him in his last days. See N. Sivaramakrishnan, 'The Late Dr. Kumarappa', Subject File, 37, Kumarappa Papers. On the first of February, Kumarappa's body was taken for cremation in a bullock cart draped in khadi and in the Tricolour. Vinaik set fire to the pyre made of cowdung cakes.

Figure 19 With Vinoba Bhave at T. Kallupatti. *Photograph courtesy of Magan Sangrahalaya Samiti, Wardha (Maharashtra).*

Figure 20 The President of India, Rajendra Prasad, called on an ailing Kumarappa at the Mission Hospital in Madurai, 15 August 1957. *Photograph courtesy of Baryalai Shalizi.*

Figure 21 Kumarappa's last place of residence at the Gandhi Niketan Ashram, T. Kallupatti. *Photograph courtesy of Venu Madhav Govindu.*

Figure 22   Kumarappa at the age of sixty-five. *Photograph courtesy of Magan Sangrahalaya Samiti, Wardha (Maharashtra).*

19   An Assessment

E ven when measured against the ethical standards of his time, the most striking aspect of Kumarappa's life is the constant endeavour to bridge the gap between practice and precept. Despite the many obstacles and challenges along the way, including his exceedingly poor health, he lived out his personal values with no let-up or compromise. Owing to such an identification with his ideals, we know far less about Kumarappa's personal life in comparison with his views on many public issues.[1] His whole life was an embodiment of the virtues of human autonomy that he strove to afford to every individual. Arguably, the freedom of thought and deed displayed by Kumarappa is of the highest order of cultural expression and self-emancipation. This is especially true in his rejection of colonial values and articulation of a new ethos, for true culture is neither imitative of alien mores nor a dogmatic assertion of static creeds. Rather, it is the self-directed and free expression of one's deepest values, ever renewed and refashioned in accordance with the demands of the time. Looking beyond his social and economic arguments, one may view Kumarappa's life-long attempt to place the agrarian economy on a

---

[1] While the archival holdings of Kumarappa's papers are extensive, there is little material that can provide us insights into his personal life.

sound footing in this light, for 'there can be no culture without contact with relevant problems'.[2]

To his eternal regret, Kumarappa never mastered an Indian language. His social background and professional training militated against his acquiring a true command of Tamil and he arrived at Hindi late in life.[3] Nevertheless, despite the handicap of communicating with fellow Indians in English, he persisted in his simple, folksy style, for the issues he wrote about were of universal concern and his intended audience was the ordinary man. Over three decades, Kumarappa seldom took recourse to the conventions of scholarship to make his point. Instead, he developed a distinct style of exposition and achieved a clarity of expression that arose out of a consistent world view shaped by a lifetime of experience. His writing was marked by simple, terse phrasing and the use of homely metaphors, often laced with biting sarcasm and a wry sense of humour. Both these traits are illustrated in an analogy that he provided to describe the overuse of artificial fertilizers. Kumarappa pointed out that an excessive application of fertilizer could be likened to a situation in which a malaria patient who, in the interest of a rapid recovery, swallows a 'laddu of quinine' instead of a small tablet.[4] Instead of being cured, he would be dead!

Kumarappa has suffered from neglect both during his lifetime and for many decades since, primarily due to the dominance of the ideologies he had vehemently opposed. Moreover, his simple and discursive style has led academics to ignore the significance of his work and writings. This is particularly true of mainstream economists who can scarcely countenance an upstart who sought to inject moral arguments into economic thought. The widespread nature of this indifference became obvious when, despite his three decades of public service, Kumarappa's death went largely unremarked. In part this was a reflection of the decline of the paradigmatic values of India's freedom movement. But it was also the case that the fire of his criticism had singed many Congress leaders and fellow constructive workers who were unlikely to mourn his departure. Strikingly, it was those outside the official folds of the Congress or Gandhian circles

---

[2] J. C. Kumarappa, *WVM*, p. 181.

[3] It is another matter that Kalelkar joked that this was a blessing in disguise for had Kumarappa known Hindi well enough, 'he would have long ago set fire to the country with his extremist views in politics and economics'. See Kaka Kalelkar, 'My Reminiscences of Kumarappa', in *Economics of Peace*, p. 349.

[4] J. C. Kumarappa, *Gandhian Economic Thought*, p. 27.

who felt that Kumarappa's harshness was not due to personal animosity but stemmed from an unyielding commitment to justice and equity. Just as S. K. Dey had recognized that Kumarappa's baptismal fire was intact, in the lone obituary of significance that can be traced, the Quaker Marjorie Sykes held a similar view. She pointed out that the resentment of Kumarappa's extravagant criticism was partly due to the guilt of those who were not 'possessed by the same selfless passion as he was, the same burning zeal to vindicate the dignity and manhood of the lowliest and weakest human being'.[5] Similarly, as an interviewer recognized, Kumarappa's 'completely frank expression' was nothing but 'an unconscious challenge to sincerity in others'.[6] While his sharp writings and utterances could be conveniently dismissed as characteristic petulance, even his worst critics had to contend with the example of a man who despite his poor health lived and worked for decades in a single-room hut in the scorching heat of central India.

Kumarappa's tiny hut at Maganvadi was furnished with 'two rough-hewn bedsteads, a small table and a stool' and had a toilet that has been delicately described as 'a simple moveable privy over a trench behind the hut'.[7] Yet, he was 'fonder and prouder of this hut than any Maharajah of his palace' and being a loner disliked 'anyone intruding inside the little space enclosed by the wooden fence of the little hut'. However, although he had a mercurial temper, Kumarappa was not a self-righteous and dour-faced killjoy as is often the fate of many who work for a public cause. As Kalelkar joked, if only Kumarappa was not 'so full of fun and frolic and put on a loin cloth he would straightaway be accepted as a pucca saint'.[8] While those at the receiving end of his admonishment had no reason to notice it, despite his 'apparent pugnacity', Kumarappa's sharp remarks were accompanied 'by a boyish twinkle in his eye' and an 'engaging grin'.[9] Although a persistent gadfly to the established order of the day, he was at peace with the world, for 'what has a man to fear when he can meet all his own wants, when he is no longer the bewildered, helpless victim of a system that is out of harmony with the deeper needs of his spirit?'

[5] Marjorie Sykes, 'Knight in Homespun', *Aryan Path*, vol. 31, no. 5 (May 1960): 196–9.

[6] 'The Economic Implications of the Teachings of Jesus: An Interview with Shri J. C. Kumarappa', *Aryan Path*, February 1950.

[7] G. Ramachandran, 'The Man', in *Economics of Peace*, p. 31.

[8] G. Ramachandran, 'The Man', p. 36.

[9] Hallam Tennyson quoted in G. Ramachandran, 'The Man', p. 35.

Such a man, as a Pacifist visiting Wardha noted, 'has everything to give and nothing to receive'.[10] One may add here that such an unflinching adherence to fundamental principles also informed Kumarappa's approach to religion and spirituality. His writings on Christian ethics are a creative and, as some see it, path-breaking interpretation of the teachings of Jesus in the context of Gandhi's principles of satya and ahimsa. Indeed, Kumarappa did disown the missionary zeal of the church, but never the ethical core of Christianity itself.

Kumarappa's personality is also discernable in his life-trajectory. Unlike many of his peers who developed their understanding of issues due to their engagement with Gandhi, it was Kumarappa's personal convictions that led him to the Mahatma. If Kumarappa's independent thinking is reflected in his early disagreement with Gandhi on the use of religious vows, the two soon developed an easy relationship that was far from the master–disciple mould that both would have abhorred. Thus, in discussing the use of wrong standards of valuation in *Economy of Permanence*, Kumarappa joked that if a race-horse dealer were to arrive at Sevagram and examine the toothless Mahatma, 'he will assign him to the *pinjrapole*[11] as being superannuated and useless'.[12] Amusing illustrations aside, it is the congruent but independent trajectory of intellectual and moral evolution that marks Kumarappa out as a most interesting Gandhian who enriched and extended the Mahatma's work and philosophy. If the fundamental economic issues at stake are more clearly visible in the debate between Kumarappa and JP than in the differences between Gandhi and Nehru, Kumarappa is also the hitherto unacknowledged influence on much of Gandhi's economic thinking from the 1930s onwards. As detailed earlier, Kumarappa's imprint is clearly visible in Gandhi's 1945 disagreement with Nehru on the future economy of India as well as in that profound and final challenge that the Mahatma mounted against his erstwhile comrades—the Lok Sevak Sangh proposal.

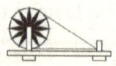

In the early decades of the twentieth century Gandhi had given both philosophical and corporeal shape to the idea of swaraj. Kumarappa further

---

[10] Hallam Tennyson quoted in G. Ramachandran, 'The Man', p. 35.
[11] A shelter for old or economically unviable cattle.
[12] J. C. Kumarappa, *EOP*, p. 43.

enriched this Indian idea of freedom by deepening the considerations of economic autonomy. In grappling with the need for both individual freedom and universal welfare, Kumarappa developed a composite approach that may be viewed as a tempered individualism that sought to curb both the excesses of Western individualism as well as traditional Indian injunctions. While the primacy of human individuality was a modern value to be nurtured and cherished, if freedom was to be available to all, the impulse for greed and unprincipled self-interest had to be contained. A legal framework of enforceable rights had its role here but to build a durable non-violent and just social order, it was imperative that a simultaneous moral transformation be effected. This objective was to be achieved by binding people into a social and economic compact of mutual obligations based on equity and justice. Resultantly, Kumarappa envisaged society and economy as a *web of freedom*.

In developing this view, Kumarappa also has much intrinsic value to offer as an imaginative interpretation of the Natural Order and a value theory to parse both the world around us and human action in it. The moral and material consequences of these principles are the basis of all of Kumarappa's insights. His prescriptions can be broadly thought of in the *spatial* terms of a local economy and a web of mutual dependence embedded within a *temporal* cyclical Natural Order. Like his mentor, Kumarappa was not a detached philosopher but a pragmatic idealist responding to the exigencies of the time. Notwithstanding the many myths that abound, the Gandhian advocacy of the agrarian economy stemmed from the radically democratic impulse to reorganize India's social, economic, and political priorities so as to afford freedom and autonomy to all and not a select few. Indeed, it is worth reiterating that the 'turn to the village' was neither sentimentality nor an advocacy of the limitation of wants as some have suggested. Rather, it was a tough-minded and clear comprehension that the demands of universal justice in modern society necessitate a decentralized economy in which ordinary individuals have both a substantial stake and measure of control. This is the only way to ensure the autonomy and dignity of the individual.

By the 1930s, intellectual consensus in India had ripened in favour of an industrial modernity. While there were substantial differences and shades of opinion, for example, between the socialists and liberals, most of India's leaders and elite held that the solution to the country's myriad problems lay in rapid industrialization. The received wisdom on economic history emphasized the advantages of economic efficiency provided by the innovations of the Industrial Revolution and its political counterpart of liberal democracy. Growth was, and indeed *is*, the mantra of the modern age. Gandhi, and later Kumarappa, recognized the fallacy of this argument and made bold to say so. Owing to the sin of swimming against a strong current of opinion, Kumarappa spent as much time dispelling the misrepresentation of Gandhian economic thought as he did in mounting a vigorous challenge to the almost universal dogma of large-scale industrialization. It was a matter of immense intellectual and moral courage to consistently argue in a poor society that the focus of economic development had to be human beings and not merely material production. Despite being mocked as a latter-day Don Quixote from Wardha, Kumarappa unflinchingly insisted that societies had to reject the theory of economic individualism and material growth as the measure of progress. While India did indeed need to provide for its people, equity and justice demanded that one search for an alternative basis to answer the many economic and political challenges.

A substantial section of Indian nationalist opinion looked to the European experience as the inspiration for India's economic and political future. While they obviously recognized the colonial exploitation of India, neither the social implications of the Industrial Revolution in England—the disembedding of the market à la Polanyi[13] or the miseries of the industrial workforce—nor the rank and unconscionable exploitation of the people and resources of the colonial tropics seem to have informed their understanding. One may argue with justice that faith in the efficacy of modernist principles in all walks of life was a form of scientism that had taken on theological proportions. Gandhi and Kumarappa were unconventional in their rejection of this view as they argued that modern industrialization could not provide a role for the vast majority of people except as a faceless pool of labour. If one desired to build a non-violent and non-exploitative society, it was imperative that this fate be avoided. While Gandhi had intuitively rejected a Hegelian understanding of economic progression of different societies, Kumarappa demonstrated an astute grasp of history in arriving at the same conclusion. Indeed, he was amongst a handful of thinkers of his time who pointed to the intimate and invidious connection between European economic development and industrialization and the exploitation of both the natural resources as well as the people of the colonized lands. Indian

---

[13] The economic historian Karl Polanyi held that in traditional societies, economic activity was embedded within social institutions and inter-personal interactions. He famously argued that it is only in modern market society that economic activity gets 'disembedded' from society and is seen as belonging to an independent realm.

evangelists of industrial modernity ignored this fact, and continue to do so even today in their pursuit of growth.

During Kumarappa's years in public life, although the individual was recognized as a political subject, the attendant economic and social dimensions got far less attention. Consequently, at least in India, the industrial economy was not adequately scrutinized in terms of its impact on the individual. In contrast, Kumarappa concluded that if the interests of the individual were to be protected, then he or she had to have control over their means of economic production. This, given India's depressed economic conditions, necessarily meant an emphasis on the limited resources available to the typical Indian poor of the time, that is, the villager. It is this understanding that shaped the impulse to modernize the village industries and not an attempt to preserve an archaic order as many critics would have it.

In his criticism of the proponents of industrialization, Kumarappa demonstrated a robust scepticism of the liberative nature of both the modern economy and the modern political state.[14] This was not an anarchist position that entirely rejected the legitimacy of the state or a degree of industrialization for that matter. The pragmatic Kumarappa recognized that the state did have a role to play especially in the deeply unequal and hierarchical context of India. Indeed, this was the reason he collaborated with the Congress as the chairman of the Agrarian Reforms Committee despite his deep disillusionment since the advent of freedom. But he remained sceptical of the ultimate ability of the state to deliver justice without intruding on the rights and autonomy of the individual. Apart from recognizing that ordinary people would have little purchase over a distant and powerful bureaucratic state, Kumarappa's position was implicitly based on a rather nuanced understanding of human nature that we may infer from his writings. While we have seen earlier that the Gandhian project was in the ultimate analysis predicated on the perfectibility of human nature, there is a clear recognition in Kumarappa's views that this was an idealized moral assumption that was not always reflected in daily living. Given the situation that obtained in society, Kumarappa was worried about entrusting the abstract instruments of state with enormous powers and resources. In adopting this position, Kumarappa demonstrated a far less romantic idea of human nature than the socialists or other modernists who took for granted that humans would cooperate for a common goal and the state would act as a benign controlling agency at the helm. At the

[14] Kumarappa's analysis of the depredations of the capitalist economy shares similarities with elements of Marxist thought but departs thereupon.

same time, one may not confuse this position of Kumarappa to imply that he accepted the current libertarian ideals of minimal interference of the state in the purported mechanisms of the free market. He was witness to the influence of money power over the decision-making processes of the colonial and the independent Indian state. This made Kumarappa a strident critic of large-scale capitalist interests as well.

While rejecting an absolute faith in either the state or the market, Kumarappa wished to tread the middle ground. Aware that most humans worked within the narrow confines of self-interest, he wished to design a system that was robust to abuse of power in the short run while promoting welfare in the long term. Arguably, while the laws and policies of the state had to be shaped to address the issue of immediate justice, Kumarappa held that it was the role of the values and norms in society to promote the long-term view, that is, to lead to an economy of permanence. Implicit in this position is the assumption that while it was a slow and arduous task to reshape society, human nature could evolve towards a higher moral basis than obtained in present circumstances. Especially after being disappointed with the government of independent India and the setback of Gandhi's assassination, Kumarappa increasingly emphasized the need for constructive workers to promote the moral basis of this long-term view amongst people. As he argued through his own actions, such a transformation could only be durably effected by moral exemplars in society and not merely by the deployment of the coercive power of the state.

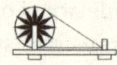

Although Gandhi and constructive workers like Kumarappa mounted a serious challenge, they failed to make a significant dent in the hold that the industrial ideal had on a generation of Indian leaders. The economic policies adopted by independent India were a direct repudiation of the values espoused by Gandhi throughout his years as a leader of the struggle for freedom. While a full consideration of the reasons for this fate of constructive work is beyond our scope here, viewing this question through Kumarappa's life provides important insights and answers. In Gandhi's conception, politics and constructive work were intimately related. At the risk of oversimplification one may state that Gandhi had established a dialectical relationship between the moral and socio-political selves of individuals which finds a homologous reflection in society as constructive work and political struggle respectively. While Gandhi embodied both these aspects in his own life, with his assassination this relationship was fully sundered to the detriment of both.

It is dubious history to claim a deep continuity between Gandhi's values and the policies of the independent Indian state. Even during Gandhi's lifetime, constructive work held little appeal within the Congress which was one of the extenuating reasons for his resignation in 1934. For instance, the nationwide chorus of applause for the satyagraha of Bardoli in 1928 did not translate into support for constructive work in the years that followed. The agrarian crisis of Indian peasantry lent itself to being framed as political campaigns against colonial rule and the landed aristocracy. But the expressions of concern seldom translated into concrete work to ameliorate the fate of those buffeted by the perils of the agrarian economy. Indeed, the fundamental character of the Congress had been decisively changed in these years and this was to have serious implications for the future. On a related note, it is a rather remarkable fact that while Kumarappa threw in his lot with Gandhi in 1929, he was the last noteworthy individual to join the cohort of constructive workers. Despite the singular success of the Salt March in 1930, the Gandhian cause failed to attract fresh recruits who could provide future leadership.

The divergence of Indian nationalism from Gandhi's agenda is also reflected in the fate of constructive work in this period.[15] The All-India Village Industries Association (AIVIA) and other measures of constructive work that Gandhi adopted in the 1930s were clearly shaped by his apprehensions about the future. With political freedom on the horizon, he wished to widen the scope of democratic practice beyond the mechanisms of conventional politics. In this sense, the AIVIA was a direct intervention in the politics of knowledge in two distinct but intimately connected ways. First, by means of a scientific and systematic reorganization of the industries and economy of the village, Gandhi sought to empower ordinary people by providing knowledge in a manner that neither the industrial mode of production nor the conventional practices of science could. Second, he sought to effect a shift in the balance of power by elevating the status of the knowledge, skills, and labour of ordinary people. Although the AIVIA was conceived to play such a role, unlike the relative success of khadi in the 1920s, its work was carried out in an adversarial atmosphere and it never had a real chance of success. It was one thing to poetically

[15] This fact is often ignored when some historians categorize khadi, village industries, and other aspects of constructive work under the rubric of Indian nationalism.

refer to khadi as the 'livery of freedom', but it was quite another to give the village its due.

Moving to the history of independent India, there were a variety of factors that militated against the economy based on village industries that Kumarappa ardently espoused. While the tangled skein of factors that led to the collapse of Gandhian ideals after the Mahatma's death needs greater elaboration elsewhere, here it will suffice to point to two significant causes. First, apart from the hostility of the intelligentsia, the decade of the 1940s was a chaotic period which saw the Second World War and the traumatic partition of India. Although Gandhi had begun attempts to reorganize constructive work to respond to the changed circumstances in 1945, the demands on his time did not allow him to finish the task. While the February 1948 meeting that Gandhi was to attend was geared towards this objective, following his assassination the Gandhian community failed to constitute itself into a significant force in India's polity. In part, the nascent cult around Vinoba was an important reason for this failure. With the exception of Kumarappa and a few others, the Gandhians also made a categorical error in interpreting the nature of the state.[16] Thus, in direct contradiction of the views of Gandhi himself, at the watershed Sevagram meeting of March 1948 Vinoba made the rhetorical argument that since the Congress was in the saddle under Nehru's leadership, the state was 'ours'. Kumarappa recognized the danger of this position but carried no influence in the new context of the growing clout of Vinoba's acolytes. Although people at large recognized Kumarappa's unimpeachable integrity and turned to him for help, he had neither the personality nor the capacities of a political leader and could not provide a fresh response to the new challenges of the time. One may add in his defence that his poor health was a factor in this equation. More widely, the Gandhians were respected for their high moral stature and sacrifice but had no real influence on the policies of the new Indian state. In the event, constructive workers ended up either compromising with the politics and power dispensation of the day or like Kumarappa stuck to their values and faded into oblivion.

The other important factor was the nature of the colonial state itself. From the perspective of high politics, 1947 marked a significant transformation when an entire subcontinent was liberated from colonial

---

[16] A major consequence of this confusion was the eventual conversion of khadi and village industries into government agencies that made a mockery of Gandhi's original agenda of self-reliance and social initiative.

rule. However, with respect to placing the agrarian economy at the heart of a decentralized economic order, the situation was far from satisfactory. The preferential bias of the colonial state towards industrial production that was accentuated during the War years was further amplified upon the Congress assuming power in 1946. While there were momentous political changes with the advent of freedom, the colonial bureaucracy remained largely untouched and as far as indifference and bias against the village economy was concerned, the Indian state showed a great degree of continuity. In this regard the colonial state proved exceedingly resilient, all to the detriment of the Indian village. If earlier the Western metropole was to be serviced, the nascent urban, capital-intensive industries of India were the new beneficiaries of policy bias while gross neglect and injustice continued to be meted out to rural India. The prior basis for this remarkable turn of events lay in the British response to the success of the 1930 Civil Disobedience campaign. By slamming everyone into prison, the British managed to extinguish the mass struggle by 1934. This was followed by the promulgation of the Government of India Act of 1935 that effectively neutralized the radical edge of the Congress and tamed it with the carrots of office. Now the Congress was looking to taking over the future governance of India and the mandate of the National Planning Committee was a clear indicator of things to come. By the end of the War years, the Congress that emerged had all but publicly repudiated Gandhi. It was almost as if those who hoped for the economic emancipation of the Indian people were told, do over.

Kumarappa spent the last decade of his life in an endless and futile battle to get the new political order to recognize the urgency of attending to the many ailments of rural India. In independent India, Kumarappa's critique of American intervention in the form of Community Projects demonstrates an accurate comprehension of geopolitics as well as the logic of bureaucratic intervention. He was prescient in his warning that the Community Projects would inexorably get reduced to an Extension Programme with serious implications for Indian agriculture. Despite its significance, this early episode of Cold War politics of development has remained largely unexplored in the literature till date. While scholars and activists have paid far greater attention to the politics of the Green Revolution in India, our understanding remains incomplete without a full consideration of the trajectory of American intervention that began in right earnest with the Community Projects initiative of the 1950s. One may also add that while Kumarappa's assessment of the American initiative was accurate enough, in his disillusionment with the rulers of independent

India, he did go rather overboard in offering the examples of China and the USSR by way of comparison. Although he eventually modified his position on these communist states in the face of public criticism, Kumarappa's failure to publicly accept this fact points to a streak of obduracy.

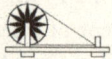

From Kumarappa's viewpoint, the shift from the charkha in the Congress flag to the 'chakra' of the independent nation was not just a simple transposition. Rather it signalled a shedding of the legacy of Gandhi's philosophy and more specifically the Mahatma's perspectives on economics. Although perfunctory homage continued to be paid to the Mahatma, the Congress continually suggested that his ideals were being implemented to the extent practicable. If Gandhi's erstwhile comrades in the Congress silently mocked his economic championing of the village, others were more direct in their criticism. Participating in a Constituent Assembly debate, B. R. Ambedkar presented his famed characterization of the village as 'a sink of localism and den of ignorance, narrow-mindedness and communalism'.[17] Kumarappa agreed with his fellow Columbia graduate and *gurubandhu*, but also added that such a characterization was only partially true. For him, the truth of such a characterization was akin to describing the late Mahatma as nothing but 'dust and ashes strewn in innumerable rivers'. While this was a materially accurate characterization of the ultimate fate of the Mahatma's body, it could hardly suffice as a true measure of the man. Similarly, with an intimate understanding of rural life, Kumarappa recognized that the acute problems of the village that Ambedkar was denouncing were indeed true. But he also argued that the solution lay in addressing the comprehensive crisis that gripped India's countryside rather than in abandoning the village. Frustrated by the widespread apathy towards the fate of the Indian village, he warned:

> As long as the villages are left in the unenviable conditions we find them in today, there can be no hope for our country as our foundations will remain rotten. The village is the unitary organism of the body politic and its state of health will affect the whole nation. It is the training ground of our future statesmen. It is the hand that feeds the nation economically. If it is to make its valuable contribution to the rebuilding of our nation, it must be restored to its pristine glory and function. It must remain an integral unit of our Political, Economic and Social life.

[17] Quoted in J. C. Kumarappa, 'What Is the Village?', *GUP*, February 1949.

While Ambedkar saw the problems of caste in the Indian village as irredeemably unjust, Kumarappa's concerns stemmed from the anxiety to preserve the economic autonomy of the individual in the face of industrialization and urbanization. Indeed, both of them were concerned with different forms of violence that persist in Indian society.

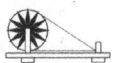

The neglect of Kumarappa was finally ended by an influential intervention on the antecedents of modern Indian environmentalism by the historian Ramachandra Guha.[18] By pointing to the many nuggets of ecological wisdom strewn through Kumarappa's writings, Guha accorded him the status of a foundational figure of environmental thought in modern India. Important as these ideas are, it is fruitful to place them in the context of Kumarappa's own work. As Guha himself recognizes, while the historiography on Indian environmentalism has been dominated by our relationship with forests and natural resources, Kumarappa locates his environmental ideas in a wholly agrarian context that is of equal importance. Moreover, much of modern Indian environmentalism has been articulated through protest movements against the direct usurpation of the natural resources of the poor that converts them into ecological refugees. Vital as these causes are, and as much as they share in a thirst for justice, most of India's recent social movements are only superficially related to Kumarappa or Gandhi's philosophy. In such a scenario, it is difficult to accept the intellectual line of descent that Guha draws between Kumarappa and some of India's activists and social leaders.[19]

As we have endeavoured to demonstrate in this biography, while it is useful to see Kumarappa as a 'green Gandhian', a fuller comprehension of his life leads to a wider range of insights and understanding. In a fundamental

---

[18] Ramachandra Guha, 'Prehistory of Indian Environmentalism: Intellectual Traditions', *Economic and Political Weekly*, vol. 27, nos 1/2 (4–11 January 1992): 57–64. Also see the chapter 'The Indian Road to Sustainability' in his *How Much Should a Person Consume? Thinking Through the Environment* (New Delhi: Permanent Black, 2006).

[19] As an aside, one may be allowed to point out that when contemporary activists extol the formulation of *sangharsh aur navnirman* (struggle and reconstruction), they are being utterly amnesiac about the far richer antecedents in satyagraha and sarvodaya respectively.

sense, Kumarappa's prescriptions regarding our relationship with the environment are driven by a non-instrumental imperative arising from his moral view of a rights–obligations dialectic applied to the Natural Order, that is, the environmental lineaments of Kumarappa's views are undergirded by a decidedly moral understanding. Indeed, the husbanding of natural resources that is seen in Kumarappa's writings arise from this philosophical position which is at many removes from a more contemporary view that sees the modern levels of material consumption as being profligate. It bears repetition that Kumarappa's green thinking should be seen in the context of Gandhi's ambitious programme of building a non-violent social and economic order. Without adequate attention to the ideological moorings of this view, one can quickly end up with a great divergence between an instrumental understanding of Kumarappa's ecological prescriptions and his teleological vision of a non-violent order of life. Conceptual clarity on this issue is also important because of the other context in which Kumarappa finds some representation, that is, Western intellectual responses to the ecological and social crises in their own societies. Many of these ideas arose out of a post–Second World War disillusionment with the promises of logical positivism and have legitimacy in their own social and historical contexts. However, it is often problematic to carelessly ascribe universal value to these specific responses. For instance, centuries of European plunder have resulted in a view that argues for the preservation of nature in its pristine form that is devoid of human presence. In densely populated India, with grave inequalities and a desperate need to improve the lives of the poor, Kumarappa sees humans as an inalienable part of the ecological landscape. Indeed, humans belong to the Natural Order of his conception and have a special role in it.[20]

If the context of constructive work is necessary to understand Kumarappa's ecological prescriptions it is even more so in comprehending his views on economics. In this regard, with some honourable exceptions, scant attention has been paid to either the body of economic thought or the practical work of constructive organizations such as the AISA or the AIVIA. Until the worldwide impact of the environmental crisis came to be finally acknowledged in the 1970s, scant attention was paid to Gandhi beyond his political work. While Gandhian political thought is slowly finding its place in scholarly literature, much of it is largely based on the easily accessible

[20] As a final aside in this context, throughout this biography we have eschewed the word 'sustainability' as a multitude of meanings has become attached to this protean term.

source of *The Collected Works of Mahatma Gandhi* or the polemical critique of *Hind Swaraj*. However, Gandhi's worldview cannot be seriously examined without attention to the philosophy and practice of constructive work. Although khadi has been examined to an extent, there is as yet no serious understanding of the comprehensive vision of the Mahatma or his cohort of constructive workers. This lack of rigorous analysis that addresses both the philosophical and historical dimensions of Gandhian thought has had two consequences that merit reference here. First, in the absence of serious scholarship, the work of Gandhi and Kumarappa has been appropriated by newer schools of thought based on superficial similarities, especially some Western brands of 'alternative economics' that do a disservice to the importance and sophistication of the life work of Gandhi and Kumarappa. Second, what is equally unsatisfactory is the growing number of scholarly volumes that are purportedly on Gandhian economics and Gandhian political economy. Often based on a perfunctory use of Gandhi's writings and utterances, most of these volumes fail to adequately grapple with the task at hand. Almost all of them have no understanding of the body of constructive work carried out by Gandhi and his compatriots and exhibit no awareness of the work of Kumarappa. Such works do far more damage to the propagation of Gandhian values in economic thought than those who vigorously oppose it.

Throughout his life Kumarappa's work was squarely focused on addressing problems of immediate relevance. However, while rooted in the specifics of his times, through a keen dialectic between thought and action, Kumarappa forged ideas and principles that are relevant for all time.[21] Indeed, apart from its historical value, this biography has been written in the belief that the importance of Kumarappa's life lies in its ability to speak to vital questions of our own times. One may not glibly suggest that everything that Kumarappa or Gandhi proposed is of direct relevance today. It is also no one's case that the application of these principles in real life is a simple and uncomplicated matter. In the years since Kumarappa's death, the world around us has changed enormously. However, Kumarappa remains relevant

[21] The discussion on Kumarappa's contemporaneity during the celebrations of his birth centenary year in 1992 is the proximate inspiration for Rajni Bakshi's *Bapu Kuti: Journeys in Rediscovery of Gandhi*.

as many of the questions that he grappled with are as alive today as they were five decades ago. For instance, the task of cultural and psychological decolonization that Kumarappa undertook in his own life is as necessary today despite the fact that India's colonizers have long departed our shores. Of equal value is the consistent focus on leading an ethical and meaningful personal life, and in this regard, Kumarappa does have many a lesson to offer. More broadly, the same may be said of his application of moral imperatives and ethical considerations to economics and indeed to all aspects of life itself. In this regard, one may point out that the significance of Gandhi's thought is not its ethical core alone. After all, such ethics are more or less available in the moral teachings of all societies. Gandhi's genius lies in the forging of ethical principles for the modern era where questions and problems are to be addressed at the mass scale. At the same time, unlike ideologies that look at society in the abstract, Gandhi made the explicit and insistent connection between individual behaviour and social outcomes. Kumarappa played a key role in developing the economic dimensions of this viewpoint.

The contemporary relevance of the multiple arguments made by this biography need not be rehearsed here. It will suffice to illustrate the point in a few instances. The absence of Gandhian thought in the foundational principles of the Indian republic is in the first instance a failure of political imagination. Having battled against the illegitimacy of colonialism, India's leadership demonstrated an inability to look beyond a specific European conception of nationhood. Admittedly, India has fared far better than most postcolonial societies but at the critical hour, it baulked and approached politics as the art of the possible. While universal adult franchise was a revolutionary step, India's democracy was not further deepened through a genuine political and economic decentralization. The result has been proof of Kumarappa's argument that one may not have political democracy without the counterpart of economic decentralization. India routinely conducts free elections, but its citizens have little influence over the actions of their elected representatives. Indeed, recent experiences both in India and elsewhere confirm the dim view that Kumarappa took when he characterized most democratic societies as nothing but delegated autocracies.[22] The crisis is particularly striking in the contemporary scenario where India's markets

---

[22] The mendacity of India's politicians apart, middle-class and affluent India views the impoverished majority as a handicap to their progress that needs to be sternly dealt with.

have been liberalized but the state continues to use its awesome powers to transfer public resources into private hands. If the policy bias against village industries was bad enough, rampant political corruption has bred a far more ominous and accelerated enclosure of the commons.

The neglect of the agrarian economy and, more widely, the village itself, as well as the massive use and abuse of India's natural resources have also had grave consequences that can hardly be detailed in the short compass of our discussion here. Suffice it to say that being an Indian farmer is such an unviable economic proposition that one is persuaded to believe that the lack of occupational mobility is the chief reason that agriculturalists continue to grow the food crops that we consume. At the same time, the ecological concerns with the overuse of water and chemical-intensive farming have translated into dangerous consequences in the past few decades. Without a doubt, Kumarappa's analysis of the connection between the political economy of agriculture and food security was prophetic. In an era that believed in the ability of science to solve many problems, Kumarappa's plumbing for food self-sufficiency was seen as antediluvian. Today we may recognize that his views were far-sighted, for despite the great leaps in food output and decades of economic growth, to India's eternal shame, millions still struggle to eke out a living and are on the verge of starvation. Even those outside this dark zone are severely affected by the poisoned food they eat, the volatility of prices, a looming threat of global shortages as well as an absence of nutritional self-sufficiency.[23]

The fundamental problem of providing adequate and meaningful employment in the village remains as serious a concern as it was during the colonial era. Unable to make ends meet in their villages, millions of Indians travel long distances to urban centres in search of livelihood. Apart from its important implications for social justice, India's internal migration of epic proportions is bound to have grave consequences that we barely comprehend today. At the same time, the commonly held view about Gandhi's economic prescriptions of khadi and village industries is nothing but a travesty of his ideas. This view that sees cottage industries as producing goods for the fickle tastes of the urban market is as far from the dictum of *local production for local consumption* as can be. For sure, the breathless media columns on the use of khadi in fashion shows for bored socialites

[23] The impact of the lopsided development in independent India's food production that focused on cereals, especially following the Green Revolution, has led to a severe undermining of the nutritional self-sufficiency of India. This also leaves it vulnerable to changed geopolitical considerations in the future.

is a mockery of the radical, emancipatory potential for self-sufficiency and self-respect that Gandhi saw in the charkha.

Kumarappa has also been demonstrably correct in his critique of the pursuit of material growth instead of the development of human potential in a just and equitable manner. Although the ideological allegiances of India's political dispensation have changed in many ways since Independence, they share in common an uncritical and dogmatic faith in the discourse of economic growth and development. If pre-liberalized India had a dismal record in the number of ecological refugees it created in the name of development, contemporary India's desire for growth and its appetite for energy has worsened the problem. The creation of new mines and nuclear and power plants are only some of the many ways in which vulnerable communities are being pushed into destitution. Indeed, the recent experiences of Indian economic choices have proved the correctness of Kumarappa's proposition that the depredations of capital are not the deliberate design of one nation on another but are inevitable due to the nature of a capitalist economy based on consumption. Nothing confirms this dismal truth and repudiates the legacy of India's freedom struggle as the growing presence of Indian companies in Africa that are taking over the lands of peasants even more vulnerable than our own. The corollary in Kumarappa's perceptive analysis of the loss of autonomy is true not only of industrial and agrarian workers in the modern world economy, but also applies across the board to many areas of work including those of the growing numbers of Indians employed as urban professionals.

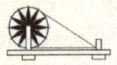

In the last years of his life, Kumarappa had a small portrait hung on the walls of his hut in Kallupatti. About the size of a postcard, it showed an old man staring into the distance. The anonymity of the person did not matter. With a wizened face burdened and creased with the cares of the world, he was Everyman. While Kumarappa's intellect ranged far and wide, in his heart he was ever aware of Gandhi's talisman. Pointing to the portrait, Kumarappa told visitors that the old man was the focus of his life's work. For that man was the master of Kumarappa's master.

Bibliography of
J. C. Kumarappa's Publications

The primary archival source on J. C. Kumarappa is the collection of his papers housed in the Manuscripts Division of the Nehru Memorial Museum and Library (NMML), New Delhi. Another important source is the archives of the Sabarmati Ashram Preservation and Memorial Trust, Ahmedabad.

Apart from books and reports, Kumarappa wrote a large numbers of essays and some book reviews, many of which appeared in the journals *Young India*, *Indian Social Reformer*, *Harijan*, *Aryan Path*, and, most importantly, the *Gram Udyog Patrika*. Many of his essays were anthologized into published volumes which are listed below. The year of publication of the first edition is indicated. Many of these volumes are not cited in the biography since the original individual essays were used and cited. Kumarappa's occasional contributions to other journals and edited volumes as well as the numerous anthologies of his writings published since his death are not listed here.

BOOKS

Kumarappa, J. C. *Public Finance and Our Poverty: The Contribution of Public Finance to the Present Economic State of India.* Ahmedabad: Navajivan Press, 1930.
———. *Public Debt of India.* Allahabad: All-India Congress Committee, 1935.

———. *Why the Village Movement? A Plea for a Village-Centred Economic Order in India*. Kashi: Akhil Bharat Sarva Seva Sangh, 1936.

———. *Economy of Permanence: A Quest for a Social Order Based on Non-violence*. Varanasi: Sarva Seva Sangh Prakashan, 1945.

———. *Practice and Precepts of Jesus*. Ahmedabad: Navajivan Publishing House, 1945.

———. *Clive to Keynes: A Survey of the History of Our Public Debts and Credits*. Ahmedabad: Navajivan Publishing House, 1947.

———. *Gandhian Economic Thought*. Bombay: Vora and Co., 1951.

———. *The Unitary Basis for a Non-violent Democracy*. Wardha: The All-India Village Industries Association. 1951.

REPORTS

Kumarappa, J. C. (Director). *A Survey of Matar Taluka: Kaira District*. Ahmedabad: Gujarat Vidyapith, 1931. A 1952 reprint was titled *An Economic Survey of Matar Taluka: Kheda District*.

Kumarappa, J. C. (Convenor). *Report on the Financial Obligations between Great Britain and India*. Bombay: All-India Congress Committee, 1931. In two volumes, of which volume 2 is an annexure prepared by K. T. Shah.

Kumarappa, J. C. (Chairman), *Report of the Industrial Survey Committee*. Nagpur: Government of the Central Provinces and Berar, 1938. Published in two parts with each part consisting of two volumes.

Kumarappa, J. C. *A Plan for the Economic Development of the North-West Frontier Province*. Peshawar: n.p., 1940. Published for private circulation.

———. *Supplement to the Report on the Economic Development of the North-West Frontier Province*, Peshawar: n.p., 1946. Published for private circulation.

Kumarappa, J. C. (Chairman). *Report of the Congress Agrarian Reforms Committee*. New Delhi: All-India Congress Committee, 1949.

Kumarappa, J. C. *Report on Agriculture and Cottage and Small-Scale Industries in Japan*. New Delhi: Ministry of Commerce and Industry, Government of India, 1952.

PAMPHLETS, COLLECTIONS OF SPEECHES, AND ESSAYS

Kumarappa, J. C. *The Organisation and Accounts of Relief Work*. Wardha: The All-India Village Industries Association, 1934.

———. *The Philosophy of the Village Movement*. Kovvur: Sanivarapu Subba Rao, 1935.

———. *The Religion of Jesus*. Rajahmundry: Hindustan Publishing Co. Ltd., 1937.

Kumarappa, J. C. *War: A Factor of Production*. Rajahmundry: Hindustan Publishing Co. Ltd., 1938.

———. *Economic Surveying and Planning*. Rajahmundry: Hindustan Publishing Co. Ltd., 1939.

———. *Currency Inflation: Its Cause and Cure*. Wardha: The All-India Village Industries Association, 1943.

Kumarappa, J. C. and V. L. Mehta. *Economics of Non-violence*. Bombay: Hamara Hindostan Publications, 1944.

Kumarappa, J. C. *Christianity: Its Economy and Way of Life*. Ahmedabad: Navajivan Publishing House, 1945.

———. *An Overall Plan for Rural Development*. Wardha: The All-India Village Industries Association, 1946.

———. *A Plan for Rural Development*. Nagpur: The All-India Village Industries Association, 1946.

———. *Stone Walls and Iron Bars*. Allahabad: New Literature, 1946.

———. *The Philosophy of Work and Other Essays*. Wardha: The All-India Village Industries Association, 1947.

———. *Women and Village Industries*. Wardha: The All-India Village Industries Association, 1947.

———. *Banishing War*. Wardha: The All-India Village Industries Association, 1948.

———. *Blood Money*. Wardha: The All-India Village Industries Association, 1948.

———. *Europe through Gandhian Eyes*. Wardha: The All-India Village Industries Association, 1948.

———. *The Gandhian Economy and Other Essays*. Wardha: The All-India Village Industries Association, 1948.

———. *Peace and Prosperity*. Wardha: The All-India Village Industries Association, 1948.

———. *Science and Progress*. Wardha: The All-India Village Industries Association, 1948.

———. *Swaraj for the Masses*. Bombay: Hind Kitabs Ltd., 1948.

———. *Our Food Problem*. Wardha: The All-India Village Industries Association, 1949.

———. *Present Economic Situation*. Wardha: The All-India Village Industries Association, 1949.

———. *The Gandhian Way of Life*. Wardha: The All-India Village Industries Association, 1950.

———. *People's China: What I Saw and Learnt There*. Wardha: The All-India Village Industries Association, 1952.

———. *Lessons from Europe*. Wardha: Akhil Bharat Sarva Seva Sangh, 1954.

———. *Planning by the People for the People*. Bombay: Vora and Co. Publishers Ltd., 1954.

———. *Sarvodaya and World Peace*. Wardha: Akhil Bharat Sarva Seva Sangh, 1954.

———. *The Non-violent Economy and World Peace*. Wardha: Akhil Bharat Sarva Seva Sangh, 1955.

Kumarappa, J. C. *A Peep behind the Iron Curtain: Life in the Soviet Union and People's China*. T. Kallupatti: J. C. Kumarappa, 1956.

Kumarappa, J. C. and others. *The Cow in Our Economy*. Kashi: Akhil Bharat Sarva Seva Sangh, 1957.

Kumarappa, J. C. *Vicarious Living*. Madras: Kumarappa Publications, 1959.

———. *Planned Economy: A Gandhian Approach*. T. Kallupatti: Gandhiniketan Ashram, 1962. Reprint of a 1941 pamphlet published by the Bombay Pradesh Congress Committee.

In addition, Kumarappa also edited the following volume:

Rajagopalachari, C. and J. C. Kumarappa (eds). *The Nation's Voice: Being a Collection of Gandhiji's Speeches in England and Sjt. Mahadev Desai's Account of the Sojourn, September to December 1931*. Ahmedabad: Navajivan Publishing House, 1932.

Index

About the Authors

Venu Madhav Govindu obtained a PhD in electrical engineering and his research interests include geometry and statistical inference in computer vision. He is also interested in the history and political economy of modern India, especially the life and work of Mahatma Gandhi.

Deepak Malghan has a PhD in ecological economics and his primary research interest is the analytical theory of scale. He is also interested in the history of modern India's political economy.

The authors live and work in Bengaluru, India.